INTRODUCTION TO CRIMINAL LAW

First Edition	January 1948
Second Edition	January 1949
Third Edition	July 1953
Fourth Edition	April 1959
Fifth Edition	June 1964
Sixth Edition	October 1968
Seventh Edition	July 1972
Eighth Edition	May 1976

CROSS AND JONES'

INTRODUCTION TO CRIMINAL LAW

EIGHTH EDITION

PHILIP ASTERLEY JONES, LL.B.
Solicitor, Head of the Department of Law at the City of Birmingham Polytechnic

RICHARD CARD, LL.M.
Reader in Common Law at the University of Reading

LONDON
BUTTERWORTHS
1976

ENGLAND:
Butterworth & Co. (Publishers) Ltd.
London: 88 Kingsway, London WC2B 6AB

AUSTRALIA:
Butterworths Pty. Ltd.
Sydney: 586 Pacific Highway, Chatswood, NSW 2067
Also at Melbourne, Brisbane, Adelaide and Perth

CANADA:
Butterworth & Co. (Canada) Ltd.
Toronto: 2265 Midland Avenue, Scarborough, M1P 4S1

NEW ZEALAND:
Butterworths of New Zealand Ltd.
Wellington: 26–28 Waring Taylor Street, Wellington 1

SOUTH AFRICA:
Butterworth & Co. (South Africa) (Pty.) Ltd.
Durban: 152-154 Gale Street, Durban

USA:
Butterworth & Co. (Publishers) Inc.
Boston: 19 Cummings Park, Woburn, Mass. 01801

ISBN Casebound: 0 406 57046 9
Limp: 0 406 57047 7

PREFACE

This is the first edition of this book of which Sir Rupert Cross has not been the prime mover, but he will recognise many passages which he wrote and which are unchanged. We hope that he is enjoying his release from his labours.

As in the past, this continues to be essentially a first book on criminal law. We have had in mind the syllabuses both for degree courses and for professional examinations, particularly those of the Bar, The Law Society and the Institute of Legal Executives. We devote most of the work to the substantive criminal law of England and Wales. In Chapters 20 to 24 we give an outline of the court system and procedure to the extent that it is required to understand the substantive law.

We have abandoned in form though not in substance the system of numbered articles and labelled explanations. We intend the opening paragraph or paragraphs on most topics to contain a simple statement of the law as it is. We have numbered all paragraphs so as to ease the identification of topics and the placing of inevitable amendments. We recognise that no teacher of law ever agrees with another's view about the order in which the subject should be taught. Probably there are many who will disagree with putting inchoate offences, duress, necessity and participation after substantive offences. To make the book as adaptable as possible to different needs we have put in a large number of cross-references which we hope will enable the topics to be taken in any order with the minimum of inconvenience.

Usually where the context and the sense permit we use the word "offence" rather than "crime" when we are describing a particular act or omission, and use "crime" mainly in its generic sense.

We thank all who have helped us. We owe special debts to Sir Norman Skelhorn Q.C., Mr. F. D. Howarth, Mr. P. K. Dodd, Mr. F. Cox, Mr. S. Carlton and Mr. C. J. A. Jones. We also thank our students past and present, our wives, and finally our publishers, not only for compiling the tables of statutes and cases and the index but also for their positive guidance and for preserving us from various errors. For the imperfections which remain in spite of all this help we are responsible.

We have tried to summarise and explain the law as it was on 1st November 1975, although by footnotes inserted in proof we have been able to indicate changes made up to 31st January 1976.

February 1976

P.A.J.
R.C.

C. & J. Cases
References throughout the book are to the Fifth Edition of *Cross and Jones: Cases on Criminal Law*.

TABLE OF CONTENTS

TABLE OF STATUTES

References to "*Statutes*" are to Halsbury's Statutes of England (Third Edition) showing the volume and page at which the annotated text of the Act will be found.
References in the right-hand column are to paragraph numbers.

LIST OF CASES

D

E

Y

1

THE CHARACTERISTICS OF CRIMINAL OFFENCES

Definition[1]

1.1 A crime or offence is an illegal act, omission or event, whether or not it is also a tort, a breach of contract or a breach of trust, the principal consequence of which is that the offender, if he is detected and the police decide to prosecute,[2] is prosecuted by or in the name of the State, and if he is found guilty is liable to be punished whether or not he is also ordered to compensate his victim.

1.2 A wrong is a breach of a rule; it may be moral or legal according to whether the rule is one of morality or law. The relations between these two types of rule are considered in the next chapter.[3] Legal wrongs may be civil or criminal, and this distinction depends upon that between civil and criminal law. The civil law is primarily concerned with the rights and duties of individuals among themselves, whereas the criminal law defines the duties which a person owes to society, but a legal wrong may be both civil and criminal.

1.3 Civil law is not exclusively concerned with the definition of wrongs, for it embraces the law of property, which largely consists of the rules governing the methods whereby property may be transferred from one person to another, and the law of succession, which concerns the devolution of property on death. There are, however, several branches of the civil law which exist in

---

1. Allen, *Legal Duties*, 221; Kenny, *Outlines of Criminal Law* (19th edition), pp. 1–5; Williams, The Definition of Crime, *Current Legal Problems*, 1955, 107; Winfield, *Province of the Law of Tort*, Ch. 8; Hughes, The Concept of Crime (An American View), [1959] Crim. L. R., 239 and 331; Fitzgerald, The Concept of Crime, [1960] Crim. L. R., 257; Seton Pollock, The Distinguishing Mark of a Crime, (1959) 22 M.L.R., 495.
2. Wilcox, A. F., *The Decision to Prosecute*.
3. Paras. 2.16 to 2.22.

whole or in part to provide redress for wrongs; the most important of these are contract, tort and trusts.

The purpose of the law of contract is to provide redress for breaches of legally binding agreements. The aggrieved party may claim damages as plaintiff in civil proceedings, and the amount which he recovers is assessed on the basis of the loss he has sustained in consequence of the non-fulfilment of the contract.

The object of the law of tort is to provide redress for breaches of duties which are owed to persons generally, and do not depend on an agreement between the parties. If B assaults A, or publishes a libel concerning him, or causes him personal injuries by the negligent driving of a motor car, he commits a tort and is liable to be sued by A in civil proceedings. In these, as in those for breach of contract, the plaintiff's damages will be assessed on the basis of the loss sustained in consequence of the tort, although the detailed rules of assessment may not be the same in each case.

The law of trusts, unlike the law of contract and tort, which depend mainly on the common law,[1] is to be gathered primarily from the rules of equity, i.e. those rules which were administered by the Court of Chancery before the Judicature Act of 1873. A breach of trust occurs where someone who holds property as trustee for another fails to carry out the duties of his office, for example by making an improper investment or wrongfully converting the trust property to his own use. He is then civilly liable to make good the loss occasioned to those on whose behalf the property was held.

1.4 The foregoing account of civil wrongs should be sufficient to indicate the two important respects in which they differ from crimes. In each instance the wrongdoer's liability is based on the loss which he has occasioned, and in each the law is brought into play at the option of the injured party. Generally speaking, no one can be obliged to sue for damages for a breach of contract or a tort, and a beneficiary cannot be forced to claim restitution of the trust property. On the other hand, where an offence has been committed, the wrongdoer is liable to punishment, which is a very different thing from being ordered to compensate the victim of the wrong, and as a general rule a criminal prosecution may proceed although the victim has been fully compensated and desires it to be discontinued.[2] The control which the State

---

1. Para. 2.1.

2. *Smith* v. *Dear* (1903), 88 L.T. 664.

exercises over criminal, as opposed to civil, proceedings is considered later.[1]

.5 The same conduct may be both a civil wrong and a crime. There are many cases in which one who commits a tort is also guilty of a crime. Assaults and collisions between vehicles are two out of numerous examples. Where a crime is also a civil wrong, criminal and civil proceedings may usually take place concurrently and the one is normally no bar to the other.

The only exception to this rule of any general importance is that where criminal proceedings are taken in a court of summary jurisdiction in respect of a common assault under s. 42 of the Offences against the Person Act 1861, or an aggravated assault upon a male child under 14 or any female under s. 43 of the Act, by or on behalf of the party aggrieved, the defendant is released from all other proceedings, civil or criminal, for the same cause, if he obtains the magistrates' certificate of the dismissal of the complaint or undergoes the punishment inflicted upon him.[2] A certificate of dismissal must be issued if the magistrates decide that the offence is not proved, or if proved is so trifling as not to merit any punishment. The power to dismiss a case even though the offence is proved, which is peculiar to assault and battery, depends on there having been a hearing "on the merits" and this will not have occurred if the accused pleaded guilty.[3]

The application and limitations of this exception may be illustrated by the cases of *Masper* v. *Brown*[4] and *Dyer* v. *Munday*.[5] In the former, an action by a husband in respect of an assault upon his wife for which the defendant had, on summary conviction, paid a fine, was held to be barred because it was for the same cause as the summary proceedings. In the latter, however, an action against a master for an assault committed by a servant in the course of his employment was held not to be similarly barred as the relief afforded to the servant by s. 45 of the Offences against the Person Act 1861 did not extend to the master.

.6 The principal criticism of the definition of a crime set out at

1. Paras. 1.7–1.9.
2. Offences against the Person Act 1861, ss. 44, 45; North, Civil and Criminal Proceedings for Assault (1966), 29 M.L.R., 16.
3. *Ellis* v. *Burton*, [1975] 1 All E.R. 395.
4. (1876), 1 C.P.D. 97.
5. [1895] 1 Q.B. 742.

the start of this chapter is that it fails to indicate what types of conduct are included in the category of crimes. The answer is that a definition is not the same thing as a description; its aim is simply to draw attention to the features which distinguish that which is being defined from other things of the same kind. In any event, it is impossible to find a concise formula which will cover every kind of criminal conduct. As Lord Atkin said in 1931,[1] "The criminal quality of an act cannot be discerned by intuition; nor can it be discovered by reference to any standard but one: is the act prohibited with penal consequences?"

It has not been necessary for Parliament to formulate a definition of a crime, but the judges have been called upon from time to time to distinguish between civil and criminal proceedings. In the former, the rules of evidence and procedure may be waived by the parties and a pardon may be granted by the Crown in the latter. Furthermore, under the provisions of s. 31 (1) (a) of the Supreme Court of Judicature (Consolidation) Act 1925, no appeal lies except as provided by that Act, the Criminal Appeal Act 1968, or the Administration of Justice Act 1960, in any criminal cause or matter from any judgment of the High Court. The authorities on the subsection show that if the direct outcome of the proceedings may be the trial and punishment of a party, they are a "criminal cause or matter".[2] The short and only answer is that the decision whether to make conduct criminal is political and social, not legal. Why politicians decide that conduct shall be criminal is beyond the scope of this book.

The initiative of the State[3]

1.7 All criminal proceedings are in theory instituted on behalf of the Crown, but in general there is nothing to prevent a private citizen from initiating criminal proceedings although certain offences can only be prosecuted by or with the consent of an official representative of the Crown or some specified person. It is not sufficient to leave the remedy for certain wrongs in the hands of private persons for various reasons:

a. Many wrongs are so serious, not only for the persons injured but for the public as a whole, that a claim for compensation would be quite inadequate to restrain the offender or to deter

---

1. *Proprietary Articles Trade Association* v. *A.G. for Canada*, [1931] A.C. 310, at p. 324.
2. *Amand* v. *Home Secretary and Minister of Defence of Royal Netherlands Government*, [1943] A.C. 147; [1942] 2 All E.R. 381; *C. & J. Cases.*
3. Williams, Discretion in Prosecuting, [1955] Crim. L. R., 222 and Williams, Power to Prosecute, *ibid.* 596; Wilcox, A. F., *The Decision to Prosecute.*

others. It is obviously in the interests of the public at large that burglars should be liable to imprisonment and not simply liable to be sued in the civil courts.

b. Many wrongful acts do no particular harm to particular individuals so that no one is sufficiently interested to institute proceedings, even if he were able to do so. Within this category come most of the offences against public order in its widest sense and certain offences against public morals, such as incest and abortion, where the parties concerned do not necessarily regard themselves as injured.

c. Many offences have been created which might be dealt with as civil matters but to do so would expose private persons to considerable trouble and expense. A good example is afforded by s. 89 (1) of the Town and Country Planning Act 1971 under which an owner of land who contravenes an enforcement notice issued by a local authority commits a crime and is liable to a fine of £400. Before the modern town planning legislation the use of land was unregulated except by private contract and restrictive covenants. The enforcement of these contracts and covenants was always a matter of some difficulty and so the new and simpler process is now gradually replacing the older and more complicated, and the type of restriction which may be imposed has been extended.

1.8 The interest of the State in the prosecution of crime is reflected in the way in which indictments are headed, e.g. *The Queen* v. *Titus Oates*, and by the way in which cases tried on indictment are named in the law reports, e.g. *R.* v. *Brown*. "R" stands for "Rex" or "Regina" (King or Queen), as the case may be. This title is retained on appeals to the Court of Appeal. In this book following the modern practice, we cite cases tried on indictment and appeals to the Court of Appeal or former appellate tribunals under the name of the accused, e.g. "Brown". If an appeal is taken from the Court of Appeal to the House of Lords, the Director of Public Prosecutions or other official conducting the appeal on behalf of the Crown appears in the title. In appeals to the Judicial Committee of the Privy Council it is the custom to place the letters "v. R." after the appellant's name.

The name of the actual prosecutor appears in summary proceedings, e.g. *Smith* v. *Jones*. Smith may be a private individual, a police officer or the representative of a government department or local authority. If Jones were unsuccessful and appealed by way of case stated to the Divisional Court, a procedure which will be described later,[1] the title of the case in the Divisional Court would be *Jones* v. *Smith*. Notwithstanding the use of the name of the individual prosecutor in summary cases, he is, in theory, the representative of the Crown.

1.9 The fact that all our prosecutions are theoretically conducted on behalf of the Crown disguises two important differences between English and continental criminal procedure. First, the police as well as private prosecutors have a much wider discretion in abstaining from a prosecution than exists in most continental countries. Secondly, the role of the private prosecutor is much more extensive in this country than it is abroad.

Private prosecutions are not possible in Scotland and the role of the police in the Scots criminal process is quite different from that in the English because the proceedings are conducted by a public official, the Procurator Fiscal.

An exception to the general rule that a private person or police officer may institute criminal proceedings in England is that there are numerous cases in which the leave of a particular official is required. For example, prosecutions for many offences cannot be begun until the consent of the Attorney-General has been obtained. These include offences under the Official Secrets Acts and several others. Other offences must be prosecuted only by or with the consent of the Director of Public Prosecutions, for example certain offences under the Bankruptcy Act 1914.[2] Sometimes a prosecution is dependent upon an order of a judge in chambers, such as the prosecution for criminal libel of a newspaper proprietor, publisher or editor.[3]

---

1. Para. 24.3.
2. Section 165.
3. Law of Libel Amendment Act 1888, s. 8.

2

THE SOURCES AND CLASSIFICATIONS OF THE CRIMINAL LAW

Common law

2.1 Common law is that part of English law which is not the result of legislation, i.e. the law which originated in the custom of the people and was unified and developed by the decisions and rulings of the judges.

Common law offences

2.2 From the twelfth to the fourteenth centuries, the judges of the Court of King's Bench elaborated the rules relating to the more serious offences which came to be known as "felonies". In the fourteenth century, less serious offences known later as "misdemeanours" were similarly evolved. A few misdemeanours were subsequently created by the rulings of the judges in particular cases and by the Court of Star Chamber.[1] After the Restoration, some of the latter were developed by the common law judges, who "always claimed the right of defining given acts as misdemeanours, although they never attempted to do so in the case of felonies",[2] but in modern times statute has played a preponderant part in the criminal law.

There are still several offences which exist at common law only. This means that their definition cannot be found in an Act of Parliament, but must be sought in the rulings of the judges. *Prima facie*, not only the definition of the offence itself, but also the punishment to be awarded (imprisonment and a fine at the discretion of the court) is contained in the common law but several statutes prescribe specific punishments for certain common law offences. For example, murder is an offence at common law; in no statute is there to be found a definition of it, but by

1. Jackson, *Modern Approach to Criminal Law*, pp. 292–300.
2. *Morris*, [1951] 1 K.B. 394, at p. 395, *per* Lord Goddard C.J.; [1950] 2 All E.R. 965, at p. 966.

reason of the wealth of judicial pronouncements it is possible to construct a comprehensive definition of the offence. The punishment for murder is, however, governed by statute.[1] Manslaughter also remains an offence at common law; imprisonment for life is laid down as the maximum punishment by s. 5 of the Offences against the Person Act 1861 but, by way of contrast with the case of murder, a lesser sentence of imprisonment, a fine, or even a conditional or absolute discharge under the Powers of Criminal Courts Act 1973 is possible. The relevant statutes content themselves with naming the offences of murder and manslaughter and assume the existence of these offences without giving any definition. Another example of a common law offence is conspiracy. This is an offence at common law although certain types of conspiracy have been covered by statute; the punishment is still prescribed by common law except in certain cases such as conspiracy to murder where the maximum punishment of ten years' imprisonment is laid down in s. 4 of the Offences against the Person Act 1861.

2.3 In *Morris*,[2] the Court of Criminal Appeal affirmed the rule that, where the punishment for an offence is not laid down by statute, the judge may sentence the accused to be imprisoned for a period to be fixed at his discretion. Normally a statute indicates the maximum punishment which may be imposed, as s. 4 of the Offences against the Person Act 1861 does. It follows that, in theory, the decision in *Morris* could lead to some very anomalous results,[3] for in the case of a common law misdemeanour for which no maximum punishment is provided by statute, the court can impose a longer sentence than it can in the case of a more serious misdemeanour, the punishment of which is dealt with by statute. There is, however, an overriding requirement that the punishment should not be excessive, and there is no reason to suppose that the decision in *Morris* will give rise to any injustice in practice.

General principles of criminal liability

2.4 The common law remains the source of virtually all the general principles of criminal liability. Examples of such principles are the defences of insanity and duress and the rules con-

1. Murder (Abolition of Death Penalty) Act 1965.
2. [1951] 1 K.B. 394; [1950] 2 All E.R. 965; approved by the House of Lords in *Verrier* v. *Director of Public Prosecutions*, [1967] 2 A.C. 195; [1966] 3 All E.R. 568; *C. & J. Cases*.
3. Williams, Common Law Misdemeanours, (1952) 68 L.Q.R., 500.

cerning participation in crime. It is intended that the general principles of criminal liability will be included in the statutory Criminal Code which is being formulated at present by the Law Commission.

The doctrine of precedent

2.5 The common law has been built up on the basis of the doctrine of precedent under which its rules must be inferred from the decisions of High Court and Appellate judges in reported cases. The decisions of the judges below the rank of High Court judge do not constitute a precedent in the technical sense so that other judges are not bound to pay attention to them in coming to a conclusion in later cases of a similar nature.

So far as the operation of the doctrine of precedent in relation to the criminal law is concerned, it will be seen later that trial on indictment involves trial by jury, and, subject to the accused's right of appeal,[1] their verdict is final. The jury is subject to the trial judge who sums up the evidence and explains the law, his explanations constituting a precedent for the future.[2] This must be distinguished from civil cases; there the principle is "found by taking account (a) of the facts treated by the judge as material, and (b) his decision as based on them"[3], whereas in criminal cases the principle must generally be ascertained without reference to the verdict of the jury, which may have been unexpected by the judge, or even contrary to his direction on the law. If the case goes to appeal, the comments made by the appellate court which directly relate to the judge's direction on the law become the precedent established by the case. Other statements on the law by the appellate court, *obiter dicta* (statements not necessary to the decision) as they are called, can never constitute a binding precedent, although they may be of persuasive authority for subsequent cases, their strength depending on the eminence of the court.

In cases tried summarily,[4] the decision of the magistrates does not, of course, constitute a precedent. Doubtful points of law may, however, be dealt with on appeal by a Divisional Court of the Queen's Bench Division, when the decision, which will constitute a legally binding precedent, will be reached on the basis of the facts which the magistrates find to be proved.

---

1. Paras. 24.5–24.7.
2. Para. 23.13.
3. Goodhart, *Essays in Jurisprudence and the Common Law*, 25.
4. Chapter 23.

Accordingly, account may have to be taken of the court's conclusion of guilty or not guilty as based on those facts in order to ascertain the principle of the case.

2.6 The doctrine of precedent depends on the principle that the courts form a hierarchy which, in the case of courts with criminal jurisdiction, is in the following descending order: House of Lords; Court of Appeal (Criminal Division); Divisional Court of the Queen's Bench Division; Crown Court, and Magistrates' Courts.[1] The rule is that a decision by an Appellate Court or High Court judge binds those courts below that in which it was given and, save in exceptional circumstances, will be followed by a court of equal status. In 1966 the House of Lords declared (reversing its former practice) that it would not be bound by its own decisions but when announcing this the Lord Chancellor emphasised the need for maintaining certainty in the criminal law.[2] This emphasis was repeated in *Knuller, Ltd.* v. *Director of Public Prosecutions*[3] where the House of Lords refused to overrule its decision in *Shaw* v. *Director of Public Prosecutions*.[4] It stated that because of the need for certainty as to the content of the criminal law the House must be sure that there is a very good reason before it departs from one of its own earlier criminal decisions. Their Lordships' speeches indicate that the House will be very slow to overrule such a decision, particularly if many convictions have been secured on the basis of it, an attitude which appears to prefer consistency to justice. The Court of Appeal (Criminal Division) takes a more liberal attitude towards its decisions and those of its predecessor, the Court of Criminal Appeal.[5] It is bound by these previous decisions except in the following situations:

a. Like the Court of Appeal (Civil Division) the Criminal Division is not bound, under the rule in *Young* v. *Bristol Aeroplane Co. Ltd.*,[6] in three situations:
    i. Where two of its previous decisions conflict; the decision which is not followed will be overruled.[7]

---

1. Chapter 20.
2. Note, [1966] 3 All E.R. 77.
3. [1973] A.C. 435; [1972] 2 All E.R. 898; *C. & J. Cases*. See Brazier, Overruling House of Lords Criminal Cases, [1973] Crim. L. R. 98.
4. [1962] A.C. 220; [1961] 2 All E.R. 446; *C. & J. Cases*.
5. See Zellick, Precedent in the Court of Appeal (Criminal Division), [1974] Crim. L. R. 222.
6. [1944] K.B. 718; [1944] 2 All E.R. 293.
7. E.g., *Gould* (No. 2), [1968] 2 Q.B. 65; [1968] 1 All E.R. 849; *C. & J. Cases*.

ii. The court must refuse to follow a previous decision of its own which, though not expressly overruled, cannot stand with a later House of Lords decision.
iii. The court is not bound to follow its previous decision if that decision was given *per incuriam* (i.e. some relevant statute or precedent, which might have affected the decision, was not brought to the attention of the court).

b. When sitting as a "full court", i.e. one constituted by more judges than usual, the Court of Appeal (Criminal Division) has power to overrule a previous decision on the ground that the law has been "misapplied or misunderstood".[1] It appears that, contrary to the previous practice,[2] an earlier decision may be overruled even though it is not in the appellant's favour to do so.[3]

The Queen's Bench Divisional Court is bound by its own previous decisions unless the *Young* v. *Bristol Aeroplane* principles[4] apply or, probably,[5] the law has been "misapplied or misunderstood". The ruling of one High Court judge is not binding on another but the latter will only refuse to follow such a decision if he is convinced that it is wrong.

Reference will occasionally be made to decisions of the Judicial Committee of the Privy Council, which is the final court of appeal from the colonies and certain Commonwealth countries. Decisions of the Judicial Committee do not bind English courts but are of very strong persuasive authority.

2.7 The theory underlying the development of the common law is that new cases simply illustrate the application of old doctrine to varying facts. Until recently this theory was strained because the courts on occasion reserved the right to create new offences, which is open to the following objections:

a. In a democratic society the creation of new offences should be done by the legislature.
b. There is a danger that the creation of new offences under the guise of developing old law promotes uncertainty concerning the extent of the legal rule.

---

1. *Taylor*, [1950] 2 K.B. 368; [1950] 2 All E.R. 170; *C. & J. Cases*; *Newsome and Browne*, [1970] 2 Q.B. 711; [1970] 3 All E.R. 455. See also Cross, *Precedent in English Law* (2nd ed.), 140–142.
2. *Taylor*.
3. *Newsome and Browne*.
4. *Huddersfield Police Authority* v. *Watson*, [1947] K.B. 842; [1947] 2 All E.R. 193.
5. *Younghusband* v. *Luftig*, [1949] 2 K.B. 354; [1949] 2 All E.R. 72.

c. The existence of a judicial power to create new offences contravenes the principle that no one should be punished for acts which were not criminal when they were performed. The principle is embodied in the Latin maxim *nulla poena sine lege*, and is sometimes spoken of as the principle of legality. It is even more important from the point of view of the liberty of the subject than other principles, such as those embodied in the doctrine of *mens rea*, and the rule that guilt must be proved beyond reasonable doubt, which are discussed at greater length in more detailed books on criminal law.

Fortunately, the judicial creation of offences is no longer possible since, in 1972 the House of Lords in *Knuller, Ltd.* v. *Director of Public Prosecutions*[1] unanimously rejected the existence of a residual power vested in the courts to create new offences or so to widen existing offences as to make punishable conduct of a type not hitherto subject to punishment.

Textwriters

2.8 In criminal law, as in other branches of English law, statements in text books have no binding force. This means that the judge is not bound to apply them in the same way as he must follow the directions contained in a statute or the principle to be inferred from a decided case. Nevertheless, some mention should be made of certain works which are treated with great respect by the judges. To go back only so far as the seventeenth century, the writings of Sir Edward Coke (d. 1634) are as important in the sphere of crime, which is dealt with in his *Third Institute*, as in other branches of the law. There is also the statement of the criminal law of a slightly later period in the unfinished *History of the Pleas of the Crown* by Sir Matthew Hale (d. 1676).

In the eighteenth century, Sir Michael Foster (d. 1763) left a valuable set of reports with notes and appendices entitled *Crown Law*, while Hawkins (d. 1746) wrote a treatise on *Pleas of the Crown* which was used by Sir William Blackstone (d. 1780) in the compilation of the fourth book of his *Commentaries* which deals with criminal law. Finally, Sir Edward Hyde East (d. 1847) published a general treatise on criminal law, known as *Pleas of the Crown*, in 1803, and the book is regarded as the successor to the treatises of Coke, Hale and Foster.

All these works are regarded as of persuasive authority on the law as it stood when they were written. Several of the standard works of the nineteenth century have been re-edited and,

1. [1973] A.C. 435; [1972] 2 All E.R. 898; *C. & J. Cases.*

although they are not authoritative in any strict sense of the word, many of them are relied on in daily practice. They include *Stephen's Digest of the Criminal Law*, *Archbold's Pleading, Evidence and Practice in Criminal Cases*, *Russell on Crime* and Kenny's *Outlines of Criminal Law*. Modern works which are frequently quoted are *Smith and Hogan's Criminal Law*, *Smith's Law of Theft* and *Grien's Theft Act 1968*. *Stone's Justices' Manual* is the standard work on summary procedure. The work of Sir James Stephen is of great importance because he was responsible for a three-volume *History of the Criminal Law* in addition to his *Digest*, and for the draft criminal code which is mentioned below.

Statute

2.9 The majority of offences are defined and regulated by statutes, i.e. Acts of Parliament which have been duly passed through both Houses and received the Royal Assent. Statute may create an entirely new offence; for example, before the passing of the Punishment of Incest Act 1908, it was not an offence for a man to have sexual intercourse with an adult female whom he knew to be his granddaughter, daughter, sister or mother, although such incestuous intercourse has generally been regarded as morally abhorrent. The Act made such conduct criminal. This is an instance of a serious offence which has been created by statute and there are many others, for, from time to time in the history of the criminal law, Parliament has thus found it necessary to punish acts which were not punished by the common law. It is in the sphere of the less morally reprehensible offences, however, that Parliament has been most active and it is true to say at the present day that the vast majority of offences have been created by statute.

2.10 Apart from the creation of new offences by statute, it is also necessary to bear in mind, in order to have a full and proper understanding of the criminal law, that many offences which now exist by virtue of statute were originally common law offences. Many statutes have replaced common law offences and in so doing have changed the common law very considerably.

This is one of the reasons for the apparent complexity of much of the statute law relating to offences. Although there are welcome signs of improvement, it must be admitted that a further reason for this complexity is the failure of those responsible for our criminal legislation to keep the statute book up to date. Enactments such as the Forgery Act 1913 and the Offences against the Person Act 1861 contain an odd assortment of sections culled from earlier legislation. Many have little or no application to modern circumstances, many of them overlap and the drafting of nearly all of them could be simplified with advantage.

2.11 It follows from what has been said that in England we have no single criminal code such as exists in many other countries. A draft code was brought before Parliament in 1878, 1879 and 1880, but it was never given statutory effect. The result is that, with the exception of common law offences and those created by subordinate legislation which are dealt with later[1] the criminal law of England is contained in a number of statutes. Some of these are concerned solely with the criminal law or with criminal procedure and each of them is in effect a code covering the particular type of offence with which it deals. The Offences against the Person Act 1861 (as amended by subsequent legislation), for example, covers a large variety of offences which are broadly defined as being committed against the person and, besides prescribing the punishment for murder and manslaughter, includes such crimes as wounding with intent to do grievous bodily harm, administering poison, using explosives, assaults, child stealing, bigamy and abortion. The Theft Act 1968 covers most offences against property, and entirely replaces the common law with regard to them. The other principal statute covering offences against property is the Criminal Damage Act 1971, which deals with damaging a person's property as distinct from depriving him of it. The two last mentioned statutes are a vast improvement on and simplification of earlier enactments dealing with the same subject matter; similar changes are contemplated with regard to the Offences against the Person Act 1861 and Forgery Act 1913.

2.12 In addition to Acts of the kind mentioned in the last paragraph, there is a large number whose main object is to set up public services of some description, or to control certain activities such as road traffic, but which contain offences for which punishments are prescribed. They are not entirely concerned with the criminal law, but they certainly create offences and as far as they do so must be regarded as one of the sources of the criminal law. This already large category is increasing because the State has embarked on many new activities and assumed the responsibility for controlling and curtailing others which previously anyone was free to undertake. Further, in the past, criminal provisions in statutes were largely concerned with punishing

1. Para. 2.14.

persons who did something which is forbidden; more frequently than before a statute punishes the failure to carry out a duty. In primitive societies, law consists of a series of prohibitions; the Ten Commandments should be called the Prohibitions and Commandments. Comparatively few omissions are punished at common law but an examination of any recent public welfare statute will demonstrate the way in which many positive duties, such as the notification of the existence of certain diseases in a particular house, are imposed on the private citizen as well as upon public bodies; the failure to carry out such duties is made a criminal offence.

Thus the field which is covered by criminal offences created by statute at the present day is very wide indeed; a glance at the Table of Statutes in *Stone's Justices' Manual* is a clear demonstration of the fact that to comprehend the extent of the criminal law, the student must not confine himself merely to those statutes which appear to be immediately concerned with it. As well as being aware of the Forgery Act 1913, the Theft Act 1968, and the Criminal Damage Act 1971, he must remember that there are penal provisions in the Bankruptcy Act 1914, the Licensing Act 1964 and a host of others.

2.13 There are certain rules relating to statutory offences which must be borne in mind. If the statute itself provides no maximum penalty, the offence is punishable with a maximum of two years' imprisonment,[1] but this does not apply where the statute merely creates a private right. Where a statute creates a new offence and also lays down the procedure for its punishment or for some other remedy, the general rule is that the procedure at common law by way of indictment is excluded. Where a statute enacts that some act shall be an offence which is already an offence at common law and also prescribes some remedy, it may be that the common law remedy by indictment will continue to exist as an alternative to the procedure provided in the statute. In other words, a statute may alter the common law, but if it does not do so, either expressly[2] or by implication, the common law continues in force.

Subordinate legislation[3]

2.14 A statute may give power to some body such as the Queen in Council, a Minister or a local authority to make regulations and prescribe for their breach.

1. Powers of Criminal Courts Act 1973, s. 18 (1).
2. E.g. Theft Act 1968, s. 32.
3. See Garner, *Administrative Law*, 4th ed., Ch. 4.

This method of creating criminal offences is of increasing importance at the present day although it is not new. A good example is the power of the Secretary of State for the Environment under the Road Traffic Acts to make regulations. Acting under this power, he has made regulations which cover a very large number of different subjects and prosecutions are regularly instituted for breach of them. Such matters as the efficiency of brakes and the avoidance of obstruction are to be found not in the Acts themselves, but in the regulations.[1]

Subordinate legislation is of two kinds. The more important kind are Orders in Council made by the Queen in Council and regulations made by Ministers. Generally, these must be made by Statutory Instrument and are subject to the rules governing publication and procedure contained in the Statutory Instruments Act 1946. The other kind of subordinate legislation, by-laws, are made by local authorities, nationalised industries and certain other bodies authorised by statute. Although general in operation, they are restricted to the locality or undertaking to which they apply.

All forms of subordinate legislation are invalid if they exceed the powers conferred by the enabling statute on the rule making body or if the prescribed procedure has not been followed and in the case of bye-laws on certain other grounds.

Social morality and the proper scope of the criminal law[2]

2.15 Although common law, statute and subordinate legislation are the only direct sources of the criminal law, allowance must be made for the very important indirect source of morality. Much of our criminal law inherited from the past has undoubtedly been influenced by Christian beliefs, but at the present day these beliefs are not the only basis of the morals of our society.

2.16 The spheres of social morals and the criminal law are co-extensive up to a point, but many of the rules enforced by the criminal law have nothing to do with social morality, and many rules of social morality are not enforced by the criminal law.

For the purposes of the present discussion, a rule may be said to be one of social morality when it is accepted by the bulk of a given society as laying down a standard of behaviour to which its members ought to conform and as justifying severe censure

1. Paras. 16.27–16.33.
2. Devlin, *The Enforcement of Morals*; Hart, *Law, Liberty and Morality*.

for those who break it. Many rules of current social morality are enforced by the criminal law, the person who breaks them thus being liable to punishment by the State as well as the censure of his fellows; obvious instances are the prohibitions of all forms of deliberate violence, theft and deliberate damage to property. No doubt it was rules of this nature which Lord Coleridge, C.J. had in mind when he said that "A legal common law duty is nothing else than the enforcing by law of that which is a moral obligation without legal enforcement."[1]

The restriction of the observation to common law duties is, however, of the utmost importance. Most, if not all, of the common law duties enforced by the criminal law are recognised by current social morality, but over the last century at least our criminal law has had added to it by statute a vast number of offences which carry no moral blame at all. We have already seen that an owner of land who uses it for a purpose which is contrary to the requirements of a local authority commits an offence, and a person who maintains a foster-child whom he received in an emergency and does not give notice of that fact within 48 hours to the welfare authority also commits an offence and is liable to imprisonment for six months and to a fine of £100.[2] These are not exceptional cases; there are many hundreds like them. To complete the quotation from Lord Atkin's speech in *Proprietary Articles Trade Association* v. *A.G. for Canada*,[3] cited in para. 1.6, "Morality and criminality are far from co-extensive, nor is the sphere of criminality necessarily part of a more extensive field covered by morality, unless the moral code necessarily disapproves of all acts prohibited by the State, in which case the argument moves in a circle."

2.17 Many rules of social morality are not enforced by the criminal law. The man who seduces his friend's wife and ruins his home, the man who stands by and watches a cruel rape without taking any steps to prevent it,[4] or the man who breaks a contract and thereby causes thousands of pounds worth of damage is free from any kind of criminal responsibility. It is not difficult to give reasons for the reluctance of the criminal law to enforce all the rules of social morality. The type of seduction which anyone

1. *Instan*, [1893] 1 Q.B. 450; *C. & J. Cases*.
2. Children Act 1958, s. 3 (1) and s. 14.
3. [1931] A.C. 310, at p. 324.
4. *Clarkson*, [1971] 3 All E.R. 344.

would wish to make criminal is difficult to define, difficult to prove and something of which proof would frequently involve gross infringement of individual privacy. The enforcement by the criminal law of a general duty to take active steps to prevent crime would give rise to insoluble problems concerning the point at which the line should be drawn. The question of the extent to which it is proper to punish one citizen for not risking his own safety in the protection of another is, like the question of the extent to which it is proper to punish people for failing to act like the Good Samaritan, very far from being susceptible of a clear answer. A similar observation may be made with regard to the question when the civil remedy for breach of contract is an adequate protection for the victims of broken promises. So drastic is the criminal sanction that its imposition is something which must be justified to the hilt.

2.18 Reflections of the kind mentioned in the last paragraph prompt the question whether the fact that conduct is prohibited by a rule of social morality can ever, without something more, justify its punishment by the criminal law. This is a matter upon which there has been, and no doubt will continue to be, a deep cleavage of opinion. Although it is possible to adopt a number of intermediate positions, two diametrically opposed answers to the question have been given; they may respectively be described as the "libertarian" and "authoritarian" answers.

2.19 The libertarian answer was given in the nineteenth century by John Stuart Mill in his essay *On Liberty* and, in the twentieth century, by the Report of the Committee on Homosexual Offences and Prostitution (the Wolfenden Committee) published in 1957.[1] Mill stated the principle underlying his essay as follows:

> "The principle is, that the sole end for which mankind are warranted, individually or collectively, in interfering with the liberty of action of any of their number is self-protection. That the only purpose for which power can be rightfully exercised over any member of a civilised community against his will is to prevent harm to others."

According to the Wolfenden Committee, the function of the criminal law is

> "to preserve public order and decency, to protect the citizen from

1. Cmnd. 247.

what is offensive or injurious and to provide sufficient safeguards against exploitation or corruption of others, particularly those who are specially vulnerable because they are young, weak in body or mind or inexperienced or in a state of special physical, official or economic dependence....

"Unless a deliberate attempt is to be made by society, acting through the agency of the law, to equate the sphere of crime with that of sin, there must remain a realm of private morality and immorality which is, in brief and crude terms, not the law's business."

The Wolfenden Committee recommended the legalisation of acts of homosexuality performed in private between consenting males of and above the age of 21, in spite of the fact that such acts may well be condemned by contemporary social morality.

2.20 The authoritarian answer to the question whether the fact that conduct is prohibited by a rule of social morality can ever, without something more, such as harm to others, justify its punishment by the criminal law was given in the nineteenth century by Stephen in his book *Liberty, Equality, Fraternity* and, in the twentieth century, by Lord Devlin in his Maccabeean lecture to the British Academy in 1959 on the enforcement of morals. According to Stephen, the criminal law affirms in a singularly emphatic manner a principle which is absolutely inconsistent with and contradictory to Mill's, namely, the principle that

"there are acts of wickedness so gross and outrageous that, self-protection apart, they must be prevented as far as possible at any cost to the offender, and punished, if they occur, with exemplary severity".

According to Lord Devlin,

"The suppression of vice is as much the law's business as the suppression of subversive activities."

He was criticising the Wolfenden Committee's view that there is a realm of private morality. Lord Devlin expressed no opinion with regard to the propriety of the Wolfenden Committee's recommendations, but he said that no society can do without "intolerance, indignation and disgust", and suggested that people should ask themselves whether, looking at the matter calmly and dispassionately, they regarded homosexuality as "a vice so abominable that its mere presence is an offence". If that turned out to be the genuine feeling of society, he did not see how society could be denied the right to try to eradicate homosexuality.

2.21 The difficulty about the libertarian view, when stated without qualification, is its inability to justify such commonly accepted prohibitions of the criminal law as those on the possession of dangerous drugs for consumption, the keeping of a brothel and cruelty to animals. The difficulty about the authoritarian view is its apparent acquiescence in the suggestion that it may sometimes be right to punish conduct simply because it is highly distasteful to a large number of people.

2.22 The libertarian view triumphed at one point when the Sexual Offences Act 1967, legalising private homosexuality between consenting males of 21 or over, was passed; the authoritarian view was supported by the speeches of the majority of the House of Lords in *Shaw* v. *Director of Public Prosecutions.*[1] Shaw published a "Ladies' Directory" designed to assist prostitutes to get custom, and he was charged, *inter alia*, with a conspiracy to corrupt public morals. He was convicted of this offence, and his conviction was upheld by the Court of Criminal Appeal and House of Lords. Lord Simonds said that he entertained no doubt that, in the sphere of criminal law,

> "there remains in the courts of law a residual power to enforce the supreme and fundamental purpose of the law, to conserve not only the safety and order but also the moral welfare of the State, and that it is their duty to guard it against attacks which may be the more insidious because they are novel and unprepared for."[2]

Lord Simonds proceeded to raise the question whether, if a time were to come when homosexuality between consenting adult males was legalised it would be an offence if, without obscenity, such practices were publicly advocated and encouraged by pamphlet and advertisement. The time having come, the question raised by Lord Simonds was answered by the House of Lords in *Knuller, Ltd.* v. *Director of Public Prosecutions*[3] where it was held that an agreement to publish advertisements to assist or encourage the commission of homosexual acts between adult males in private was a conspiracy to corrupt public morals. However, the House emphasised that the courts did not have a residual power to extend the criminal law, by creating new offences or widening existing ones, to enforce good morals. Lord Simon of Glaisdale said that what the courts could and

1. [1962] A.C. 220.
2. *Ibid.*, at p. 267.
3. [1973] A.C. 435; [1972] 2 All E.R. 898.

should do was to recognise the applicability of established offences to new circumstances to which they were relevant. Obviously a fine line has to be drawn but this decision does show that the authoritarian view of the criminal law is losing ground.

The proper scope of the criminal law

2.23 Whatever view be taken about the enforcement of social morality as such, it must be recognised that it is something which, like the concept of crime, varies from country to country and from time to time. Under the conditions prevailing in contemporary England, a case can be made out for the abolition of such crimes as incest between adults, bigamy and, where there is no evidence of exploitation, brothel keeping; but it by no means follows that the case should be accepted. In the case of the first and third examples, it may be urged that the criminal sanction is necessary for the protection of women in a vulnerable position, and it is possible that the decision to cease to regard bigamy as a crime would undermine the institution of marriage. A case can also be made out for the legalisation of euthanasia, but here again it by no means follows that the case should be accepted because well nigh insuperable difficulties can be raised with regard to the method of determining that the deceased really was a consenting party to his death. A case can also be made out for the legalisation of the possession for sale and consumption of cannabis but many people think that the case is met by our ignorance of the long-term effects of this substance.

In 1971, a conference of directors of criminological research institutes, having opined that the only acceptable definition of crime is behaviour which seriously interferes with the life of society, suggested that modern trends in dealing with shoplifting and worthless cheques showed that such actions are no longer regarded as true crimes, whereas pollution of the environment, noise and invasions of privacy were being treated more and more often as criminal offences. Although a very great deal of shoplifting and obtaining of property by means of worthless cheques is not prosecuted, it is doubtful whether many English lawyers would favour their removal from the criminal calendar. The allusion to new offences is significant because discussions of the proper scope of the criminal law are apt to concentrate on whether there are too many offences to the exclusion of whether there are too few; but a new offence should be created only if there is a strong demand for it, and if there is a reasonable prospect of that demand continuing. It is much easier to make than to unmake criminal law.

The classification of offences

2.24 Offences may be classified according to:

a. their source, into statutory and common law offences;

b. their effect on the law of arrest, into arrestable and other offences;

c. the survival of certain special rules, into treasons and other offences; or

d. the method by which they are tried, into indictable and summary offences.

The sources of the criminal law have already been discussed and nothing more need be said about the first division. The second and third divisions can be understood only in the light of history.

2.25 We have already seen that the serious offences created by the judges from the twelfth to the fourteenth century were called felonies, and the less serious came to be known as misdemeanours. The principal original felonies were homicide, rape, theft, robbery, burglary and arson. The main characteristics of a felony were that the punishment was generally capital, that the felon's goods were forfeited to the Crown, while his lands escheated to his feudal lord and that there was a general power of arrest without warrant.

The rigours of the first characteristic were mitigated by the institution known as "benefit of clergy". This evolved out of the twelfth-century controversy about whether the royal or ecclesiastical courts should try priests accused of felony. By the end of the middle ages, the privilege of claiming benefit of clergy had been extended to all laymen who could read, the test for this being their capacity to get through the first verse of the fifty-first Psalm: "Have mercy upon me, O God, after Thy great goodness, according to the multitude of Thy mercies do away with mine offences." This came to be known as the "neck verse". The practice was for the privilege to be claimed after conviction in the royal courts and, if the claim was made good, the only punishment which those courts could administer was branding (to prevent the privilege from being claimed again by the same person) and a year's imprisonment. Benefit of clergy therefore in effect afforded relief to first offenders in the case of felonies.

From the sixteenth century onwards, various statutes provided that in the more serious felonies, for example murder, the privilege could not be claimed. Thus arose the distinction between clergyable offences and those which were not clergyable. Various felonies were brought into the latter category from time to time by statute down to the abolition of benefit of clergy in 1827. From then on the death penalty was abolished in the case of most felonies, and it only exists today in treason and as a theoretical possibility in piracy with violence.

Forfeiture of goods and lands remained possible consequences of a conviction for felony until it was abolished by the Forfeiture Act 1870. Both before and after 1870, statutes declared a number of crimes to be felonies, and the result is that a felony can best be defined as an offence which, before 1870, involved forfeiture of the convict's lands and goods or an offence subsequently declared to be a felony by statute.

Benefit of clergy never applied to misdemeanours because none of them were ever capital, a conviction of a misdemeanour did not entail forfeiture of land or goods and there was no general power of arrest without warrant. The procedure at a trial for felony differed somewhat from that at a trial for misdemeanour and, at one time, there was a further important difference between the two categories of offence due to the fact that felonies were more serious offences. This had ceased to be so long before the abolition of the distinctions between felonies and misdemeanours by the Criminal Law Act 1967 which provides that on all matters on which a distinction between felonies and misdemeanours had previously been made, the law applicable at the commencement of the Act to misdemeanours applies.

Arrestable offences and treason

.26 The Criminal Law Act 1967 contains special provisions with regard to arrest in the case of certain offences described as "arrestable offences". A further possible division of crimes is therefore that between arrestable offences and other offences. Arrestable offences are defined in para. 22.7.

Benefit of clergy never applied to treason, on a conviction for which the convict's lands and goods were permanently forfeited to the Crown. Before the Treason Act 1945, treasons were subject to special rules of procedure and this led many of the older writers to treat treasons as a separate category of offence. Despite drastic reduction by the 1945 Act, some of the procedural differences between treasons and other offences remain. Moreover, the Criminal Law Act 1967 expressly provided that nothing in the Act should apply to treason. Accordingly it is still necessary to recognise a possible division of crimes into treasons and other offences.

Indictable and summary offences

2.27 This method of classifying crimes, which is dealt with in more detail later,[1] is essentially procedural. An indictable offence is one triable on indictment. Trial on indictment takes place in the Crown Court and is always with a jury.[2] A summary offence is one triable summarily. Summary trial invariably takes place before a magistrates' court where there is no jury.[3] Since the thirteenth century trial upon indictment has been the typical method of trial at common law, although the proceedings are now regulated by statute. Broadly speaking, summary trial is only applied to the less serious offences but naturally they are much more numerous.

---

1. Paras. 22.10–22.11 and 23.17–23.18.
2. Paras 23.1–23.16.
3. Paras. 23.17–23.24.

3

CRIMINAL LIABILITY[1]

Actus reus and *mens rea*

3.1 A cardinal principle of criminal law is embodied in the maxim *actus non facit reum, nisi mens sit rea*—an act does not make a person legally guilty unless the mind is legally blameworthy.[2] In this chapter it is proposed to deal generally with what must be proved in order to secure a conviction although it may be that the accused person can rely on a defence which the prosecution must disprove. Two points are involved—first the outward conduct, and secondly the state of mind of the accused. It has become customary to consider the definition of every offence under two heads—the *actus reus* and the *mens rea*.

3.2 It is convenient to begin with a few general observations before analysing these expressions. The full implications of the requirement of *mens rea* cannot be appreciated until not only the entire chapter and the entire book but many others have been studied. The maxim has not escaped criticism. When commenting on the similar phrase "*non est reus nisi mens sit rea*" Stephen, J., said "though this phrase is in common use, I think it most unfortunate, and not only likely to mislead, but actually misleading, on the following grounds. It naturally suggests that, apart from all particular definitions of crimes, such a thing exists as a '*mens rea*', or 'guilty mind', which is always expressly or by implication involved in every definition. This is obviously not the case, for the mental elements of different crimes differ widely."[3] This remains true today. *Mens rea* means in murder

---

1. Barnes, Criminal Liability, (1946) 9 *Cambridge Law Journal*, 210; Holmes, *Common Law*, lecture 2; *Modern Approach to Criminal Law*, pp. 195–272; Stallybrass, The Eclipse of *Mens Rea*, (1936) 52 L.Q.R. 60; Stephen, *History of Criminal Law*, Vol. II, Ch. xviii; Williams, *Criminal Law: The General Part*, 2nd ed.; Williams, *The Mental Elements in Crime*. We are heavily indebted to Professor Williams' books. They should be consulted as further reading on this and other chapters.
2. *Younghusband* v. *Luftig*, [1949] 2 K.B. 354, at p. 370.
3. *Tolson* (1889), 23 Q.B.D. 168, at p. 187; *C. & J. Cases.*

an intention to kill or do grievous bodily harm; in theft that the accused acted "dishonestly" and with the intention of permanently depriving another of the property; and in criminal damage an intention to damage property belonging to another, or recklessness as to whether any such property would be damaged. In some cases, such as manslaughter, *mens rea* can denote mere blameworthy inattention.

The maxim can also be criticised in that *mens rea* is not always required for criminal liability; in some offences a person can be convicted despite the fact of his blameless inattention.

Notwithstanding these strictures, the significance of the maxim has been stressed in a number of modern judgments. In *Brend* v. *Wood*,[1] Lord Goddard, C.J., said "It is of the utmost importance for the protection of the liberty of the subject that a court should always bear in mind that, unless a statute either clearly or by necessary implication rules out *mens rea* as a constituent part of a crime, the court should not find a man guilty of an offence against the criminal law unless he has a guilty mind."

3.3 Most people would agree that, as a general rule, the infliction of punishment is only justified when the accused was at fault, and, in order to ascertain whether the accused was at fault it is necessary to pay attention to such matters as his control over his bodily movements at the material time, his knowledge of relevant facts and his foresight of relevant consequences.

The requirement of *mens rea* is thus designed to give effect to the idea of just punishment. For those who believe that everyone who does an act prohibited by the criminal law should be liable to therapeutic treatment rather than punishment, the state of mind with which the act was performed is a relevant consideration only when the method of treatment falls to be determined,[2] but the holders of these beliefs have not supplied a blueprint of the practical means of giving effect to their views.

Nonetheless, these views at least have the merit of emphasising the fact that the requirement that an *actus reus* should always be proved is even more important than the requirement of *mens rea*. The Christian moral code may condemn evil intentions just as much as evil deeds, but it is unnecessary for the law to go to such lengths. Evil intentions only become sufficiently dangerous to society to merit punishment when the agent has gone

1. (1946), 175 L.T. 306.
2. Wootton, *Crime and the Criminal Law*.

a considerable distance towards carrying them out. Even the most diehard believers in punishment concede that a system of law according to which wishes were equivalent to deeds would be even less satisfactory than one which punished deeds without considering the mental state of the doer. "The reasons for imposing this great leading restriction upon the law are obvious. If it were not so restricted it would be utterly intolerable; all mankind would be criminals and most of their lives would be passed in trying and punishing each other for offences which could never be proved".[1]

3.4 Not only does the maxim *actus non facit reum, nisi mens sit rea* serve the important purpose of stressing two basis requirements of criminal liability but it also suggests a useful framework for the analysis of the definitions of specific offences. This task is undertaken in Chapters 7 to 17 and we generally divide our discussion into a consideration of the *actus reus* and *mens rea* required in each case. It is, however, most important that the maxim should not be allowed to become the master rather than the tool of the criminal lawyer. A perfectly coherent account of the criminal law could be given without it, and time is sometimes wasted by the consideration of pointless questions concerning the heading under which certain undeniable requisites of, or exemptions from, criminal liability should be discussed. Thus there is no doubt that excusable automatism is generally a defence, even when the accused is sane. This means that, if there is sufficient evidence that the accused did not know what he was doing at the material time, the prosecution will fail unless it can satisfy the jury that the accused did know what he was doing. No useful purpose is served by considering whether the requirement that the accused must generally have acted voluntarily, i.e. when not in a state of automatism, relates to *actus reus* or *mens rea*.

Actus reus

3.5 It is necessary to refer to the definition of the offence charged in order to ascertain the precise nature of the prohibited conduct, and even the most cursory consideration of the different offences makes it plain that, if the phrase *actus reus* is to be used as a description of the requisite external conduct, it must be given a far wider meaning than "criminal act". Rarely, if ever, is a mere act sufficient for criminal liability. The definitions of offences

1. Stephen, *History of the Criminal Law*, Vol. II, 78.

invariably specify surrounding circumstances, such as time or place, which are essential to render the act criminal. Sometimes the definition requires a consequence to result from the act, such as the consequence of death in murder. Thus, the expression *actus reus* is understood as meaning the act (or sometimes the omission or other event) indicated in the definition of the crime charged as being proscribed by the criminal law together with any surrounding circumstances, other than the accused's state of mind, and any consequences of that act which are indicated by the definition.

Acts, omissions and events

3.6 An act is the most common basis of the *actus reus*. The nature of the requisite act, of course, varies from offence to offence. Some indicate it precisely, so that in rape an act of sexual intercourse is required and in causing death by dangerous driving an act of driving. However, the relevant act is specified less precisely in the definitions of other offences, particularly where they use words which comprise two concepts, that of an act and of a consequence flowing from it; for example the common law definitions of murder and manslaughter simply require the "killing" of another. Where the act is left undefined in this way, any act which results in the death of another will suffice. Thus, murder can be committed by an act of shooting or hitting or strangling or planting a bomb or poisoning or by any other of the many ways which men and women have devised for killing each other.

An omission to act is a less common basis of criminal liability.[1] Offences where an omission can give rise to criminal liability can be divided into two groups:

a. Those whose definition requires a particular omission to act, such as the offences of failing to accord precedence to a pedestrian on a pedestrian crossing and of failing, without reasonable excuse, to provide a specimen of breath under the breathalyser legislation.[2] Apart from the common law offence of misprision of treason (a failure to report a treason), all offences of this type are statutory.
b. Those which, according to the interpretation given to them by the courts, can be committed either by an act or an omission. Here an omission to act will only suffice as an alternative to an act if the accused was under a legal duty to act but did not do so. This duty can arise in two principal ways—under

1. Para. 2.12.

2. Para. 16.32.

a contract[1] or by virtue of a particular relationship, such as parent and child or doctor and patient, where one person has care of another.[2] Murder or manslaughter, for example, may be committed by someone who fails to feed his child.[3]

Sometimes the definition of a offence refers to a mere external event rather than an act or omission. All offences where a mere event is sufficient are statutory. One example is provided by s. 25 of the Theft Act 1968, whereby a person is guilty of an offence if, when not at his place of abode, he has with him any article for use in the course of or in connection with any burglary, theft or cheat.

Circumstances and consequences

3.7 The accused's act or omission may be required to result in a particular consequence. In murder and manslaughter it must be proved that the accused's act or omission resulted in the death of a human being and in obtaining property by deception it must be proved that the property belonging to another was obtained as the result of the accused's deception.

The circumstances in which the act, omission or external event must occur vary widely from offence to offence and are expressed with varying degrees of precision. The offence under s. 25 of the Theft Act can be committed only by someone who is not at his place of abode; the act of entry in burglary must be by a trespasser, and bigamy can be perpetrated only by a person who is already married. These circumstances are clearly required by the relevant definitions but in other cases less exact words are used. One example is the word "unlawfully" which is particularly common in the definitions of offences against the person. Probably the use of such a word does no more than express what would otherwise be implied, namely that no *actus reus* is committed if some appropriate justification or excuse exists, such as self-defence or prevention of crime or the alleged victim's valid consent.

3.8 There can be no criminal liability unless the whole *actus reus* is proved. In *White*,[4] for instance, the accused put potassium of cyanide in his mother's drink, intending to kill her. Shortly afterwards the mother was found dead with the glass, partly full,

1. *Pittwood* (1902), 19 T.L.R. 37.
2. *Gibbins and Proctor* (1918), 13 Cr. App. Rep. 134; *Bonnyman* (1942), 28 Cr. App. Rep. 131.
3. *Gibbins and Proctor*.
4. [1910] 2 K.B. 124.

beside her. The medical evidence was that she had died from a heart attack, and not from poisoning, and that the quantity of potassium cyanide administered was insufficient to cause her death. The accused was acquitted of murder (but convicted of attempted murder) because although the intended consequence —death—had occurred it had not been caused by his conduct and thus an element of the *actus reus* of murder was missing. Similarly, one who handles goods, mistakenly believing that they are stolen goods, cannot be convicted of handling stolen goods since the necessary circumstance that the goods are stolen is absent.[1]

Mens rea

3.9 Despite occasional judicial utterances to the contrary,[2] it is clear from the application of *mens rea* in the courts that it has nothing necessarily to do with notions of an evil mind or knowledge of the wrongfulness of the act. The accused's ignorance of the criminal law is no defence, nor generally is the fact that the accused did not personally consider his conduct to be immoral or know that it was regarded as immoral by the bulk of society. Moreover, it is generally irrelevant to liability whether the accused acted with a "good" or "bad" motive.

The expression *mens rea* means the mental state expressly or impliedly required by the definition of the offence charged. This varies from offence to offence but typical instances are intention, recklessness, guilty knowledge and malice. In the course of our examination of typical mental states it will be necessary to refer to negligence, although this can hardly be said to be a mental state.

Intention

3.10 Where the definition of the *actus reus* of the offence charged requires the accused's conduct to produce a particular consequence he has a sufficient mental state if he intended it to occur. Thus, if it is proved that A has obtained property from B by deception, A is guilty of the offence of obtaining property by deception if, when he made the deception which resulted in property being obtained, he intended to obtain property and fulfilled the other requirements of s. 15 of the Theft Act 1968.[3]

---

1. *Haughton* v. *Smith*, [1975] A.C. at p. 485; [1973] 3 All E.R. 1109.
2. See, for example, *Sherras* v. *de Rutzen*, [1895] 1 Q.B. 918, at p. 921, *per* Wright, J.; *Sweet* v. *Parsley*, [1970] A.C. 132, at p. 152, *per* Lord Morris of Borth-y-Gest.
3. Paras. 11.13–11.19.

3.11 There are two types of intention with regard to prohibited consequences, "direct" intention and "oblique" intention. The distinction was drawn by Jeremy Bentham, although he spoke of consequences as being intentional, whereas it is now more common to speak of acts as being intentional with reference to their consequences.

> "A consequence, when it is intentional, may either be directly so, or only obliquely. It may be said to be directly or lineally intentional, when the prospect of producing it constituted one of the links in the chain of causes by which the person was determined to do the act. It may be said to be obliquely or collaterally intentional, when, although the consequence was in contemplation, and appeared likely to ensue in case of the act's being performed, yet the prospect of producing such consequences did not constitute a link in the aforesaid chain."[1]

Direct intention

3.12 Intention has recently been defined by the Court of Appeal in *Mohan*[2] as: "a decision to bring about, insofar as it lies within the accused's power, [a particular consequence], no matter whether the accused desired that consequence of his act or not". As the court recognised,[3] this can be described more briefly as the "aim". According to the definition adopted in *Mohan* the accused acts intentionally with reference to a particular consequence in the following cases:

a. If he aimed at achieving a particular consequence and believed he was likely to succeed, he acted intentionally with reference to it.
b. If he aimed at achieving a particular consequence although he did not expect that his act would do so, he acted intentionally with reference to it. Suppose A were to fire a pistol at B, hoping that the bullet would travel beyond what he took to be the weapon's normal range, but without believing that it would do so, A can be said to have killed B intentionally if his hope was fulfilled.
c. If he aimed at achieving a particular consequence (although he did not desire it in itself) in order to achieve an objective which he desired, he acted intentionally with reference to the particular consequence. Suppose T, a desperate criminal, finds his way of escape blocked by a policeman and, having

---

1. *Principles of Morals and Legislation* (ed. Harrison, Oxford, 1960) 202.
2. [1975] 2 All E.R. 193, at p. 200.
3. *Ibid.*, at p. 198.

no desire to harm him but having no other means of escape, shoots him dead. T can be said to have killed the policeman intentionally since he decided to kill him, insofar as it lay within his power. This example shows that, under the definition in *Mohan*, a man can be said to intend a consequence which is not desired in itself if that consequence is a condition precedent to the achievement of a desired consequence and he decides to cause that consequence, insofar as it lies within his power.

Oblique intention

3.13 So far as ordinary language is concerned, the only occasions on which it is proper to speak of a person having intended a consequence or having acted intentionally with reference to it is when he decided to bring it about, insofar as it lay within his power (i.e. he aimed at producing it). However, some such concept as oblique intention is essential for law and morals because it is generally considered that there are many situations in which a person who acts with the knowledge that a particular consequence will, or will probably, ensue is just as blameworthy as the man who aimed at producing those consequences. According to the moral doctrine of "double effect" a person is less blameworthy in respect of the unwanted consequences of his conduct however clearly he must have realised that they would occur, than for those which he sought to achieve, but the doctrine certainly does not represent English law.

3.14 A consequence is said to have been intended obliquely in two cases. The first is when, although not aimed at by the accused, it was foreseen by him as substantially certain to result. Suppose that F, wishing to collect the insurance on a cargo, puts a time bomb on an aircraft to blow it up in flight. He realises that the explosion is certain to kill those on board. The death of these persons is obliquely intended but can F be said to have acted intentionally with reference to these deaths in the legal sense of intention? F's state of mind would seem to fall outside the definition of intention postulated in *Mohan* since it does not look as if he has decided to bring about the deaths, insofar as it lies within his power. However, the opinion of Lord Hailsham in *Hyam v. Director of Public Prosecutions*,[1] decided by the House of Lords the year before *Mohan*, suggests that the case can be brought within the definition of intention adopted in *Mohan*. Lord Hail-

1. [1974] 2 All E.R. 41, at p. 52.

sham adopted a definition of intention similar to that in *Mohan* and went on to say that the definition should be held to include "the means as well as the end and the inseparable consequences of the end as well as the means", namely the consequences which are foreseen as substantially certain to result, although they were not the aim. On this basis, Lord Hailsham thought that the deaths of the occupants of the aircraft were intended by F, but this seems not merely to alter but to destroy the definition of intention in *Mohan*. If a person foresees a consequence as certain to result from his act but does not aim to produce it, it cannot be said that he has decided to bring about that consequence (the deaths in the above example), insofar as it lies within his power. The reason is that these words, particularly "insofar as it lies within his power", connote that the accused's efforts are directed towards producing the consequence in question and in the case under discussion F's efforts are not directed towards producing the deaths of the passengers; he is indifferent as to their fate or may even hope that they survive the explosion by a miracle. The case is different from that where the desperate criminal decided to kill the policeman in order to achieve his desired objective (escape) because the desperate criminal did direct his efforts towards the consequence in question (the policeman's death).

Of course, the fact that foresight of a substantially certain consequence does not fall within the definition postulated in *Mohan* does not necessarily mean that it is not a legally sufficient species of intention. There is clear authority that foresight of certainty constitutes intention in a legal sense. To be liable as an accomplice, it must be proved that the accused person intended to aid the commission of the principal offence. In *National Coal Board* v. *Gamble*,[1] Devlin, J. said, with regard to the "intent to aid":

> "If one man deliberately sells to another a gun to be used for murdering a third, he may be indifferent about whether the man lives or dies and interested only in the cash profit to be made out of the sale, but he can still be an aider and abettor. To hold otherwise would be to negative the rule that *mens rea* is a matter of intent only and does not depend on desire or motive..."

.15 The second instance of oblique intent is where a person foresees that a consequence will probably result from his act, although he does not aim to produce it. *A fortiori*, this falls outside the species of intent defined in *Mohan*, statements to this

1. [1959] 1 Q.B. 11, at p. 23; [1958] 3 All E.R. 203.

effect being made in that case. Some writers,[1] as well as Lord Hailsham in *Hyam* v. *Director of Public Prosecutions* deny that foresight of probability constitutes intention in a legal sense. Other writers,[2] including ourselves, consider that the legal concept of oblique intention extends to foresight of probability. The same view was taken *obiter* by Viscount Dilhorne in *Hyam* v. *Director of Public Prosecutions*:[3]

> "A man may do an act with a number of intentions. If he does it deliberately and intentionally, knowing that when he does it it is highly probable that grievous bodily harm will result, I think most people would say and be justified in saying that whatever other intentions he may have had as well, he at least intended grievous bodily harm."

3.16 Theorising about whether the same terminology should be applied to foresight of probability as is applied to foresight of certainty is arid because, whatever terminology is used, it is difficult if not impossible to point to a decided case which suggests that there may be liability where the prohibited consequence (which is not aimed at) is foreseen as certain, but not where it is foreseen as probable. It is equally unimportant whether either type of what is called "oblique" intention here constitutes intention in law since it is quite clear that foresight of a consequence as certain or probable provides a sufficient *mens rea* for most crimes whatever term is used to describe such a state of mind. This point was clearly made by Lord Diplock in *Hyam* v. *Director of Public Prosecutions*:[4]

> "... I agree with those of your Lordships who take the uncomplicated view that in crimes of this class no distinction is to be drawn in English law between the state of mind of one who does an act because he desires it to produce a particular evil consequence and the state of mind of one who does the act knowing full well that it is likely to produce that consequence although it may not be the object he was seeking to achieve by doing the act. What is common to both these states of mind is willingness to produce the particular evil consequence: and this, in my view, is the *mens rea* needed to satisfy a requirement whether imposed by statute or existing at common law, that in order to constitute the offence with which the accused is charged he must have acted with 'intent' to produce a particular evil consequence ..."

---

1. E.g., Williams, *Mental Elements in Crime*.
2. Lord Denning, *Responsibility Before the Law*; Cross (1967) 83 L.Q.R. 215.
3. [1974] 2 All E.R. 41, at p. 59.
4. *Ibid.*, at pp. 62–63.

17 There are, however, offences for which the courts have insisted on a direct intention although there is no doubt about the existence of an oblique intention with regard to the prohibited consequences. In *Steane*,[1] for instance, the accused was charged with doing acts likely to assist the enemy, with intent to assist the enemy, contrary to Defence Regulations which have since been repealed. He broadcast for the Germans after he had been beaten up and after his family had been threatened with detention in a concentration camp. Steane did not directly intend to assist the enemy because, unlike the desperate criminal in the example given above, he had not decided to assist the enemy, insofar as it lay within his power, in order to achieve his desired objective of saving himself and his family. He could not be said to have aimed at assisting the enemy. Steane's conviction was quashed by the Court of Criminal Appeal because the trial judge merely told the jury that the accused must be taken to have intended the natural consequences of his act, whereas he should have told them that it was for the prosecution to prove that the accused had the specific intent of assisting the enemy, and that he was entitled to be acquitted if, on a review of all the evidence, there was any doubt about its existence. Lord Goddard gave some illustrations which seem to show that belief in the probability or even the certainty of a consequence does not mean that the requisite intent existed with regard to it. For example, shooting with intent to murder (a species of attempted murder no longer separately provided for by statute) and shooting with intent to resist arrest were distinct offences. Lord Goddard said that, if the accused shot at a policeman at close range, the jury should acquit him on a charge of shooting with intent to murder if they thought that he shot with intent to resist arrest. The judgement does however give rise to awkward problems. For instance, Professor Glanville Williams assumes that Steane would have had no defence if he had acted as he did in order to obtain a packet of cigarettes.[2]

.18 It is uncertain in how many offences proof of a direct intention is necessary even where there is no doubt about the existence of an oblique intention. It was established in *Mohan*[3] that only a direct intention will suffice for liability for attempt. The accused was convicted of attempting by wanton driving to cause

1. [1947] K.B. 997; [1947] 1 All E.R. 813; *C. & J. Cases.*
2. *Criminal Law: The General Part*, 2nd ed., 41.
3. [1975] 2 All E.R. 193.

bodily harm to a policeman after the trial judge had directed the jury that it was not necessary to prove that the accused intended to cause bodily harm, but that he could be convicted if he realised that his driving, unless interrupted, was likely to cause bodily harm, or was reckless as to whether bodily harm was caused. The Court of Appeal allowed the accused's appeal against conviction on the ground a. that intention was an essential ingredient of the offence of attempt and b. that "intention", when that word was used to describe the *mens rea* in attempt, meant, as we have seen, "a decision to bring about, insofar as it lies within the accused's power, the commission of the offence which it is alleged the accused attempted to commit, no matter whether the accused desired that consequence of his act or not".

Other offences which may require a direct intention may include treason by adhering to the Queen's enemies[1] and assisting offenders.[2] The use of the words "with intent" (to produce the consequences prescribed by the definition of the *actus reus*) in the statutory definition of an offence may indicate that only a direct intention will suffice even where there can meaningfully be said to be an oblique intent with reference to the requisite consequences.

In view of these uncertainties, the proposals for reform mentioned later,[3] which abandon the logic of Lord Goddard in *Steane*, are welcome. Lest it be thought that, by suggesting that oblique intention should suffice in cases like *Steane*, a draconian view is being advanced, it should be pointed out that a verdict of acquittal would still be available in extreme cases of that type on the basis of the defence of duress.

Further intention

3.19 This type of intention is alternatively known as "ulterior intention". These terms are used to describe an intention on the part of the accused which does not relate to a consequence of his conduct required by the definition of the *actus reus* of the crime charged but relates instead to something ulterior to it. Certain acts are made criminal only if they were performed with some further intent, or in order to do some further act. For example, it is not an offence to enter a building as a trespasser, but a person who does so with intent to steal anything in the building is guilty of burglary.[4] Very often the criminal law

1. *Ahlers*, [1915] 1 K.B. 616; *C. & J. Cases.*
2. *Andrews and Craig*, [1962] 3 All E.R. 961; *C. & J. Cases.*
3. Para. 3.31.
4. Theft Act 1968, s. 9. paras 11.3–11.6.

punishes what would otherwise be a comparatively minor offence with much greater severity if it was committed with the further intent of perpetrating a more serious offence. For example, a common assault is punishable, even on indictment, with only one year's imprisonment, but assault with intent to rob is punishable with imprisonment for life. In these and the fairly numerous similar cases, it must be proved that, when he did the prohibited act, the accused had decided to do all that he could towards the performance of the subsequent act. Talk of an oblique intent would obviously be quite out of place.

Specific intention

0 This phrase is used frequently in the reports and should be treated with caution since, although it does not connote an additional species of intention, it can bear three different meanings:

a. the intention which must be proved to secure a conviction for a particular offence;
b. a direct as opposed to an oblique intention;[1] and
c. a further intention.

"Specific intention" is discussed further in Chapter 5.[2]

Recklessness[3]

21 "Recklessness" is used in two senses. In the first (subjective) sense, it means the conscious taking of an unjustified risk. In the second (objective) sense it means the conscious taking of an unjustified risk of which the accused ought to have been aware, and in this second sense, "recklessness' is the equivalent of gross negligence, discussed later.[4]

We have seen that intention with reference to the consequences of an act normally means that the accused aimed at achieving them and expected them to occur ("direct intention"), although allowance has to be made for the extended sense in which the accused knew that consequences were likely to occur, although his conduct was not aimed at achieving them ("oblique intention"). A person would certainly never be said to have been reckless with regard to consequences which he set himself to

---

1. E.g. *Steane*, [1947] K.B. 997; [1947] 1 All E.R. 813; *Mohan*, [1975] 2 All E.R. 193.
2. Paras. 5.26–5.31.
3. White, Carelessness, Indifference and Recklessness, (1961) 24 M.L.R., 592; Fitzgerald, Carelessness, Indifference and Recklessness, 25 *ibid.*, 49; see also Glanville Williams, *ibid.*, 55; White, The Rejoinder, *ibid.*, 437.
4. Para. 3.28.

achieve, whether he expected them to occur or not. It must be admitted, however, that the oblique intention can be regarded as a species of recklessness, the use of the word "intention" in this context being justified by the magnitude of the foreseen risk.

Let us assume that A's purpose (direct intention) is to frighten B by pointing a revolver at him and pulling the trigger; he has no wish to kill B but realises that there is a risk of doing so in the following situations in which he takes a revolver from a crate containing a thousand revolvers some of which he knows to be loaded:

a. A knows that all the revolvers save one are loaded;
b. A knows that more than five hundred are loaded;
c. A knows that less than five hundred are loaded;
d. A knows that some may be loaded, it may be only one, it may be many, and he has no means of assessing the risk.

If A shoots and kills B, it is at least sensible to indicate the difference between cases a. and b. on the one hand and c. and d. on the other hand by describing B's death as in some way intended in the first two cases. Whatever be the appropriate terminology, the law appears to distinguish the first two cases from the others for there is little doubt that A would be guilty of murder in them, but only of manslaughter in cases c. and d.

Knowledge of a risk is not of itself sufficient to constitute recklessness. The risk must have been unjustified. All that can be said by way of generalisation with regard to this second point is that it raises a variety of questions. How great was the risk? How beneficial to society or to the victim was the object which the accused was seeking to achieve? Every doctor foresees the risk of the death of the patient upon whom he is thinking of operating, but this fact will not render him legally liable if he does operate without negligence and the patient dies in consequence.

3.22 In the case of many offences, intention and recklessness in its subjective sense are alternative bases of liability. For example, under s. 1 of the Criminal Damage Act 1971, a person who destroys or damages any property intending to do so or being reckless as to whether any property is damaged or destroyed is guilty of the same offence although the distinction may sometimes be reflected in the sentence.

Malice

3.23 In some statutory offences, notably those defined by the Offences against the Person Act 1861, the prosecution has to prove that the accused acted "maliciously". In this context, "malice" means either intention or recklessness, in the subjective sense, with reference to the consequences. In *Cunningham*[1] the accused stole a gas meter from a cellar. He tore the meter from the wall, with the result that the gas percolated into an adjoining house in which one W was sleeping. W was made ill by the gas, and the accused was charged with unlawfully and maliciously causing W to take a noxious thing so as to endanger life contrary to s. 23 of the Offences against the Person Act 1861. The trial judge told the jury that "maliciously" meant wickedly, and the accused was convicted. The Court of Criminal Appeal held that it should have been left to the jury to decide whether, even if the accused did not intend to injure W, he foresaw that the removal of the meter might have this effect, and yet proceeded to remove it. The conviction under s. 23 was quashed, although the accused's convictions on separate counts of larceny of the meter and its contents stood.

The Court of Criminal Appeal approved the following statement of the late Professor Kenny:[2]

> "In any statutory definition of a crime, 'malice' must be taken, not in the old vague sense of wickedness in general, but as requiring either (1) an actual intention to do the particular kind of harm that in fact was done; or (2) recklessness as to whether such harm should occur or not. (I.e. the accused has to have foreseen that the particular kind of harm might be done and yet has gone on to take the risk of it.) It is neither limited to, nor does it indeed require any ill will towards the person injured."

Mowatt[3] shows that it is necessary to construe the words "particular kind of harm" in the above passage in a broad sense. It is an offence under s. 20 of the Offences against the Person Act 1861 to wound, or inflict grievous bodily harm maliciously.[4] After saying that the word "maliciously" imports on the part of the person who unlawfully inflicts the wound or other grievous bodily harm an awareness that his act may have the consequence of causing some physical harm to some other person, Diplock, L.J., speaking for the Court of Appeal (Criminal Division), added: "It is quite unnecessary that the accused should have foreseen that his unlawful act might cause physical harm of the gravity described in the statute, i.e. a wound or serious physical injury. It is enough that he should have foreseen that some physical harm to some person albeit of a minor nature

1. [1957] 2 Q.B. 396; [1957] 2 All E.R. 412; *C. & J. Cases.*
2. *Outlines of Criminal Law*, 19th ed., 211.
3. [1968] 1 Q.B. 421; [1967] 3 All E.R. 47; *C. & J. Cases.*
4. Paras 7.11–7.13.

might result." This is a modern instance of what is sometimes called "constructive crime".[1] An accused who intends or foresees only slight harm is treated by the law as if he had intended or foreseen grave harm. The problem of the extent to which it is right to punish a man more severely because he has caused harm greater than that which he intended or foresaw, or even could reasonably be expected to have foreseen, arises at several points in the criminal law. Further instances are provided by the type of manslaughter, sometimes called "constructive manslaughter" in which the accused kills the deceased in the course of a minor assault, or while performing an unlawful abortion on the deceased with her consent, and by the offence of causing death by dangerous driving, which is punishable with five years imprisonment in contradistinction to the two years maximum for dangerous driving *simpliciter*.[2]

3.24 The word "malice" is used with a different meaning in other contexts than that of statutory offences. In relation to murder malice means intention to kill or to cause grievous bodily harm. We shall see[3] that, in relation to the criminal liability of children, malice means knowledge that an act is morally, as well as legally, wrong. The expression is undoubtedly one which the modern criminal law could do without. It is highly improbable that words like "maliciously" will ever be used in the definitions of offences in future, and it is highly probable that they will be supplanted by words like "intentionally" or "recklessly" as has already happened in the case of the criminal destruction of or damage to property, the Criminal Damage Act 1971 having largely superseded the Malicious Damage Act 1861.

Unforeseen victim or mode

3.25 Provided the accused acted intentionally or recklessly in the way required by the definition of the offence charged, it is irrelevant that the actual object (whether person or property) was unintended or unforeseen. Where an injury intended for X, or foreseen as possibly occurring to him, falls on Y by accident, the accused's state of mind is said to be transferred towards Y under the doctrine of "transferred malice". In *Latimer*,[4] A aimed a blow at B which glanced off him and struck C who was standing beside B, wounding her severely. It was held that A could be convicted of maliciously wounding C because he had an intent

1. Para. 5.1. 2. But see Cmnd. 6323, Appendix K, para. 2.
3. Buxton, Negligence and Constructive Crime, [1969] Crim. L. R., 112.
4. (1886), 17 Q.B.D. 359.

to injure and it was irrelevant that he had not intended to injure C.

Of course, the doctrine of transferred malice cannot apply where harm of a particular type (e.g. injury to the person) is intended but harm of a different type (e.g. damage to property) is caused. In such a case the accused must be acquitted unless the offence is one where recklessness suffices and he is proved to have been reckless as to the risk of the type of harm which he actually caused. This is shown by *Pembliton*,[1] where the accused, who had been fighting with persons in the street, threw a stone at them, which missed but went through the window of a nearby public house. His conviction for maliciously damaging the window was quashed because he had acted with intent to injure persons and not with intent to injure property. The Court for Crown Cases Reserved pointed out that if the jury had found the accused had been reckless as to the risk of the window being broken the conviction would have been upheld, because recklessness was a sufficient state of mind for the offence in question.

It is irrelevant as far as the question of *mens rea* is concerned that the consequence in relation to which the accused acted intentionally or recklessly occurred in an unexpected manner.

Guilty knowledge

26 Our attention now turns to *mens rea* in relation to the circumstances in which the relevant act or omission must occur. This issue is of special importance in relation to statutory offences. What is said here is of equal application to those offences where a mere event is required.

Knowledge of the circumstances by virtue of which an act or omission is criminal is expressly required in the case of many statutory offences on account of the inclusion of some such word as "knowingly" in the definition but "knowingly" is not the only word which will have this effect, since it merely says expressly what is normally implied.[2] Even when no appropriate word appears in the definition, a requirement of guilty knowledge is frequently implied by the courts. In *Sleep*,[3] for example, the accused was charged with being in possession of naval stores marked with the broad arrow, an offence under a statute of William III which has since been repealed. It was held that he

---

1 (1874), L.R. 2 C.C.R. 119.

2. *Roper* v. *Taylor's Central Garages (Exeter), Ltd.*, [1951] 2 T.L.R. 284, *per* Devlin, J.

3. (1861), Le. & Ca. 44; see also *Cugullere*, [1961] 2 All E.R. 343.

must be acquitted as there was no proof that he knew that the stores in question were marked with the broad arrow as was in fact the case. In the opinion of the Court for Crown Cases Reserved, the fact that the accused ought, as a reasonable man, to have known of the marking was immaterial. Similarly, in *Sweet* v. *Parsley*,[1] after a different opinion had prevailed in the lower courts, the House of Lords held that a person could not be guilty of "being concerned in the management of premises used for the purpose of smoking cannabis" (an offence which has subsequently been modified) in the absence of proof of knowledge of such user.

3.27 As Lord Devlin has indicated, there are three degrees of knowledge known to the criminal law.[2] The first is actual knowledge which may be inferred from the conduct of the accused. Where a person has actual knowledge of the circumstances in which he is acting he is said to act intentionally in relation to them. Knowledge of the second degree consists of wilful blindness, where a person realises the risk that a surrounding circumstance may exist and deliberately refrains from making inquiries, the results of which he may not care to have; this is actual knowledge in the eyes of the law. Wilful blindness is a species of recklessness with reference to surrounding circumstances, and it is often called connivance.[3] The first reported instance of the recognition of wilful blindness is *Sleep* where several members of the Court for Crown Cases Reserved would clearly have been prepared to treat it as a basis for liability. In a more recent case, it was held that a person cannot be convicted of permitting a vehicle to be used on a road with a defective braking system unless he actually knew of this or shut his eyes to the obvious not caring whether a contravention occurred or not.[4]

Actual knowledge and wilful blindness must be sharply distinguished from knowledge of the third degree, otherwise described as constructive knowledge, which exists where a person did not know but ought to have known. Thus, a person has knowledge of the third degree if he fails to make the inquiries which a reasonable and prudent person would make. It is distinguishable from wilful blindness in that the failure to inquire is not deliberate; and unlike wilful blindness it is only a sufficient

1. [1970] A.C. 132; [1969] 1 All E.R. 347; *C. & J. Cases.*
2. *Roper* v. *Taylor's Central Garages (Exeter), Ltd.*, [1951] 2 T.L.R. 284.
3. Edwards, *Mens Rea in Statutory Offences*, 203; see also *Ross* v. *Moss*, [1965] 2 Q.B. 396; [1965] 3 All E.R. 145.
4. *James & Son, Ltd.* v. *Smee*, [1955] 1 Q.B. 78; [1954] 3 All E.R. 273.

basis in exceptional cases,[1] being necessarily irrelevant where words such as "knowingly" are used. Constructive knowledge is a species of negligence and will be discussed further under that head.[2]

For the avoidance of doubt it should be mentioned that guilty knowledge need extend only to the circumstances as prescribed in the definition of the offence in question.[3] Thus, a person is guilty of the offence of knowingly selling intoxicating liquor to a person under 18 if he knows, or is wilfully blind, that he is selling intoxicating liquor to such a person, it being irrelevant, for instance, that he thinks the person is 16 when he is in fact 17 years old.

Negligence[4]

28 Negligence is non-compliance with a standard of conduct in relation to a risk which is reasonably intelligible. It is distinguishable from intention, recklessness and guilty knowledge of the first and second degree since it connotes blameworthy inadvertence on the part of the accused.

A person is negligent with regard to a consequence of his conduct when, although he did not realise the risk of it occurring, he ought to have done so, and would have avoided it if he had acted reasonably. The only important instance of negligence as to consequence as a basis of criminal liability is manslaughter which may be committed by someone who is grossly negligent, in the sense that he fails to comply with a low standard of care in relation to a reasonably foreseeable risk of death or grievous bodily harm to another, which he would himself have foreseen if he had been moderately careful.

A person is negligent with regard to a circumstance relevant to his conduct when, although unaware of it, he ought to have been aware of it, and would have been if he had not unreasonably failed to make inquiries. Such constructive knowledge will suffice for liability only in exceptional cases, such as the following:

a. In statutory offences by whose definition the accused can be convicted on the ground that he had "reasonable cause to believe", "reason to believe" or "ought to have known" that the circumstance existed. For example, under s. 25 of the

---

1. *Roper* v. *Taylor's Central Garages (Exeter) Ltd.*, [1951] 2 T.L.R. 284, *per* Devlin, J.
2. Para. 3.28.
3. *McCullum*, (1973), 57 Cr. App. Rep. 645.
4. Hart, Negligence, Mens Rea and Criminal Responsibility, *Oxford Essays in Jurisprudence*, 29.

Firearms Act 1968: "It is an offence for a person to sell ... any firearm or ammunition to another person whom he knows or has reasonable cause for believing to be drunk or of unsound mind".

b. Where phrases of the above type have been introduced into the offence by judicial interpretation of its definition. There are a few modern instances where this has been done,[1] but the tendency has been deplored.[2]

c. Where a material mistake is required to be reasonable in order to exculpate the accused. This is discussed further in the next chapter.[3]

3.29 Some writers object to describing negligence as "*mens rea*", preferring to confine that term to guilty knowledge and foresight of prohibited consequences. Others have no objection to treating negligence as a kind of *mens rea*, and there is no uniform judicial practice.

This difference concerning the inclusion of negligence under the head of *mens rea* is less important than it appears for most people would agree that negligence involves fault, though it is usually less blameworthy than intentional or reckless wrongdoing. The accused who was negligent is culpable because he could have avoided behaving as he did, if he had only exercised a reasonable degree of self-control, been reasonably thoughtful, or exerted himself to a moderate extent. The question whether he should be said to have had *mens rea* thus resolves itself into the semantic question whether a guilty mind can be said to include weakness of will or defects in the conative faculties.

3.30 There is a troublesome question of terminology in this branch of the law. The gross inadvertent negligence which suffices as one ground of liability in manslaughter is often spoken of as "recklessness", a term which is also used in some other branches of the law in the objective sense of negligence.[4] "Criminal negligence" is sometimes said to consist of gross inadvertent negligence as well as recklessness in the subjective sense of the conscious assumption of a risk. There are no commonly accepted words by which these different attitudes may be distinguished,

---

1. *Browning* v. *J. W. H. Watson (Rochester), Ltd.*, [1953] 2 All E.R. 775.
2. *Gray's Haulage Co., Ltd.* v. *Arnold*, [1966] 1 All E.R. 896; *C. & J. Cases.*
3. Para. 4.14.
4. *Bates*, [1952] 2 All E.R. 842; but see *Mackinnon*, [1959] 1 Q.B. 150; [1958] 3 All E.R. 657. See also *Grunwald*, [1963] 1 Q.B. 935; [1960] 3 All E.R. 380 and *Shawinigan, Ltd.* v. *Vokins & Co., Ltd.*, [1961] 3 All E.R. 396.

and it would be pointless to invent a special terminology: the expressions are confusing.

Proposals for reform

.31 The broad effect of the suggestions contained in a working paper published by the Law Commission in 1970[1] is that, unless it is expressly excluded, all future offences should be based on fault. In the case of offences of commission, the fault should be intention or recklessness with regard to prohibited consequences, while it should be negligence in the case of offences of omission. The working party responsible for the paper were not entirely in agreement with regard to the definition of what has been described above as "oblique intention", as we can see from these proposed definitions:

"A person intends an event not only

a. when his purpose is to cause that event but also;

b. (first alternative) when he has no substantial doubt that that event will result from his conduct;

(second alternative) when he foresees that that event will probably result from his conduct."

The first alternative was preferred by the majority because it emphasises more clearly the difference between intention and recklessness; a point made in favour of the second alternative was that it represents more closely the existing law. There was a similar difference of opinion with regard to guilty knowledge:

"A person knows of circumstances not only when he knows that they exist but also when

(first alternative) he has no substantial doubt that they exist

(second alternative) he knows that they probably exist."

The proposed definitions of recklessness and negligence are as follows:

"A person is reckless if,

a. knowing that there is a risk that an event may result from his conduct or that a circumstance may exist, he takes that risk, and

b. it is unreasonable for him to take it having regard to the degree and nature of the risk which he knows to be present."

"A person is negligent if he fails to exercise such care, skill or foresight as a reasonable man in his situation would exercise."

---

1. Published Working Paper No. 31. It does not represent the final views of the Commission, but has been circulated for comment.

Contemporaneity[1]

3.32 It is a cardinal rule that the accused's *mens rea* must exist at the time of his prohibited conduct.[2] Where the *actus reus* comprises an event, such as unauthorised possession of a controlled drug, there is continuing rather than momentary conduct, and the same is often true in the case of omissions. Although normally momentary, an act may be of the continuing variety. Where there is continuing conduct it is enough if *mens rea* exists at some period during its continuance. This is illustrated by *Fagan* v. *Metropolitan Police Commissioner*.[3] A motorist, having been asked by a police officer to draw into the kerb, drove his car on to the officer's foot. The magistrates were not satisfied that he did so either intentionally or recklessly, but he refused to drive his car off the officer's foot for some little time after being requested to do so. The Divisional Court held by a majority that the motorist's conduct amounted to a battery (an act resulting in the application of force to another accompanied by an intention to do so or recklessness as to this result).[4] The problem was to find an act of application of force accompanied by the appropriate *mens rea* since the original driving on to the foot might have been unintentional. The majority concluded that the driving of the car on to the officer's foot and allowing it to remain there could be treated as a continuing act with the result that the motorist's act was not complete and spent by the time his *mens rea* began, as would have been the case if the driving on to the foot had been treated as a single complete act. His *mens rea* could therefore be superimposed on his existing continuing act.

Exceptions to the requirement of contemporaneity in two types of situations will be dealt with later.[5]

Motive

3.33 A person's motive is his reason for acting as he did. Thus A's motive for killing B may be financial gain, and C's motive for stealing may be his wish to feed his starving children. The general rule is that the accused's motives, good or bad, are irrelevant to his criminal liability. In *Sharpe*,[6] where the accused, motivated by affection for his mother and religious duty, had

---

1. Marston, Contemporaneity of Act and Intention, (1970) 86 L.Q.R., 208.
2. *Fowler* v. *Padget* (1798), 7 Term Rep. 509, *per* Lord Kenyon, C.J.
3. [1969] 1 Q.B. 439; [1968] 3 All E.R. 442; *C. & J. Cases.*
4. *Venna* (1975), 119 Sol. Jo. 679.
5. Paras. 5.34, 8.14.
6. (1857), 7 Cox C.C. 214.

removed her corpse from a grave in a cemetery belonging to Protestant Dissenters in order to bury it with the body of his recently deceased father in a churchyard, it was held that his motives, however estimable they might be, did not provide a defence to a charge of removing a corpse without lawful authority. However, Sharpe's "good" motives were reflected in the punishment awarded, a fine of one shilling being imposed.

Intention, whether relating to an element required for the *actus reus* or ulterior to it, must be distinguished from motive. Motive is secondary intention; the distinction between further intention and motive is difficult to draw, the former being relevant simply because it is specified in the definition of a particular offence.

An illustration of the distinction between intention and motive is provided by *Smith*.[1] The accused was charged with corruptly offering a gift to the mayor of a borough. He had handed an I.O.U. to his agent with the intention that it should be given to the mayor to induce him to promote the sale of land by the borough council to the accused. The accused did not intend to go through with the transaction, his reason for causing the offer to be made being his desire to expose what he believed to be the corrupt habits of those connected with the local administration. It was held that "corruptly" in the definition of the relevant offence meant "with intent that the donee should enter into a corrupt bargain" and that, even though his motive was not corrupt, the accused was guilty of the offence since he had offered the money with the requisite further intent.

Ignorance of law and morals

.34 The account which has been given of *mens rea* shows that essentially it connotes ideas of foresight of consequence and guilty knowledge. It does not mean that the accused must have been aware of the illegality of his conduct. Ignorance or mistake of law is usually no defence. Various reasons have been given for this rule. First, it is said that everyone knows the law, but this is palpably untrue. Secondly, it is said that it would be difficult to prove that the accused knew the law; if this were the real reason for the rule, ignorance of the law should be a defence when it can be clearly proved. However, it has been held that a person who was on the high seas, in circumstances in which he could not have been informed of the contents of a recent

1 [1960] 2 Q.B. 423; [1960] 1 All E.R. 256.

statute, might be convicted of contravening it.[1] The best reason for the rule is expediency.

> "Every man must be taken to be cognisant of the law, otherwise there is no knowing of the extent to which the excuse of ignorance might be carried. It would be urged in almost every case."[2]

Even a foreigner who proves that he mistakenly believed his conduct to be lawful would not, under the rule, be exempt from criminal liability in England.[3]

The rule that ignorance or mistake of law is no excuse (which is applied more strictly in England than in many other countries) is only rendered compatible with most people's idea of justice by the fact that many offences are also moral wrongs and even when this is not so the ordinary member of the public or, at least, the ordinary member of the class most affected (as motorists are affected by traffic legislation) has a rough idea of the provisions of the criminal law. The rule is liable to be particularly harsh where a person has reasonably relied on the advice of a lawyer or someone in authority that a proposed course of action is not criminal. It has been suggested that a person should have a defence to a charge concerning that action in such circumstances;[4] at present reasonable reliance on erroneous advice can only be reflected in mitigation of the sentence imposed.[5]

As an exception to the general rule, ignorance or mistake of civil law frequently provides a defence where it tends to show that the accused lacked the *mens rea* of the offence charged. For instance, if, because of a mistake relating to the law of property, a person believes that property belongs to him and damages it for some reason he cannot be convicted on a charge of intentionally or recklessly damaging property belonging to another contrary to the Criminal Damage Act 1971 since he lacks the necessary intention, or recklessness, to damage property belonging to another.[6] Some offences contain mental elements which expressly envisage the defence of mistake of law. In theft, the prosecution must prove that the accused acted dishonestly, and the appropriation of property belonging to another is not to be regarded as dishonest if the person who appropriated it believed that he had in law the right to deprive the other of it.[7]

---

1. *Bailey* (1800), Rus. & Ry. 1.
2. *Bilbie* v. *Lumley* (1802), 2 East 469.
3. *Esop* (1836), 7 C. & P. 456.
4. Ashworth, Excusable Mistake of Law, [1974] Crim. L. R. 652.
5. *Surrey County Council* v. *Battersby*, [1965] 2 Q.B. 194; [1965] 1 All E.R. 273. See also *Arrowsmith*, [1975] 1 All E.R. 463.
6. *Smith (D. R.)*, [1974] Q.B. 354; [1974] 1 All E.R. 632.
7. Para. 10.20.

The fact that the accused did not personally consider his conduct to be immoral or know that it was regarded as immoral by the bulk of society is generally irrelevant to his criminal liability. The principal exceptional cases where it is relevant that the accused was aware of the moral turpitude of his conduct are those of the child between the ages of 10 and 14[1] and the offence of blackmail.[2]

---

1. Para. 5.1.
2. Para. 11.32.

4

PROOF

4.1 The general rule is that the prosecution has the burden of proving the *actus reus* and *mens rea* beyond reasonable doubt, but the burden of adducing evidence sufficient to raise an issue is often borne by the accused in the first instance. Exceptionally the accused has the burden of proving an exculpating matter on the balance of probabilities.

4.2 Although the great majority of criminal cases are tried before magistrates, and therefore without a jury,[1] it is convenient for the student to think in terms of a trial by judge and jury when considering the following paragraphs. All questions of fact have to be determined by the jury, but the judge exercises a considerable degree of control at two stages in particular. One is for the judge to withdraw a case, or an issue in a case, from the jury on the ground that the supporting evidence is in law insufficient. This step is sometimes taken on a submission by the defence, at the close of the prosecution's evidence, that there is no case to answer; an acquittal is directed if the submission is successful. The other is by means of his summing-up.[2]

The two burdens

The burden of proof

4.3 The party who bears the burden of proof on a given issue will lose on that issue if, after reviewing all the evidence, the jury or magistrates entertain the appropriate degree of doubt whether the proposition in question has been established. As the prosecution bears the burden of proving most issues in a criminal case beyond reasonable doubt, it is generally true to say that the guilt of the accused must be established beyond reasonable doubt. This has been the recognised position for a long time so far as most criminal charges are concerned, but before 1935 there

1. Paras. 23.17–23.21.
2. Para. 23.13.

was believed to be an exception in the case of murder. It was thought that, if the deceased was shown to have met his death as a result of the conduct of the accused, it was incumbent on the accused to satisfy the jury of his innocence, or of the existence of a mitigating circumstance, such as provocation, which would justify a verdict of manslaughter.

There were several authorities which seemed to support this view concerning the law of murder, but they were overruled or explained on other grounds by the House of Lords in *Woolmington* v. *Director of Public Prosecutions.*[1] Woolmington was charged with murdering his wife by shooting. He admitted that she was killed by a bullet fired from a rifle which he was handling, but said that he squeezed the trigger involuntarily while endeavouring to induce her to return to live with him by threatening to shoot himself. Woolmington was convicted after a summing up which contained the following sentences: "The Crown has got to satisfy you that this woman ... died at the prisoner's hands ... If they satisfy you of that, then he has to show that there are circumstances to be found in the evidence which has been given from the witness box in this case, which alleviate the crime so that it is only manslaughter, or which excuse the homicide altogether by showing that it was a pure accident." An appeal to the Court of Criminal Appeal was dismissed, but a further appeal to the House of Lords succeeded and Woolmington was acquitted. The following important sentences are taken from the speech of Lord Sankey.

> "If it is proved that the conscious act of the prisoner killed a man and nothing else appears in the case, there is evidence upon which the jury may, not must, find him guilty of murder. It is difficult to conceive so bare and meagre a case, but that does not mean that the onus is not still on the prosecution ... throughout the web of the English criminal law one golden thread is always to be seen, that it is the duty of the prosecution to prove the prisoner's guilt. ... If, at the end of and on the whole of the case, there is a reasonable doubt, created by the evidence given by either the prosecution or the prisoner, as to whether the prisoner killed the deceased with a malicious intention, the prosecution has not made out the case and the prisoner is entitled to an acquittal. No matter what the charge or where the trial, the principle that the prosecution must prove the guilt of the prisoner is part of the common law of England and no attempt to whittle it down can be entertained."

---

1. [1935] A.C. 462; *C. & J. Cases.*

4.4 The rule that the prosecution must prove the accused's guilt beyond reasonable doubt means that it is generally incumbent on the prosecution to negative any defence raised by the accused. In *Woolmington* v. *Director of Public Prosecutions* Lord Sankey said that the prosecution bears the burden of negativing a plea that a verdict of manslaughter should be returned on a charge of murder because of provocation caused by the conduct of the deceased, and the Court of Criminal Appeal has substituted a verdict of manslaughter for one of murder when the trial judge left it to the jury to decide whether the accused had been provoked, but failed to tell them that the burden of disproving provocation rested on the prosecution.[1] The Court of Criminal Appeal has also held that the burden of negativing a plea of duress,[2] and of self-defence[3] is borne by the prosecution. The House of Lords has held that the burden of negativing automatism, when it is not caused by insanity, is likewise borne by the prosecution[4] and there are *obiter dicta* (which may safely be assumed to represent the law) to the effect that at common law every defence except insanity, and possibly those described in para. 4.5.c below, must be negatived by the prosecution.[5]

4.5 In three exceptional cases the burden of proving certain exculpating facts is placed on the accused, but when this is so the burden borne by him is lighter than that borne by the prosecution on the issues on which it has to prove guilt, for the accused has only to prove the exculpating fact on the balance of probabilities, not beyond reasonable doubt.[6] He will succeed in doing this if the jury are reasonably satisfied of the particular fact or find it more probable than not.[7] The situations where the accused bears the burden of proof are:

a. Defence of insanity. It was said in *M'Naghten's Case*,[8] which contains the leading statement on the subject, that everyone

---

1. *Macpherson* (1957), 41 Cr. App. Rep. 213.
2. *Gill*, [1963] 2 All E.R. 688; *C. & J. Cases*; *Bone*, [1968] 2 All E.R. 644.
3. *Lobell*, [1957] 1 Q.B. 547; [1957] 1 All E.R. 734.
4. *Bratty* v. *A.-G. for Northern Ireland*, [1963] A.C. 386; [1961] 3 All E.R. 523; *C. & J. Cases*.
5. *Chan Kau*, [1955] A.C. 206; [1955] 1 All E.R. 266; *Warner* v. *Metropolitan Police Commissioner*, [1969] 2 A.C. 256, at p. 303 *per* Lord Pearce.
6. *Sodeman*, [1936] 2 All E.R. 1138; *C. & J. Cases*; *Carr Briant*, [1943] K.B. 607; [1943] 2 All E.R. 156; *Patterson*, [1962] 2 Q.B. 429; [1962] 1 All E.R. 340.
7. *Miller* v. *Minister of Pensions*, [1947] 2 All E.R. 372, at p. 373–374.
8. (1843), 10 Cl. & Fin. 200; *C. & J. Cases*.

is to be presumed to be sane until the contrary is proved to the satisfaction of the jury. There is therefore no doubt that under the present law an accused person who raises the defence of insanity has the burden of proving it.[1]

b. Express statutory provision. A statute sometimes provides that it shall be for the defence to prove certain facts. For instance, under s. 1 of the Prevention of Crime Act 1953 it is an offence for a person to have with him an offensive weapon in a public place "without lawful authority or reasonable excuse, the proof whereof shall lie on him".

c. Provisos and exemptions in statutory offences. Where a statute on its true construction prohibits the doing of an act save in specified circumstances or by persons of specified classes or with specified qualifications or with the licence or permission of specified authorities, the onus of proving such an exemption is cast on the accused. This rule is provided in the case of summary proceedings by s. 81 of the Magistrates' Courts Act 1952 and applies in the case of trials on indictment as the result of the decision in *Edwards*[2] where a number of authorities were reviewed. In *Edwards*, the accused was charged with selling intoxicating liquor without holding a justices' licence authorising such sale contrary to s. 160 (1) of the Licensing Act 1964. The Court of Appeal, having construed the enactment, held that the offence was one which prohibited the doing of something subject to an exemption and that the onus of proving the exemption (that he was the holder of a licence) was on the accused.

The burden of adducing evidence

4.6 The prosecution must adduce *prima facie* evidence of the accused's guilt for otherwise there is no case to answer and the judge directs an acquittal; this means only that the prosecution must adduce sufficient evidence of the *actus reus* and *mens rea* mentioned in the definition of the offence charged. It is not necessary to negative every special defence that might be available to the accused. In the words of Devlin, J., "It would be quite unreasonable to allow the defence to submit at the end of the prosecution's case that the Crown had not proved affirmatively and beyond reasonable doubt that the accused was at the time of the crime sober, or not sleep walking or not in a trance or blackout."[3] It follows that it is incumbent on the accused to

1. Para. 5.4.
2. [1975] Q.B. 25; [1974] 2 All E.R. 1085.
3. *Hill* v. *Baxter*, [1958] 1 Q.B. 277, at p. 284.

adduce sufficient evidence to raise a particular defence although the burden of disproving it finally rests on the Crown.

For example, in murder the prosecution must dispel all reasonable doubt on the question of provocation for otherwise a verdict of manslaughter must be returned, but this duty of the prosecution only arises if there is sufficient evidence to raise the issue of provocation. If there is no sufficient evidence, the judge need not allude to the question in his direction to the jury. In *Mancini* v. *Director of Public Prosecutions*,[1] the principal plea in answer to a charge of murder was self-defence. The accused alleged that he had been attacked in a night club by the deceased and another man and that the deceased had an open pocket knife in his hand. The jury returned a verdict of guilty after a full direction on the question of self-defence. The summing up did not refer to the question of provocation, and the House of Lords held that, on the particular facts of the case, the judge had rightly withdrawn the issue of provocation from the jury. This does not mean that, in all cases in which self-defence is pleaded, it would be proper for the judge to make no allusion to the subject of provocation. Generally it is necessary for him to do so, but everything depends upon the facts of the particular case.[2] It is common practice to speak of the accused's burden of adducing evidence, but it should never be forgotten that the burden may have been discharged for the accused by the witnesses for the prosecution. If a Crown witness says that he saw the deceased aim a blow at the accused just before the fatal injury was inflicted, the judge might well leave the issue of provocation to the jury even if the accused neither gave evidence himself nor called witnesses.

Proposals for Reform

4.7 The exceptional cases where the burden of proof on the balance of probabilities is cast on the accused are open to the grave objection that a jury may have to convict a man although they think it as likely as not that he has a defence. This unfortunate situation would be avoided if clause 8 of the Draft Bill attached to the 11th Report of the Criminal Law Revision Committee[3] were adopted. The effect of the clause would be to place the ultimate burden of disproving all common law defences, including insanity, on the prosecution as well as the

1. [1942] A.C. 1; [1941] 3 All E.R. 272; *C. & J. Cases.*
2. *Bullard,* [1957] A.C. 635; *Rolle,* [1965] 3 All E.R. 582.
3. Cmnd. 4991, paras. 137–142.

burden of disproving statutory defences, exemptions etc., the accused merely having an evidential burden in respect of them. The sole exemptions to this provision would be the statutory "third party defences"[1] and any exceptions expressly created by subsequent enactments, in which cases the accused would bear the burden of proving his defence on the balance of probabilities.

Presumptions

4.8 Proof may be aided by certain presumptions which are classified as irrebuttable presumptions of law, rebuttable presumptions of law and presumptions of fact.

A presumption is the product of a rule according to which on proof of one fact the jury may or must find that some other fact (often called the "presumed fact") exists. The "may" or "must" in the last sentence gives the clue to the classification of presumptions into presumptions of law and presumptions of fact.

When the jury must find that the presumed fact exists, the presumption is a presumption of law. There are two kinds of presumption of law, rebuttable and irrebuttable. When the presumption is irrebuttable, no evidence can be received to contradict the presumed fact. Examples of irrebuttable presumptions of law are provided by the rules[2] that a child under 10 is incapable of committing an offence and a boy under 14 is presumed incapable of rape or any other form of unlawful intercourse. Irrebuttable presumptions of law are sometimes called conclusive presumptions.

Where there is a rebuttable presumption of law, the jury must find that the presumed fact exists unless sufficient evidence to the contrary is adduced. The amount of evidence required in rebuttal varies somewhat in different presumptions. Examples of rebuttable presumptions of law are provided by the presumption that a child born in wedlock is legitimate and the presumption that a marriage ceremony constitutes a valid union. If a child is proved to have been born in wedlock, the jury must find that he was legitimate unless sufficient evidence to the contrary is adduced. When a marriage ceremony has been proved, the jury must assume that it constituted a valid marriage until sufficient evidence to the contrary is adduced.

When the jury may find that the presumed fact exists on proof of some other fact, the presumption is one of fact. Presumptions

---

1. Para. 6.10.
2. Paras. 5.1 and 9.1.

of fact are sometimes called provisional presumptions and they play a very important part in the administration of the criminal law because they are frequently the only means by which the state of the accused's mind can be proved. The judge will tell the jury that they are entitled to infer guilty knowledge or criminal intent from the fact that the prohibited act was done by the accused, and if the accused offers no explanation the inference will usually be drawn. This is a matter of common sense, because people generally are aware of the circumstances in which they act, and they generally do foresee that what does result from their conduct will result from it. If a credible explanation is offered, the jury must consider the evidence as a whole, and if they entertain any reasonable doubt, the general rule that the prosecution has the burden of proof obliges the jury to give the accused the benefit of that doubt.

Proof of *mens rea*

4.9 The extent to which it is possible to prove the past state of the accused's mind is apt to trouble the student. Regard must be had to the statements of the accused at the time, or at a later date or in the course of his testimony. If the statements out of court amount to admissions, great weight is attached to them on the assumption that what people say adverse to their case is probably true. Regard must also be had to the conduct and circumstances of the accused. The mere doing by him of the prohibited act can justify an inference that he did it intentionally, with knowledge of the surrounding circumstances, and where relevant with the intention of producing its normal consequences, although it must never be forgotten that this is only an inference, and the jury may well conclude that it is not warranted on the particular facts of the case. The presence or absence of motive is another important consideration.

The following is a typical extract from a summing-up in a murder case:

> "It is a trite observation that there is no scientific means of analysing the state of a person's mind at a particular moment of time. There is no scientific instrument which enables you to do that; nothing comparable to a pressure gauge on an engine or a speedometer of a car which enables you to ascertain what is going on inside. So one usually looks—you may think this is common sense—at the man's actions, at all the surrounding circumstances, at the conduct which precedes and very often the conduct which follows the killing, and in particular the way in which the killing was carried out, the nature, the number, the quality of the injuries,

the nature and kind of weapon that was used, if one was used, to ask yourselves whether you are satisfied that at the time of the killing there must at least have been an intention, if not to kill, to inflict serious physical harm."[1]

.10 Since it is a common cause of difficulty for the student, the so-called presumption that a man intends the natural consequences of his acts requires further comment. Certain acts are known to be likely to produce certain consequences which are frequently spoken of as the "natural" consequences of those acts. This fact, coupled with the fact that people usually do foresee the normal consequences of their conduct has led people to talk of a presumption that everyone intends the natural consequences of his conscious acts. The phrase is a harmless one provided it is always remembered that the presumption is one of fact. If this point is forgotten, it is fatally easy to suggest that once a particular act is proved against him, it is incumbent on the accused as a matter of law to adduce evidence to disprove that he intended the natural consequences of that act; it may even come to be suggested that the accused bears the burden of disproving such an intention. On one possible interpretation of the case, *Director of Public Prosecutions* v. *Smith*,[2] decided that in certain circumstances the presumption of intention might be irrebuttable. This was the culminating point of a tendency to direct the jury that they must, not merely that they could, infer that the accused foresaw what a reasonable man would have foreseen and that the accused's testimony to the contrary must as a matter of law be ignored. The matter has now been put right by s. 8 of the Criminal Justice Act 1967 which reads as follows:

"A court or jury in determining whether a person has committed an offence (a) shall not be bound in law to infer that he intended or foresaw a result of his actions by reason only of its being a natural and probable consequence of those actions, but (b) shall decide whether he did intend or foresee that result by reference to all the evidence, drawing such inferences from the evidence as appear proper in the circumstances."

Although it will probably become less and less common for judges to direct juries in terms of the presumption that a man intends the natural consequences of his act (a practice deplored in *Smith's* case itself), juries will no doubt continue to act on the sound principle of common sense that, because most people

---

1. *Ives*, [1970] 1 Q.B. 208, at p. 214, *per* Melford Stevenson, J.
2. [1961] A.C. 290; [1960] 2 All E.R. 450; *C. & J. Cases*.

would foresee certain consequences as the probable result of their action, it is proper to assume that the accused did in the absence of evidence to the contrary. The evidence to the contrary may require the jury to believe such incredible facts as to leave them with no alternative but to continue to make the assumption that the accused foresaw the consequences of his conduct. The evidence to the contrary may even be of such a nature as to amount, on analysis, to an admission of criminal intent. For example, A is charged with causing grievous bodily harm with intent to cause grievous bodily harm.[1] It is proved that he struck B a severe blow with a hatchet. A says "I knew I was hitting B with a hatchet, and that is what I intended to do, but the idea of causing him any serious harm never entered my mind." A's evidence is a contradiction in terms. Hitting people severe blows with a hatchet is, by definition, causing grievous bodily harm. If it were necessary for the jury to be satisfied in every case that the idea of hurting or injuring his victim must have been in the accused's mind, however momentarily, a lot of people who deliberately aim blows or shoot in bad temper or panic would be entitled to be acquitted.

The negation of *mens rea*

4.11 In this and the following paragraphs we deal with cases in which there is no doubt that the conscious conduct of the accused caused the prohibited occurrence. The question at issue is whether he had the necessary *mens rea*, something which he denies on account of accident, ignorance of fact, or mistake of fact or civil law. It is customary to speak of pleas of this nature as defences, but they are not matters on which the accused bears the burden of proof. Indeed it is only in the plea of reasonable mistake that he even bears the burden of adducing evidence.

The cases about to be considered differ from those discussed in the next chapter because the accused is assumed to have been above the age of criminal responsibility, mentally normal, conscious and sober.

Accident

4.12 "Accident" is a word which has several shades of meaning but, when we speak of the defence of accident when the conscious conduct of the accused constitutes the *actus reus* of the crime charged, the allegation always is that the accused did not intend to produce the prohibited consequences.

---

1. Para. 7.15.

The typical instance is one in which someone who was conscious of and in control of his bodily movements and aware of all relevant circumstances did not foresee that his conduct would have the prohibited consequences. The accused aims a bullet at a crow, but owing to the presence of a high wind or the fact that he is a poor shot he hits a house pigeon. In either event, he is said to have killed the bird accidentally.[1]

An accident may be caused by conscious reflex action. Thus Hale gives as a case of excusable homicide that in which a man's hand shakes while shooting at the butts, with the result that the arrow kills a bystander.[2]

When an accused alleges that an occurrence was an accident, he may simply mean that he had no causal connection with it; but this is a denial of the *actus reus* and accordingly outside the purview of these paragraphs.

Even when the prohibited consequences occur in a way which would be described as an "accident" because they were unintended,[3] an accused who has been negligent or reckless will not escape liability if the offence charged is one in which liability may be based on negligence or recklessness since an accident caused by negligence or recklessness cannot constitute a defence to a charge of such an offence.

The accused cannot be said to bear the burden of adducing evidence of accident because, however weak his evidence may be, the issue of his intention must be left to the jury as it is raised by the prosecution.

Ignorance of fact

13 The accused's ignorance of fact is a defence if it results in him lacking the intention, recklessness or guilty knowledge which is expressly or impliedly required by the definition of the offence charged. Thus, in *Hibbert*,[4] a man was charged with an offence against s. 55 of the Offences against the Person Act 1861 (substantially re-enacted by s. 20 of the Sexual Offences Act 1956), which provided that "whosoever shall unlawfully take ... any unmarried girl, being under the age of 16 years, out of the possession and against the will of her father or mother, or of any other person having lawful care or charge of her, shall be guilty of

---

1. *Horton* v. *Gwynne*, [1921] 2 K.B. 661.
2. Hale, P. C. 472; *Woolmington* v. *Director of Public Prosecutions*, [1935] A.C. 462; *C. & J. Cases.*
3. *Gray* v. *Barr*, [1971] 2 Q.B. 554; [1971] 2 All E.R. 949.
4. (1869), L.R. 1 C.C.R. 184; *C. & J. Cases.*

a misdemeanour …". The accused met a girl of 14 in the street, took her to another place where he seduced her, and left her where he had found her. The girl was in the custody of her father, but it was held that, in the absence of a finding by the jury that the prisoner was aware of this fact, he must be acquitted. This case is of special interest because of the problem of reconciling it with *Prince*,[1] discussed later.[2] To avoid possible confusion, it should be pointed out that having intercourse with a girl under 16 has since been made an offence, as it was an offence in 1869 to have intercourse with a girl under 12, but the crime with which the section quoted above is concerned may be committed by a person who abducts a girl without any improper intention.

Where the prosecution has to prove *mens rea*, the accused does not bear the burden of adducing evidence with regard to his lack of it because the issue of *mens rea* must be left to the jury as it is part of the prosecution's case. In most cases the accused will adduce evidence of ignorance but its sufficiency is no concern of the judge at a trial with a jury.

Simple ignorance of fact (i.e. where the accused's mind is a complete blank as to a particular fact) is comparatively rare because lack of knowledge is normally connected with a mistake, in that the accused has thought about the possible existence of the fact but wrongly concluded that it does or does not exist as the case may be.

Mistake

Mistakes negativing the mental element which the prosecution must prove

4.14 A mistake of fact or civil law on the part of the accused is a defence if it results in him lacking the intention, recklessness or guilty knowledge which the prosecution is required to prove. Where the accused seeks to contradict the prosecution's case with evidence of mistake, the judge does not have to consider whether the evidence is sufficiently weighty to be left to the jury. Furthermore, there is no rule of law that the mistake must be a reasonable one. This was affirmed by the majority of the House of Lords in *Morgan*,[3] where it was stated that, since the *mens*

1. (1875), L.R. 2 C.C.R. 154; *C. & J. Cases*.
2. Para. 6.1.
3. [1975] 2 All E.R. 347. See also *Wilson* v. *Inyang*, [1951] 2 K.B. 799; [1951] 2 All E.R. 237; (1951) 14 M.L.R. 485 (note); *Smith (D.R.)*, [1974] Q.B. 354; [1974] 1 All E.R. 632.

rea of rape which had to be proved by the prosecution was an intention to have sexual intercourse with a woman without her consent or recklessness as to whether or not she consented, an honest but unreasonably mistaken belief that she was consenting would afford a defence to a charge of rape. Thus, on a charge of murder by shooting, however weak the accused's evidence that he believed the gun was unloaded may be, the jury must acquit of murder if they are not sure that he knew it was loaded, even if they think that his alleged belief was utterly unreasonable, since the prosecution will have failed to prove an intent to kill or do grievous bodily harm, which is the *mens rea* for murder. The fact that in the present context the accused's mistake is not required as a matter of law to be reasonable does not mean that the reasonableness of his mistake is entirely irrelevant. As was recognised in *Morgan*, the reasonableness of his belief is of considerable evidential significance because the more reasonable the belief, the more likely it is that the jury will accept his story that he was acting under a mistake.

Mistakes relating to a new issue which the accused raises by way of defence

.15 Where the accused's mistake leads to a belief in the existence of facts which would constitute a defence, whether a general one such as necessary self-defence, or specific to the particular offence charged, there is a rule of law that to be a defence the mistake, whether of fact or of civil law, must have been reasonable; the accused bears the burden of adducing evidence of such a mistake, i.e. the judge may tell the jury that they are obliged, as a matter of law, to disregard the evidence of mistake if he considers it to be insufficient. If the issue of mistake is left to the jury, the prosecution bears the burden of disproving the accused's allegation on the principle of *Woolmington*'s case. The operation of these principles can be illustrated as follows. On a charge of murder, the accused is entitled to be acquitted of both that offence and of manslaughter if: a. the person he killed was about to kill him or some other person and b. there was no other means of preventing such an occurrence. If these two conditions did not exist but the accused mistakenly believed that they did and if he adduces sufficient evidence that he reasonably believed in their existence and this allegation is not disproved by the prosecution,[1] he is entitled to be acquitted of murder and manslaughter. The difference between the present type of case

1. *Rose* (1884), 15 Cox, C. C. 540; *C. & J. Cases.*

and those mentioned in the last paragraph is that a new issue is raised by the accused (supposedly necessary self-defence), whereas in the latter he alleges that, because of a mistake, he lacks the *mens rea* which the prosecution must prove as an essential ingredient of the offence.

4.16 The distinction between cases in which the mistake need not, as a matter of law, be a reasonable one and those in which evidence of the reasonableness of the mistake must be available, may also be illustrated by bigamy.[1] The offence, which is contained in s. 57 of the Offences against the Person Act 1861, is committed by a person who "being married, shall marry any other person during the life of the former (sic) husband or wife". The *mens rea* required to be proved by the prosecution is merely the intent to go through the second marriage ceremony.[2] If there is evidence, accepted by the jury, that the accused mistakenly believed that the marriage ceremony was a mere betrothal, he is entitled to be acquitted however unreasonable his belief may have been because he would lack the intention to go through a marriage ceremony which the prosecution must prove. Section 57 provides that it shall not extend to those cases in which, at the time of the accused's second marriage, either i. his former spouse had been continuously absent for a period of seven years and was not known by him to be alive or ii. the first marriage had been dissolved or annulled. These provisos furnish the accused with defences. Since the first proviso would be pointless otherwise, it is unnecessary for the prosecution to prove in the first instance that the accused knew, at the time of the ceremony of marriage, that his or her spouse was alive. However, if the accused adduces evidence of seven years' absence, the prosecution must prove either that there was no such absence or that he knew his wife to be living during it.[3]

If the defence is that the accused believed that the first spouse was dead, it is necessary for there to be evidence showing that the belief was based on reasonable grounds. The accused here will not be seeking to negative the mental element which the prosecution must prove, proof of knowledge that the first spouse was alive at the time of the second ceremony being unnecessary, but will be raising a new issue by way of defence. The avail-

1. Paras. 9.11–9.16.
2. *Director of Public Prosecutions* v. *Morgan*, [1975] 2 All E.R. at p. 383, *per* Lord Fraser of Tullybelton.
3. *Curgerwen* (1865), L.R. 1 C.C.R. 1; *Lund* (1921), 16 Cr.App.Rep. 31.

ability of the defence of reasonable mistake of fact in such a case was established in *Tolson*.[1] Mrs Tolson could not rely on either of the provisos because she married for a second time within less than seven years of the disappearance of her first husband from whom she had not been divorced. Nevertheless, she was found by the jury to have believed on reasonable grounds and in good faith that he was dead, and her conviction was quashed by a majority decision of the Court for Crown Cases Reserved.

The Court of Criminal Appeal and its successor, the Criminal Division of the Court of Appeal, have since held that a mistaken belief on the part of someone charged with bigamy that his first marriage was void,[2] or had been dissolved,[3] is a defence. In each case, had the facts been as the accused believed, he would have been acting lawfully and innocently. In each case, however, it was said that the mistake must be reasonable and, in the first case, the judge was held to have acted rightly in refusing to allow the defence of mistake to go to the jury because there was no sufficient evidence that the accused had made reasonable inquiries before concluding that his first marriage was void.

When it is incumbent on the accused to adduce evidence of reasonable grounds for the mistake on which he acted, he may be held liable on the basis of constructive knowledge, because he is deemed to know of facts of which he would have been aware if he had made the inquiries which a reasonable man would have made in the circumstances. This is a concept which usually has no place in the criminal law.[4]

Mistake in crimes where proof of negligence suffices

.17 Where negligence, if proved by the prosecution, is a sufficient basis of liability, a material mistake must be reasonable in order to exculpate the accused since if he acts under a mistake which is not based on reasonable grounds he is necessarily negligent. We have seen[5] that on a charge of murder by shooting, the jury must acquit of murder if the prosecution does not disprove an allegation by the accused that he did not know that the gun was loaded; this is so even if they think that his alleged mistake was utterly unreasonable because he should have ascertained whether the gun was loaded. The reason is that the prosecution has not

1. (1889), 23 Q.B.D. 168; *C. & J. Cases*.
2. *King*, [1964] 1 Q.B. 285; [1963] 3 All E.R. 561; *C. & J. Cases*.
3. *Gould*, (No. 2), [1968] 2 Q.B. 65; [1968] 1 All E.R. 849: *C. & J. Cases*.
4. Para. 3.27.
5. Para. 4.14.

proved the necessary intent to kill or do grievous bodily harm, but the jury may convict of manslaughter on the grounds of gross negligence.

We shall see in Chapter 6 that there are offences in which not even a reasonable mistake excuses an accused.

5

CAPACITY

Children

5.1 The age of an accused person may provide him with a defence on a criminal charge or may result in him being dealt with by civil care proceedings[1] instead.

It is irrebuttably presumed that no child under the age of 10 years can be guilty of an offence.[2] Such a child is said to be *doli incapax* (not capable of crime). At common law the age of immunity from responsibility was seven. It was raised to 8 by statute in 1933 and, again by statute, to 10 in 1963.

The common law lays down a special rule concerning children of 10 years or over but under the age of 14. They are presumed to be incapable of committing an offence, but this presumption may be rebutted by proof of a "mischievous discretion" i.e. knowledge that what was done was wrong.[3] Thus, a child aged between 10 and 14 can be convicted only if the prosecution proves that he committed the *actus reus* with *mens rea* and knew he was doing wrong. This additional requirement is often expressed by the phrase *malitia supplet aetatem* (malice makes up for want of age). As used here, "malice" (or the "mischievous discretion") means knowledge that the act is legally wrong or, if there is no such knowledge, that it is morally wrong.[4]

In *Gorrie*,[5] a boy of 13 jabbed another boy with his penknife and caused his death. He was charged with manslaughter and the jury was directed that it was not sufficient to prove the presence of such a state of mind as would suffice in the case of a person of 14 or over; it was necessary to go further and prove that, when the boy did the act, he knew he was doing what was wrong—not merely what was wrong but what was gravely wrong, seriously wrong.

1. Para. 23.24.
2. Children and Young Persons Act 1963, s. 16.
3. *Owen* (1830), 4 C. & P. 236.
4. *Smith* (1845), 1 Cox C.C. 260; *B.* v. *R.* (1958), 44 Cr. App. Rep. 1; *Gorrie* (1918), 83 J.P. 136.
5. (1918), 83 J.P. 136.

The evidence in rebuttal of the presumption of incapability may consist of proof that the child is well brought up and comes from a good home.[1] The ironical result is that a child who would benefit more by court action is less likely to be found guilty than a child from a good home. It is open to question whether any useful purpose is served by the rebuttable presumption of incapability to commit crime in the case of children between 10 and 14.

5.2 Boys under 14 are irrebuttably presumed incapable of sexual intercourse or sodomy and thus cannot be convicted, as perpetrators on charges of rape,[2] other offences involving sexual intercourse or sodomy.[3] In *Waite*,[4] it was held that a boy under 14 could not be convicted of having sexual intercourse with a girl under 13. Youthful sexual athletes should, however, be warned that in *Waite* and other similar cases[5] convictions for indecent assault (which does not require sexual intercourse) have been upheld. Where the evidence shows that the boy was capable of intercourse it seems indefensible that he should be irrebuttably presumed incapable.

5.3 With the exceptions of prosecutions for homicide and for indictable offences where a child is charged jointly with a person aged 17 or over,[6] all criminal charges against children between the ages of 10 and 14 are dealt with summarily, normally in the juvenile court. On a finding of guilt that court can make a number of orders,[7] e.g. an order committing the child to the care or supervision of the local authority.

Insanity

5.4 The defence of insanity is contained in the *M'Naghten Rules* which were laid down by the judges in their advice to the House of Lords in *M'Naghten's Case*.[8] Their advice was sought in consequence of the acquittal of M'Naghten, who was found to be insane on a charge of murdering Sir Robert Peel's private secretary. Although the rules are not laid down in a case decided by

---

1. *B.* v. *R.* (1958), 44 Cr. App. Rep. 1. 2. *Philips* (1839), 8 C. & P. 736.
3. *Tatam* (1921), 15 Cr. App. Rep. 132; *Cratchley* (1913), 9 Cr. App. Rep. 232.
4. [1892] 2 Q.B. 600.
5. E.g. *Williams*, [1893] 1 Q.B. 320.
6. Children and Young Persons Act 1969, s. 6 (1).
7. Paras. 23.22–23.24.
8. (1843), 10 Cl. & Fin. 200; *C. & J. Cases*.

the House of Lords, they have been recognised again and again as representing the present law.

The *M'Naghten Rules* can be summarised thus:

a. Everyone is presumed sane until the contrary is proved.
b. It is a defence to a criminal prosecution for the accused to show that he was labouring under such a defect of reason, due to disease of the mind, as *either* not to know the nature and quality of his act, *or* if he did know this, not to know that he was doing wrong.

We have seen that when insanity is pleaded the onus of proof is exceptionally on the accused, but he may rebut the presumption of sanity by adducing evidence which satisfies the jury on the balance of probabilities that he was insane within the terms of the *M'Naghten Rules* when he committed the alleged offence.

5.5 In order to succeed with his defence of insanity the accused must prove three things:

a. He must show that he was suffering from a disease of the mind when he did the prohibited act. "Disease of the mind" connotes a malfunctioning of the mind caused by disease.[1] It makes no difference that the disease was physical in origin; a temporary blackout due to arteriosclerosis will suffice.[2] The requirement that the mental malfunctioning should be caused by disease must be stressed. "A malfunctioning of the mind of transitory effect caused by the application to the body of some external factor such as violence, drugs, including anaesthetics, alcohol and hypnotic influences cannot fairly be said to be due to disease" and does not constitute a disease of the mind.[3] Similarly, mere "brutish stupidity without rational power" is not enough.[4] However, if the accused is shown to have done a criminal act while suffering from a malfunctioning of the mind due to disease, it matters not whether the disease is curable or incurable, temporary or permanent.[5] The question whether a disease is a "disease of the mind" within the *M'Naghten Rules* is to be decided by the judge; he does not have to leave the point to the jury.[6]

---

1. *Quick*, [1973] Q.B. 910; [1973] 3 All E.R. 347, at p. 356.
2. *Kemp*, [1957] 1 Q.B. 399; [1956] 3 All E.R. 249; *C. & J. Cases*.
3. *Quick*.
4. *Kemp*, [1957] 1 Q.B. 399, at p. 408.
5. *Kemp*.
6. *Bratty* v. *A.-G. for Northern Ireland*, [1963] A.C. 386; [1961] 3 All E.R. 523; *C. & J. Cases*; *Kemp*.

b. He must show that he was suffering from a defect of reason due to disease of the mind. It must be more than a momentary confusion and amount to a complete deprivation of reasoning power[1] which would usually render him insane for medical purposes.
c. The defect of reason must affect legal responsibility,[2] something to which a person's capacity to appreciate what he was doing and whether it was lawful is highly relevant, and the accused must go on to prove that because of his insanity *either* he did not know the nature and quality of his act *or*, if he did know this, he did not know he was doing wrong.

5.6 The words "nature and quality" refer to the physical nature of the act.[3] The jury must be satisfied that the accused did not know what he was doing, or was quite incapable of appreciating the probable effects of his conduct, or of realising the material circumstances (i.e. those which expressly or impliedly constitute the *actus reus* of the offence) in which he was acting. An insane person who was acting in a state of complete automatism, or who stabbed another with a knife without knowing that he was using the implement at all would be held not to have known the nature and quality of his act. So would a person who cut a sleeper's head off because "it would be great fun to see him looking for it when he woke up".[4] He would know that he was engaged on the act of decapitation, but would be manifestly incapable of appreciating its physical effects. Similarly, if an insane person squeezes someone's throat, thinking that he is squeezing an orange, he does not know the nature and quality of his act but if he kills a boy, mistakenly believing the victim is a girl, he knows the nature and quality of his act since his mistake is not material.

5.7 Turning to the alternative limb of the test of responsibility, the jury must be asked whether, assuming the accused knew what he was doing, he also knew that it was wrong. Some difficulty has been experienced with regard to the meaning of "wrong" in this context. It is settled that a person is not able to establish a case of insanity within the *M'Naghten Rules* if he knew that his conduct was prohibited by law. Thus, in *Windle*,[5]

1. *Clarke*, [1972] 1 All E.R. 219.
2. *Rivett* (1950), 34 Cr. App. Rep. 87.
3. *Codère* (1916), 12 Cr. App. Rep. 21, at p. 28.
4. Stephen, *History of the Criminal Law*, Vol II, 166.
5. [1952] 2 Q.B. 826; [1952] 2 All E.R. 1; *C. & J. Cases*.

where the accused induced his wife, who had frequently spoken of committing suicide, to consume 100 aspirins, because he thought it would be beneficial for her to die, it was held that the trial judge was justified in withdrawing the case from the jury on the question of insanity. The accused had said that he would be hanged for what he had done, and there was no doubt that he knew it was contrary to law. The High Court of Australia has declined to follow *Windle*, being of the opinion that "wrong" in the *M'Naghten Rules* means contrary to the moral views of the majority of the members of society.[1] According to this opinion, if Windle had believed his wife to be suffering from a painful incurable illness, and, if he had also believed that euthanasia was approved by the bulk of ordinary Englishmen, he ought to have been acquitted even though he knew that mercy killing was prohibited by law.[2] Sir James Stephen once said that the absence of the power of self-control would involve an incapacity to know right from wrong.[3] But this was at a time when it was not clear whether, according to English law, "wrong" in the *M'Naghten Rules* meant legally wrong or morally wrong. Since it was decided that "wrong" means legally wrong the Privy Council has held that the absence of the power of self-control is not *per se* evidence of incapacity to distinguish right from wrong, although, on the facts of a particular case, there may be medical evidence warranting the conclusion that a disease which impairs the accused's power of self-control also impairs his ability to distinguish right from wrong.[4]

8 In their advice in *M'Naghten's Case* the judges enunciated a third test: that where a man commits a criminal act under an insane delusion, he is under the same degree of responsibility as he would have been if the facts had been as he imagined them to be. This test is generally regarded as redundant since it merely re-states a principle provided by the two tests just mentioned. To illustrate their third test the judges said:

> "For example, if, under the influence of his delusion, the accused supposes another man to be in the act of attempting to take away his life, and he kills that man, as he supposes in self-defence, he would be exempt from punishment. If his delusion was that the deceased had inflicted a serious injury to his character and fortune,

1. *Stapleton* v. *R.* (1952), 86 C.L.R. 358.
2. Norval Morris, "Wrong" in the M'Naghten Rules, (1953) 16 M.L.R. 435.
3. *History of the Criminal Law*, Vol. II, 171.
4. *A.-G. for State of South Australia* v. *Brown*, [1960] A.C. 423; [1960] 1 All E.R. 734; *C. & J. Cases.*

and he killed him in revenge for such supposed injury, he would be liable to punishment."[1]

The same answers would have been provided by the "knowledge of wrong" or the "nature and quality" tests.[2] The third test can also be criticised as defective in that it suggests that if the accused kills his wife under the insane delusion that he is killing a cat he can be convicted of an offence in relation to a cat, since, said the judges, one who acts under an insane delusion is under the same degree of responsibility as he would have been if his delusion had been true. This clearly cannot be so since the accused would not have committed any *actus reus* in relation to a cat. A study of the directions made in insanity cases shows that the third test has fallen into desuetude and it can safely be ignored.[3]

Verdict and procedure

5.9 Until 1800, the verdict, in cases of insanity, was simply "not guilty". The Criminal Lunatics Act 1800 gave the court power to detain the accused in such cases and provided that the jury should declare that the accused was acquitted on the ground of insanity. The Act of 1800 applied only to felonies, but it was extended to misdemeanours by the Trial of Lunatics Act 1883, which also provided that, in cases tried with a jury, the verdict should be "Guilty of the act or omission charged against him but insane at the time" or, more tersely, "guilty but insane". This alteration was made at the wish of Queen Victoria who was distressed by the finding that one McLean who fired a pistol at her was "not guilty" on account of his insanity. The verdict provided for by the Act of 1883 was illogical, and s. 1 of the Criminal Procedure (Insanity) Act 1964, provides that the verdict shall be "not guilty by reason of insanity".

5.10 It was decided in *Felstead* v. *R.*[4] that there was no appeal against a verdict of "guilty but insane" because it was tantamount to an acquittal. This rule, though logical, could produce hardship in a case in which the accused's defence to a charge of murder, or other offence against the person, was accident, as well as insanity,[5] or in a case in which the accused pleaded diminished responsibility in answer to a murder charge and was

1. (1843), 10 Cl. & Fin. 200, at p. 211; *C. & J. Cases.*
2. Williams, *Criminal Law: The General Part*, 2nd ed., p. 499.
3. Williams, *op. cit.*, para. 160.
4. [1914] A.C. 534.
5. *Duke*, [1963] 1 Q.B. 120; [1961] 3 All E.R. 737.

found to be insane. Accordingly s. 12 of the Criminal Appeal Act 1968 provides that there shall be an appeal against the special verdict of acquittal on the ground of insanity.[1]

11 The cases conflict on the question whether, if the accused puts his state of mind in issue by pleading automatism, the prosecution can adduce evidence of insanity but the better view would seem to be that it can.[2] Section 6 of the Criminal Procedure (Insanity) Act 1964 provides that, where in the case of murder the accused pleads insanity, the court shall allow the prosecution to adduce or elicit evidence of diminished responsibility, and *vice versa*.

12 When the accused is found not guilty by reason of insanity he does not go free. Instead, he is ordered to be detained at the Queen's pleasure in a hospital to be selected by the Home Secretary,[3] in practice one of the secure hospitals such as Broadmoor. The effect of the order is the indefinite detention of the accused until the Home Secretary is satisfied that this is no longer required for the protection of the public.[4] The number of cases in which insanity is pleaded as a defence is very small;[5] partly this is reaction against the prospect of prolonged, even lifelong, detention in a secure hospital, but it also reflects the very strict test of responsibility laid down by the *M'Naghten Rules* and the existence since 1957 of the defence of diminished responsibility.[6]

Criticisms of the M'Naghten Rules

13 Five criticisms may be made of the *M'Naghten Rules:*

a. The rule concerning the burden of proof is anomalous. In most other criminal cases, the accused merely bears the burden of adducing evidence sufficient to raise a particular defence, and there is no reason why someone who pleads insanity should be any worse off.
b. It may be maintained that the word "wrong" should be interpreted to mean morally wrong in accordance with the

1. This right of appeal was introduced by the Criminal Procedure (Insanity) Act 1964, s. 2.
2. *Kemp*, [1957] 1 Q.B. 399; [1956] 3 All E.R. 249; *Bratty* v. *A.-G. for Northern Ireland*, [1963] A.C. 386, at pp. 411–412; [1961] 3 All E.R. 523, at p. 534; but see *Charlson*, [1955] 1 All E.R. 859; *C. & J. Cases*.
3. Mental Health Act 1959, s. 71.
4. Criminal Procedure (Insanity) Act 1964, Sched. 1, para. 2.
5. The special verdict of "not guilty by reason of insanity" was only returned in 3 cases in 1974. *Criminal Statistics*, 1974, Cmnd. 6168.
6. Paras. 5.17 and 5.18.

opinion of the High Court of Australia. This is a very debatable point. The decision in *Windle*[1] to the effect that "wrong" in the *M'Naghten Rules* means legally wrong has been supported extra-judicially by Lord Devlin in the following words: "I do not see how an accused man can be heard to say that he knew he was doing an act which he knew to be contrary to law, and yet that he is entitled to be acquitted at the hands of the law. Guilt, whether in relation to the *M'Naghten Rules*, or any other rules, means responsibility in law."[2] In any event, the "knowledge of wrong" test as interpreted in *Windle* provides a very narrow ground of exemption since even grossly disturbed persons generally know that murder, for instance, is a crime.[3]

c. It is said that the *M'Naghten Rules* are based on the outmoded theory that partial insanity is possible. Lawyers cannot pronounce on the validity of this criticism, but partial insanity is regarded as a possibility in several other branches of the law in which the *M'Naghten Rules* are not applied.[4]

d. The *Rules* are limited to cognitive factors, excluding all matters concerning volition, or the emotions, and thus make no allowance for so-called "irresistible impulse". It is said that it should be a defence for a person to show that, although he was aware of the nature and quality of his act and knew it to be wrong, he found, owing to insanity, that it was difficult, if not impossible, to prevent himself from doing what he did. Nevertheless, there are obvious practical dangers in allowing such a defence, and what was until comparatively recently the attitude of the courts may be summed up in the following remarks of Lord Hewart, C.J., in a case in which it was urged that the trial judge should have directed the jury with regard to irresistible impulse: "It is a fantastic theory of irresistible impulse which, if it were to become part of our criminal law, would be merely subversive. It is not yet part of the criminal law, and it is to be hoped that the time is far distant when it will be made so."[5] Yet the Infanticide Act 1922, re-enacted in 1938, had already shown that Parliament was willing to depart from the *M'Naghten Rules* by providing that if a mother killed her newly born child while she was

1. Para. 5.7.
2. [1954] Crim. L. R., 681–682.
3. Butler Committee on Mentally Abnormal Offenders, Cmnd. 6244, para. 18.8.
4. *Hill* (1851), 2 Den. 254; *In the Estate of Bohrmann, Caesar and Watmough* v. *Bohrmann*, [1938] 1 All E.R. 271.
5. *Kopsch* (1925), 19 Cr. App. Rep. 50, at pp. 51–52.

suffering from the effects of childbirth or lactation she should not be convicted of murder if the balance of her mind was disturbed. Moreover a committee presided over by Lord Atkin recommended that irresistible impulse due to insanity should be a defence as long ago as 1924, and a similar recommendation was made by the Royal Commission on Capital Punishment whose recommendations were published in 1953. Allowance is made for irresistible impulse in a number of Commonwealth and North American jurisdictions and the defence of diminished responsibility admits it on a charge of murder.

e. It is not clear that the *M'Naghten Rules*[1] apply to cases in which the mental development of the accused is incomplete since it is uncertain whether mental deficiency is a disease of the mind.

.4 These criticisms are of no great practical importance because of the infrequency of a plea of insanity; in the past the plea was generally raised only in murder cases but in such cases now reliance is rarely placed on the *M'Naghten Rules* owing to the availability, since the Homicide Act 1957 came into force, of a plea of diminished responsibility on a charge of murder in cases in which the accused was substantially mentally abnormal at the material time. When such a plea succeeds, the accused is not automatically detained at the Queen's pleasure, and a substantial sentence of imprisonment is often preferred by the accused. In 1974, there were only two murder cases in which the *M'Naghten Rules* were successfully pleaded by adults as contrasted with 72 findings of diminished responsibility.[2]

Summary Trials

5 The following variations to what has been said above apply to summary trials in Magistrates' Courts. The *M'Naghten Rules* apply to cases tried in Magistrates' Courts but the legislation concerning the special verdict of acquittal, and the results thereof, do not apply to Magistrates' Courts which must, as at common law, give an ordinary acquittal if the defence is made out and the defendant goes free. This is satisfactory if the interests of the accused or society do not require protection, but some power is clearly necessary to deal with cases tried by magistrates where the public or the accused's interests demand further action. This need is met by s. 60 (2) of the Mental Health Act

1. Para. 5.4.

2. *Criminal Statistics*, 1974, Cmnd. 6168.

1959 under which, when the accused is suffering from mental illness or severe subnormality, the magistrates may make a hospital order without registering a conviction, if satisfied merely that the accused did the act or made the omission charged. No causal connection between the offence and the disorder need exist. In 1974, 61 orders under s. 60 (2) were made.[1]

Relevance of the accused's state of mind at different times

5.16 There are four other periods in the history of an accused person at which his mental condition may be relevant, not to provide a defence, but to prevent him being tried or to introduce special provisions concerning the sentence passed on him, even though there may be no doubt that he was sane when he did the act charged. These matters are discussed later.[2]

Proposals for reform

5.17 The Butler Committee on Mentally Abnormal Offenders,[3] which reported in 1975, found the *M'Naghten Rules* unsatisfactory and proposed a complete re-casting of the law relating to the legal responsibility of mentally abnormal offenders. Its recommendations can be summarised as follows:

a. There should be a new special verdict, "not guilty on evidence of mental disorder". The power to give this special verdict should be extended to Magistrates' Courts and as a result s. 60(2) of the Mental Health Act 1959 should be repealed.
b. There should be two alternative grounds for the special verdict:
   i. The special verdict could be returned if the jury or magistrates found that the accused did the act or omission charged but, by reason of evidence of mental disorder as defined by s. 4 of the Mental Health Act 1959, did not find that it had been proved that the accused had the state of mind required for the offence and further found on the balance of probability that the accused was mentally disordered at the time. According to s. 4 of the Mental Health Act "mental disorder" means mental illness, arrested or incomplete development of mind psychopathic, and any other disorder or disability of the mind; and "mentally dis-

---

1. *Ibid.*
2. Paras. 23.6, 23.7 and 23.16.
3. Cmnd. 6244, paras. 18.1–18.50.

ordered" is to be construed accordingly. The present ground would work as follows: if the prosecution failed to prove the requisite state of mind, although it had proved the *actus reus*, the accused would be entitled to a complete acquittal unless the jury or magistrates were satisfied on the balance of probabilities that he was mentally disordered at the time of the offence.

ii. The special verdict could also be returned where the jury or magistrates were satisfied on the balance of probabilities that, at the time of the act or omission charged, the accused was suffering from severe mental illness or severe subnormality. This provision would extend the law considerably. It covers not only cases at present covered by the "knowledge of wrong" test under the *M'Naghten Rules* but also any other case where at the time of the act or omission charged the accused, although able to form intentions and carry them out, was suffering from mental illness or severe subnormality. This ground would be of importance where the prosecution succeeded in proving the necessary *mens rea* for the offence charged.

c. If the special verdict was returned the court should have a discretion as to disposal, except that an overtly penal disposal should be excluded. Thus, it would be open to the court to order an absolute discharge but not to pass a sentence of imprisonment.

Diminished responsibility

18 The concept of diminished responsibility, which has been known to Scots law for some time, was introduced into English law by s. 2 of the Homicide Act 1957, sub-s. (1) of which provides:

> "Where a person kills or is a party to the killing of another, he shall not be convicted of murder if he was suffering from such abnormality of mind (whether arising from a condition of arrested or retarded development of mind or any inherent causes or induced by disease or injury) as substantially impaired his mental responsibility for his acts or omissions in doing or being a party to the killing."

The defence of diminished responsibility is quite different from that of insanity. Insanity covered by the *M'Naghten Rules* is a complete defence, whatever the offence charged, and leads to an acquittal. Diminished responsibility, on the other hand, is merely a mitigating factor limited to charges of murder and, if successfully pleaded, reducing liability from murder to manslaughter.[1] This means that the court has a discretion in the matter of punishment which may vary from imprisonment for life to an absolute discharge, and where considered appropriate, a hospital or guardianship order may be made under s. 60 of the Mental Health Act 1959 which is discussed later.[2]

Section 2 (1) makes it plain that the accused may rely on the defence although he knew what he was doing and knew that it was wrong, and soon after the section came into force it was held that the fact that a killing was premeditated does not destroy a plea of diminished responsibility.[3] At first, there was a tendency to direct the jury to consider whether the case came on the borderline of insanity under the *M'Naghten Rules* and to refrain from explaining the words of the statute to them,[4] but all the earlier decisions have to be read in the light of the judgment of the Court of Criminal Appeal in *Byrne*,[5] which will be discussed shortly. Since *Byrne* was decided, it has been held that, if a judge invites a jury to consider whether someone pleading diminished responsibility was on the borderline of insanity, he should make it plain that he is not using the word "insanity" in the narrow legal sense of the *M'Naghten Rules*.[6] It has also been held that it is not right for the judge merely to refer the jury to the terms of s. 2 of the Act of 1957 without some guidance on their meaning.[7]

5.19 The wording of s. 2 (1) can be broken down into three elements which by s. 2 (2) the accused has the burden of proving, and it has been held that the burden is discharged by proof on the balance of probabilities.[8] The Court of Appeal will quash a conviction for murder and substitute one for manslaughter where there is sufficient evidence to shift the onus of proof with regard to diminished responsibility and that evidence is not contradicted by the Crown.[9] These three elements are:

a. The accused must have been suffering from "abnormality of mind" at the material time. This phrase was explained by the

---

1. Homicide Act 1957, s. 2 (3).
2. Para. 23.16.
3. *Matheson*, [1958] 2 All E.R. 87.
4. *Walden*, [1959] 3 All E.R. 203; *Spriggs*, [1958] 1 Q.B. 270; [1958] 1 All E.R. 300.
5. [1960] 2 Q.B. 396; [1960] 3 All E.R. 1; *C. & J. Cases*.
6. *Rose* v. *R.*, [1961] A.C. 496; [1961] 1 All E.R. 859.
7. *Terry*, [1961] 2 Q.B. 314; [1961] 2 All E.R. 569. See also *Gomez* (1964), 48 Cr. App. Rep. 310.
8. *Dunbar*, [1958] 1 Q.B. 1; [1957] 2 All E.R. 737.
9. *Matheson*, [1958] 2 All E.R. 87.

Court of Criminal Appeal in *Byrne.*[1] Byrne was a sexual psychopath who strangled a girl and mutilated her body. He was charged with murder and pleaded diminished responsibility. The trial judge told the jury that the accused would not have established the defence even if he satisfied them that he found it difficult or impossible to control his perverted sexual impulses. Byrne was convicted, and he successfully appealed to the Court of Criminal Appeal who substituted a verdict of manslaughter on the ground of diminished responsibility. It held that "abnormality of mind" meant a state of mind so different from that of an ordinary person that the reasonable man would term it abnormal. The term was wide enough to cover the mind's activities in all its aspects, not only the perception of physical acts and the ability to form a rational judgment as to whether the act is wrong, but also the ability to exercise will-power to control physical acts in accordance with that rational judgment. Seriously impaired self-control, though irrelevant to the *M'Naghten Rules* as construed in this country, is thus highly relevant to the question whether the accused was suffering from diminished responsibility.

b. The abnormality of mind must result from one of the specified causes, i.e. from a condition of arrested or retarded development of mind or any inherent causes or induced by disease or injury.

c. The abnormality of mind must have substantially impaired his mental responsibility for his acts in doing or being a party to the killing. In *Byrne* the Court of Criminal Appeal held that "mental responsibility for his acts" pointed to a consideration of the extent to which the accused's mind was answerable for his physical acts. This had to include a consideration of the extent of his ability to exercise will-power to control his physical acts. Whether there had been a substantial impairment of the accused's mental responsibility was a question of degree. Where there was inability to exercise will-power to control acts due to abnormality of mind from one of the specified causes there would clearly be substantial impairment, but where there was difficulty due to abnormality of mind from a specified cause to exercise will-power to control acts it would depend on the degree of difficulty. In this connection "substantial" means what it says. The impairment of the accused's ability to resist the impulse under

1. [1960] 2 Q.B. 396; [1960] 3 All E.R. 1; *C. & J. Cases.*

which he acts need not be "total" but it must be more than "trivial" or "minimal". "Substantial" means something in between.[1] The difficulty which the accused had in controlling his conduct must have been substantially greater than would have been experienced by an ordinary person, without mental abnormality, in the circumstances in question.[2]

Whether the accused was suffering from abnormality of mind such as to substantially impair his mental responsibility is a question for the jury. The jury should approach these issues in a broad, commonsense way, taking into account all the evidence, including the acts or statements of the accused and his demeanour.[3] Of course, the medical evidence is important but the jury is not bound to accept it if there is other material before it which, in its opinion, conflicts with and outweighs it.[4] Sometimes the jury are faced with the difficult task of weighing conflicting medical evidence.[5] On the other hand, the aetiology of the mental abnormality (i.e. whether it arose from a specified cause) does seem to be a matter to be determined on expert evidence.[6]

Proposals for reform

5.20 The Butler Committee[7] found s. 2 of the Homicide Act 1957 unsatisfactory, particularly because of the imprecision of "abnormality of mind" and "mental responsibility". Clearly, the only substantial justification for the existence of the defence of diminished responsibility is the mandatory life sentence for murder. The Committee thought there was a strong case for giving the judge a discretion in passing sentence for murder, in which case the defence could be abolished. If this preferred solution was rejected, the Committee proposed that the defence should be amended as follows:

> "Where a person kills or is party to the killing of another, he shall not be convicted of murder if there is medical or other evidence that he was suffering from a form of mental disorder as defined in section 4 of the Mental Health Act 1959 and if, in the opinion

1. *Lloyd*, [1967] 1 Q.B. 175; [1966] 1 All E.R. 107.
2. *Simcox*, [1964] Crim. L. R. 402.
3. *Simcox*; *Byrne*, [1960] 2 Q.B. 396, at pp. 403–404.
4. *Byrne*, [1960] 2 Q.B. 396, at p. 403.
5. *Jennion*, [1962] 1 All E.R. 689.
6. *Byrne*.
7. Committee on Mentally Abnormal Offenders, Cmnd. 6244, paras. 19.1–19.21.

of the jury, the mental disorder was such as to be an extenuating circumstance which ought to reduce the offence to manslaughter." Under this rather imprecise provision the accused would no longer bear the burden of proving the defence but only a burden of adducing evidence to raise an issue. Moreover, if the defence agreed, it would be open to the prosecution to charge manslaughter where there was evidence that a case of diminished responsibility could be made out. As an alternative to this proposal, although they favoured it least of all, the Committee proposed the abolition of the defence of diminished responsibility and the provision that on a conviction for murder the judge should have a discretion to make a hospital or psychiatric probation order instead of imposing life imprisonment where there was appropriate medical evidence.

Automatism and other involuntary conduct[1]

5.21 The basic requirement of criminal liability is that the act or omission in respect of which the accused is charged should have been voluntary. Generally, an involuntary act or omission is not punishable.[2] An act or omission to act is involuntary where it is beyond the control of the person who acts or fails to act; where it is beyond the control of that person's mind the situation is known as one of automatism. For convenience acts and omissions will be discussed in turn.

One of the best known examples of an involuntary act is where the act is compelled by external physical force. Hale gave the following example: "If there be an actual forcing of a man, as if A by force take the arm of B and the weapon in his hand, and therewith stabs C whereof he dies, this is murder in A, and B is not guilty."[3] In *Hill* v. *Baxter*[4] it was stated that a man could not be said to be driving where at the material time he was attacked by a swarm of bees and was prevented from exercising any directional control over the vehicle, any movements of his arms and legs being solely caused by the action of the bees. However, most involuntary acts are not directly caused by external

1. See Edwards, Automatism and Criminal Responsibility, (1959) 21 M.L.R. 375; Hart, *Punishment and Responsibility*, 90.
2. *Woolmington* v. *Director of Public Prosecutions*, [1935] A.C. 462, at p. 482; *Bratty* v. *A.-G. for Northern Ireland*, [1963] A.C. 386, at p. 409; [1961] 3 All E.R. 523, at p. 532; *C. & J. Cases; Kilbride* v. *Lake*, [1962] N.Z.L.R. 590; *Ryan* v. *R.* (1967), 121 C.L.R. 205.
3. Hale, I P.C., 434. Also see Hawkins, I P.C., ch. 29, s. 3.
4. [1958] 1 Q.B. 277; [1958] 1 All E.R. 193.

physical force and the following have also been held to be involuntary acts: reflex actions, spasmodic or convulsive acts;[1] acts done during a state of somnambulism,[2] or concussion,[3] or in a hypoglycaemic coma.[4] In *Hill* v. *Baxter*,[5] Lord Goddard, C.J., said this about a man who had been charged with dangerous driving:

> "Suppose he had had a stroke or an epileptic fit, both instances of what may properly be called acts of God; he might well be in the driver's seat, even with his hands on the wheel, but in such a state of unconsciousness that he could not be said to be driving."

It is clear from the cases that the phrase "automatism and other involuntary conduct" has a meaning limited to cases of unconscious or reflex actions and other actions beyond the control of the accused. Thus acts done under an irresistible impulse are not regarded as "involuntary acts". In the case of an irresistible impulse a person's act will not be beyond his control although he may not be able to control the impulse which prompts his act, but this does not make his act involuntary.[6] The narrow meaning given to "involuntary conduct" also prevents that phrase covering acts done under duress (where there is a threat of physical force unless an act is done),[7] although the threat may afford a justification for the voluntary act and, as we shall see later,[8] provide a defence.

An omission to act is involuntary (i.e. beyond the accused's control) where he is physically restrained from acting or otherwise incapable of acting. Thus in *Leicester* v. *Pearson*,[9] which was concerned with the offence of failing to accord precedence to a pedestrian on a zebra crossing, it was held that if the failure was beyond the control of a driver, e.g. because he had been pushed onto the crossing by a bump from a car behind, he would not be liable.

---

1. *Bratty* v. *A.-G. for Northern Ireland.*
2. *Ibid.*
3. *Ibid.*
4. *Watmore* v. *Jenkins*, [1962] 2 Q.B. 572; [1962] 2 All E.R. 868; *Quick*, [1973] Q.B. 910; [1973] 3 All E.R. 347.
5. [1958] 1 Q.B. 277, at p. 293; [1958] 1 All E.R. 193, at p. 195.
6. *Bratty* v. *A.-G. for Northern Ireland*, [1963] A.C. 386, at p. 409.
7. Edwards, (1958) 21 M.L.R. 376, at p. 381; Williams, *Criminal Law: The General Part*, 2nd ed., 11.
8. Paras. 18.1–18.9.
9. [1952] 2 Q.B. 668; [1952] 2 All E.R. 71. Also see *Kilbride* v. *Lake*, [1962] N.Z.L.R. 590; *Burns* v. *Bidder*, [1967] 2 Q.B. 227; [1966] 3 All E.R. 29.

The distinction between insane and non-insane automatism

5.22 Where the accused is suffering from non-insane automatism he must be acquitted, but if the case is one where the accused was suffering from a "defect of reason due to disease of the mind" the *M'Naghten Rules* apply and, if the trial is on indictment, he is found not guilty by reason of insanity and detained during Her Majesty's pleasure. This distinction was established by the House of Lords in *Bratty* v. *A.-G. for Northern Ireland.*[1] Bratty was charged with the murder of a girl. It was not disputed that he had strangled her. Bratty said that he had had a blackout and there was some evidence that he was suffering from psychomotor epilepsy, which is undoubtedly a disease of the mind. The accused relied on the defences of automatism and insanity, but the trial judge only directed the jury on the issue of insanity. Bratty was convicted, and his appeals to the Northern Irish Court of Criminal Appeal and the House of Lords were dismissed. It was held that, where the only evidence of the cause of automatism is a disease of the mind, the case is one of insane automatism and the *M'Naghten Rules* apply. If, on the other hand, the evidence is that automatism was caused, not by a disease of the mind but by some other cause such as a blow on the head or somnambulism, the case is one of non-insane automatism.[2]

Naturally, an accused who wishes to plead his automatism will be reluctant to claim that it is of the insane variety and the question arises whether, on a plea of automatism, the court or the prosecution can raise the issue of insanity when insanity is not pleaded by the defence. A negative reply was given by Barry, J., in *Charlson*,[3] where the accused was charged with unlawfully and maliciously causing grievous bodily harm. He struck his small son with a mallet, and threw him out of the window. He may have been suffering from a cerebral tumour; there was no evident motive or anger prompting the accused's action, and his defence was that he was, for practical purposes, unconscious at the material time. Barry, J., directed the jury that the case did not involve the defence of insanity since that defence had not been raised by the accused who was alone competent to do so. The accused was acquitted after the jury had

---

1. [1963] A.C. 386; [1961] 3 All E.R. 523; *C. & J. Cases.*
2. Also see *Quick*, [1973] Q.B. 910; [1973] 3 All E.R. 347.
3. [1955] 1 All E.R. 859; *C. & J. Cases.*

been told that he would not be guilty if his acts were purely automatic and his mind had no control over them but later cases have held that the issue of insanity can be raised by the prosecution or the judge where the accused pleads automatism. In *Kemp*,[1] a man was charged with causing grievous bodily harm to his wife with intent to murder her, a statutory offence which has since been repealed because it was identical with the common law offence of attempted murder. It was not disputed that the accused had struck his wife with a hammer in a moment of unconsciousness, caused by the effect on his brain of arteriosclerosis. The defence asked for an acquittal on the authority of *Charlson*, but Devlin, J., distinguished *Charlson* on the ground that in that case the doctors were apparently agreed that the accused was not suffering from any "disease of the mind", whereas it was not denied that arteriosclerosis had affected Kemp's mind. Devlin, J., accordingly directed the jury to consider the question of insanity, and the old style verdict of guilty but insane[2] was returned. With respect, the two cases are not so easily reconciled since the question of whether the accused is suffering from a "disease of the mind" is a question of law to be decided by the judge and not a medical question to be decided by medical witnesses.[3] *Charlson* was doubted by Lord Denning in *Bratty's* case.[4] Lord Denning said that the old notion that only the defence can raise the issue of insanity has gone. The approach adopted in *Kemp* would now seem to represent the law and it is preferable that this should be so since, if a man is subject to uncontrolled outbursts of violence, it is desirable that he should be made subject to restraint.

The distinction between insane and non-insane automatism is one of great importance because, in the case of non-insane automatism, the accused simply bears the burden of adducing evidence;[5] once the issue is raised, the burden of disproving automatism is borne by the Crown in accordance with the general principles enunciated in *Woolmington's* case.[6] If, however, the case is one of insane automatism the accused bears the burden of proof as well as the burden of adducing evidence.[7]

---

1. [1957] 1 Q.B. 399; [1957] 3 All E.R. 249; *C. & J. Cases*.
2. Para. 5.9.
3. Para. 5.5.a.
4. [1963] A.C. 386, at p. 411.
5. *Bratty* v. *A.-G. for Northern Ireland*.
6. Para. 4.3.
7. Para. 5.4.

The accused bears the burden of adducing evidence of non-insane automatism because there is a rebuttable presumption of law that everyone has sufficient mental capacity to be responsible for his crimes. If the prosecution had to adduce evidence of capacity in every case, its position would be intolerable. It is up to the accused to indicate the nature of his alleged incapacity, and since, generally speaking, the mere statement "I had a black-out" or "I can't remember what happened" will be totally insufficient,[1] the accused must support his claim with medical evidence.[2]

Prior fault

5.23 The accused cannot rely on the defence of automatism or other involuntary conduct if the incapacitating condition was the foreseeable consequence of his own previous behaviour and was capable of prevention by taking a precaution which he could and should have taken. This principle was laid down initially in a number of cases concerning driving offences. In *Kay* v. *Butterworth*,[3] for instance, a motorist was held to have been driving without due care and attention when he went to sleep at the steering wheel of his car, which was in motion, and the court took the view that he must have felt drowsy and ought thereupon to have stopped driving. It was said that the accused would not have been liable if he had been rendered unconscious by a sudden illness or a blow from a stone, or if without any fault on his part the car had got out of control. In other cases it has been held, in relation to the strict liability offence of failing to accord precedence at a zebra crossing, that an involuntary failure to accord precedence would not be criminal if it was occasioned by a circumstance beyond the reasonable or possible control of the driver, and of which he did not know and could not reasonably be expected to know.[4]

In *Quick*,[5] the principle that prior fault prevents reliance on the defence of automatism or other involuntary conduct was applied to an offence against the person. Quick was a male nurse

---

1. *Cook* v. *Atchison*, [1968] Crim. L. R. 266.
2. *Bratty* v. *A.-G. for Northern Ireland*, [1963] A.C. 386, at p. 414; [1961] 3 All E.R. 523, at p. 535, *per* Lord Denning.
3. (1945), 173 L.T. 191. Also see *Hill* v. *Baxter*, [1958] 1 Q.B. 277; [1958] 1 All E.R. 193; *Watmore* v. *Jenkins*, [1962] 2 Q.B. 572; [1962] 2 All E.R. 868; *Sibbles*, [1959] Crim. L. R. 660.
4. *Leicester* v. *Pearson*, [1952] 2 Q.B. 668; [1952] 2 All E.R. 71; *Burns* v. *Bidder*, [1967] 2 Q.B. 227; [1966] 3 All E.R. 29.
5. [1973] Q.B. 910; [1973] 3 All E.R. 347.

who as a diabetic was taking prescribed doses of insulin and was under strict dietary control. One day, when he had had very little to eat and had drunk some alcohol, he attacked and injured a hospital patient. He was charged with assault occasioning actual bodily harm and at his trial he adduced medical evidence to suggest that lack of food and excessive alcohol would react on his condition so as to bring about a hypoglycaemic episode, with temporary loss of consciousness and outbursts of violence. The Court of Appeal held that conduct could not be treated as involuntary if the incapacitating condition, the hypoglycaemic episode in this case, could have been foreseen as a result of either doing or not doing something, such as taking alcohol against medical advice after using the prescribed insulin or failing to have regular meals while taking insulin.

The cases on driving offences mentioned above specify an objective test of foresight of the incapacitating condition, i.e. one of reasonable foreseeability. *Quick* is ambiguous on this point, one passage suggesting an objective test, another a subjective test, i.e. whether the accused foresaw that he would get into the incapacitating condition. Subsequently, the Court of Appeal in *Burns*[1] adopted the subjective test in a case concerning indecent assault and this test now seems to be the one to apply outside those offences where liability is strict or based on negligence, as in driving offences, in which case the objective test is applicable.

Although, if the accused's incapacitating condition is caused by prior fault, he cannot escape liability on the ground of automatism or other involuntary conduct, if the offence charged requires proof of subjective *mens rea* the accused may still escape liability on the basis of lack of *mens rea*. However, as we shall see in the next paragraphs, if his automatism was caused by self-induced intoxication he will only escape if the offence charged requires proof of a specific intent.

Intoxication[2]

5.24 All that the leading cases establish is that voluntary or self-induced intoxication by alcohol or other drugs is a defence to a criminal prosecution only if:

a. it causes such a disease of the mind as to bring the *M'Naghten Rules* into play; or

1. (1973), 58 Cr. App. Rep. 364.
2. Paras. 5.24–5.36 will probably need to be read in the light of the House of Lords' decision on the appeal pending in *Majewski*, [1975] 3 All E.R. 296.

b. a specific intent is an essential element of the offence and because of intoxication the accused lacks this intent.

Even to this limited extent voluntary intoxication has been recognised as a defence only within the last 150 years; before that it was regarded as an aggravating factor warranting a punishment of more than ordinary severity. Alcohol and other drugs[1] are substances which are capable of altering mood, perception or consciousness, of loosening inhibitions and self-control, of impairing movements, reactions and judgment and of giving the taker an exaggerated sense of his own capacity. Intoxication is a contributory factor in many offences,[2] and in some is the essence of the offence, as in driving under the influence of drink or drugs, but the vital question is the extent to which it may be a defence where it is a factor but not of the essence.[3] More precisely, it is necessary to consider the effect of intoxication on *mens rea*. The legal position is unsatisfactory. Logically, no one ought to be convicted of an offence unless his mind is guilty, but public and judicial consciences object to acquitting those who are intoxicated solely on that ground. The truth is that the substantial offence is to become intoxicated in the first place, at all events with knowledge and foresight that violent or other criminal conduct may be the result.

25 In England and Wales the general rule remains that voluntary intoxication is no defence.[4] It is no excuse that the accused's powers of perception were impaired so that he was not able to foresee or measure the consequences of his actions as he would if he were sober, nor that his power to judge between right and wrong was impaired so that he would not have acted as he did but for his drunkenness, nor that his powers of self-control were relaxed so that he more readily gave way to temptation than if he were sober[5] and it is not a defence in itself that the accused's voluntary drunkenness caused him to become an automaton.[6]

1. *Lipman*, [1970] 1 Q.B. 152; [1969] 3 All E.R. 410; *C. & J. Cases*; *Majewski*, [1975] 3 All E.R. 296.
2. See Walker, *Crime and Punishment in Britain*, (1968), pp. 32 and 62, and the studies mentioned therein.
3. Singh, A History of the Defence of Drunkenness in the English Criminal Law, (1933), 49 L.Q.R. 528; Orchard, Drunkenness, Drugs, and Manslaughter, [1970] Crim. L. R. 132, 211.
4. *Director of Public Prosecutions* v. *Beard*, [1920] A.C. 479; *C. & J. Cases*; *A.-G. for Northern Ireland* v. *Gallagher*, [1963] A.C. 349; [1961] 3 All E.R. 299; *C. & J. Cases*.
5. *Ibid.*
6. *Bratty* v. *A.-G. for Northern Ireland*, [1963] A.C. 386, at p. 410; [1961] 3 All E.R. 523; *C. & J. Cases*, *per* Lord Denning.

The first exception

5.26 The first exception to the general rule that drunkenness is no defence is where drinking produces a distinct disease of the mind so that the accused is insane within the *M'Naghten Rules*,[1] so that he has a defence if he proves that at the material time he was suffering from a defect of reason, due to the disease of the mind caused by intoxication, such that he did not know the nature and quality of his act or that it was wrong.

Although mere malfunctioning of the mind due to intoxication does not constitute a "disease of the mind",[2] habitual drinking can sometimes lead to such permanent changes in the brain tissues as to be accounted insanity, such as delirium tremens or alcoholic dementia. Presumably because of the serious consequences of a verdict of "not guilty by reason of insanity", a plea of insanity based on drunkenness is extremely rare but an old example is *Davis*.[3] At his trial for wounding with intent to murder (an offence which no longer exists in those words), the accused raised the defence of insanity. There was evidence that at the time, although sober, he was suffering from delirium tremens resulting from excessive drinking. Stephen, J., directed the jury that "drunkenness is one thing and the diseases to which drunkenness leads are different things".[4] He said that if a man by drink brought on a disease of the mind which caused a defect of reason, albeit temporary, which would have relieved him from responsibility if it had been produced in any other way, he would not be criminally responsible. The jury were told to find a verdict of not guilty on the ground of insanity if they thought that the accused had been suffering from a distinct disease of the mind caused by drinking, but differing from drunkenness, and that by reason thereof he did not know that his act was wrong.

5.27 Two observations may be made about this first exception to the general rule. First, it is only where it applies that the accused's appreciation of the legal implications of his conduct becomes relevant; ignorance of the wrongfulness of conduct is irrelevant in the case of those who are sane but drunk, as has been stated

---

1. *Davis* (1881), 14 Cox C.C. 563; *Director of Public Prosecutions* v. *Beard*, [1920] A.C. 479; *A.-G. for Northern Ireland* v. *Gallagher*, [1963] A.C. 349; [1961] 3 All E.R. 299.
2. *Quick*, [1973] Q.B. 910; [1973] 3 All E.R. 347.
3. (1881), 14 Cox C.C. 563.
4. *Loc. cit.* at p. 564.

above. Secondly the distinction between temporary insanity caused by drink and simple drunkenness is not easy to make. This is unfortunate since the distinction is important where the accused alleges that because of excessive drinking he did not know his conduct was wrong.

Stephen, J.'s direction was approved by the House of Lords in both *Director of Public Prosecution* v. *Beard*[1] and *A.-G. for Northern Ireland* v. *Gallagher.*[2] The latter case is particularly important in this context since the judgments emphasise that if the accused was suffering from a disease of the mind which was insufficient to bring him within the *M'Naghten Rules*, e.g. because it would never induce anything more than lack of control, the fact that the disease was exacerbated by drunkenness at the material time would not make the defence of insanity available to him. When sober, Gallagher formed the intention of killing his wife. He then purchased a bottle of whisky, and he may have drunk some of it before he in fact killed his wife with a knife. At his trial the defences of insanity and drunkenness negativing specific intent were raised. There was evidence that the accused was a psychopath, and that his psychopathy was a disease of the mind which would be aggravated by drink in such a way as to cause him the more readily to lose his self-control. The trial judge told the jury that, in considering whether the *M'Naghten Rules* applied to the case, they should have regard to the accused's state of mind just before he took the whisky. Gallagher was convicted. He successfuly appealed to the Northern Irish Court of Criminal Appeal, but his conviction was subsequently reinstated by the House of Lords. The basis of the House of Lords' decision was that Gallagher's psychopathy was quiescent and, without the drink, could not have brought the *M'Naghten Rules* into play because it merely weakened his power of self-control and the defence of insanity could not be made good by getting drunk on whisky. It would have been different, it was said, if Gallagher's psychopathy had been caused by drink and he had been insane within the *M'Naghten Rules*.

A plea of diminished responsibility cannot be based on drunkenness itself[3], although it is probable that a permanent injury to the brain produced by drink would be held to be an "injury" for the purposes of s. 2 of the Homicide Act 1957.

---

1. [1920] A.C. 479; *C. & J. Cases.*
2. [1963] A.C. 349; [1960] 1 All E.R. 734; *C. & J. Cases.*
3. *Fenton* (1975), 119 S.J. 695.

The second exception

5.28 The courts have repeatedly stated that drunkenness affords a defence where a specific intent is an element of the offence in question and the drunkenness is such as to prevent the formation of that intent. A leading authority is *Director of Public Prosecutions* v. *Beard*:[1] this was a case of murder which is unlawful homicide with malice aforethought. Malice aforethought consists, at present, of an intention to kill or to cause grievous bodily harm, but when *Beard* was decided, it also consisted of an intention to commit a felony such as robbery or rape. This meant that a man who unintentionally caused death by giving someone with a weak heart a slight push would be guilty of murder if the push were given in furtherance of rape or robbery, although he would only be guilty of manslaughter if his intentions were not felonious.

5.29 In *Beard*, the accused placed his hand over the mouth of a child in furtherance of the felony of rape. He unintentionally killed her by pressing his thumb on her throat when endeavouring to prevent her from screaming. The Court of Criminal Appeal substituted a conviction of manslaughter for one of murder because the jury had not been told to consider whether Beard, who pleaded drunkenness, knew that what he was doing was dangerous. The House of Lords restored the conviction for murder as "The capacity of the mind of the prisoner to form the felonious intent which murder involves" was "to be explored in relation to the ravishment". It was not suggested that Beard was so drunk as to be incapable of forming the intention to commit the felony of rape and, because of this intention he had malice aforethought according to the law as it stood when his case was decided.

The law relating to voluntary drunkenness was reviewed in *Beard* and, leaving aside the issue of drunkenness resulting in insanity, two principal points were made by Lord Birkenhead in the course of his judgment:

a. Evidence of drunkenness rendering the accused incapable of forming the specific intent essential to constitute the offence charged should be taken into consideration with the other facts proved in order to determine whether or not he had this intent.
b. Evidence of drunkenness falling short of a proved incapacity

---

1. [1920] A.C. 479; *C. & J. Cases.*

in the accused to form the intent necessary to constitute the offence in question, and merely establishing that his mind was affected by drink so that he more readily gave way to some violent passion, affords no defence. (Lord Birkenhead's reference to a "proved incapacity to form the intent" must be read in the light of the subsequent decision in Woolmington's case. The burden of proving drunkenness is not borne by the accused although he must adduce evidence of his drunkenness at the relevant time.)[1]

The first of these two points must be read in conjunction with a later passage in the same judgment. Lord Birkenhead went on to say that the proposition to be deduced from the earlier authorities on drunkenness was not an exceptional rule applicable only to cases in which it is necessary to prove a specific intent, for "speaking generally (and apart from certain special offences), a person cannot be convicted of a crime unless the *mens* was *rea*."[2] The fact that Lord Birkenhead was plainly of the opinion that the defence of drunkenness is available in cases other than those in which a specific intent must be proved has been ignored in subsequent cases, such as *A.-G. for Northern Ireland* v. *Gallagher*[3] the facts of which will be mentioned later, and *Lipman*.[4]

30 In *Gallagher*, Lord Denning (who was the only Law Lord to discuss the point) said that, apart from drunkenness leading to insanity, the only exception to the general rule that drunkenness was no defence was where the offence in question required a specific intent (as murder did) and drunkenness prevented the formation of that specific intent. This degree of drunkenness was reached when a man was rendered so stupid by drink that he did not know what he was doing. Shortly afterwards, Lord Denning made a similar statement in *Bratty* v. *A.-G. for Northern Ireland*[5] where he pointed out that if the drunken man was so drunk that he did not know what he was doing, he had a defence to any charge, such as murder or wounding with intent contrary to s. 18 of the Offences against the Person Act 1861, in which a specific intent is essential, but could nevertheless be convicted of manslaughter or unlawful wounding contrary to s. 20 of the

---

1. *Broadhurst* v. *R.*, [1964] A.C. 441; [1964] 1 All E.R. 111; *C. & J. Cases.*
2. [1920] A.C. 479, at p. 501.
3. [1963] A.C. 349; [1961] 3 All E.R. 299; *C. & J. Cases.*
4. [1970] 1 Q.B. 152; [1969] 3 All E.R. 410; *C. & J. Cases.*
5. [1963] A.C. 386; [1961] 3 All E.R. 523; *C. & J. Cases.*

same Act for which no specific intent is required. Although Lord Denning purported to be following *Beard* in both cases, his restriction of the defence of drunkenness to offences in which a specific intent must be proved seems to be inconsistent with the later part of Lord Birkenhead's speech in *Beard* in which Lord Birkenhead treated the law with regard to drunkenness as an application of the ordinary requirement of *mens rea*. On this view, though drunkenness should not be a defence when liability is based on negligence as it can be in manslaughter, it should, if of the requisite degree, be a defence when liability is based on recklessness or malice, such as unlawful wounding, and the courts of New South Wales, a jurisdiction in which the defence of drunkenness is governed by the common law, have reached this conclusion.[1]

5.31 Lord Birkenhead's proposition in *Beard* that drunkenness which renders the accused incapable of forming the specific intent essential to constitute the offence should be taken into account along with the other factors "proved" in order to determine whether he had that intent is not easy to grasp. As Lord Devlin said in *Broadhurst*,[2] a Privy Council case, if the accused is rendered incapable of forming an intent by drunkenness, whatever the other factors in the case may be, he cannot have formed it, and it would not be sensible to take the incapacity into consideration with the other facts in order to determine whether he had the necessary specific intent. Moreover if, through drunkenness, the accused lacks the necessary specific intent it is arbitrary to exculpate him if his drunkenness was such that he did not have the capacity to form the specific intent but to convict if his drunkenness did not render him incapable of forming that intent although because of it he did not have that intent.

Fortunately, it is clear that the harshness of the present proposition of Lord Birkenhead has been mitigated to some extent by s. 8 of the Criminal Justice Act 1967. As we have seen,[3] under s. 8 a man is no longer to be presumed to intend the natural and probable consequences of his act; instead the question whether the accused had the necessary intent is to be decided by the jury or magistrates on all the evidence. Thus, the jury in deciding whether the accused had the necessary specific intent must take into account all the evidence. The strongest evidence

1. *Stones*, [1956] S.R. (N.S.W.) 25.
2. [1964] A.C. 441; [1964] 1 All E.R. 111; *C. & J. Cases*.
3. Para. 4.10.

of course is that the accused was too drunk to be capable of forming the specific intent, but it is enough if, on all the evidence, the jury find that while the accused's drunkenness was not such as to make him incapable of forming a specific intent, i.e. he could have intended, he did not in fact have that intent. Authority for this new interpretation is *Pordage*,[1] where the accused pleaded drunkenness on a charge of wounding with intent to do grievous bodily harm. The trial judge directed the jury to consider the question of the accused's capacity to form the necessary specific intent. The Court of Appeal held that this was wrong; the judge should have told the jury to take drunkenness into account in deciding whether the accused did have the specific intent to do grievous bodily harm.

32 This amendment to Lord Birkenhead's proposition does not remove its major limitation—the restriction of the defence of drunkenness to offences requiring proof of a specific intent. The effect of this limitation is demonstrated by *Lipman*[2] where the accused was charged with the murder of a girl and convicted of manslaughter. He and the girl had taken L.S.D. together in her room, and Lipman alleged that, while under the influence of the drug, he had the illusion of descending to the centre of the earth and being attacked by snakes. His case was that he must have killed the girl during this experience. She had received two severe blows on the head, but the immediate cause of death was asphyxia due to having had part of a sheet crammed into her mouth. The Court of Appeal affirmed the conviction because "when the killing results from the unlawful act of the prisoner, no specific intent has to be proved to convict of manslaughter, and self-induced intoxication is no defence". The court took the view that, for this type of manslaughter, it was enough that the accused had done such an act "as all sober and reasonable people would inevitably recognise must subject the other person to, at least, the risk of some harm resulting therefrom, albeit not serious harm".[3]

To justify the exclusion of the defence that his drugged condition rendered the accused's act involuntary, the court relied on Lord Denning's statement in *Bratty* that an involuntary act which proceeds from a state of drunkenness would not provide

---

1. [1975] Crim. L. R. 575.
2. [1970] 1 Q.B. 152; [1969] 3 All E.R. 410.
3. *Per* Edmund Davies, J., in *Church*, [1966] 1 Q.B. 59; [1965] 2 All E.R. 71; *C. & J. Cases*.

a complete acquittal; although it would excuse a person from liability for murder, for which a specific intent was required, he would be convicted of manslaughter since no such intent was necessary.

In *Hayward*,[1] Crockett, J., sitting in the Supreme Court of Victoria, declined to follow *Lipman* and the dicta in the House of Lords upon which the decision was based on the ground that they ignored the need to have regard to the mental state of the accused in respect of the foremost element of criminal liability, namely that the act in question must be a conscious, voluntary and deliberate act.

We shall see in the next paragraph that several further criticisms can be made of the proposition that, insanity apart, voluntary drunkenness can only provide a defence where the offence in question requires a specific intent. Nevertheless that rule is still being applied by the courts[2] and must be accepted as being the present law.

Criticism of the second exception

5.33 One criticism can be based on the fact of the ambiguity of the phrase "specific intent". It is sometimes used to mean the intent which must be specified in the indictment, as an intent to cause grievious bodily harm or resist arrest must be specified on charges of wounding or causing grievous bodily harm with intent contrary to s. 18 of the Offences against the Person Act 1861. Sometimes "specific intent" is used as a synonym for further (or ulterior) intent, e.g., the further intent to steal which must be proved in addition to the intentional trespass in burglary. On other occasions "specific intent" is used in the sense of direct as opposed to oblique intent, i.e. the aim to produce a particular result as distinct from knowledge that such a result is likely or even certain.[3] All that can be said with confidence is that, in this context, murder, wounding with intent, burglary and theft[4] require a specific intent, although the list could no doubt be extended to cover a number of other offences, especially those with statutory definitions in which the words "with intent" are employed. So far as murder is concerned the specific intent is the intention (which may be direct or oblique) to cause

1. [1971] V.R. 755.
2. *Bolton* v. *Crawley*, [1972] Crim. L. R. 222; *Majewski*, [1975] 3 All E.R. 296; *McPherson*, [1973] Crim. L. R. 457.
3. Para. 00.0.
4. *Ruse* v. *Read*, [1949] 1 K.B. 377; [1949] 1 All E.R. 398; *Kindon* (1957), 41 Cr. App. Rep. 208.

death or really serious bodily harm. Conversely, it is possible to draw up a list of those offences which do not require a specific intent: manslaughter, unlawful wounding, assault occasioning actual bodily harm,[1] assaulting a constable in the execution of his duty,[2] indecent assault[3] and taking a conveyance without lawful authority[4] can be included in this list. Manslaughter can be established merely by proving an intention to do the unlawful act which caused death. The act must be one obviously likely to cause some degree of physical harm but it is unnecessary for the prosecution to prove that the accused intended to cause any physical harm to the deceased. The intent to do the unlawful act is not a specific intent.[5]

Nevertheless, the fact that, in the light of decided cases, it is possible to draw up lists of offences which do, or do not, require a specific intent, does not lessen the ambiguity which surrounds "specific intent" nor does it help us in ascertaining, in advance of judicial decision on the nature of an intent in a particular offence, whether it is specific or not.

5.34 A second criticism is that the courts have not explained satisfactorily the relationship between the defence of drunkenness and s. 8 of the Criminal Justice Act 1967.[6] We have seen that according to Lord Denning, the defence of drunkenness, applies only to offences requiring a specific intent and that unlawful wounding contrary to s. 20 of the Offences against the Person Act 1861 is not such an offence.

One way of stating Lord Denning's view would be to say that, on a charge of unlawful wounding where the only excuse raised is drunkenness, the court or jury is bound to infer that the accused foresaw that his act would cause bodily harm to his victim, however drunk the accused may have been; but, if this is the correct formulation of *Beard* and Lord Denning's view, and the Court of Appeal in *Sheehan*[7] stated *obiter* that it was, it is inconsistent with s. 8 of the Criminal Justice Act 1967, which directs the court or jury to refer to all the evidence and to draw such inferences as it thinks proper in determining whether the

1. *Bolton* v. *Crawley*, [1972] Crim. L. R. 222.
2. *Majewski*, [1975] 3 All E.R. 296.
3. *Burns* (1973), 58 Cr. App. Rep. 364.
4. *McPherson*, [1973] Crim. L. R. 457.
5. *Lipman*, [1970] 1 Q.B. 152; [1969] 3 All E.R. 410.
6. Para. 4.10.
7. [1975] 2 All E.R. 960.

accused had the necessary intention or foresight, and is no longer good law. This view was taken in *Sheehan*, although it was necessarily *obiter* since the Court of Appeal did not need to decide the point. However, in *Majewski*,[1] which was decided shortly afterwards, this proposition was rejected by the Court of Appeal. The Court held that s. 8 is an evidential provision concerned only with proof of the intent which has to be proved, whereas Lord Denning was stating the substantive law with regard to drunkenness as a defence to a criminal charge. In effect he was saying that where drunkenness is the only excuse raised in an offence not requiring a specific intent but some other form of *mens rea*, that offence is transformed into one not requiring proof of *mens rea*. This means that the rules with regard to drunkenness are not exclusively based on the negation of *mens rea*[2] and are best explained as rules of judicial policy aimed at maintaining law and order. Those who are drunk and dangerous should certainly be punished but it is artificial to convict them of an offence for which they lacked the *mens rea* otherwise required. What is required is an offence of being drunk and dangerous but this is necessarily a matter for Parliament.[3] *Majewski* is at present (February 1976) before the House of Lords and we hope that, at the very least, their Lordships will simplify the present law. The Butler Committee[4] has proposed that it should be an offence for a person while voluntarily intoxicated to do an act, or make an omission, that would amount to a dangerous offence if it was done or made with the requisite state of mind for such an offence. This offence of being drunk and dangerous would not be charged in the first instance but the jury would be directed to return a verdict on this offence in the event of intoxication being raised successfully as a defence.

A restriction on the two exceptions

5.35 A restriction on the exceptions to the general rule that voluntary drunkenness is no defence was postulated by Lord Denning in *A.-G. for Northern Ireland* v. *Gallagher*.[5] His Lordship dealt with the issues raised in that case in a way different from that of his colleagues and introduced what may be called the "Dutch courage" rule which is particularly important in the case of the

---

1. [1975] 3 All E.R. 296.
2. Also see *Howell*, [1974] 2 All E.R. 806.
3. Para. 2.7.
4. Committee on Mentally Abnormal Offenders, Cmnd. 6244, paras. 18.51–18.59.
5. [1963] A.C. 349; [1961] 3 All E.R. 299; *C. & J. Cases*; para. 5.27.

second exception (drunkenness negativing the necessary specific intent).

Lord Denning said that the case had to be decided on the general rule that drunkenness is no defence to a criminal charge. He recognised that there are two exceptions to this rule but held that neither of them was applicable because Gallagher had deliberately made himself drunk in order to give himself Dutch courage to commit the offence.

His Lordship said:

> "If a man, whilst sane and sober, forms an intention to kill and makes preparation for it, knowing it is a wrong thing to do, and then gets himself drunk so as to give himself Dutch courage to do the thing, and whilst drunk carries out his intention, he cannot rely on this self-induced drunkenness as a defence to a charge of murder, nor even as reducing it to manslaughter. He cannot say that he got himself into such a stupid state that he was incapable of an intent to kill. So, also, when he is a psychopath, he cannot by drinking rely on his self-induced defect of reason as a defence of insanity. The wickedness of his mind before he got drunk is enough to condemn him, coupled with the act which he intended to do and did do. A psychopath who goes out intending to kill, knowing it is wrong, and does kill, cannot escape the consequences by making himself drunk before doing it."[1]

Lord Denning suggested that the case would have been different if Gallagher had resiled from his intention to kill his wife before taking the drink. In that event, the question would have been whether the drunkenness was such as to bring the case within the second exception to the general rule.

Although Lord Denning's formulation of the Dutch courage rule is to be welcomed as a matter of policy, it does provide an apparent exception to the rule that *mens rea* and *actus reus* must be contemporaneous.[2]

Involuntary drunkenness

5.36 Intoxication is involuntary where it is not self-induced[3] as where the accused's friends have slipped vodka into his ginger beer or where he has been drugged by his enemies. Intoxication is also involuntary, even though it might be regarded as self-induced, where it results from the taking of drugs prescribed by a doctor and the accused has acted perfectly properly. The

1. *Ibid.*, at p. 382.
2. Para. 3.32.
3. *Quick*, [1973] Q.B. 910; [1973] 3 All E.R. 347.

accused will not have acted properly, and his drunkenness will be voluntary, if he does or omits to do something which causes his intoxication to be foreseeable, e.g. taking alcohol against medical advice after using certain prescribed drugs or failing to take regular meals while taking prescribed insulin.[1]

Where the accused was involuntarily drunk he is not limited to the defences which apply in the case of voluntary drunkenness. Thus, he has the defence of non-insane automatism[2] or, if he was not a drunken automaton, that his drunkenness prevented him having the necessary *mens rea* for the offence (whether or not a specific intent is required).

Corporations[3]

5.37 The general rule is that a corporation, such as an incorporated company, a public corporation like those formed for nationalised industries or a local authority, may be criminally liable to the same extent as a natural person, subject to two exceptions:

a. in the case of offences which from their very nature cannot be committed by corporations; and

b. where the only punishment the court can impose is physical.

In law a corporation is a separate person distinct from its members. There has never been any doubt that the members, like the servants, of a corporation cannot shelter behind the corporation and may be successfully prosecuted for criminal acts performed or authorised by them; the problem with which we are concerned is the extent to which the corporate body itself may be criminally liable. The law on this subject has been developed comparatively recently and is due to the growth in the activities of limited liability companies. The chief obstacle to the acceptance of the concept of the criminal liability of a corporation has been the combination of its artificiality with the traditional need for the proof of *mens rea* in crime "... did you ever expect a corporation to have a conscience, when it has no soul to be damned and no body to be kicked?"[4] In 1700, a corporation was not indictable at all;[5] today the situation is as we have described it.

5.38 The courts had little difficulty in holding that a corporation

1. *Ibid.*
2. *Ibid.*
3. Leigh, *The Criminal Responsibility of Corporations in English Law;* Welsh, Criminal Liability of Corporations, (1946) 62 L.Q.R. 345; Burrows, Criminal Responsibility of Corporations, (1948) 1 *Journal of Criminal Science*, 1.
4. Attributed to the second Baron Thurlow.
5. *Anon* (1702), 12 Mod. 559.

can be guilty of breach of a statutory duty, such as the duty imposed on the "occupier" of a factory to fence its machinery or on the "keeper" of a dog to license it. Since the middle of the nineteenth century it has been clear that, like anyone else, a corporation is liable if it is in breach of a statutory duty imposed on it as an occupier or keeper or in some other similar capacity.[1] In *Evans & Co., Ltd.* v. *London County Council*,[2] the defendant company was charged that, being the occupier of a shop, it did not close it on the afternoon of an early closing day in breach of the duty imposed on the occupiers of shops by the Shops Act 1912. The Divisional Court held that the company was liable for breach of this statutory duty. Unlike the other methods of imposing corporate liability, it is not necessary to find an act or omission by a servant which is imputable to the corporation.

There was equally little difficulty in holding a corporation vicariously liable for the acts of servants and others in the same way as an individual.[3] These two grounds of liability can render a corporation criminally liable only for a relatively small number of offences, essentially statutory offences of strict liability; the issue of principle was settled in 1944 at the latest[4] since when it has been possible to impose criminal liability on a corporation, whether as a perpetrator or as an accomplice, for virtually any offence, notwithstanding that *mens rea* is required by the use of the principle of identification.

The principle of identification

39 In one of the earliest cases in which this principle was applied, *I.C.R. Haulage, Ltd.*,[5] a company was held indictable for a common law conspiracy to defraud, an offence which requires *mens rea* and to which vicarious liability cannot apply. As this case shows, whereas the other kinds of corporate liability are creatures of statute and statutory construction, the present principle is a judicial creation which depends on the fiction that the acts and state of mind of certain superior officers who are seen as composing the very personality of the organisation are the acts and state of mind of the corporation. In such a case liability

1. *Birmingham and Gloucester Rail. Co., Ltd.* (1842), 3 Q.B. 223.
2. [1914] 3 K.B. 315.
3. Para. 19.25; also see *Mousell Brothers, Ltd.* v. *London and North Western Rail. Co.*, [1917] 2 K.B. 836, at p. 846.
4. Three cases in 1944 went far to establish the present law: *Director of Public Prosecutions* v. *Kent and Sussex Contractors, Ltd.*, [1944] K.B. 146; [1944] 1 All E.R. 119; *I.C.R. Haulage, Ltd.*, [1944] K.B. 551; [1944] 1 All E.R. 691; *C. & J. Cases*; *Moore* v. *I. Bresler, Ltd.*, [1944] 2 All E.R. 515.
5. [1944] K.B. 551; [1944] 1 All E.R. 691; *C. & J. Cases*.

is not vicarious in that the corporation is not held responsible on the basis of liability for the acts of its agents; instead the corporation, as in the case of breach of duty, is regarded as having committed the offence personally.

5.40 The nature of the principle of identification and the clear distinction which exists between corporate liability by virtue of it and the corporation's vicarious liability as an employer is shown in the following passage from Lord Reid's speech in *Tesco Supermarkets, Ltd.* v. *Nattrass*:[1]

> "A living person has a mind which can have knowledge or intention or be negligent and he has hands to carry out his intentions. A corporation has none of these: it must act through living persons, though not always one and the same person. Then the person who acts is not speaking or acting for the company. He is acting as the company and his mind which directs his acts is the mind of the company. There is no question of the company being vicariously liable. He is not acting as a servant, representative, agent or delegate. He is an embodiment of the company, or, one could say, he hears and speaks through the *persona* of the company, within his appropriate sphere, and his mind is the mind of the company. If it is a guilty mind then that guilt is the guilt of the company."

It is a question of law whether a person in doing a particular thing is to be regarded as the company or merely as the company's servant or agent. It follows that the judge should tell the jury that if they find certain facts proved then they must find that the acts and state of mind of that person are the acts and state of mind of the company.[2]

5.41 A widely approved dictum on the question of who can be identified with the corporation is that of Lord Denning in the civil case of *H. L. Bolton (Engineering) Co., Ltd.* v. *P. J. Graham Sons, Ltd.*[3]:

> "A company may in many ways be likened to a human body. It has a brain and nerve centre which controls what it does. It also has hands which hold the tools and act in accordance with directions from the centre. Some of the people in the company are mere servants and agents who are nothing more than hands to do the

---

1. [1972] A.C. 153, at p. 170; [1971] 2 All E.R. 127, at pp. 131–132. *C. & J. Cases*. Para. 5.43.
2. *Ibid.*, and at pp. 173 and 134 respectively. See also *Andrews Weatherfoil, Ltd.*, [1972] 1 All E.R. 65.
3. [1957] 1 Q.B. 159, at p. 172; [1956] 3 All E.R. 624.

work and cannot be said to represent the mind or will. Others are directors and managers who represent the directing mind and will of the company, and control what it does. The state of mind of these managers is the state of mind of the company and is treated by the law as such."

This dictum was approved in *Tesco Supermarkets, Ltd.* v. *Nattrass*[1] by Lords Reid, Dilhorne and Pearson who held that only those who constitute the "directing mind and will" of the corporation can be identified with it. These were people such as directors and others who manage the affairs of the corporation. In addition, they include a person to whom those responsible for the general management of the corporation had delegated some part of their functions of management, giving to that person full discretion to act independently of instructions from them. Within the scope of the delegation, the delegate could act as the corporation. In assessing whether a particular person could be identified with the company in this way account should be taken of the constitution of the corporation.[2]

.42 The corporation may on these criteria be identified with a manager to whom the directors have delegated full power in the running of its affairs[3] but not with the branch manager of a company with a large number of branches who was required to comply with the general directions of the board of directors,[4] nor with a depot engineer,[5] nor with the operator of a weighbridge belonging to the corporation.[6]

The person identified with the corporation renders it liable only so long as he acts within the scope of his authority,[7] but this does not mean that activities contrary to the corporation's interests will exclude its liability. A corporation may be convicted even though it is itself defrauded, provided that the offence was committed by a person identified with the corporation acting within the scope of his authority.[8]

---

1. [1972] A.C. 153; [1971] 2 All E.R. 127; *C. & J. Cases.*
2. *Ibid.*, at pp. 190–191, and p. 132 respectively, *per* Lord Pearson. See also the speech of Lord Diplock.
3. *Lennard's Carrying Co., Ltd.* v. *Asiatic Petroleum Co. Ltd.*, [1915] A.C. 705.
4. *Tesco Supermarkets, Ltd.* v. *Nattrass*, para. 5.40.
5. *Magna Plant, Ltd.* v. *Mitchell*, [1966] Crim. L. R. 394.
6. *John Henshall (Quarries), Ltd.* v. *Harvey*, [1965] 2 Q.B. 233; [1965] 1 All E.R. 725; *C. & J. Cases.*
7. *Director of Public Prosecutions* v. *Kent and Sussex Contractors, Ltd.*, [1944] K.B. 146; [1944] 1 All E.R. 119.
8. *Moore* v. *I. Bresler, Ltd.*, [1944] 2 All E.R. 515.

Offences to which the principle of identification cannot apply

5.43 In the *I.C.R. Haulage, Ltd.* case,[1] although it was said that a corporation was *prima facie* criminally liable to the same extent as a natural person, two exceptions to this general rule were mentioned and it was recognised that there might be others. The first exception was said to consist of "cases where from its very nature, the offence cannot be committed by a corporation".[2] The court gave perjury and bigamy as examples, and sexual offences such as rape and incest also fall within this category. It is open to question whether a corporation cannot be indicted for perjury, for the act of the corporate representative in swearing a false oath, and his guilty knowledge, could be attributed to the corporation. Therefore it has been suggested[3] that a company whose governing body authorised one of its number to swear a false affidavit could be convicted of perjury. In the case of perjury in judicial proceedings, the false statement must be made by a person who has been lawfully sworn, and the corporation cannot be so described. Nevertheless, if a governing body were to authorise the making of a false statement on oath in court, a corporation might be convicted of subornation (i.e. procuration) of perjury. Similarly, although a corporation cannot commit bigamy as a perpetrator, if a marriage bureau is managed by a limited company, one of whose directors knowingly negotiates a bigamous marriage, it is difficult to see why the company should not be convicted of aiding and abetting bigamy, for a natural person may be convicted of aiding and abetting an offence which he could not commit himself as a perpetrator.[4] Clearly, although a corporation cannot be convicted as a perpetrator of offences involving sexual intercourse, theoretically it could be convicted as an accomplice but it is difficult to visualise a situation where the responsible officer would be acting within the scope of his authority.

The second exception to the general rule of corporate liability for crime referred to in the *I.C.R. Haulage, Ltd.* case arises from the fact that "the court will not stultify itself by embarking on a trial in which, if a verdict of guilty is returned, no effective order by way of sentence can be made".[5] This exception is now

1. [1944] K.B. 551; [1944] 1 All E.R. 691; *C. & J. Cases.*
2. *Ibid.*, at pp. 594 and 693 respectively.
3. Stephen, *Digest of Criminal Law*, 9th ed., 4.
4. Para. 19.12.
5. [1944] K.B. at p. 554; [1944] 1 All E.R. at p. 693.

confined to murder and treason for which the only punishment which the court can impose is imprisonment or death.

It was said, *obiter*, in several old cases that a corporation could not be indicted for a crime of violence.[1] These dicta were acted upon by Finlay, J., in *Cory Brothers, Ltd.*,[2] where he held that a company could not be indicted for manslaughter or the statutory offence of setting up an engine (in this case an electric fence) calculated to destroy life with intent to injure a trespasser. This decision is no longer good law: it was questioned in *I.C.R. Haulage, Ltd.* and a company has since been convicted of aiding and abetting the causing of death by dangerous driving.[3] This discussion of the boundaries of corporate liability should not obscure the fact that most prosecutions involving *mens rea* against corporations under the present principle are concerned with commercial fraud.[4]

Social policy

4 Neither Parliament nor the courts have ever considered comprehensively the merits or otherwise of imposing criminal liability on corporations, either in principle or in its practical applications. As we have seen, the idea has developed on a pragmatic and expedient basis. Writers have demonstrated the unreality of imputing to a corporation the mind or minds of its chief officers, the absurdity of imposing fines which are trifling when compared with the profits or losses of the body concerned and the injustice of penalising shareholders, consumers or taxpayers, who ultimately bear the burden of fines imposed on corporations, for acts or omissions of which usually they are unaware. These and others are fair points, but few people seem reluctant to accept the principle of corporate personality and it is but a short step to accept its full implications. In modern society, many decisions or failures to decide are collective and many individuals share the credit or the blame. It is often difficult to identify blameworthy individuals with the precision and weight of proof which the criminal law demands and, whatever may be the intellectual arguments, the conception of corporate responsibility by now is well entrenched in the public mind. No doubt this is one of the many topics which call for systematic research and consideration but it is one of the least urgent.

---

1. E.g. *Birmingham and Gloucester Rail. Co., Ltd.*, (1842), 3 Q.B. 223, at p. 232.
2. [1927] 1 K.B. 810.
3. *Robert Millar (Contractors), Ltd.*, [1970] 2 Q.B. 54; [1970] 1 All E.R. 577.
4. Possible reforms of the law of corporate liability are discussed in Law Commission Working Paper No. 44, *Criminal Liability of Corporations*.

Identification and statutory defences

5.45 The principle of identification can also excuse a corporation from liability for certain regulatory offences. As we shall see later,[1] some statutes provide that it is a defence for a person, who would otherwise be vicariously liable, to show that he has exercised all due diligence and that the commission of the offence was due to the act or default of "another person". As far as corporations are concerned, "another person" means a person other than those officers of the corporation who are identified with it. In *Tesco Supermarkets, Ltd.*, v. *Nattrass*,[2] a local shop manager employed by a company running a chain of 800 supermarkets was not identified with the company. His faulty supervision had caused a shop assistant to sell goods in circumstances in which the company was *prima facie* guilty under the principles of vicarious liability of an offence under the Trade Descriptions Act 1968, but the House of Lords held that the manager, though a servant, could not be identified with the corporation and could be treated as "another" through whose fault the offence had been committed for the purposes of the defence provided by s. 24 of the Act.[3]

Liability of directors and similar persons

5.46 Where a corporation has been held criminally liable the natural persons involved may be liable of course as perpetrators or accomplices. In addition, many statutes now provide for the guilt of senior officers of the corporation who would not be criminally liable under ordinary principles, or whose guilt it would otherwise be hard to prove. The following is a common example of this type of provision:

> "Where an offence under this Act which has been committed by a body corporate is proved to have been committed with the consent and connivance of, or to be attributable to any neglect on the part of, any director, manager [i.e., someone managing the affairs of the corporation[4]] secretary or other similar officer of the body corporate, or any person who was purporting to act in that capacity, he, as well as the body corporate, shall be guilty of that offence".[5]

---

1. Para. 16.24.
2. [1972] A.C. 153; [1971] 2 All E.R. 127; *C. & J. Cases*; paras. 5.38 and 5.39.
3. Para. 16.21.
4. *Tesco Supermarkets, Ltd.* v. *Nattrass*, [1972] A.C., at p. 178.
5. Trade Descriptions Act 1968, s. 20.

The words "attributable to any neglect on the part of" are important since they considerably extend the ambit of the criminal law in this context, rendering a person of the stipulated type liable for his negligence in failing to prevent the offence committed by the corporation.

6

STRICT LIABILITY[1]

6.1 In some exceptional offences the accused may be convicted although his conduct was neither intentional nor reckless nor negligent with reference to one or more of the consequences or circumstances mentioned in the definition of the offence charged.

We have seen that a person acts intentionally with reference to the consequences of his conduct when he either aims at achieving them or foresees them as probable; a person is reckless with regard to consequences when he consciously takes the unjustified risk of their occurrence; he is negligent when, though unaware of that risk, he ought to have been aware of it. A person is said to act intentionally with reference to circumstances when he knows of their existence, i.e. he has actual knowledge, or knowledge of the first degree spoken of by Lord Devlin;[2] a person acts recklessly with reference to circumstances when he knows that there is a risk of their existence but disregards that risk without justification; the case is one of connivance, wilful blindness, or knowledge of the second degree spoken of by Lord Devlin; a person acts negligently with reference to circumstances when he unreasonably fails to make inquiries concerning them; the case is one of constructive knowledge. When someone is held guilty of an offence although he acted neither intentionally, nor recklessly nor negligently with reference to either a circumstance or consequence of the *actus reus*, he is rendered liable to punishment in the absence of any fault on his part and is said to be under strict liability, of which there are many critics. It is not a satisfactory answer to say that it is always possible to subject the offender to a small fine, or even to discharge him absolutely under s. 7 of the Powers of Criminal Courts Act 1973.[3]

One of the earliest and most important cases on the exceptions

---

1. Edwards, *Mens Rea in Statutory Offences*; Howard, *Strict Responsibility*; Law Commission Working Paper No. 30, *Strict Liability and Enforcement of the Factories Act 1961*.
2. Para. 3.27.
3. Wootton, *Crime and the Criminal Law*.

to the application of the doctrine of *mens rea* in statutory offences is *Prince*.[1] The charge was one of taking a girl under the age of 16 out of the possession of her father contrary to s. 55 of the Offences against the Person Act 1861[2] (re-enacted by s. 20 of the Sexual Offences Act 1956). Prince knew that the girl was in the custody of her father but he believed, on reasonable grounds, that she was 18. Had this been so, the offence would not have been committed but Prince was held by a majority of fifteen to one to have been rightly convicted since knowledge that the girl was under 16 was not required. The decision that such knowledge was not required was based variously on the views that, even on the facts as he supposed them to be, the accused's conduct would have been immoral,[3] or a tort against the father's parental rights[4] and he took the risk that the girl was under the statutory age, and that a requirement of knowledge as to age would render the offence nugatory.[5] The court clearly took the view that an intention to take the girl out of the possession of her father was required to be proved, proof of which intention was not disputed. Although the contrary has been maintained,[6] *Prince* is distinguishable from *Hibbert*,[7] discussed above,[8] because Hibbert did not intend to take the girl he abducted from anybody's possession. The jury appear to have found that he did not have actual or constructive knowledge that she was in anybody's guardianship.

Most cases of strict liability are ones in which the defences of excusable ignorance of fact or mistake, even though reasonable, as in *Prince*, are held not to be available, but there are other isolated instances in which the total absence of fault has been held to be no defence. In *Salter*,[9] a bankrupt trader was held guilty of having failed to give a satisfactory explanation of his losses contrary to s. 157 (1) (c) of the Bankruptcy Act 1914, although he might have done his best to provide full accounts. It was no defence for him to show that he had acted honestly and reasonably with regard to his explanations.

There are three exceptional offences of strict liability at common law—public nuisance, criminal libel and criminal contempt

---

1. (1875), L.R. 2 C.C.R. 154; *C. & J. Cases*.
2. Para. 9.7.
3. Judgment of Bramwell, B.
4. Judgment of Denman, J.
5. Judgment of Blackburn, J.
6. (1936), 52 L.Q.R. 64.
7. (1869), L.R. 1 C.C.R. 184; *C. & J. Cases*.
8. Para. 4.13.
9. [1968] 2 Q.B. 793; [1968] 2 All E.R. 951.

of court—but for the most part strict liability in criminal cases is imposed in statutory offences as the result of the court's interpretation of a particular statute.

Strict liability at common law

6.2 a. *Public nuisance.*—A person may be vicariously liable, on a criminal charge, for a nuisance committed by those under his control although he did not know of its existence.[1] A public nuisance has been defined as an act not warranted by law, or the omission to discharge a legal duty which obstructs or causes inconvenience or damage to the public in the exercise of rights common to all Her Majesty's subjects;[2] a section of the public must be so affected.[3] Typical examples are the obstruction of the highway or the emission of noise or smells from a factory in such a way as to cause serious inconvenience to the neighbourhood.

b. *Private libel.*—Criminal libels may be directed against a private individual or else they may affect the public at large on account of their seditious, blasphemous or obscene nature. In public libels there must be *mens rea* on the part of the accused, as he must be shown to have published a statement with a seditious intent or with the intention of disseminating blasphemous or obscene matter but the position in criminal law is not so clear in private libel. In the law of tort, a person may, subject to a special statutory defence,[4] be liable in defamation although he did not know that that which he published applied to the plaintiff, as where someone says that a couple are engaged, when unknown to him, the man is in fact married to a third person who complains that her reputation has been impugned.[5] If, on such facts, a criminal prosecution would be successful, the case would undoubtedly be one of strict liability, but there is no decision directly covering this point.

c. *Criminal contempt of court.*—In some areas of the law of contempt, particularly as it affects the press, liability does not for the most part depend upon proof of knowledge or intent.[6]

---

1. *Stephens* (1866), L.R. 1 Q.B. 702.
2. Stephen, *Digest of Criminal Law*, 9th ed., 179.
3. *Madden*, [1975] 1 All E.R. 155.
4. Defamation Act 1952, s. 4.
5. *Cassidy* v. *Daily Mirror Newspapers, Ltd.*, [1929] 2 K.B. 331.
6. *Evening Standard*, [1954] 1 Q.B. 578; [1954] 1 All E.R. 1026; paras 13.9–13.17.

Strict liability in statutory offences

.3 Often it is made clear in the statutory definition of an offence that *mens rea* is required in relation to the elements of the *actus reus* by the use of such qualifying adverbs as "maliciously" or "knowingly"[1] or by the use of words which connote the need for advertence; for example people who "permit" certain things to be done on their premises or by their employees are frequently punishable under statutory provisions, and "It is of the very essence of the offence of permitting someone to do something that there should be knowledge".[2]

Strict liability in statutory offences is normally the result of the courts' refusal to read into a statutory provision which is silent on the point such a word as "knowingly" in relation to an element of the *actus reus* of a particular offence or, at the very least, to imply a proviso about the defence of reasonable mistake of fact or civil law.

Most of the statutory offences of strict liability arise under the regulatory legislation controlling such matters as the sale of food, the conduct of licensed premises and the use of false or misleading trade descriptions. Similarly, many of the offences in statutes regulating road traffic have been held to be of strict liability,[3] as have certain financial provisions.[4]

.4 The courts, particularly in recent years, have been understandably reluctant to interpret an offence as one of strict liability and the decision of the House of Lords in *Sweet* v. *Parsley*[5] suggests that any further expansion of strict liability will be closely scrutinised and confined within narrow limits. Nevertheless, given the necessary circumstances, the courts are still prepared to hold that, on the true interpretation of a statutory offence, Parliament intended to rule out the need

---

1. Paras. 3.23, 3.26 and 3.27.
2. *Per* Lord Parker, C.J., in *Gray's Haulage Co., Ltd.* v. *Arnold*, [1966] 1 All E.R. 896; *C. & J. Cases*, following *James & Sons, Ltd.* v. *Smee*, *Green* v. *Burnett*, [1955] 1 Q.B. 78; [1954] 3 All E.R. 273. Contrast *Lyons* v. *May*, [1948] 2 All E.R. 1062; *Baugh* v. *Crago*, [1975] R.T.R. 453.
3. *Lyons* v. *May*, [1948] 2 All E.R. 1062; *Taylor* v. *Kenyon*, [1952] 2 All E.R. 726; *Cummerson*, [1968] 2 Q.B. 534; [1968] 2 All E.R. 863.
4. *St. Margaret's Trust, Ltd.*, [1958] 2 All E.R. 289; *Patel* v. *Customs Controller*, [1966] A.C. 356; [1965] 3 All E.R. 593.
5. [1970] A.C. 132; [1969] 1 All E.R. 347; *C. & J. Cases*.

for *mens rea* in relation to an element of its *actus reus*.[1] The approach adopted by the courts is as follows:

a. *Presumption that* mens rea *is required*.—In interpreting a criminal statute which is silent on the point, there is a presumption that *mens rea* is required but this may be rebutted by clear evidence that Parliament intended the contrary. These principles were re-affirmed in *Sweet* v. *Parsley*,[2] where the House of Lords (reversing the Court of Appeal and overruling previous decisions of that court) held that a person could not be convicted of the offence of "being concerned in the management of premises used for the purpose of smoking cannabis" in the absence of evidence of knowledge of the user. Parliament has made this requirement doubly sure by inserting the word "knowingly" in the definition of the corresponding offence in the Misuse of Drugs Act 1971, which replaces the previous provision.
b. *Rebuttal by words of the statute*.—The wording of the statute may cause the court to hold that the presumption that *mens rea* is required is rebutted. In this context, the appearance in the definition of other offences in the statute of words such as "knowingly" is likely to lead to a finding that *mens rea* is not required in relation to an element or elements of the offence in question, although, as is shown by a comparison of *Cundy* v. *Le Cocq*[3] and *Sherras* v. *De Rutzen*,[4] this will not necessarily be so. The former case concerned the offence under s. 13 of the Licensing Act 1872 (re-enacted by s. 172 (3) of the Licensing Act 1964) of sale by a publican of liquor to a drunken person. It was held that the accused licensee's belief, even if founded on reasonable grounds, in the sobriety of his customer was no defence. This conclusion was reached in the light of the general scope of the Act, which was for the repression of drunkenness, and of a comparison of the various sections in the relevant part of the Act, some of which, unlike the section in question, contained the word "knowingly". In *Sherras* v. *De Rutzen*, a licensee had supplied liquor to a police officer who was on duty, contrary to s. 16 (2) of

---

1. *Warner* v. *Metropolitan Police Commissioner*, [1969] 2 A.C. 256; [1969] 2 All E.R. 356; *C. & J. Cases; Alphacell, Ltd.* v. *Woodward*, [1972] A.C. 824; [1972] 2 All E.R. 475; *C. & J. Cases*.
2. Also see *Sherras* v. *De Rutzen*, [1895] 1 Q.B. 918, at p. 920; *C. & J. Cases*, *per* Wright, J; *Lim Chin Aik*, [1963] A.C. 160; [1963] 1 All E.R. 223; *C. & J. Cases*.
3. (1884), 13 Q.B.D. 207; [1881–5] All E.R. Rep. 412; *C. & J. Cases*.
4. [1895] 1 Q.B. 918; [1895–9] All E.R. Rep. 1167; *C. & J. Cases*.

the Licensing Act 1872. The licensee reasonably believed that the officer was off duty because he had removed his armlet which at that time, to the knowledge of the licensee, was worn by police officers in the locality when on duty. The licensee was convicted by the magistrates but his conviction was quashed on appeal, the Divisional Court holding that the presumption that *mens rea* was required was not rebutted even though the other subsection of the section in question used the word "knowingly".

c. *Rebuttal by reference to extrinsic factors.* Where no clear indication of Parliament's intention is given by the words of the statute, the courts will go outside the Act and examine all the relevant circumstances to determine whether Parliament intended to displace the need for *mens rea*. The following are among these circumstances:

   i. The subject-matter of the enactment. In many cases this is the only extrinsic factor referred to by the court in deciding whether the presumption is rebutted. An offence is more likely to be construed as one of strict liability if it falls within the three classes enumerated by Wright, J., in *Sherras* v. *De Rutzen*:[1]

   > "Apart from isolated and extreme cases [such as *Prince*], the principal classes of exceptions [to the general rule that *mens rea* is required] may perhaps be reduced to three. One is a class of acts which, in the language of Lush, J., in *Davis* v. *Harvey*,[2] are not criminal in any real sense, but are acts which in the public interests are prohibited under a penalty. Several such instances are to be found in the decisions on the Revenue Statutes, e.g. *A.-G.* v. *Lockwood*,[3] where the innocent possession of liquorice by a beer retailer was held to be an offence. So under the Adulteration Acts, *Woodrow*[4] as to innocent possession of adulterated tobacco; *Fitzpatrick* v. *Kelly*[5] and *Roberts* v. *Egerton*[6] as to the sale of adulterated food.... to the same head may be referred *Bishop*,[7] where a person was held rightly convicted of receiving lunatics in an unlicensed house, although the jury found that he honestly and on reasonable grounds believed that they were not lunatics.

1. [1895] 1 Q.B. 918, at p. 921.
2. (1874), L.R. 9 Q.B. 433.
3. (1842), 9 M. & W. 378.
4. (1846), 15 M. & W. 404.
5. (1873), L.R. 8 Q.B. 337.
6. (1874), L.R. 9 Q.B. 494.
7. (1880), 5 Q.B.D. 259.

> Another class comprehends some, and perhaps all, public nuisances.... Lastly, there may be cases in which, although the proceeding is criminal in form, it is really only a summary mode of enforcing a civil right: see *per* Williams and Willes, JJ., in *Morden* v. *Porter*,[1] as to unintentional trespass in pursuit of game.... But except in such cases as these, there must in general be guilty knowledge on the part of the defendant...."

This dictum was referred to by the House of Lords in *Alphacell, Ltd.* v. *Woodward*,[2] where the accused company, whose settling tanks overflowed into a river, was convicted of causing polluted matter to enter a river contrary to the Rivers (Prevention of Pollution) Act 1951, despite the fact that there was no evidence that it knew that pollution was taking place from its settling tanks or had been in any way negligent. In construing the offence as one of strict liability, Viscount Dilhorne and Lord Salmon regarded the statute as dealing with acts which "are not criminal in any real sense,[3] but are acts which in the public interest are prohibited under a penalty", while Lord Pearson thought that the offence fell within the second class enumerated, saying "*mens rea* is generally not a necessary ingredient in an offence of this kind which is in the nature of a public nuisance".[4] The first of Wright, J.'s, three classes is particularly important since it covers many statutes regulating particular activities involving potential danger to public health or safety which a person may choose to undertake.

ii. The mischief of the crime. In offences which are aimed at the prevention of some grave social evil, such as inflation or pollution, the need for *mens rea* is particularly likely to be displaced. This is illustrated by *St. Margaret's Trust, Ltd.*,[5] where the accused finance company was charged with offences against the Hire-Purchase and Credit Sales Agreements (Control) Order 1956, article 1 of which prohibited a person from disposing of any goods in pursuance of a hire-purchase agreement unless 50 per cent of the cash price had been paid. This requirement was not satisfied in the case of a number of hire-purchase transactions relating to motor cars because, although the company had acted innocently, it had been misled as to the true cash price and

1. (1860), 7 C.B. N.S. 641.
2. [1972] A.C. 824; [1972] 2 All E.R. 475; *C. & J. Cases.*
3. Para. 16.2.
4. [1972] A.C., at p. 842.
5. [1958] 2 All E.R. 289.

had been informed that the requisite 50 per cent had been paid. The Court of Criminal Appeal dismissed the company's appeal against conviction, holding that the offence was one of strict liability. Donovan, J., had this to say about the mischief of the offence:

> "The object of the order was to help to defend the currency against the peril of inflation which, if unchecked, would bring disaster on the country. There is no need to elaborate this. The present generation has witnessed the collapse of the currency in other countries and the consequent chaos, misery and widespread ruin. It would not be at all surprising if Parliament, determined to prevent similar calamities here, enacted measures which it intended to be absolute prohibition of acts which might increase the risk in however small a degree. Indeed, that would be the natural expectation. There would be little point in enacting that no one should breach the defences against a flood, and at the same time excusing anyone who did it innocently. For these reasons we think that art. 1 of the order should receive a literal construction [under which *mens rea* was not required]".[1]

iii. The maximum punishment. Not surprisingly, this is a factor to be taken into account in interpreting the statute, as was pointed out by Lord Pearce in *Sweet* v. *Parsley*.[2] If the offence is punishable with imprisonment, particularly if the maximum term is severe, this suggests that Parliament cannot have intended it to be one of strict liability, partly because it can hardly be said to be concerned with acts "which are not criminal in any real sense". Nevertheless, on occasions the courts have construed such offences as not requiring *mens rea*. In *Warner* v. *Metropolitan Police Commissioner*,[3] the offence of unauthorised possession of drugs was held not to require proof that the accused knew that what he was in possession of was a drug, despite the fact that the offence in question was punishable with a maximum of two years' imprisonment, and could, if the drug had been of a different type, have been punished with a maximum of ten years. The law on this subject has been changed since *Warner*.[4] Again the offence of abduction in *Prince* is

---

1. *Ibid.*, at p. 293.
2. [1970] A.C., at p. 156.
3. [1969] 2 A.C. 256; [1968] 2 All E.R. 356; *C. & J. Cases*.
4. Para. 6.9.

punishable with two years' imprisonment, as is the bankruptcy offence of which the accused in *Salter*[1] was convicted.

iv. Whether strict liability would assist the enforcement of the law. In *Lim Chin Aik*,[2] a case concerned with Singapore immigration regulations, it was said not to be enough merely to label the statute before the court as one dealing with a grave social evil, and from that to infer that strict liability was intended. It is also necessary to inquire whether putting the accused under strict liability will assist the enforcement of the law. There must be something he could do "directly or indirectly, by supervision or inspection, by improvement of his business methods or by exhorting those whom he may be expected to influence or control, which will promote the observance of the regulations. . . . Where it can be shown that the imposition of strict liability would result in the prosecution and conviction of a class of persons whose conduct would not in any way affect the observance of the law, their Lordships consider that, even where the statute is dealing with a grave social evil, strict liability is not likely to be intended".[3] Lim Chin Aik had been convicted under the Singapore Immigration Ordinance which makes it an offence for someone prohibited from entering Singapore to enter or remain there. He had been prohibited from entering Singapore, but the prohibition had not been published or made known to him. The Privy Council advised that his conviction should be quashed on account of the futility of imposing punishment in such a case.

6.5 Some of the judgments in earlier cases undoubtedly do what is condemned in *Lim Chin Aik*, and simply assume that strict liability must have been intended because the statute under consideration deals with a grave social evil, without inquiring whether the enforcement of the law would be assisted by placing the defendant under strict liability. But in the main, the principles stated in *Lim Chin Aik* had previously been followed by the English courts.

---

1. Para. 6.1.
2. [1963] A.C. 160; [1963] 1 All E.R. 223; *C. & J. Cases*.
3. [1963] A.C. 160. at pp. 174–175. See also *Reynolds* v. *G. H. Austin & Sons, Ltd.*, [1951] 2 K.B. 135, at p. 150; [1951] 1 All E.R. 606, at p. 612, *per* Devlin, J.

Thus, in *Harding* v. *Price*,[1] it was held that if a duty is imposed after the occurrence of an event, such as a duty to report an accident under s. 22 (2) of the Road Traffic Act 1930 (re-enacted by s. 25 of the Road Traffic Act 1972) it must be shown that the accused was aware of the occurrence of the event before he can be convicted of a breach of the duty. Otherwise a person will be required to do the impossible.

Nevertheless, the distinction between this case and *Chajutin* v. *Whitehead*,[2] a typical decision on strict liability according to which it is no defence for someone charged with being in possession of an altered passport contrary to the Aliens Order 1920 to show that he believed, on reasonable grounds, that the passport in his possession was genuine, has perplexed at least one Law Lord.

> "Both in ignorance do something which is forbidden—the one carries an altered passport, the other drives on after an accident. But for some reason which escapes me the man who carries a passport acts at his peril, while the one who drives on does not. Both do forbidden acts but the one is guilty and the other is not ... I think that the explanation of this case [*Harding* v. *Price*] must be that the court, disliking some of the older authorities but being unable to overrule them, seized on an insubstantial distinction to prevent any extension of the doctrine of absolute liability".[3]

How strict is strict liability?

6.6 Strict liability is sometimes spoken of as "absolute liability" and the corresponding expressions of "absolute prohibition" and "absolute offences" are occasionally used. They are, however, like "absolute liability" open to the suggestion that no defences are available to the accused. Certainly, the wording of certain so-called "status offences", such as that in issue in *Larsonneur*,[4] may lead to such a conclusion.

In *Larsonneur*, an alien who had not got leave to land in the United Kingdom was deported from Eire. She was brought to England under police custody, and was "found", still in custody, in a cell at Holyhead. She was held guilty of an offence under orders made under the Aliens Restriction Acts according to which it was an offence for an alien to whom leave to land in the

---

1. [1948] 1 K.B. 695; [1948] 1 All E.R. 283; *C. & J. Cases*; see also *Hallam*, [1957] 1 Q.B. 569; [1957] 1 All E.R. 665.
2. [1938] 1 K.B. 506; [1938] 1 All E.R. 159.
3. Lord Reid in *Warner* v. *Metropolitan Police Commissioner*, [1969] 2 A.C. 256, at p. 278.
4. (1933), 149 L.T. 542.

United Kingdom had been refused, to be found in any place within the United Kingdom. The accused came precisely within the wording of the relevant order, and it is a matter of speculation whether she might not equally have been held guilty if she had been insane, or if she had mistakenly believed that she was not an alien, or even if she had been parachuted from an aeroplane against her will. Such cases are most exceptional, because very few offences are defined in the same way as that with which Madame Larsonneur was charged and we think it highly unlikely that the case would have been decided in the same way today.

However, apart from such rare offences, most of the general defences of the criminal law (some of which were discussed in the last chapter, while others are discussed later[1]) are probably available to a person accused of an offence of strict liability. Admittedly, on a charge of failing to comply with a traffic sign contrary to s. 22 of the Road Traffic Act 1972, an offence which has been described as absolute, the defence of necessity does not apply,[2] but it is very doubtful, to say the least, whether there are any offences, except perhaps those whose wording is similar to that of the offence in *Larsonneur*, to which the general defences of insanity, duress, compulsion and automatism would not apply. Not the least of the troubles about strict liability is that no one knows how strict it is.

The justification for strict liability

6.7 One justification for strict liability is that the commission of many regulatory offences is very harmful to the public and, it being very difficult to prove that the accused had acted knowingly or negligently, they would often go unpunished and the legislation rendered nugatory.[3] Again, it is sometimes said that too many bogus defences would succeed if excusable ignorance or mistake were always accepted as defences. It is also argued that the great pressure of work upon the minor criminal courts nowadays makes it impractical to inquire into *mens rea* in each prosecution for a regulatory offence.[4] Moreover, it is urged that the imposition of strict liability does something towards ensuring that the controllers of business organisations do everything possible to see that important welfare regulations are carried

1. See Chapter 18.
2. *Buckoke* v. *Greater London Council*, [1971] Ch. 655; [1971] 2 All E.R. 254.
3. *Alphacell, Ltd.* v. *Woodward*, [1972] A.C. 824, at pp. 839 and 848, [1972] 2 All E.R. at pp. 483 and 491, *per* Viscount Dilhorne and Lord Salmon.
4. Sayre, 33 *Columbia Law Review* 69.

out.[1] Repeated convictions may discourage or oblige the incompetent to refrain from certain undertakings and ensure that the competent stay competent.

There are many who remain unconvinced by these arguments[2] and who reply that the fact that the prosecution may find proof of *mens rea* difficult is of itself no reason for depriving the accused of his customary safeguards; they argue, in any event, that it does not follow that, even if proof of *mens rea* is impossible in certain types of cases, the only solution is to go to the other extreme by denying that the accused's mental state is relevant to the question of responsibility, since there are other possibilities such as a defence of no negligence. They add that it is improper to jettison the requirements of *mens rea* simply to facilitate the flow of judicial business, and that the courts' time is taken up anyway by considerations of *mens rea* in determining sentence. In addition, they point out that strict liability cannot make an improvement in the systems of those who infringe regulatory legislation despite taking all possible care to avoid doing so.

6.8 To those who remain unconvinced by the arguments for strict liability the following developments are particularly welcome:

a. the re-affirmation in *Sweet* v. *Parsley* of the presumption in construing a criminal statute that *mens rea* is required although as the subsequent case of *Alphacell, Ltd.* v. *Woodward* shows, the House of Lords is still prepared to construe a statute in such a way as to impose strict liability;
b. the increase in the number of statutes providing "no-negligence" and other defences;[3] and
c. the proposals in the Law Commission Working Paper on the Mental Element in Crime.[4]

Statutory Defences

6.9 Since the purpose of many offences of strict liability is to catch the person who negligently performs an activity, it is odd that the courts have interpreted as imposing strict liability statutes which catch the person who took reasonable care as well as the one who did not. The injustice involved is mitigated in some

1. *Alphacell, Ltd.* v. *Woodward*, [1972] A.C. 824 at p. 848, [1972] 2 All E.R. at p. 491; Smith and Pearson, The Value of Strict Liability, [1969] Crim. L.R. 5.
2. For instance Howard, *Strict Responsibility*, pp. 9–28.
3. Paras. 16.24: 16.37.
4. Para. 3.31.

statutes by the provision of defences which come into operation once the prosecution has proved that the accused has committed the *actus reus* of the offence in question.

A "no-negligence" defence is one whereby a burden is placed on the accused of proving that he had no knowledge of, and was not negligent as to, a particular element of the offence. An example is provided by reference to the recent legislation on drugs which modifies the law relating to the unauthorised possession of dangerous drugs.[1] In *Warner* v. *Metropolitan Police Commissioner*,[2] a majority of the House of Lords held that a person could not be in possession of dangerous drugs unless he was at least aware of the general nature of that which was under his control, although on the preponderant view within the majority it was unnecessary for the prosecution to show that he knew of its quality. This meant that a man could be convicted of the unauthorised possession of dangerous drugs, such as amphetamine tablets, provided he knew he was in control of a bottle of tablets, even though he believed them to be aspirins and thus lacked *mens rea* as to this circumstance of the *actus reus*; it would be different if he thought that the bottle contained scent because he would not know he was in control of tablets at all and he would be unaware of the nature of that which was under his control and therefore would not be in possession of it. Section 28 of the Misuse of Drugs Act 1971 provides that the accused shall be acquitted if he proves that he neither believed, nor suspected, nor had reason to suspect that the substance he possessed was a controlled drug, although it is not generally a defence for him to show that he neither knew nor suspected, nor had reason to suspect that the drug was the particular controlled drug it was alleged to be.[3]

Another example of a "no-negligence" defence is s. 24 of the Trade Descriptions Act 1968, which provides the accused with a defence if he proves that he exercised due diligence to avoid committing the offence in question.[4] Such defences solve the problems of proof of *mens rea* urged by the supporters of strict liability.

6.10 "Third party defences" provided in some statutes[5] require the

1. Paras. 16.34–16.39.
2. [1969] 2 A.C. 256; [1969] 2 All E.R. 356; *C. & J. Cases*.
3. Para. 16.37.
4. Para. 16.24.
5. An example is s. 113 (1) of the Food and Drugs Act 1955. For another example see para. 16.23.

accused to prove not only lack of negligence on his part but also that the contravention was due to the act or default of a third party (who is liable to conviction).

Proposals for reform

11 In *Sweet* v. *Parsley*, Lords Reid and Pearce suggested a "half-way house"[1] based on their understanding[2] of the Australian solution to the problems engendered by regulatory offences, whereby statutory offences which appear at first sight to be offences of strict liability would be construed as subject to the defence that the accused acted under an honest and reasonable belief in a state of facts which, if they existed, would make his act innocent, the burden of proving this being on the accused. The effect of this suggestion would be to generalise the "no-negligence" defences mentioned above and the suggestion would be open to the same objection concerning the burden of proof.

This objection does not apply to Lord Diplock's solution which he put forward in *Sweet* v. *Parsley*,[3] and which was based partly on his interpretation of the Australian case law. His Lordship said:

> "Even where the words used to describe the prohibited conduct would not in any other context connote the necessity of any particular mental element, they are nevertheless to be read as subject to the implication that a necessary element in the offence is the absence of a belief, held honestly and upon reasonable grounds, in the existence of facts which, if true, would make the act innocent."

Lord Diplock went on to say that the accused did not bear the burden of proving such a mistake, although the burden of adducing evidence of it was borne by him. The adoption of the course taken by Lord Diplock as a general principle of construction of criminal statutes would be welcomed by opponents of strict liability and would come near to the tentative suggestions of the Law Commission.

In its Working Paper on the Mental Element in Crime,[4] the Commission suggests that in the case of offences created by future statutes, where no mental state is expressly mentioned it

---

1. [1970] A.C., at pp. 150 and 158; [1969] 1 All E.R. at pp. 351 and 357.
2. Brett, Strict Responsibility: Possible Solutions, (1974) 37 M.L.R. 417, argues that the Australian cases were misunderstood by their Lordships.
3. [1970] A.C. at p. 163; [1969] 1 All E.R., at p. 361.
4. Law Commission Published Working Paper No. 31.

should be assumed that intention or recklessness with regard to the relevant circumstances and consequences is required in the case of acts but, if this assumption is expressly excluded in the definition from some or all of the elements of the offence, negligence will be required as to them; in the case of omissions negligence will be assumed to suffice. These assumptions will not prevail if there is an express provision that the offence is one of strict liability. So far as existing offences of strict liability are concerned, the suggestion is that negligence with reference to circumstances and consequences should be required, subject to any specific exceptions. When negligence is required, either with regard to future offences or existing offences, the suggestion is that the accused should bear the burden of adducing evidence of absence of negligence on proof by the prosecution of the *actus reus*, although, as with the course taken by Lord Diplock, the prosecution should bear the burden of proving negligence in accordance with the principle of *Woolmington's* case once the accused has satisfied his evidential burden.

7

NON-FATAL OFFENCES AGAINST THE PERSON

7.1 The most serious offences against the person—murder and manslaughter—are not defined by any statute. The Offences against the Person Act 1861 deals in detail with those offences against the person, such as assaults and wounding, which are not fatal. These were treated very leniently by the common law, but have been dealt with by statute for some time. The Act of 1861 also covers abortion and bigamy, while sexual offences are now governed by the Sexual Offences Act 1956. There is plenty of scope for simplification as the present law is unnecessarily fragmented.

Consent

7.2 Many offences against the person, such as rape and assault, cannot be committed if the victim gives a valid consent. On the other hand, no one can lawfully consent to his own death at the hands of another.[1] Although suicide is no longer an offence, euthanasia still is. However excellent his motives may be, someone who kills another at that other's request is guilty of murder unless he acted in pursuance of a suicide pact, in which case his offence is manslaughter.[2] It is also an offence to assist another to commit suicide.[3]

Whether consent renders lawful what would otherwise be unlawful in the case of non-fatal offences against the person depends upon the following principles:

a. A person cannot always give a valid consent to bodily harm falling short of death. It would seem, following the case of *Donovan*,[4] that ordinarily a person cannot consent to the infliction upon himself of harm which constitutes, or exceeds, "bodily harm" as defined in that case.

---

1. *Young* (1838), 8 C. & P. 644; *Cuddy* (1843), 1 Car. & Kir. 210.
2. Para. 8.20.
3. *Ibid.*
4. [1934] 2 K.B. 498; *C. & J. Cases*.

Donovan was convicted of an indecent assault upon a girl of 17. He had caned her, with her consent, for the sake of sexual gratification. He successfully appealed to the Court of Criminal Appeal on the ground that the jury had been misdirected with regard to the burden of proof; but, although they quashed the conviction, the Court stressed the point that the jury should have been asked whether the blows struck by the accused were likely or intended to do "bodily harm" to the girl because her consent to such harm would afford no defence. The Court defined "bodily harm" as "any hurt or injury calculated to interfere with the health or comfort of the prosecutor which need not be permanent, but must, no doubt, be more than merely transient and trifling".

The Court of Criminal Appeal in *Donovan* stated that there were "well established exceptions" to the rule that a valid consent could not be given to an act likely or intended to cause bodily harm. It enumerated some, but not all, of these, e.g. "lawful" sports such as wrestling, which could be justified on the basis (*inter alia*) that they are "manly diversions, they intend to give strength, skill and activity, and may fit people for defence, public as well as personal, in time of need".[1] It is clear that a "manly diversion" such as boxing, which has caused serious injury, has been put in a different category from a sexual deviation, such as flagellation, which seldom has serious physical consequences.

The principle governing this and other exceptions may be contained in the following words by Stephen, J., in *Coney*[2] (a case in which the participants in a prize fight with bare fists were held guilty of assault):

> "When one person is indicted for inflicting personal injury upon another, the consent of the person who sustains the injury is no defence to the person who inflicted the injury, if the injury is of such a nature, or was inflicted under such circumstances, that its infliction is injurious to the public as well as to the person injured. The injuries given and received in prize fights are injurious to the public, both because it is against the public interest that the lives and health of the combatants should be endangered by blows, and because prize fights are disorderly exhibitions, mischievous on many grounds. Therefore the consent of the parties to the blows which they mutually receive does not prevent those blows from being assaults. . . . In all cases the ques-

1. Foster, *Crown Law*, 3rd ed., p. 259.
2. (1882), 8 Q.B.D. 534, at p. 549; *C. & J. Cases*.

tion whether consent does or does not take from the application of force to another its illegal character is a question of degree depending on the circumstances."

This approach was not mentioned in *Donovan* but Denning, L.J., in the civil case of *Bravery* v. *Bravery*,[1] said that it was "well illustrated" by *Donovan*. Applying this test, which is ultimately one of public policy, an example of bodily harm to which consent can validly be given is a therapeutic operation, and possibly a non-therapeutic operation as a sex-change or cosmetic operation can be performed by properly qualified doctors.[2]

It should not be thought that under the exceptions to the rule in *Donovan* it will necessarily be possible to consent to any degree of physical harm. Stephen, J.'s, criterion must be borne in mind and while a participant in a sport such as boxing or football validly consents to any bodily harm ordinarily incidental to it,[3] he does not and in law cannot consent to the infliction of really serious harm[4] since such an injury would make him liable to become a burden on society and thus the injury would be "of such a nature, or . . . inflicted under such circumstances, that its infliction is injurious to the public as well as the person injured".

The application of Stephen, J.'s, criterion will not always be easy. This is shown by the case of *Bravery* v. *Bravery* where Denning, L.J., held that a sterilisation operation performed on a man for non-eugenic reasons (to enable him to enjoy sexual intercourse without the risk of becoming a father) would be unlawful as being injurious to the public interest, whereas the other two Lords Justices expressly dissociated themselves from this view, saying they were not prepared "in the present case" to hold that such operations were injurious to the public interest.[5]

b. In most sexual offences, the consent of young people under certain ages is no defence.[6]

c. An apparent consent will be treated as unreal, and thus no defence where:

---

1. [1954] 3 All E.R. 59.
2. See Skegg, Medical Procedures and the Crime of Battery, [1974] Crim. L. R. 693.
3. *Per* Cave, J., in *Coney* (1882), 8 Q.B.D. 534, at p. 537.
4. *Coney*; *Moore* (1898), 14 T.L.R. 229; *Bradshaw* (1878), 14 Cox C.C. 83. Also see paras. 7.11 and 8.12.
5. [1954] 3 All E.R. 59, at p. 64.
6. Paras. 9.3–9.9.

i. The victim is very young and unable to comprehend the nature of the act committed.[1]

ii. The victim's apparent consent has been procured by duress. In *Day*[2] the accused was charged (*inter alia*) with an assault on a girl of nine. The girl had not resisted his conduct and it was argued that, since she had submitted to his acts, she must be taken to have consented and that therefore Day was not guilty. The jury were directed that if the girl had submitted to Day's acts out of fear there would have been no real consent on her part and they would be without her consent.

iii. There is no real consent if a person, apparently consenting, is induced to do so by fraud as to the nature of the act or identity of the accused, but provided that the victim knows of the nature of the act, it is irrelevant that he is mistaken about a collateral detail of it.[3] Thus, it was held that no assault had occurred in *Clarence* where a man had intercourse with his wife knowing that he had venereal disease and thereby infected her. The wife did not know of her husband's disease. It was argued that the accused's concealment of his condition amounted to a fraud which negatived his wife's consent to the intercourse and thus rendered the bodily contact an assault; it was held that even if the husband's conduct did amount to a fraud it would not vitiate the wife's consent because she understood the nature of the act; her ignorance of the husband's disease was not enough.

d. Consent may be express or implied. One impliedly consents to the risk of accidental bodily contact in ordinary activities[4] in the street, in queues or on buses to name a few places.

Assault and battery

7.3 Assault and battery are common law misdemeanours but their punishment is now provided for by the Offences against the Person Act 1861. They are separate offences and for that reason a conviction of assault or battery will be quashed because a person cannot be convicted of alternative offences.[5] A person is guilty

1. *Burrell* v. *Harmer*, [1967] Crim. L. R. 169. *Howard*, [1965] 3 All E.R. 684.
2. (1841), 9 C. & P. 722.
3. *Clarence* (1888), 22 Q.B.D. 23 at p. 44; *C. & J. Cases*; and paras. 7.4 and 7.5.
4. *Tuberville* v. *Savage* (1669), 1 Mod. Rep. 3; *Cole* v. *Turner* (1704), 6 Mod. Rep. 149.
5. *Jones* v. *Sherwood*, [1942] 1 K.B. 127.

of an assault if he intentionally or recklessly causes another person to apprehend immediate and unlawful force: a person is guilty of battery if he intentionally or recklessly uses unlawful force to another person.[1] A battery generally includes an assault (and for this reason the two offences are frequently referred to generically though misleadingly as assaults),[2] but this is not always so. One who hits another without having previously caused him to fear that unlawful force was about to be used against him because, for example, he had crept up behind him, would commit battery even though no assault had been committed.

Assault[3]

7.4 The *actus reus* of assault is an act which causes the victim to fear the immediate application of unlawful force against him. An omission to act which creates such a fear is not enough.[4] In principle there is no reason why a verbal threat of the immediate use of force should not suffice for an assault, even if the threat is not accompanied by instant action,[5] but such authority as there is may be against this view.[6] It would be unfortunate if threatening words should not suffice. To go up behind a person and shout "Hit him, boys", is probably more frightening for him than to confront him with a raised fist. However, such conduct could usually be prosecuted under the Public Order Act 1936 s. 5 or under a local Act or bye-law provided that the threat was in a public place.[7] The requirement that the application of unlawful force must be apprehended means that:

a. pointing an unloaded gun at one who is unaware of its harmlessness may amount to an assault;[8]
b. inviting another to touch the invitor cannot amount to an assault on the invitee,[9] and

---

1. *Fagan* v. *Metropolitan Police Commissioner*, [1969] 1 Q.B. 439; [1968] 3 All E.R. 442; *C. & J. Cases*; *Venna*, [1975] 3 All E.R. 788.
2. *Rolfe* (1952), 36 Cr. App. Rep. 4.
3. Turner, *Modern Approach to Criminal Law*, pp. 344–356.
4. *Fagan* v. *Metropolitan Police Commissioner*, [1969] 1 Q.B. 439; [1968] 3 All E.R. 442; *C. & J. Cases*.
5. Williams, Assaults and Words, [1957] Crim. L. R. 216.
6. *Meade's and Belt's Case* (1823), 1 Lew C.C. 184, but see *Fairclough* v. *Whipp*, [1951] 2 All E.R. 834; *C. & J. Cases*.
7. Para. 15.6.
8. *St George* (1840), 9 C. & P. 483; *C. & J. Cases*; cf. *James* (1844), 1 Car. & Kir. 530; *Kwaku Mensah*, [1946] A.C. 83.
9. *Fairclough* v. *Whipp*, [1951] 2 All E.R. 834; *C. & J. Cases*.

c. a man may be guilty of this offence if he shakes his fist at another in a threatening manner, although he thereafter was prevented from touching him.[1] Clearly, if the circumstances are such that there cannot possibly be any fear that the threats will be carried out, as where a person on a rapidly moving train shakes his fist at someone who is standing on a station platform, there is no assault. Moreover, the threatening gesture may be accompanied by words indicating that there is no intention to carry it out, as in the old case of *Tuberville* v. *Savage*[2] where a man put his hand menacingly upon his sword but said "If it were not assize time I'd run you through the body", and it was held that an assault had not been committed.

Battery

7.5 The *actus reus* of battery is an act which results in the application of unlawful force to the person of another. Thus, it has been held that a person who put Spanish flies (harmful irritants) into the guests' beer at a wedding reception was not guilty of a battery[3] although he could be charged under s. 24 of the Offences against the Person Act 1861 for administering a noxious thing with intent to injure or annoy. Similarly, the use of force merely to pull away from another does not constitute a battery.[4] An omission to act which results in force to another e.g. failing to step aside so that another runs into you will not suffice.[5] The slightest degree of force, even mere touching, will suffice. Blackstone justified this by saying that the law cannot distinguish between criminal and non-criminal violence and therefore prohibits the lowest degree of it.[6]

The force may be applied directly, for example, hitting the victim with a fist or cosh, or throwing a stone at him, or by treading or driving on to his foot[7] or indirectly, as where the victim falls into a hole which the accused has dug[8] or where the accused causes a theatre audience to panic and rush down

1. *Stephens* v. *Myers* (1830), 4 C. & P. 349; *C. & J. Cases.*
2. (1669), 1 Mod. Rep. 3.
3. *Walkden* (1845), 1 Cox C.C. 282.
4. *Sheriff*, [1969] Crim. L. R. 260.
5. *Fagan* v. *Metropolitan Police Commissioner*, [1969] 1 Q.B. 439; [1968] 3 All E.R. 442; *C. & J. Cases.*
6. Blackstone, 4 Comm. 217, referring to 3 Comm. 120.
7. *Fagan* v. *Metropolitan Police Commissioner.*
8. This example was given by Stephen and Wills, JJ., in *Clarence* (1882), 22 Q.B.D. 23; *C. & J. Cases.*

an unlighted staircase across whose exit doorway he has placed an iron bar and against which those at the front of the crowd are injured.[1] The act may be momentary or continuing, e.g. stepping on a person's foot and maintaining that position. This is of obvious importance in relation to the principle of contemporaneity of *actus reus* and *mens rea*.[2]

Unlawful force

7.6 The force used in battery or threatened in assault must be unlawful and it will be so unless:

a. the victim validly consents to it;[3] or
b. the accused uses reasonable force in self-defence, the prevention of crime or the furtherance of lawful arrest;[4] or
c. the accused is acting in the exercise of the right of corporal punishment.

Parents, teachers and other persons in *loco parentis* are entitled as a disciplinary measure[5] to apply a reasonable degree of force to their children or pupils old enough to understand its purpose,[6] but if the punishment is given out of spite or for some other non-disciplinary reason or if the degree of force is unreasonable it is unlawful.[7]

Mens rea in assault and battery

7.7 Liability for assault and battery requires an intention to cause the victim to apprehend the immediate application of force (assault) or to apply force (battery) or recklessness in its subjective sense as to whether such a consequence occurred.[8]

It is clear that a person cannot be held liable for a negligent assault. In this respect English criminal law differs from that of some parts of the United States.[9]

Procedural matters and punishment

7.8 There is, as we have seen,[10] in cases of assault and battery, an exception to the rule that where a tort is committed which is

---

1. Stephen and Wills, JJ. in *Clarence* referring to *Martin* (1881), 8 Q.B.D. 54, [1881–5] All E.R. Rep. 699.
2. Para. 3.32.
3. Para. 7.2.
4. Para. 18.11.
5. *Cleary* v. *Booth*, [1893] 1 Q.B. 465; *Donovan*, [1934] 2 K.B. 498 at p. 509; *C. & J. Cases*; *Mackie* (1973), 57 Cr. App. Rep. 453.
6. *Griffin* (1869), 11 Cox C.C. 402.
7. *Hopley* (1860), 2 F. & F. 202.
8. *Venna*, [1975] 3 All E.R. 788.
9. Perkins, *Criminal Law*, 2nd ed., 112.
10. Para. 1.5.

also an offence civil and criminal proceedings may be taken concurrently.

Very often summary proceedings are brought by both parties to a fight, each alleging that the other started it, a procedure known as taking out cross-summonses for assault; in many such cases the court finds it difficult to ascertain the facts and often suggests to both parties that they should be bound over to keep the peace.

In ordinary cases of assault and battery, known as common assault, the maximum punishment which can be imposed on summary conviction is two months' imprisonment or a fine of £50,[1] but it is six months' imprisonment or £100 where the victim was a male child below the age of 14 or a female, and it was accompanied by aggravating circumstances.[2] Aggravation here means violence and not indecency.[3] In the rare case where common assault is tried on indictment, the maximum sentence is one year's imprisonment.[4]

Aggravated assaults

7.9 There are several statutory offences of assault (which term includes battery) which by virtue of defined aggravating circumstances are subject to higher penalties; in the following examples the punishments specified are the maximum permissible on conviction on indictment:

a. An assault with intent to rob is punishable with life imprisonment.[5]
b. An assault with intent to resist arrest is punishable with two years' imprisonment.[6]
c. An assault occasioning actual bodily harm is punishable with five years' imprisonment.[7] "Actual bodily harm" means any hurt or injury (whether physical or mental) calculated to interfere with the health or comfort of the victim.[8]

   The connection between the accused's assault and the actual bodily harm is purely one of causation and does not have to be foreseen by him. In *Roberts*,[9] the accused tried to remove

1. Offences against the Person Act 1861, s. 42.
2. *Ibid.*, s. 43.
3. *Baker* (1883), 47 J.P. 666.
4. Offences against the Person Act 1861, s. 47.
5. Theft Act 1968, s. 8.
6. Offences against the Person Act 1861, s. 38.
7. Offences against the Person Act 1861, s. 47.
8. *Miller*, [1954] 2 Q.B. 282, at p. 292; [1954] 2 All E.R. 529, at p. 534.
9. (1971), 56 Cr. App. Rep. 95.

the coat of a girl in a moving car, indicating that he meant to take liberties with her against her will. She jumped out of the car and was injured. He appealed against conviction for assault occasioning actual bodily harm on the ground that the jury were not directed to consider whether he foresaw that she would jump and suffer injury. The Court of Appeal rejected this, saying that the only issue was one of causation; the question was whether the victim's actions were the natural result of the accused's conduct, in the sense that it was something that could reasonably have been foreseen as the consequence of what he was saying and doing.

d. An assault on a police officer acting in the execution of his duty is punishable with two years' imprisonment under s. 51 of the Police Act 1964. The phrase "in the execution of his duty" is discussed later.[1] There is authority in support of the view that it is unnecessary for the prosecution to prove that the accused knew that his victim was a police officer acting in the execution of his duty.[2]

   A police officer has no general power to detain for questioning; if he does so he is not acting in the execution of his duty and the use of force to escape from such detention is not an assault on him in the execution of his duty.[3] However, if unreasonable force is used to escape, the person using it may be convicted of common assault, assault occasioning actual bodily harm or affray (as the circumstances warrant).[4] Belief that another is being unlawfully arrested is no defence.[5] The absence of a general power to detain for questioning is often made good by local powers and emergency legislation.[6]

e. Indecent assault whose punishment varies depending on the victim is discussed later.[7]

Wounding and grievous bodily harm

10 The offences under ss. 18 and 20 of the Offences against the Person Act 1861 resemble each other in that the accused must be proved to have acted unlawfully and maliciously. The first

---

1. Para. 15.2.
2. *Forbes and Webb*, (1865), 10 Cox C.C. 362; *Maxwell and Clanchy*, (1909), 2 Cr. App. Rep. 26; *Kenlin* v. *Gardiner*, [1967] 2 Q.B. 510; [1966] 3 All E.R. 931; *C. & J. Cases*; Howard, Assaulting Policemen in the Execution of their Duty, (1963) 79 L.Q.R. 247.
3. *Kenlin* v. *Gardiner*, [1967] 2 Q.B. 510; [1966] 3 All E.R. 931; *C. & J. Cases*.
4. *Purdy*, [1975] Q.B. 288; [1974] 3 All E.R. 465.
5. *Fennell*, [1971] 1 Q.B. 428; [1970] 3 All E.R. 215.
6. Para. 22.8.
7. Para. 9.4.

of these requirements means that the fact that he was using reasonable force in self defence, or to prevent crime or effect a lawful arrest[1] justifies the conduct of the accused and so does the fact that he was performing a lawful surgical operation.[2]

Section 20

7.11 Section 20 of the Offences against the Person Act 1861 provides that it is an offence, punishable with a maximum of imprisonment for five years, unlawfully and maliciously to wound or inflict any grievous bodily harm upon any other person, either with or without a weapon or instrument. The last phrase adds nothing to the definition but was presumably added for the avoidance of doubt. The *actus reus* of this offence requires an act resulting in the wounding of another or the infliction of grievous bodily harm on him. To constitute a wound, the inner and outer skin must actually be broken;[3] a bruise is not sufficient, but the wound need not be grievous. "Grievous bodily harm" means really serious harm.[4]

7.12 It is often said that without an assault there can be no infliction of grievous bodily harm under s. 20. This view is based on the statement of Stephen, J., in *Clarence*,[5] where the accused, knowing that he had venereal disease but concealing this fact from her, had intercourse with his wife as the result of which she contracted that disease. The Court for Crown Cases Reserved held that he could not be convicted of unlawfully inflicting grievous bodily harm on his wife because "inflict" implied the need for an assault (which term includes battery) and since the wife had consented to the bodily contact involved, there had been no assault. A similar view is implicit in *Snewing*[6] where, on a charge of unlawfully inflicting grievous bodily harm, it was held that the accused could be convicted of assault occasioning actual bodily harm, which would only be permissible if the former offence requires proof of an assault.[7]

However, a number of cases suggest that an assault is not required for "infliction" and that it will suffice in the alternative if the accused frightens another who injures himself in trying

1. Para. 18.11.
2. Para. 7.2.
3. *Moriarty* v. *Brooks* (1834), 6 C. & P. 684; *McLoughlin* (1838), 8 C. & P. 635.
4. *D.P.P.* v. *Smith*, [1961] A.C. 290, *Metharam*, [1961] 3 All E.R. 200.
5. (1888), 22 Q.B.D. 23. Para. 7.2.
6. [1972] Crim. L. R. 267.
7. Para. 7.3.

to escape. In *Cartledge* v. *Allan*,[1] the accused while in the company of other youths threatened N and, as a result, N panicked and ran off. He was pursued by some of the youths but not by the accused and sought refuge in a public house. As he entered, he put his hand through the glass panel of the door and injured it. The accused's conviction of unlawfully inflicting grievous bodily harm on N was upheld by the Divisional Court. The Court stated that the justices having found that N had acted under a reasonable apprehension of violence caused by the accused's actions and his injuries resulting from the panic caused by those actions, there was a causal nexus between the accused's actions and the consequence of grievous bodily harm. Therefore there had been an "infliction" of grievous bodily harm. It seems doubtful whether there had been an assault *stricto sensu* by the accused since nothing seems to have occurred to put N in apprehension of immediate violence; nor would the events here seem to be a battery of the indirect type, the unintended injury being far more remote than the examples given above,[2] so that it is likely that grievous bodily harm is "inflicted" even though it does not result from an assault or battery.

13 The *mens rea* required for this offence is comprised by the word "maliciously", which does not connote spite or ill-will.[3] It means that the accused must have been aware that his act might have the consequence of causing some physical harm to some other person, i.e. that he acted intentionally or recklessly in relation to such harm; it is not necessary to prove that he foresaw the possibility of the infliction of a wound or grievous bodily harm.[4]

There is some slight authority that in the context of s. 20 "maliciously" bears an alternative meaning, viz., an intention to frighten. In *Ward*,[5] the accused fired at A who was in a punt, causing him grievous bodily harm. The trial judge directed the jury that, if the accused fired near A with the intention of frightening him, they should convict the accused of unlawful wounding. The accused was convicted and 12 out of the 15 judges in the Court for Crown Cases Reserved held that the direction and conviction founded on it were correct. In this case,

1. [1973] Crim. L. R. 530. Also see *Halliday* (1889), 61 L.T. 701 and *Lewis*, [1970] Crim. L. R. 647.
2. Para. 7.5.
3. *Cunningham*, [1957] 2 Q.B. 396; [1957] 2 All E.R. 412; *C. & J. Cases*.
4. *Mowatt*, [1968] 1 Q.B. 421; [1967] 3 All E.R. 47; *C. & J. Cases*.
5. (1872), L.R. 1 C.C.R. 356.

on the facts taken as proved, the accused did not mean to inflict on A any actual physical injury at all, but meant merely to frighten him. If this alternative meaning for "maliciously" does exist it is particularly apt to deal with cases where the victim injures himself in trying to escape from the accused.

7.14 The offence under s. 20 may in many cases overlap with the offences of common assault and assault occasioning actual bodily harm, but a person may be guilty of these offences even though he does not cause bodily harm which can be regarded as "grievous".

Section 18

7.15 Section 18 of the Offences against the Person Act 1861[1] provides that it is an offence, punishable with a maximum of imprisonment for life, unlawfully and maliciously to wound or cause grievous bodily harm to any person by any means whatsoever with intent to do grievous bodily harm, or to resist or prevent the lawful apprehension or detainer of any person.

"Wound" and "grievous bodily harm" mean the same as in s. 20. However, s. 18 speaks of "causing", as opposed to "inflicting", grievous bodily harm. This, coupled with the fact that the wounding or causing of grievous bodily harm may be "by any means whatsoever", suggests that any act which results in grievous bodily harm, will suffice for a s. 18 offence. Section 18 also differs significantly from the s. 20 offence in relation to its *mens rea* because the prosecution must prove that the accused had the intent to do grievous bodily harm or resist the lawful apprehension of himself or another. Thus, in *Abraham*,[2] a gamekeeper who shot at retreating poachers, who were too far away to be seriously hurt, in order to "warm their tails", was acquitted on a charge of shooting with intent to do grievous bodily harm. Similarly, one who causes grievous bodily harm by means of a practical joke may be guilty of the s. 20 offence, but not of the s. 18 offence on account of the absence of intent. It is uncertain whether mere foresight that grievous bodily harm was a probable consequence will suffice for s. 18. This depends upon whether, in this instance, the words "with intent to" are satisfied by an oblique as well as a direct intent.[3]

---

1. As amended by the Criminal Law Act 1967.
2. (1845), 1 Cox C.C. 208.
3. Paras. 3.10 to 3.19, and see Lord Denning, *Responsibility Before the Law*, p. 28, and Smith, (1975) 39 *Journal of Criminal Law* 187.

16 Another debatable point is the precise import of the word "maliciously" in s. 18. If it means the same thing as "maliciously" in s. 20, it is redundant in s. 18, at least where the accused has the intent to do grievous bodily harm.[1] Causing grievous bodily harm or wounding with intent to do grievous bodily harm must, whether the requisite intent be direct or oblique, include foresight of the possibility of some physical harm which, as we have seen, is the meaning to be attached to "maliciously" in s. 20; but it is possible to attach some force to the word "maliciously" in s. 18 when the alleged intent is to resist lawful apprehension. If A gently seizes a policeman's jacket, or even gently trips him up, in order to prevent him giving instant chase to B, an escaping criminal, A would undoubtedly have acted with intent to avoid B's apprehension, but, if the policeman suffered serious injury wholly unforeseen by A, A would not have acted "maliciously", i.e. with foresight of the risk of some harm to the policeman. We suggest that that meaning should be given to "maliciously" in this context since it would seem unduly harsh to convict a person of the serious offence under s. 18 where he accidentally but seriously injured another in trying to prevent or resist arrest. It was said in *Mowatt*[2] that "'maliciously' adds nothing" in s. 18, but the case was concerned with causing grievous bodily harm with intent to do so.

Similar offences

17 There are many other offences, similar to those which have been discussed, in which some specific intent, or the use of particular means, is an essential ingredient. They are all contained in ss. 17–35 of the Offences against the Person Act 1861, and they cover such things as choking, drugging, poisoning, exposing children, causing injury by explosion, using spring guns and endangering life.

1. See the article by Sir Bernard Mackenna, [1966] Crim. L. R. 548.
2. [1968] 1 Q.B. 421; [1967] 3 All E.R. 47; *C. & J. Cases.*

8

HOMICIDE AND RELATED OFFENCES

Homicide generally

Actus reus

8.1 Homicide may be lawful or unlawful and, if it is unlawful, it may be murder, manslaughter, infanticide, genocide, or causing death by dangerous driving. For convenience the last offence will be dealt with elsewhere,[1] although what is said here is equally applicable to it: genocide is in a class by itself.

Murder, manslaughter and infanticide share a common *actus reus*: unlawfully killing a human being, death following within a year and a day.[2] The three offences are distinguished by the state of mind which they require on the part of the accused and by the availability of certain mitigating defences which are available to a person otherwise guilty of murder.

The victim

8.2 Before any question of a person's liability for homicide can arise, it must be established that he killed a human being. On rare occasions the offspring of human parentage may be so deformed as to be unrecognisable as a human being, or barely so recognisable. Such offspring are usually a freak of nature but they can result from radiation or the use of drugs. They may be acephalous or ectocardiac. Sometimes they belong to a fish stage of development with gills, webbed arms and feet and sightless eyes. If a person kills such a being the question may arise whether he has committed homicide. There is no reported case in which the problem has arisen. Professor Williams expresses the tentative view that a "monster" is not protected by the law,[3] but it seems more probable that the courts would regard any offspring of a human mother as itself human.

---

1. Para. 16.30.
2. Coke, 3 Inst. 47.
3. Williams, *The Sanctity of Life and the Criminal Law*, pp. 31–35.

.3 The issues of when life begins and ends are clearly relevant to homicide. It is not homicide to destroy a baby who is not yet born alive or the corpse of a man already dead. The law states that a child is born alive when two conditions are satisfied: a. the whole body of the child must have emerged into the world,[1] and b. thereafter the child must have had an existence independent of its mother.[2] It is not necessary that the umbilical cord should have been severed.[3] There is no modern authority on the test of post-natal "independence" but earlier case law reveals that some judges favoured the test of breathing[4] while others favoured that of independent circulation.[5] This difference of opinion remains unresolved. Medically, breathing by the child is indicative of live birth. Moreover, the "independent circulation" test is not very realistic as a determinant of when life begins since it is now known that within a month of conception the embryonic heart is maintaining the foetal blood stream, with no direct communication with the mother's blood.[6]

The wilful destruction of a child capable of being born alive before it is born alive may amount to the offence of child destruction, while the intentional procuring of a miscarriage may constitute the offence of abortion.[7] If a child is born alive, and dies because of ante-natal injuries which were inflicted, the person who inflicted them is guilty of murder[8] or manslaughter[9] depending on the state of mind with which he acted.

The point of time at which life ends for legal purposes is obscure. Medical science recognises that death is a continuing process and not instantaneous, but a different approach was taken by an American court[10] which held that death occurs at a precise time, when the heart stops beating and breathing ends. This is not very satisfactory since these symptoms can occur in conditions like barbiturate overdosage and hypothermia, from both of which recovery is possible. It will be interesting to see

---

1. *Poulton* (1832), 5 C. & P. 329.
2. *Enoch* (1833), 5 C. & P. 539; *Handley* (1874), 13 Cox C.C. 79.
3. *Reeves* (1839), 9 C. & P. 25.
4. *Handley*, contrast *Brain* (1834), 6 C. & P. 349.
5. *Enoch*.
6. Williams, *op. cit.*, pp. 19–23.
7. Paras. 8.36 to 8.39.
8. *West* (1848), 2 Cox C.C. 500.
9. *Senior* (1832), 1 Mood, C.C. 346.
10. *Thomas* v. *Anderson* (1950), 96 Ca. App. 2d. 371. Also see Hillman and Aldridge, Towards a Legal Definition of Death, (1972) 116 Sol. Jo. 323.

the reaction of our courts if, and when, a person is charged with the homicide of one whose heart had just stopped beating from some independent cause.

Any human being can be the victim of homicide with the exception of alien enemies killed in the actual heat and exercise of war and, perhaps, rebels who are at the time actually engaged in hostile operations against the Crown.[1] The deliberate and unjustified shooting of prisoners of war amounts to murder.[2]

The killing

8.4 A homicide may be punishable even if it is the outcome of an omission rather than a positive act, but the omission must consist of a failure to perform a duty recognised by the criminal law and, up to the present, that law has been slow to impose duties to do positive acts. The problem has generally been raised on prosecutions for manslaughter; but where there is a duty to act, as there is a duty on the part of a parent to provide food for his or her helpless child, a person may be guilty of murder by omitting to perform it with the intention of causing death,[3] and the possibility of infanticide by omission is expressly contemplated by the Infanticide Act 1938.

8.5 The death with which it is sought to charge the accused must be shown to have occurred not more than a year and a day after the act or omission by which it is alleged to have been caused. This rule was evolved by the common law because of the difficulty of proving that an act or omission outside the period did cause the death in question. It is now possible to diagnose the cause of death even though it occurred a substantial time afterwards and it is unfortunate that the rule should allow a person to escape liability for a homicide which he is scientifically shown to have caused. The rule could produce an anomalous result where the victim is kept alive for a substantial period, say in a coma, before dying.

The application of the year and a day rule is well illustrated by the facts of *Dyson*.[4] The victim died in March 1908, having been injured by the accused in November 1906, and again in December 1907. The Court of Criminal Appeal quashed a conviction for manslaughter on the ground that the jury had been

1. Hale, 1 Pleas of the Crown, 433; *Page*, [1954] 1 Q.B. 170; [1953] 2 All E.R. 1355.
2. *Maria* v. *Hall* (1807), 1 Taunt. 33, at p. 36.
3. *Gibbins and Proctor* (1918), 13 Cr. App. Rep. 134.
4. [1908] 2 K.B. 454.

directed wrongly that they could convict if they found that death had been caused wholly by the injuries inflicted in 1906. The jury should have been asked whether the death had been accelerated by the injuries of 1907, in which case they could have properly convicted the accused. There is, of course, no objection in such cases to an indictment founded on some offence less than homicide, such as one under s. 20 of the Offences Against the Person Act 1861.

.6 Finally, the prosecution must prove that the victim's death was caused by the conduct of the accused.[1] This issue of attribution involves a question of fact and a question of law. In so far as it is a factual question, the accused's conduct will not be a factual cause of death unless the death would not have occurred, when and as it did, without it. If the conduct is a factual cause, a question of law arises whether, for the purposes of liability, it can be said to be a cause of death. The answer is provided by a number of legal rules which discriminate between factual causes, labelling some as legally operative (so that death is attributed legally to the conduct) and others as too remote (in which case there is no such attribution). Provided that there is some evidence that the accused's conduct was a legal cause of death the judge leaves the case to the jury, directing them on the legal rules they must apply. The questions of fact and of law can be illustrated as follows:

a. A stabs B. C subsequently decapitates B.
b. A administers a slow-working poison to B. Before it can take effect B dies of a heart attack induced by natural causes.
c. A stabs B. B is treated in hospital. After his wound has healed B is operated on for appendicitis and dies as a result.

In none of these cases is A's conduct a factual cause of death since the death occurred, when and as it did, independently of it. Contrast the following:

d. A stabs B who is later stabbed by C. B dies from the effects of both wounds.
e. A stabs B who receives emergency treatment in hospital from which he dies.

In these two cases the death would not have occurred, when and as it did, without A's conduct which is therefore a factual cause. However, whether B's death in these two cases is attributable to A for the purposes of liability is a question of law. On

1. Hart and Honoré, *Causation in the Law*, Chs. XII–XIV; Williams, Causation in Homicide, [1957] Crim. L. R. 420 and 510.

the authorities, it is impossible to formulate any general theory of causation so far as the law is concerned.

8.7 All that can be done here is to state a number of rules, general and specific, which determine issues of causation. In what follows, it should be borne in mind that questions of foreseeability of death are irrelevant to the issue of causation, although, of course, they may be highly relevant to liability in terms of the *mens rea* required.

a. *General principles of causation.*—Judges have often said that death can only be attributed to the accused if he substantially caused it.[1] However, "substantial" in this context merely seems to mean "more than minimal",[2] and "cause" simply means "accelerate". Thus, it is no defence that the victim was already dying from some mortal illness if the accused has "substantially" accelerated death.[3]

As already implied, the accused's conduct need not be the sole cause of death.[4] Thus, even though a third party has substantially contributed to the death, the accused can be convicted if his act is also a substantial cause. In *Benge*,[5] the accused, a foreman platelayer, misread the timetable so that the track was up when a train arrived. The accused had sent a signalman with a flag up the line but he went only half the distance required by the company's rules and the engine driver, who was not keeping a very sharp lookout, did not see the signal in time to stop. The resulting accident caused several deaths. If the signalman and driver had not been negligent there would not have been an accident, but the foreman platelayer was convicted of manslaughter, his negligent reading of the timetable being a substantial cause of the fatal accident. Of course in a case like this the other railwaymen could also be convicted of homicide in relation to the same death, and this would be possible whether or not they were acting in combination.

Unless it is so gross as to prevent the accused's act being a substantial cause,[6] the contributory negligence of the victim is no defence. In *Longbottom*,[7] the victim, who was deaf, was

1. See, for example, *Smith*, [1959] 2 Q.B. 35; [1959] 2 All E.R. 193; *C. & J. Cases*.
2. *Hennigan*, [1971] 3 All E.R. 133; *Cato*, [1976] Crim. L.R. 59.
3. *Dyson*, [1908] 2 K.B. 454.
4. *Smith*.
5. (1865), 4 F. & F. 504.
6. *Martin* (1827), 3 C. & P. 211.
7. (1849), 3 Cox C.C. 439. Also see *Swindall and Osborne* (1846), 2 Car. & Kir. 230.

walking in the middle of the highway and was run over by the accused, who was driving too fast. It was held that the accused could be convicted of manslaughter notwithstanding any contributory negligence on the part of the victim in walking as he had done.

On a charge of manslaughter by gross negligence it must be shown not merely that the accused caused the death but that the death followed from the particular feature of the accused's conduct which is regarded as negligent. In *Dalloway*,[1] the accused was driving a horse and cart without reins when he ran down and killed a child who suddenly jumped into the road. The jury were told not to convict him of manslaughter unless satisfied that he could have stopped in time if he had been using reins. The question was not simply whether death was caused by the accused's driving, but whether it was due to his negligent driving.

b. *Pre-existing conditions in the victim.*—The existence of a medical condition which rendered the victim more susceptible to mortal injury, e.g. haemophilia, does not prevent attribution of the death to the accused. In *Hayward*,[2] the accused arrived home in a state of agitation, saying that he was "going to give his wife something" when she came home. On her arrival there was an altercation and the wife ran into the road, closely pursued by the accused who was making violent threats towards her. The wife fell down in the road and was found to be dead when she was picked up. The medical evidence was that the wife was in good health apart from a persistent thyrus gland, but that in this condition death might result from a combination of fright and physical exertion. The jury were directed that the wife's suceptibility to death, whether the accused knew of it or not, was irrelevant if they were satisfied that her death was accelerated by his threats of violence.

c. *Where the victim dies in trying to escape.*—If the victim brings about his own death under a reasonable apprehension, occasioned by the accused, of immediate violence to himself, the death will be attributable legally to the accused. Thus, in *Pitts*,[3] it was held that if a person drowns after throwing himself into a river in order to avoid immediate acts of violence against him, which he reasonably apprehends, the death

1. (1847), 2 Cox C.C. 273.
2. (1908), 21 Cox C.C. 692.
3. (1842), Car. & M. 284. Also see *Mackie* (1973), 57 Cr. App. Rep. 453.

could be attributable to his assailant. In *Pitts* it was said that the victim's action must be such as a reasonable man might take but this requirement has not been made in other cases.[1]

d. *Victim's neglect of treatment or maltreatment of self.*—In *Wall*,[2] the governor of a colony was held guilty of the murder of a soldier whom he had sentenced to an illegal flogging, although it was argued that the victim might not have died if he had refrained from drinking spirits while in hospital in consequence of the blows he had received. Macdonald, L.C.B., directed the jury that:

> "There is no apology for a man if he puts another in so dangerous and hazardous a situation by his treatment of him, that some degree of unskilfulness and mistaken treatment of himself may possibly accelerate the fatal catastrophe."

A case involving neglect of treatment by the victim is *Holland*.[3] The accused deliberately inflicted some wounds on the deceased. One of these caused blood poisoning in a finger, and the deceased was advised to have it amputated. Had he done so, his surgeon stated, his life would probably have been saved. However, lockjaw set in and death ensued. The jury were directed that it made no difference whether the wound was instantly mortal of its own nature, or became the cause of death only by reason of the deceased's not having adopted the best mode of treatment. A verdict of guilty of murder was returned. The dictum of Macdonald, L.C.B. cited above did not preclude the possibility that the victim's neglect or maltreatment of himself might provide a defence if it constituted negligence of an extreme degree, in which case a direction given today of the type in *Holland* might have been incorrect because, medical science having advanced greatly since 1841, a refusal of an operation might now be regarded as grossly negligent. However, such an argument was scotched in 1975 by the Court of Appeal in *Blaue*,[4] where the deceased, who had been stabbed by the accused, was a Jehovah's Witness and consequently refused to have a blood transfusion which was required before surgery and which might have saved her life. The Court of Appeal held that a

---

1. *Evans* (1812), 1 Russell on Crime, 12th ed., p. 414; *Hickman* (1831), 5 C. & P. 151; *Mackie*.
2. (1802), 28 State Tr. 51.
3. (1841), 2 Mood. & R. 351; for a full account of the facts see [1957] Crim. L. R. 702.
4. [1975] 3 All E.R. 446.

victim's refusal to have medical treatment could not provide a defence. In such a case the accused would be liable if his act was still an operative and substantial cause of death. Blaue was liable because the physical cause of death was the bleeding in the pleural cavity arising from the penetration of the lung. This was not brought about by any decision of the girl but by the stab wound. While the decision in *Blaue* seems to be right, particularly since the adjudication of the reasonableness of religious objections to medical treatment would raise a number of difficulties, it is intolerable that the victim of a petty wound can make the wounder guilty of manslaughter by obstinately refusing medical treatment, and so bringing about his own death.

e. *Intervening events.*—An intervening event which causes death will only prevent the legal attribution of the death to the accused if its occurrence was not likely (i.e. not reasonably foreseeable). Thus, if A injures B and leaves him lying injured on the ground, it is immaterial that B died of exposure or from an infection caused by the wound or from a combination of the wound and the supervening event. Conversely, the death would not be attributable to A if B had been killed by an unlikely event such as an earthquake or a stroke of lightning.[1]

f. *Intervening acts by a third party.*—Here we are concerned with cases where, although the death would not have occurred without the accused's act, an intervening act by another also contributed to the death. Where the accused's act directly contributes to the death, that result is attributable legally to him. Suppose E stabs F and shortly afterwards G stabs F. F dies from the cumulative effect of the two wounds, the second merely aggravating the effect of the first. The death can be attributed to both E and G, whether or not they were acting in combination and whether or not either wound was mortal in itself. There is no authority on the point but it seems that E is not excused merely because G's wound was later in time since his own act substantially contributed to the death when and as it occurred.

The position is more complicated where the accused's act does not directly cause death but does so indirectly, in that the intervening act, from which the victim's death directly results, would not have occurred but for the accused's act. Here the death is attributable to the accused as well as to the

---

1. Perkins, *Criminal Law*, 2nd ed., pp. 722–723.

intervener, unless the intervening act was not likely to occur (i.e. not reasonably foreseeable) in the circumstances. Thus, if J knocks K unconscious in a busy road and leaves him lying there, K subsequently being killed by a car, K's death can be attributed to J. However, if during an altercation L knocks M down, whereupon a bystander acting independently steps up and kicks M, thereby causing his death, the death is not attributable to L since the fatal intervening act was unlikely.[1]

g. *Intervening medical treatment.*—The fact that the victim subsequently receives medical treatment for his injury which kills him will not generally excuse the person who injured him. In *Smith*,[2] a person who had been stabbed in a barrack room brawl was twice dropped on the way to hospital and when he got there was given treatment which was "thoroughly bad" and might have affected his chances of recovery. He died some two hours after being stabbed. The Courts Martial Appeal Court held that these events did not break the chain of causation between the stabbing and the death. Lord Parker, C.J., said:

> "It seems to this court that if at the time of death the original wound is still an operating cause and a substantial cause, then the death can properly be said to be the result of the wound, albeit that some other cause of death is also operating. Only if it can be said that the original wound is merely the setting in which another cause operates can it be said that the death did not result from the wound. Putting it another way, only if the second cause is so overwhelming as to make the original wound merely part of the history can it be said that the death does not flow from the wound".[3]

The facts in *Smith* clearly fell within the first sentence of this dictum. Where the original wound is not "an operating cause" at the time of death, e.g. because it is healing, the medical treatment will only be "so overwhelming as to make the original wound merely part of the history" if it is performed with gross negligence. It was held in *Jordan*,[4] where the accused had stabbed the deceased, that the death could not be attributed to the accused since it had been caused by the adminstration of terramycin after the deceased had shown he was intolerant (which was described as "palpably wrong" treatment), and when his wound was nearly healed.

1. Perkins, *op. cit.*, pp. 728–729.
2. [1959] 2 Q.B. 35; [1959] 2 All E.R. 193; *C. & J. Cases*.
3. [1959] 2 Q.B. at pp. 42–43.
4. (1956), 40 Cr. App. Rep. 152.

Unlawful killing

8.8 A killing is unlawful unless it falls within one of the following categories of lawful homicide:

a. *Advancement of justice.*—If a hangman duly carries out the lawful sentence of a competent court, the homicide is lawful. If he acts contrary to his authority, by poisoning the convict, for instance, or if the sentence is not one which the court could impose, the hangman is guilty of murder, unless the facts are such that the defences of mistake or superior orders[1] are available to him.

   Force may be used against someone resisting or escaping from arrest, and homicide caused by the exercise of lawful force in such circumstances would be justifiable. Section 3 (1) of the Criminal Law Act 1967 provides that a person may use such force as is reasonable in the circumstances when effecting or assisting in the lawful arrest of offenders or suspected offenders or of persons unlawfully at large.

b. *Self-defence and the prevention of crime.*—Section 3 also provides that a person may use such force as is reasonable in the circumstances in the prevention of crime. As we shall see,[2] it is not clear whether the section expressly refers to self-defence, but the point is immaterial because it has been said in the Court of Appeal that the degree of force permissible in self-defence is similarly limited by the requirement of reasonableness.[3] So far as the prevention of crime is concerned paragraph 23 of the Seventh Report of the Criminal Law Revision Committee,[4] on which the Criminal Law Act 1967 is based, says:

   > "No doubt . . . the court, in considering what was reasonable force, would take into account all the circumstances, including in particular the nature and degree of force used, the seriousness of the evil to be prevented and the possibility of preventing it by other means; . . . Since the clause [s. 3] is framed in general terms, it is not limited to arrestable or other class of offences, though in the case of very trivial offences it would very likely be held that it would not be reasonable to use even the slightest force to prevent them."

   These words are equally applicable to the use of force when effecting an arrest, when acting in defence of the person or property, or when preventing offences against third parties.

---

1. Paras. 4.14–4.17 and 18.18.
2. Para. 18.11.
3. *McInnes*, [1971] 3 All E.R. 295; *C. & J. Cases*.
4. Cmnd. 2659.

Somewhat surprisingly, it seems that the rule of English law is that, if death results from the use of an unreasonable degree of force in effecting an arrest, self-defence or the prevention of crime, the offence will be murder and not manslaughter provided, of course, that the accused intended to kill or cause grievous bodily harm (the *mens rea* of murder). In *Palmer* v. *R.*,[1] an appeal to the Privy Council from the West Indies, the accused was a member of a party believed to have stolen ganja who were being pursued by another party. A member of the second party was shot and killed by a member of the first. The accused's defence was that he had not got possession of a gun at the material time, but the trial judge took the view that he ought also to direct the jury with regard to the possibility that the accused had acted in self-defence. He did not direct the jury that they should convict of manslaughter if they concluded that, although the accused believed on reasonable grounds that his life was in danger, he used more force than was reasonably necessary. The Privy Council held that there was no need for such a direction. "The defence of self-defence either succeeds so as to result in an acquittal or it is disproved in which case as a defence it is rejected".[2]

Palmer's case has been followed, in preference to Australian decisions which went the other way,[3] by the Court of Appeal in England.[4] There is no English authority dealing with the use of excessive force in effecting an arrest or preventing an offence against a third party, but the logical consequence of the advice given in *Palmer's* case would be a conviction of murder provided death resulted and the accused intended either to kill or cause grievous bodily harm.

The result is no more surprising than the apparent rule that, if A kills B, intending to do so or to cause B grievous bodily harm, but believing, on unreasonable grounds, either that B was about to kill him or to kill someone else, he is nonetheless guilty of murder and not manslaughter.[5] This rule and the decision in *Palmer's* case are open to the same objection, namely, that it is improper to convict of murder someone

---

1. [1971] A.C. 814; [1971] 1 All E.R. 1077; *C. & J. Cases.*
2. Lord Morris of Borth-y-Gest. See articles by Morris, [1960] Crim. L. R., 468, Howard, [1964] Crim. L. R. 448, and Smith, [1972] Crim. L. R. 524.
3. *McKay*, [1957] V.R. 560; *Howe* (1958), 100 C.L.R. 448.
4. *McInnes*, [1971] 3 All E.R. 295; *C. & J. Cases.* Contrast the acceptance in Ireland of the Australian decisions, *People (A.-G.)* v. *Dwyer*, [1972] I.R. 416.
5. Para. 4.15.

whose intention was to commit a lawful homicide or lawfully to seriously injure so that the case against him is simply that he was guilty of an error of judgment in a difficult situation.

c. *Misadventure*.—Death is caused by misadventure where it results, by an accident not involving gross negligence, from the doing of a lawful act. An obvious instance is where death results from a lawful operation carried out with due care by a surgeon. Further examples are death resulting from lawful punishment and lawful acts done in the course of lawful games, such as football, but in such cases the violence must not be immoderate, for otherwise the act is unlawful,[1] and so is the homicide.

Murder

8.9 Murder, an offence for which the only punishment is imprisonment for life, is unlawful homicide with "malice aforethought".

Murder was a purely capital offence until the law was modified by the Homicide Act 1957, which drew a distinction between capital and non-capital murder. Capital murder included murders done in the course or furtherance of theft; by shooting or causing an explosion; in resisting, avoiding or preventing lawful arrest, and murders of a police officer acting in the execution of his duty. Non-capital murder was punished with life imprisonment.

As a result of the Murder (Abolition of Death Penalty) Act 1965, the only sentence in all cases of murder is imprisonment for life. Under the Act the judge has a discretion to recommend to the Home Secretary the minimum period which should be served by the prisoner before the Home Secretary exercises the powers of release on licence which he possesses in the case of all life prisoners. These powers cannot be exercised in the case of a murderer without the consent of the Parole Board and consultation with the Lord Chief Justice together with the trial judge, if available.

The mandatory life sentence for murder can be supported by the argument that at the time of sentence neither the judge nor the Court of Appeal can have the foresight to know when the murderer can be released compatibly with the safety of society, but further thought should be given to a proposal that in certain tragic cases such as mercy killings the judge should be able to

1. Para. 7.6.

make a hospital order or probation order or a conditional discharge where he is satisfied that it would be contrary to the interests of justice for the convicted person to serve any term of imprisonment.[1]

In 1974 there were convictions for murder in respect of 114 victims.[2]

Malice aforethought

8.10 Malice aforethought consists of an intention on the part of the accused:

a. to kill another human being; or
b. to do grievous bodily harm to another human being.

Malice aforethought does not imply either premeditation or ill-will. The sudden unprovoked killing of a total stranger is no less murder than the cunningly contrived assassination of a deadly enemy. Malice aforethought is thus a misleading term of art and its abolition would improve the precision and lucidity of the law of murder.[3]

Exposition has been greatly helped by the Homicide Act 1957 and the judgment of the Court of Criminal Appeal in *Vickers*.[4] Although this case has recently been held to be wrong by a minority of the House of Lords,[5] the judgment entitles us to make use of some terms which had not previously been employed precisely in any textbook or judicial statement of the law. Before the Act of 1957 came into force, there were three kinds of malice aforethought. It might have been "express", "implied" or "constructive". Constructive malice aforethought has been abolished, but malice aforethought may still be express or implied.

It is said to have been "express" in cases in which there was an intention to kill, and "implied" when there was an intention to do grievous bodily harm.

There used to be two kinds of constructive malice aforethought, for it was murder to cause death in furtherance of a felony or when resisting lawful arrest. This doctrine was capable

---

1. For a recent discussion of the penalty for murder see the 12th Report of the Criminal Law Revision Committee, Cmnd. 5184, and the Report of the Butler Committee on Mentally Abnormal Offenders, Cmnd. 6244, paras. 19.8–19.15.
2. *Criminal Statistics*, 1974, Cmnd. 6168.
3. Stephen, *History of the Criminal Law*, 1883, Vol. 3, p. 83; *Hyam* v. *Director of Public Prosecutions*, [1974] A.C. 55; [1974] 2 All E.R. 41, at p. 45, *per* Lord Hailsham.
4. [1957] 2 Q.B. 664; [1957] 2 All E.R. 741; *C. & J. Cases*.
5. Para. 8.13.

of operating very harshly for it meant that someone would be technically guilty of murder if, when committing robbery, he gave his victim a slight push which happened to prove fatal through an unforeseen contingency such as a heart attack. It also meant that a man would be technically guilty of murder if he unintentionally killed a policeman when using no more than a moderate degree of violence in resisting arrest. These cases of constructive malice were quite distinct from those in which malice was express or implied, for the accused might not have intended to kill or to do grievous bodily harm. There was much uncertainty concerning the proper formulation of the rules with regard to constructive malice, but this is no longer of practical importance on account of s. 1 of the Homicide Act 1957. The marginal note reads "Abolition of constructive malice", and the section reads:

"(1) Where a person kills another in the course or furtherance of some other offence, the killing shall not amount to murder unless done with the same malice aforethought (express or implied) that is required for a killing to amount to murder when not done in the course or furtherance of another offence.

(2) For the purposes of the foregoing subsection, a killing done in the course or for the purpose of resisting an officer of justice, or of resisting or avoiding or preventing a lawful arrest, or of effecting or assisting an escape or rescue from legal custody, shall be treated as a killing in the course or furtherance of an offence."

The effect of these provisions is that, in considering whether the accused is guilty of murder, the fact that he killed the deceased in furtherance of another offence or in resisting an arrest can be ignored. The question is always did he have that which would have constituted express or implied malice aforethought if the Act of 1957 had not been passed?

The different types of express and implied malice aforethought must now be discussed in greater detail, and the discussion will conclude with some proposals of the Law Commission.

Intention to kill

.11 The accused is of course guilty of murder if he had the direct intention to kill, i.e. if the death of some other person was the aim of his act or omission. The phrase "malice aforethought" also includes foresight on the part of the accused that his act or omission is likely to cause death.[1] Such a state of mind is, as we

1. *Hyam* v. *Director of Public Prosecutions*, [1975] A.C. 55; [1974] 2 All E.R. 41.

have seen,[1] sometimes spoken of as "oblique intention" although some writers and judges prefer to speak of it as a separate head of malice aforethought.[2] The classic illustration is *Desmond, Barret and others*.[3] The accused exploded a barrel of gunpowder in a crowded street in order to facilitate the escape of prisoners from Clerkenwell gaol. They did not aim at killing anyone, but someone was nonetheless killed. Cockburn, C.J. told the jury that, "if a man did an act, more especially if that were an illegal act, although its immediate purpose might not be to take life, yet if it were such that life was necessarily endangered by it—if a man did such an act, not for the purpose of taking life, but with the knowledge or belief that life was likely to be sacrificed by it, that was murder." The accused were convicted.

In *Serné and Goldfinch*,[4] the accused set fire to a house with the result that one of Serné's children who he knew was in the house was burned to death. Somewhat surprisingly they were acquitted on a charge of murder after Stephen, J. had expressed himself as follows:

> "It is alleged that he [Serné] arranged matters in such a way that any person of the most common intelligence must have known perfectly well that he was placing all those people in deadly risk. It appears to me that if that were really done, it matters very little indeed whether the prisoners hoped that the people would escape or whether they did not."

Before the Suicide Act 1961 came into force, an intention on the part of the accused to kill himself constituted malice aforethought; accordingly someone who killed another while endeavouring to kill himself was guilty of murder. The principle underlying this odd rule was that suicide was self-murder. The Act of 1961 provides that it shall no longer be an offence for a person to commit or attempt to commit suicide, and it seems to follow that someone who kills another while endeavouring to kill himself is at most guilty of manslaughter. Murder involves an unlawful killing of another and someone who is endeavouring to kill himself does not intend to kill another unlawfully, although he may be guilty of sufficient criminal

---

1. Paras. 3.13–3.16.
2. E.g. Stephen, *Digest of Criminal Law*, art. 264; Lord Cross in *Hyam* v. *Director of Public Prosecutions*, [1975] A.C., at p. 96.
3. Cited in Stephen, *op. cit.*, art. 264, illustration 8; for further details see Hogan, Funeral in Dublin, [1970], Crim. L. R. 452.
4. (1887), 16 Cox C.C. 311; *C. & J. Cases*; see also *Walters* (1841), Car. & M. 164.

negligence to render himself liable to be convicted of manslaughter.

Intention to do grievous bodily harm

.12 As before, "intention" is used here to include both direct and oblique intention to do grievous bodily harm to another.

An old example of this second type of "malice aforethought" is afforded by the case of *Errington*,[1] where the accused, having placed large quantities of straw on a man who was asleep, threw a shovel of hot cinders on it. The straw ignited and the man was burnt to death. There was no evidence of an intention to kill but the jury were directed that if they believed that the accused intended to do any serious bodily injury to the deceased, although not to kill him, it was murder.

Vickers[2] is a modern instance of the same doctrine. The accused broke into a shop with intent to steal. On being approached by an elderly lady, who lived above the shop, he struck her several blows in consequence of which she died although the violence used was only of a moderate degree. Vickers was convicted of capital murder, and his conviction was affirmed by the Court of Criminal Appeal because the jury had been properly directed that "malice aforethought" would be implied if the accused intended to do some grievous bodily harm.

"Grievous bodily harm" has since been held to mean really serious harm,[3] and the older authorities suggesting that any serious interference with health or comfort will suffice have been overruled. The direction in *Vickers* followed the older authorities and the verdict might have been one of manslaughter if the jury had been told that, to constitute murder, an intention to cause really serious bodily harm was necessary.

The argument in *Vickers* was mainly concerned with the construction of s. 1 of the Homicide Act 1957. We have seen that the effect of this is that, in deciding whether he had malice aforethought express or implied, the court must disregard the fact that the accused killed the deceased in the course or furtherance of some other offence. Vickers killed his victim in the course or furtherance of the offences of burglary and causing grievous bodily harm with intent to do so. It was argued on his behalf

1. (1838), 2 Lew. C.C. 217.
2. [1957] 2 Q.B. 664; [1957] 2 All E.R. 741; *C. & J. Cases*.
3. *Director of Public Prosecutions* v. *Smith*, [1961] A.C. at p. 303; [1960] 3 All E.R. 161; *C. & J. Cases*.

that, just as it could no longer be said that he had malice aforethought simply because he was committing burglary, so he did not have malice aforethought merely because he intended to do grievous bodily harm as that was the *mens rea* of the offence of causing grievous bodily harm, contrary to s. 18 of the Offences against the Person Act 1861, which he was committing. The court held that, because intention to do grievous bodily harm had always been sufficient to imply malice aforethought independently of the constructive malice doctrine and because implied malice had been preserved by s. 1 of the Homicide Act, the words "in the course or furtherance of some other offence" referred to some other offence, e.g. burglary, than that of intentionally causing grievous bodily harm, which was the means by which death was caused. The decision in *Vickers* was approved by the House of Lords in *Director of Public Prosecutions* v. *Smith*,[1] although it was not considered at any length.

8.13 The question whether intention to do grievous bodily harm constitutes malice aforethought was considered again in *Hyam* v. *Director of Public Prosecutions*.[2] Although the House of Lords in this case did not overrule *Vickers*, some of the speeches make the present position less certain than it was previously thought to be. The accused, Mrs Hyam, had been associating with J, who transferred his affections to B. The accused set fire to the house where B was living and two of B's children were killed; the accused knew that people were, or were very probably, in the house at the time. She was charged with murder. At the trial she said that her object had been to frighten B into leaving the district and that she did not aim to cause bodily harm, let alone death, to anyone. The jury was directed that the prosecution had to prove that the accused intended to do B serious bodily harm, and that if the prosecution proved that when she had set fire to the house she had known it was highly probable that that would cause serious bodily harm the necessary intent would be established; it mattered not that the accused's motive had been to frighten B. The accused was convicted and her appeal against conviction was dismissed by the Court of Appeal, who granted leave to appeal to the House of Lords. The point certified was whether malice aforethought in the crime of murder was established by proof beyond reasonable doubt that when doing the act which led to the death of another the accused had known

1. *Ibid.*
2. [1975] A.C. 55; [1974] 2 All E.R. 41.

that it was highly probable that the act would result in death or serious bodily harm.

The House of Lords, by a majority of three to two, answered "yes" to this question and dismissed the appeal. Lord Hailsham and Viscount Dilhorne expressly approved *Vickers* but the third member of the majority, Lord Cross, said that he was not prepared to decide on the validity of *Vickers* and would content himself "with saying that on the footing that *R.* v. *Vickers* was rightly decided the answer to the question put to us should be 'yes' and that this appeal should be dismissed".[1]

Lords Diplock and Kilbrandon, who dissented, held that an intention to cause grievous bodily harm was not sufficient *mens rea* for murder unless the accused realised his act was likely to endanger life. They thought that *Vickers* was wrongly decided and should be overruled along with that part of *Director of Public Prosecutions* v. *Smith* which approved it. Lord Diplock's reasoning was that the Court of Criminal Appeal in *Vickers* had been wrong to say that an intention to do grievous bodily harm had itself always supplied "malice aforethought", that it had only become "malice aforethought" by virtue of the doctrine of constructive malice when the intentional causing of grievous bodily harm had been made a felony by statute in 1803, and that consequently it had ceased to constitute malice aforethought when constructive malice was abolished by the Homicide Act 1957.

The even split between those Lords who wished to uphold and to overrule *Vickers* means that the question of the correctness of that decision is still open in the House of Lords; the Court of Appeal is still bound by *Vickers*, because the decision in *Hyam*, in which Lord Cross concurred, was on the basis that *Vickers* was correct.[2]

General comments on express and implied malice aforethought

14 a. In *Hyam*, Lord Hailsham rejected the concept of oblique intention. He was not prepared to accept that a person who foresees that a thing is a highly probable consequence of his act intends it. Thus, while he took the view that intention to kill or do grievous bodily harm constituted "malice aforethought", he refused to hold that foresight of death or grievous bodily harm constituted such an intention. However,

---

1. [1975] A.C. at p. 98.
2. See the note by Professor Williams in [1974] 34 *Cambridge Law Journal* 200.

he postulated a third category of malice aforethought, a (direct) intention to expose the victim to the serious risk of death or grievous bodily harm. It is submitted that the difference between this formulation and that of Lords Dilhorne and Cross (who were prepared to accept that foresight that death or grievous bodily harm was a likely consequence constituted "malice aforethought", whether or not it was described as intention) is purely verbal and no practical distinction exists, even if a philosophical one does.

b. The decision in *Hyam* shows that if death or grievous bodily harm are not directly intended it will suffice that they are foreseen as a highly probable consequence. However, *Hyam* does not decide that foresight of some lesser probability of death or grievous bodily harm will not suffice. The speeches of Lords Hailsham and Cross state that it will, and this point remains open for future decision by the courts.

c. An intention to kill or do grievous bodily harm generally which would be manifested, for instance, by a person who planted a bomb in a crowded department store, will suffice for malice aforethought.

d. In the law of homicide, as in the rest of the law relating to offences against the person, a generic intent suffices. This means that, if the accused is shown to have done an act with the intention of killing one person, and in fact another is killed, he is on the principle of "transferred malice" guilty of murder. Thus, in the old case of *Salisbury*,[1] the jury were directed that footpads were guilty of murdering a servant when they had lain in wait for his master with the intention of killing the latter but had killed the servant.

e. The intention to kill or do grievous bodily harm must of course be directed against a human being. If someone shoots and kills a man in the dark believing that he is a pig,[2] he cannot be guilty of murder, although he may well be guilty of manslaughter on account of criminal negligence. This would also be the case if someone destroyed what he believed to be a dead body, although it was in fact the body of a living being.[3] As it is not murder to kill an enemy in time of war, a soldier who killed one of his officers under the mistaken impression that he was an enemy ought not to be guilty of this offence, although the court might require the mistake to

1. (1553), 1 Plowd. 100; *C. & J. Cases*; see also *Gore* (1611), 9 Co. Rep. 81a; *C. & J. Cases*.
2. Williams, Homicide and the Supernatural, (1949) 65 L.Q.R. 491.
3. *Shoukatallie* v. *R.*, [1962] A.C. 81; [1961] 3 All E.R. 996.

have been reasonable, because the soldier would have had the requisite *mens rea* which the prosecution must prove as an essential ingredient of the offence, and would be relying on the defence of mistake on the ground that, had the facts been as he supposed them to be, he would not have been responsible for an *actus reus*.[1] In the other hypothetical cases mentioned in this paragraph, the mistake would negative an intention to kill any human being at all.

f. Generally, the intent to kill or do grievous bodily harm must exist at the time of the accused's act which caused death.[2] However, if death is caused by one act in a series of acts which it is impossible to divide, e.g. because they formed part of a preconceived plan, it is irrelevant that the accused lacked the necessary intent for murder when that act was done if he had that intent when another act in the series was done. In *Thabo Meli* v. *R.*,[3] the accused planned to kill the deceased in a hut and thereafter to roll his body over a cliff so that it might appear to be a case of accidental death. The deceased was rendered unconscious in the hut and, believing him to be dead, the accused rolled him over the cliff. There was medical evidence that the deceased was not killed by the injuries received in the hut, but died from exposure where he had been left at the bottom of the cliff. It was argued that the accused were not guilty of murder because, while the first act was accompanied by *mens rea*, it was not the cause of death; and because the second act, while it was the cause of death, was not accompanied by *mens rea*, the accused believing their victim to be dead already. The Privy Council rejected this argument, holding that the two acts formed part of a series which could not be divided up. Accordingly, the accused were guilty of murder, and not of attempted murder or culpable homicide (manslaughter), as would have been the case if the rejected argument had prevailed. The advice of the Privy Council suggests that its decision might have been different if the acts done with intent to kill and the actual act of killing had not formed part of a preconceived plan. However, *Thabo Meli* was applied by the Court of Criminal Appeal in *Church*[4] to a case where the act which caused death was not part of a plan, being quite unforeseen at the time of the act done with *mens rea*. The accused had a sudden fight

1. Paras. 4.14–4.16.
2. Para. 3.32.
3. [1954] 1 All E.R. 373; *C. & J. Cases*; also see *Moore and Dorn*, [1975] Crim. L. R. 229.
4. [1966] 1 Q.B., 59; [1965] 2 All E.R. 72; *C. & J. Cases*.

with a woman and rendered her unconscious. Then, believing that she was dead, he threw her body into a river, where she drowned. His conviction for manslaughter was upheld on appeal on the basis that his conduct constituted a series of acts which culminated in the woman's death. These decisions seem to be right, although it will often be difficult to decide whether the accused's acts form a series which cannot be broken up.

D.P.P. v. *Smith* and a possible further kind of malice aforethought

8.15 In *Director of Public Prosecutions* v. *Smith*,[1] a police officer asked the accused, who was driving a car which had been stopped in the ordinary course of traffic, to draw into the kerb so that his interrogation concerning the contents of the car might continue. Instead of drawing in as requested, the accused drove his car, with the officer clinging on to it, very close to oncoming cars at an increasing speed. The officer was eventually shaken off the car and run over and killed by another car. The accused was convicted of murder after the jury had been asked whether he must, as a reasonable man, have contemplated grievous bodily harm as a likely result of his conduct. The conviction was altered to one of manslaughter by the Court of Criminal Appeal, but the House of Lords reinstated the conviction of capital murder. The House took the view that, once the jury were satisfied that he was unlawfully and voluntarily "doing something to someone, it matters not what the accused in fact contemplated as the probable result, or whether he ever contemplated at all. The sole question is whether the unlawful and voluntary act was of such a kind that grievous bodily harm was the natural and probable result. The only test available for this is what the ordinary responsible man would, in all the circumstances of the case, have contemplated as the natural and probable result."

What exactly was decided in *Director of Public Prosecutions* v. *Smith* is a matter of dispute. Three interpretations of the case are possible.

a. *A third type of malice aforethought.*—One possible interpretation of the decision is that it recognises the existence of a third kind of malice aforethought different from an intention (direct or oblique) to kill and an intention (direct or oblique) to cause grievous bodily harm. The precise formulation of this kind of malice aforethought is a matter of some nicety.

1. [1961] A.C. 290; [1960] 3 All E.R. 161; *C. & J. Cases.*

Very old authority could be cited in support of the view that malice aforethought may consist of an intention to do an act which, in the circumstances of which the accused was aware, is intrinsically likely to kill or cause grievous bodily harm. Thus, a case which has been much discussed in textbooks was put by Blackstone as follows:[1]

> "When a workman flings down a stone or piece of timber into the street and kills a man; this may be either misadventure, manslaughter, or murder, according to the circumstances under which the original act was done; if it were in a country village, where few passengers are, and he calls out to all people to have care, it is misadventure only; but if it were in London, or other populous town, where people are continually passing, it is manslaughter, though he gives loud warning; and murder, if he knows of their passing, and gives no warning at all."

The basis of liability for murder seems to have been that the accused did an act which, in the circumstances known to him, was likely to kill. It seems to have been immaterial whether he was aware of this latter fact. He would have been equally guilty if he had drawn the obvious inference from the known facts and deliberately taken a grave risk of killing someone, or if he had failed to draw the inference owing to loss of temper, stupidity or thinking about other things.

The Lord Chancellor's speech in *Smith's* case certainly does not sanction the recognition, in modern law, of a kind of malice aforethought as broad as that which has been stated. The intention recognised in the speech must not merely be an intention to do an act which, in the circumstances known to the accused, is intrinsically likely to kill or cause grievous bodily harm; the intention must be to do an act in the nature of an assault, an unlawful attack on another human being.

b. *Further explanation of "intention to do grievous bodily harm"*.—It is at least arguable that all that the House of Lords was saying in *Smith's* case was that there are certain acts with regard to which it would be a contradiction in terms for a man to say "I meant to do the act, but I did not intend to cause grievous bodily harm." Examples are exerting great pressure on someone's throat, or banging the person clinging to a car up against oncoming traffic.[2] Doing these things is by definition causing grievous bodily harm. If someone intentionally (i.e. meaning to do so) gives another a violent blow on the head

1. Blackstone, 4 Comm. 192; *Hull* (1664), Kel. 40.
2. See *per* Lord Parker, C.J., in the course of argument in *Grimwood*, [1962] 2 Q.B. 621; [1962] 3 All E.R. 285.

and exerts extreme pressure on his throat, he intends to do grievous bodily harm even though, owing to panic or bad temper, the thought of his victim suffering such harm never crossed his mind. If this interpretation is the right one, no third kind of "malice aforethought" was recognised in *Smith's* Case.

c. *Proof of intention to do grievous bodily harm.*—According to this interpretation, also, no third kind of "malice aforethought" was accepted in *Smith*. On this interpretation the decision is simply concerned with how an intention to do grievous bodily harm could be proved and the House of Lords merely decided that if the accused knowingly did something unlawful to someone and grievous bodily harm was the natural and probable consequence of that unlawful act, the accused was to be irrebuttably presumed to have intended grievous bodily harm, in the absence of insanity or incapacity to form an intent.

The effect of s. 8 of the Criminal Justice Act 1967 on *D.P.P.* v. *Smith*

8.16 As we have seen,[1] the problem of the precise import of *Smith's* case led to the passing of s. 8 of the Criminal Justice Act 1967 which reads:

> "A court or jury, in determining whether a person has committed an offence, (a) shall not be bound in law to infer that he intended or foresaw a result of his actions by reason only of its being a natural and probable consequence of those actions; but (b) shall decide whether he did intend or foresee that result by reference to all the evidence drawing such inferences from the evidence as appear proper in the circumstances."

The section was the first of three proposals made by the Law Commission with regard to proof of criminal intent and reforming the law of murder. The other two have not yet been made law. They are a. that "where a person kills another the killing shall not amount to murder unless done with an intent to kill"; b. "A person has an intent to kill if he means his actions to kill or if he is willing for his actions, though meant for another purpose, to kill in accomplishing that purpose."[2]

No doubt the Commission meant all three proposals to be enacted together. Had this been done, there could have been no doubt about the law of murder. "Malice aforethought", if there

1. Para. 4.10.
2. *Imputed Criminal Intent*. See (1967) 111 Sol. Jo. 183; (1967) 30 M.L.R. 431.

would have been any point in continuing to use that phrase, would have meant an intent to kill, and proof of an intent to kill would, like the proof of any other criminal intent, have been governed by what is now s. 8 of the Criminal Justice Act. As it is, we are left with a theoretical difficulty. If *Director of Public Prosecutions* v. *Smith* does decide that there is still, in modern law, a kind of malice aforethought different from an intention (direct or oblique) to kill, or an intention (direct or oblique) to do grievous bodily harm, i.e. an intention to do an act which, in the circumstances known to the accused, is intrinsically likely to kill or cause grievous bodily harm, the decision was unaffected by s. 8; it strictly still represents the law since the House of Lords in *Hyam* v. *Director of Public Prosecutions*[1] did not overrule it. If, on the other hand, *Smith's* case was solely concerned with proof of an intention to cause grievous bodily harm, then it has ceased to have any authority since s. 8 came into force except in so far as it illustrates the point that an intention to do certain acts, such as to hit a man violently with a hatchet, is in reality an intention to do grievous bodily harm, and except in so far as it authorises the definition of grievous bodily harm as "really serious bodily harm" and approves *Vickers*. The question of the combined effect on the law of murder of *Director of Public Prosecutions* v. *Smith* and s. 8 of the Criminal Justice Act 1967 is theoretical because, in practice, there can be little doubt, particularly in view of the subjective terms of the discussion in *Hyam's* case, that juries will be directed in all murder cases in subjective terms.[2]

The Law Commission's unenacted proposal

17 The merit of the Law Commission's proposal to base liability for murder solely on an intention to kill is that it would bring the law into accord with what are probably the views of the ordinary layman. So far as the proposed definition of an intent to kill is concerned, it is not so clear what its effect would be. It is expressly stated by the Commission to be intended to cover the case of a man who puts a bomb in an aeroplane so as to destroy it in flight in order to recover the insurance on the freight. This is a very strong case of oblique intention, and it is not clear how far the Commission intended to change the existing law with regard to oblique intention to kill as illustrated by such cases as *Desmond, Barret and others*.

1. [1975] A.C. 55; [1974] 2 All E.R. 41.
2. *Wallett*, [1968] 2 Q.B., 367; [1968] 2 All E.R. 296; *Cooper*, [1969] 3 All E.R. 118; *Hyam* v. *Director of Public Prosecutions*.

Manslaughter

8.18 Generally, any unlawful homicide which is not classified as murder is manslaughter, the punishment for which may vary from imprisonment for life[1] to an absolute discharge.

There are two generic types of manslaughter—voluntary and involuntary. A person is guilty of voluntary manslaughter where, although he may have killed with malice aforethought, he has done so under circumstances which the law regards as mitigating the gravity of his offence. These are that the accused was suffering from diminished responsibility, acting pursuant to a suicide pact or was provoked. Involuntary manslaughter is an unlawful killing where the accused has some blameworthy mental state less than an intention to kill or do grievous bodily harm.

Diminished responsibility

8.19 Diminished responsibility was discussed earlier.[2] It is expressly provided by s. 2 (4) of the Homicide Act 1957 that the fact that one party to the killing is not liable to be convicted of murder on account of his diminished responsibility does not affect the question whether the killing amounted to murder in the case of any other party to it.

Suicide pacts

8.20 At common law, where a person agreed with another to kill that other, or be a party to him being killed by a third person, and then to kill himself, but survived, he was guilty of murder. However, s. 4 of the Homicide Act 1957 now provides that the survivor of such a suicide pact is only guilty of manslaughter. On a charge of murder the burden of proving that he was acting pursuant to a suicide pact between him and the other is borne by the accused.[3]

It is convenient here to describe the related offence of aiding and abetting suicide. At common law, a person who aided and abetted another to kill himself was guilty of murder as an accomplice, because suicide was self-murder. Under s. 4 of the Homicide Act 1957 the liability of one who aided and abetted suicide was reduced to manslaughter, provided that he had agreed to die also; but when the Suicide Act 1961 abolished the crime of

---

1. Offences against the Person Act 1861, s. 5.
2. Paras. 5.18 and 5.19.
3. Homicide Act 1957, s. 4 (2).

suicide, s. 2 created the lesser offence of aiding and abetting suicide, punishable with a maximum of 14 years' imprisonment, which applies to all cases of such conduct. Should the facts warrant it, there may be a conviction for aiding and abetting suicide on a trial for murder or manslaughter.[1] Prosecutions under s. 4 of the Homicide Act or s. 2 of the Suicide Act are extremely rare.

Provocation

.21 While evidence that the accused was provoked is a circumstance which the jury must take into account, along with all the other circumstances, in deciding whether he intended to kill or do grievous bodily harm,[2] the statutory defence of provocation is concerned with the situation where the accused did intend to kill or do grievous bodily harm but acted under a sudden loss of self-control.[3]

Unlike the other two types of voluntary manslaughter, the defence of provocation is a creature of the common law, although its terms have been extensively amended by s. 3 of the Homicide Act 1957 (hereafter referred to as s. 3) which provides:

> "Where on a charge of murder there is evidence on which the jury can find that the person charged was provoked (whether by things done or by things said or by both together) to lose his self control, the question whether the provocation was enough to make a reasonable man do as he did shall be left to be determined by the jury; and in determining that question the jury shall take into account everything both done and said according to the effect which, in their opinion, it would have on a reasonable man."[4]

Provocation is not a defence to any charge other than murder,[5] not even to attempted murder.[6] The reasoning behind this is that in most offences it is possible to make allowance for provocation in sentence, but this is not possible in murder because the sentence is fixed by law. The mitigating factor of provocation is quite distinct from the justification of

1. Suicide Act 1961, s. 2 (2).
2. Criminal Justice Act 1967, s. 8; *Ives*, [1970] 1 Q.B. 208; [1969] 3 All E.R. 470.
3. *A.G. of Ceylon* v. *Kumarasinghege Don John Perera*, [1953] A.C. 200; *Lee Chun-Chuen* v. *R.*, [1963] A.C. 220; [1963] 1 All E.R. 73; *C. & J. Cases*; *Martindale*, [1966] 3 All E.R. 305.
4. P. English, What did s. 3 do to the Law of Provocation?, [1970] Crim. L. R. 249; S. White, A note on provocation, *ibid.* 446.
5. *Cunningham*, [1959] 1 Q.B. 288; [1958] 3 All E.R. 711.
6. *Bruzas*, [1972] Crim. L. R. 367; see P. English, Provocation and Attempted Murder, [1973] Crim. L. R. 727.

self-defence. It is based on a sudden loss of self-control in circumstances where the accused does not entertain a reasonable, or generally speaking any kind of belief that his life is in danger. In the absence of authority, we suggest that someone who without provocation aids and abets a person who is entitled to a verdict of manslaughter on the ground of provocation would be guilty of murder as an accomplice.

8.22 Before the Homicide Act 1957 only limited types of conduct were sufficient to constitute provocation. Physical violence or the detection of a spouse in the act of adultery[1] was almost invariably required in order to found a case of provocation. Thus, the man who killed his mistress or fiancée detected in intercourse could not plead provocation and had to be convicted of murder.[2] In *Holmes* v. *Director of Public Prosecutions*,[3] the House of Lords stated that, save in circumstances of a most extreme and exceptional nature, words could not constitute provocation. The House held that a confession of adultery by one spouse to another could not constitute sufficient provocation to justify a verdict of manslaughter if the injured spouse killed his spouse or the adulterer. Section 3 has removed these restrictions and, provided the elements of the defence of provocation are satisfied, anything done or said (or a combination of acts and words) will suffice.

The provocative conduct need not have been done by the person who is killed. Assuming that all the elements of the defence are present, if a person accidentally kills someone other than the one who provoked him, when aiming at the latter, he is only guilty of manslaughter.[4] However, apart from this, at common law the provocation had to be by the person whom the accused killed.[5] It is now clear that this rule has been amended by s. 3 and that acts or words amounting to provocation are not excluded from consideration merely because they emanate from some person other than the victim.[6]

The provocative conduct must normally have been directed

1. *Maddy* (1671), 2 Keb. 829.
2. *Greening*, [1913] 3 K.B. 846; *Palmer*, [1913] 2 K.B. 29; but see *Larkin*, [1943] K.B. 174; [1943] 1 All E.R. 217; *C. & J. Cases*, and *Gauthier* (1943), 29 Cr. App. Rep. 113 where the fact that the women were mistresses was ignored.
3. [1946] A.C. 588; [1946] 2 All E.R. 124.
4. *Gross* (1913), 23 Cox C.C. 455.
5. *Simpson* (1915), 84 L.J.K.B. 1893.
6. *Davies*, [1975] 1 All E.R. 890.

at the accused. This is certainly the position at common law.[1] although an exception is where the provocation is directed at a near relative.[2] However, it may be that s. 3 has changed this rule since if it can be interpreted as not requiring the provocation to have been done by the deceased it would also seem to be interpretable as not requiring the provocation to be directed at the accused or a near relative.

.23 Two conditions must be fulfilled before murder is reduced to manslaughter by provocation:

a. *The accused himself must have been provoked.*—The plea of provocation is not open to an unusually cool man confronted with conduct which would cause a normal person to lose control of himself. In *Duffy*,[3] Devlin, J. said that there must be "a sudden and temporary loss of self control, rendering the accused so subject to passion as to make him or her for the moment not master of his mind". In deciding whether the accused had been provoked to lose self control when he acted the jury should take into account all the relevant circumstances, but particularly relevant is whether a sufficient "cooling time" had elapsed between the provocation and the fatal act. It is possible that at common law the defence of provocation necessarily failed if there had been a sufficient time between the occurrence of the provocation and the killing for the accused's "blood to cool and for reason to resume its seat".[4] It is probable, however, that this requirement of "cooling time" was never anything more than a most important item of evidence on the issue of whether the accused was in fact provoked when he did the fatal act. Since the passing of the Homicide Act 1957, s. 3, there is no doubt that "cooling time" is merely an evidential factor, albeit important, which the jury must weigh when deciding whether the accused had been provoked to lose self control when he acted.

b. *The provocation must have been enough to provoke a reasonable man to do as the accused did.*—Before the Homicide Act 1957 the judge had the power to withdraw the issue of provocation from the jury not only when he thought there was insufficient evidence that the accused was in fact provoked, but also if he thought the provocation insufficient to affect a reasonable

1. *Duffy*, [1949] 1 All E.R. 932n.
2. *Harrington* (1866), 10 Cox C.C. 370; *Porritt*, [1961] 3 All E.R. 463.
3. [1949] 1 All E.R. 932n.
4. *Jervis* (1833), 6 C. & P. 157, at p. 159.

man (or cause him to act as the accused did). It was under this latter power of withdrawal that restrictive rules grew up that words and non-violent acts would not generally suffice, that provocation must have been given by the deceased and so on. This latter power of withdrawal was thought to be excessive and has been abolished by the Homicide Act 1957.[1]

In deciding whether the reasonable man would have been provoked to lose his self-control, the reasonable man is not invested with those characteristics and idiosyncracies of the accused which would not be found in a reasonable man, even though these may have made the accused particularly liable to be provoked. Thus, no allowance can be made for the fact that the accused is unusually excitable.[2] Similarly, the fact that the accused was under the influence of drink must be ignored if its only relevance is to show that he might have yielded to provocation more readily than a sober man.[3] It is likewise irrelevant that the accused is sexually impotent and therefore particularly susceptible to taunts from the prostitute he stabs after an unsuccessful attempt to have intercourse with her.[4]

The theory underlying this second requirement is that the rule with regard to provocation is a concession to ordinary human frailty, not to extraordinary bad temper or abnormal excitability, but the law's refusal to make any allowance for physical disabilities which seems to follow from the refusal to make allowance for sexual impotence is unduly harsh. What should be required is a reasonable explanation of the accused's loss of self-control. It may well be impossible to give a reasonable explanation for a sudden outburst of rage where most other people would be unperturbed, and intoxication may well be considered not to be a reasonable explanation for a surrender to passion where the average sober man would restrain himself. Yet it certainly seems unjust to expect a sexually impotent man to react to taunts on the subject of his infirmity with the same disdain as that which would be shown by a potent man in such circumstances.

The decisions concerning the remarkable qualities of the reasonable man were made before the Homicide Act 1957

---

1. Para. 8.24, for the powers of the judge under the Homicide Act 1957.
2. *Lesbini*, [1914] 3 K.B. 1116.
3. *McCarthy*, [1954] 2 Q.B. 105; [1954] 2 All E.R. 262; *C. & J. Cases*.
4. *Bedder* v. *Director of Public Prosecutions*, [1954] 2 All E.R. 801; *C. & J. Cases*.

but, in view of the use of the phrase "reasonable man" in s. 3 of that Act, it would be difficult to argue that Parliament intended to change this part of the law. In addition, it is clear that s. 8 of the Criminal Justice Act 1967 has not swept s. 3 of the Homicide Act away by a side wind; the former deals with the proof of *mens rea*, the latter with a mitigating defence which is not concerned with issues of *mens rea*.

The provocation must have been enough to cause a reasonable man, if provoked,[1] to do what the accused did. The common law required that the accused must have acted in a reasonable fashion after he had lost self-control.[2] The mode of resentment had to bear a reasonable relationship to the provocation. "Fists might be answered with fists, but not with a deadly weapon".[3] This rule was criticised because it was unrealistic to expect that a person who has been provoked to lose his self-control would act reasonably.

The reasonable relationship rule has been abolished as a rule of law by s. 3 of the Homicide Act 1957. In *Brown*,[4] the Court of Appeal stated that s. 3 required the jury to decide whether the provocation was enough to make the reasonable man do as the accused did. It stated that, in answering this question, the jury should be told to take into account the proportion or relationship between the provocation and the retaliation. But it was not a rule of law that a plea of provocation would fail if there was no reasonable relationship; it should be made clear to the jury that the issue of reasonable relationship was merely a factor which they should take into account in deciding whether, if provoked, the reasonable man would have done as the accused did.

The function of judge and jury

.24 Section 3 of the Homicide Act requires the judge to leave the defence of provocation to the jury if there is evidence on which it might find that the accused himself was provoked. This provision applies even if the defence of provocation was not raised during the trial.[5] If the judge, determining that there is such

---

1. *Phillips* v. *R.*, [1969] 2 A.C. 130 at p. 137; *C. & J. Cases*.
2. *Mancini* v. *Director of Public Prosecutions*, [1942] A.C. 1; [1941] 3 All E.R. 272; *C. & J. Cases*; *Gauthier* (1943), 29. Cr. App. Rep. 113; *McCarthy*, [1954] 2 Q.B. 105; [1954] 2 All E.R. 262.
3. *Duffy*, [1949] 1 All E.R. 932n.
4. [1972] 2 Q.B. 229; [1972] 2 All E.R. 1328.
5. *Cascoe*, [1970] 2 All E.R. 833.

evidence, leaves the issue to the jury he must direct that they can only return a verdict of manslaughter on account of provocation if they find that the two conditions mentioned above are fulfilled.[1] As we have already seen,[2] if the issue of provocation is left to the jury the prosecution has the burden of negativing one or more elements of the defence.

Mistaken belief and provocation

8.25 As in the case of other defences, the accused who acts under a reasonably mistaken belief that he was being provoked must be judged as if the facts were as he mistakenly believed them to be. Moreover, if his mistake resulted from intoxication he is to be so judged,[3] even though a drunken mistake cannot be said to be reasonable. This should not be confused with the rule that the accused's drunkenness must be ignored in deciding whether the reasonable man would have been provoked;[4] while drunkenness is irrelevant to questions of the self-restraint of the reasonable man, it is relevant to the question of whether the accused thought he was being provoked.

No other categories of voluntary manslaughter

8.26 The question arises whether or not there are other mitigating circumstances reducing murder to manslaughter. The cases of *Palmer* and *McInnes*[5] suggest that there are not. The common law has been extraordinarily reluctant to allow for mitigating circumstances in murder. If necessity[6] and duress (in the case of a perpetrator[7]) are not absolute defences to murder one would have thought that, at the very least, they ought to be treated as mitigating factors reducing liability to manslaughter, but when *Dudley and Stephens*[8] was argued the possibility of a verdict of manslaughter seems never to have been considered.

8.27 We now turn to those situations where the accused is not guilty of murder because he lacked an intention either to kill

---

1. *Brown*.
2. Para. 4.4; *Macpherson* (1957), 41 Cr. App. Rep. 213.
3. *Letenock* (1917), 12 Cr. App. Rep. 221; *Wardrope*, [1960] Crim. L. R. 770.
4. Para. 8.23b.
5. Para. 8.8b.
6. Para. 18.15.
7. Para. 18.6.
8. (1884), 14 Q.B.D. 273. See para. 18.15.

or do grievous bodily harm, but acted with some other blameworthy state of mind.

Killing by an unlawful act likely to cause bodily harm which is not serious

28 This mode of committing manslaughter is commonly known as "constructive manslaughter". At one time the unlawful act could consist of a tort[1] but now only a criminally unlawful act will suffice,[2] and there are these two further qualifications on the nature of the unlawful act:

a. An act which has become criminally unlawful simply because it was negligently performed does not constitute an unlawful act for the purposes of "constructive manslaughter". In *Andrews* v. *Director of Public Prosecutions*,[3] the accused had killed another while committing the offence of dangerous driving and was convicted of manslaughter. On appeal to the House of Lords, Lord Atkin said that where an otherwise lawful act (e.g. driving) was unlawful merely because it was negligently performed this did not necessarily make the driver guilty of manslaughter if death resulted. The doctrine of "constructive manslaughter" did not apply to such acts, although there might be liability for manslaughter under the head of killing by criminal negligence.[4]
b. It was formerly thought that, provided there was a duty to act, an omission to act which was likely to cause harm would suffice instead of an unlawful act for the purposes of constructive manslaughter. There are cases where the unintentional causing of death by non-performance of a duty owed to someone by the accused has been held to be manslaughter. The most obvious instance is the neglect of a child by its parent or guardian which, if wilful, is an offence under s. 1 of the Children and Young Persons Act 1933. In *Senior*,[5] for instance, where owing to the religious belief of the accused his child was not provided with medical attendance and died in consequence, it was held that manslaughter had been committed, but the Court of Appeal in *Lowe*[6] held that *Senior*

---

1. *Fenton* (1830), 1 Lew C.C. 179.
2. *Lamb*, [1967] 2 Q.B. 981; [1967] 2 All E.R. 1282; *C. & J. Cases*.
3. [1937] A.C. 576.
4. Para. 8.31.
5. [1899] 1 Q.B. 283. Also see *Watson and Watson* (1959), 43 Crim. App. Rep. 111.
6. [1973] 1 Q.B. 702; [1973] 1 All E.R. 805.

was no longer good law and that an omission would not suffice for constructive manslaughter. The accused's baby died some 10 weeks after birth and at the time of her death was grossly dehydrated and emaciated. The father was convicted of manslaughter and of wilfully neglecting the child. His appeal against the former conviction was allowed by the Court of Appeal who held that a finding of manslaughter did not inexorably follow from a finding of wilful neglect (which offence required a deliberate failure). There was a clear distinction between an omission and act likely to cause harm: "... if I strike a child in a manner likely to cause harm it is right that if the child dies I may be charged with manslaughter. If, however, I omit to do something with the result that it suffers injury to health which results in death, we think that a charge of manslaughter should not be an inevitable consequence, even if the omission is deliberate".[1] It is difficult to see the distinction between the person who causes the death of his child by deliberate inaction and the one who does so by positive action.

A second reason for the decision was that *Senior* could no longer be regarded as good law in the light of the House of Lords decision in *Andrews* v. *Director of Public Prosecutions*[2] but the Court seems to have misunderstood *Andrews*. It relied on a passage in that case concerned with the other type of involuntary manslaughter, killing by criminal negligence. Lord Atkin said that mere negligence would not suffice; it must be gross. The Court seems to have confused "negligence" with "neglect" (i.e. omit to maintain and care) in concluding that, following *Andrews*, mere neglect does not suffice for manslaughter and that the doctrine of constructive manslaughter cannot apply to omissions, even if deliberate.

8.29 To secure a conviction on the basis of constructive manslaughter the prosecution must prove three things:

a. *Commission of the* actus reus *of an unlawful act.*—Common examples of unlawful acts in this context are assaults and batteries.[3] All the elements of the *actus reus* of the unlawful act must be proved. Thus, manslaughter is not committed if a child unexpectedly dies as a result of reasonable punishment by a parent, since such punishment does not constitute an assault or battery or any other offence[4]; this is homicide by

1. *Per* Phillimore, L.J., [1973] 1 All E.R. at p. 809. 2. [1937] A.C. 576.
3. *Cato: Morris: Dudley*; (1975), *The Times*, 16th October. 4. Para. 7.6.

misadventure. If unreasonable force is used,[1] or if the person punishing has no right to do so (e.g. because he is a brother not *in loco parentis*),[2] the punishment constitutes an assault and battery and the person inflicting it is guilty of manslaughter if death unexpectedly results even though he had no intention of causing grievous bodily harm. As we have seen, in many instances an act which would otherwise be unlawful is rendered lawful by the consent of the person against whom it is directed, and if death results it is death by misadventure. However, a person cannot consent lawfully to the infliction of bodily harm in certain circumstances, and so a person who performs an unlawful operation, such as an illegal abortion, without reason to suspect that it will cause serious bodily harm to the patient, is guilty of manslaughter if death unexpectedly results.[3]

b. *The* mens rea *for the unlawful act.*—Subject to what is said below concerning intoxication the unlawful act can be established only if the necessary *mens rea* for that unlawful act is proved. This was stated by the Court of Appeal in *Lamb.*[4] The accused as a joke pointed a loaded gun at his friend whom he did not intend to alarm and who also was treating the thing as a joke. The gun had two bullets in the chambers but neither bullet was in the chamber opposite the barrel. However, when the accused pulled the trigger, still as a joke, the gun fired and killed his friend. This was because, unknown to the accused who was ignorant of how the gun worked, the action of the gun was to place a bullet behind the barrel when the trigger was pulled. The Court of Appeal held that the accused could not be convicted of constructive manslaughter because the unlawful act must at least constitute a "technical assault" and there had been no proof of "that element of intent without which there can be no assault".[5] Thus, if death is caused by the inadvertent firing of a gun, which the accused had pointed at another under the impression that it was unloaded with the intention of causing alarm (the *mens rea* for assault[6]), he is guilty of manslaughter, because pointing a gun at another is an assault.[7]

---

1. *Hopley* (1860), 2 F. & F. 202; *Conner* (1835), 7 C. & P. 438; *C. & J. Cases.*
2. *Woods* (1921), 85 J.P. 272.
3. *Lumley* (1911), 76 J.P. 208; *Buck and Buck* (1960), 44 Cr. App. Rep. 213; *C. & J. Cases*; *Creamer*, [1966] 1 Q.B. 72; [1965] 3 All E.R. 257.
4. [1967] 2 Q.B. 981; [1967] 2 All E.R. 1282.
5. *Ibid.*, at p. 989.
6. Paras. 7.3–7.4.
7. *Kwaku Mensah* v. *R.*, [1946] A.C. 83.

A similar view to that taken in *Lamb* was expressed by Lord Denning in *obiter dicta* in the civil case of *Gray* v. *Barr*:[1]

> "In the category of manslaughter relating to an unlawful act, the accused must do a dangerous act with the *intention* of frightening or harming someone, or with the *realisation* that it is likely to frighten or harm someone, and nevertheless he goes on and does it regardless of consequences."

c. *Unlawful act must be likely to cause bodily harm.*—Not every unlawful act will suffice. At one time it was thought that death occasioned by any unlawful act would amount to manslaughter, although it was not likely to cause physical harm to anyone. It is now clear that the unlawful act causing death must be dangerous, in the sense that it is likely to injure someone, as well as unlawful. In *Larkin*[2] the accused produced a razor at the house of a man with whom his mistress had been associating: he did so in order to frighten him. His mistress, who was drunk, blundered against the razor and was killed. The Court of Criminal Appeal, in dismissing an appeal against conviction, held that where the act which a person is engaged in performing is unlawful, then, if at the same time it is an act likely to injure another person, and that person dies, the accused is guilty of manslaughter.

The leading case on this subject is now *Church* where the Court of Criminal Appeal said:[3]

> "An unlawful act causing the death of another cannot, simply because it is an unlawful act, render a manslaughter verdict inevitable. For such a verdict inexorably to follow, the unlawful act must be such as all sober and reasonable people would inevitably recognise must subject the other person to, at least, the risk of some harm resulting therefrom, albeit not serious harm."

Of course, very often the accused will have foreseen such harm but he is not required to do so. This objective test is not concerned with proving a risk which the accused must foresee but with delimiting the type of unlawful act which will suffice for liability for manslaughter. Thus this test remains unaffected by s. 8 of the Criminal Justice Act 1967 which requires foresight to be subjectively proved.[4]

---

1. [1971] 2 Q.B. 554, at p. 568; [1971] 2 All E.R. 949, at p. 956; *C. & J. Cases.*
2. [1943] K.B. 174; [1943] 1 All E.R. 217; *C. & J. Cases.* Also see *Hall* (1961), 45 Cr. App. Rep. 366.
3. [1966] 1 Q.B. 59 at p. 70; [1965] 2 All E.R. 72 at p. 75; *C. & J. Cases.* Also see *Mackie* (1973), 57 Crim. App. Rep. 453.
4. *Lipman*, [1970] 1 Q.B. 152; [1969] All E.R. 410; *C. & J. Cases.*

In the nature of things, the unlawful acts in question are generally assaults or batteries. This being so, the objective limitation discussed here is often redundant because in the normal case of battery, at least, the accused will have foreseen some harm to the victim; the limitation adds nothing to the need to prove the *mens rea* of the unlawful act. The limitation is of more importance where the accused merely assaults another: here the intention to make the victim apprehend the immediate application of physical force suffices as the *mens rea* of that unlawful act and the objective limitation operates so as to restrict liability for manslaughter where death results from an assault to those assaults which are objectively likely to cause harm.

Some recent cases[1] decided at first instance, where the victim has died as the result of an assault, appear to have ignored the objective limitation in *Church* and other cases and required that the accused himself should have foreseen that the victim might suffer some harm, albeit not serious harm. While any move towards criminal liability based solely on the accused's realisation is in accordance with the present trend towards subjective liability, decisions at first instance cannot affect the objective limitation laid down by the Court of Criminal Appeal in *Church*. It is true that the distinction between the two approaches is often academic because the questions (i) "Would all reasonable people realise . . .", and (ii) "Did the accused realise . . .", are usually likely to receive the same answer. The distinction is only crucial where the accused fails to realise the risk of bodily harm, e.g. because he is simple-minded; of course in such a case he may well, like the accused in *Lamb*, lack the necessary *mens rea* for the unlawful act and thus still escape liability.

The special case of self-induced intoxication

30 *Lipman*[2] shows that where the accused commits an unlawful act which causes death it is irrelevant to his liability for manslaughter that, through self-induced intoxication, he lacked the *mens rea* for that unlawful act. Lipman and a girl had taken the

---

1. *Hosken*, [1974] Crim. L. R. 48; *Boswell*, [1973] Crim. L. R. 307. The House of Lords have given leave to appeal on the following point certified by the Court of Appeal: "Can a defendant be properly convicted of manslaughter, when his mind is not affected by drink or drugs, if he did not foresee that his act might cause harm to another?" *Director of Public Prosecutions* v. *Newbury* (1975), *Times*, 28th November.
2. [1970] 1 Q.B. 152; [1969] 3 All E.R. 410; *C. & J. Cases.*

drug lysergic acid diethylamide (L.S.D.) together in her room, and Lipman alleged that, while under the influence of the drug, he had the illusion of descending to the centre of the earth and being attacked by snakes. His case was that he must have killed the girl during this experience. She had received two severe blows on the head, but the immediate cause of death was asphyxia due to her having had part of a sheet crammed into her mouth. The Court of Appeal affirmed the conviction for manslaughter and held, following previous authority,[1] that self-induced intoxication is a defence only where the offence requires a specific intent and the intoxication prevents the formation of that intent. It said that manslaughter did not require proof of a specific intent (whatever that phrase may mean), and in particular that the intent required to constitute the unlawful act was not a specific intent. The accused's intoxication was thus no defence. He had committed an unlawful act which was such "as all sober and reasonable people would inevitably recognise must subject the other person to, at least, the risk of some harm resulting therefrom, albeit not serious harm"[2] and was therefore guilty of manslaughter.

It must be emphasised that the decision in *Lipman*, that the accused can be convicted of manslaughter even though he lacked the *mens rea* for the unlawful and fatal act, is limited to cases where the accused was voluntarily intoxicated at the material time. Proof of the *mens rea* for the unlawful act is still required in other cases. This was acknowledged by Wien, J., in *Howell*.[3] This special rule is clearly based on policy, viz., that one who voluntarily takes drink or drugs and thereafter kills another should, at the very least, be convicted of manslaughter whatever his mental state may have been, for he had no business to get intoxicated and subject others to the possible risk of violence.[4]

Manslaughter by criminal negligence

8.31 Manslaughter is committed if death is caused by the criminally negligent performance of an act, even though that act is lawful.[5] Similarly where there is a duty of care recognised by the criminal law,[6] a person is guilty of manslaughter if he fails to perform it and his failure is due to criminal negligence. In *Bonnyman*,[7]

1. For a discussion of the relevance generally of intoxication to liability, see paras. 5.24–5.36.
2. *Church*, [1966] 1 Q.B. 59; [1965] 2 All E.R. 71; *C. & J. Cases*.
3. [1974] 2 All E.R. 806.
4. Para. 5.34.
5. *Andrews* v. *Director of Public Prosecutions*, [1937] A.C. 576, at p. 583.
6. Para. 8.4.
7. (1942), 28 Cr. App. Rep. 131.

for instance, where a doctor's wife was held to have died in consequence of his omission to treat her, the case was said to have been rightly left to the jury on the basis that it was one of manslaughter by criminal negligence.

The analysis of the relevant case law is complicated by an ambiguity apparent in some cases where judges have said that the accused is liable only if he acted "recklessly" without defining that term. As we have seen,[1] "recklessness" has two senses. Recklessness in its subjective sense covers cases where the accused himself foresees the risk (but not the probability) of death and cases in which he foresees the risk of bodily harm (but not the probability of really serious bodily harm), and nonetheless takes either of these risks without justification. In the instances excepted in brackets, the accused would be guilty of murder. While there is some authority[2] indicating that manslaughter by criminal negligence is limited to recknlessness in its subjective sense, most of the cases concerning manslaughter by criminal negligence have concerned recklessness in its objective sense.

Recklessness in its objective sense is normally known as gross inadvertent negligence and in the context of manslaughter connotes a failure to comply with a low standard of care in relation to a reasonably foreseeable risk of death (or possibly grievous bodily harm)[3] to another which the accused does not foresee, although he would have done so if he had been moderately careful. A substantial number of cases show that gross negligence suffices for liability for manslaughter. In *Pittwood*,[4] for instance, the accused, a level crossing keeper, forgot to close the gates after opening them to let a cart pass through, and went off to lunch. Ten minutes later, a person using the crossing in another cart was struck by a train and killed. It was held that he could be convicted of manslaughter, the case being one of "gross and criminal negligence". *Finney*[5] is to similar effect. The accused, an attendant at a lunatic asylum, had been bathing the deceased inmate. He had emptied the bath and told the deceased, who was capable of understanding him, to get out of it. The accused's attention was momentarily diverted and he turned on the hot tap, mistaking it for the other. The deceased was still in the bath and was scalded to death. Lush, J., directed the jury that they could convict the accused if they thought that there had been

1. Para. 3.21.
2. *Nicholls* (1874), 13 Cox C.C. 75.
3. Williams, *Criminal Law: The General Part*, 2nd ed., p. 111.
4. (1902), 19 T.L.R. 37.
5. (1874), 12 Cox C.C. 625; *C. & J. Cases*.

inadvertence amounting to culpability. While these and other cases demonstrate that killing by gross negligence constitutes manslaughter, it would of course be no defence that the accused was reckless in its subjective sense.

8.32 Not every slip makes a man criminally negligent. The leading authority is *Bateman*[1] which shows that the accused must have been guilty of a much higher degree of negligence than that which will suffice to establish liability in tort. Lord Hewart, C.J., said:

> "In explaining to juries the test which they should apply to determine whether the negligence, in the particular case, amounted to or did not amount to a crime, judges have used many epithets, such as 'culpable', 'criminal', 'gross', 'wicked', 'clear', 'complete'. But whatever epithet he used and whether an epithet be used or not, in order to establish criminal liability the facts must be such that, in the opinion of the jury, the negligence of the accused went beyond a mere matter of compensation between subjects, and showed such a disregard for the life and safety of others as to amount to a crime against the State, and conduct deserving punishment".[2]

In *Andrews* v. *Director of Public Prosecutions*,[3] Lord Atkin said that, while these words were not, and were not intended to be, a precise definition of the crime, he thought that their substance was valuable and correct.

In the case from which the above quotation is taken a doctor's conviction for manslaughter was quashed because of the trial judge's failure to emphasise the difference between civil and criminal negligence. In *Dant*,[4] the accused was held guilty of criminal negligence in leaving a dangerous horse to graze on a common. It caused the death of a child for which he was convicted of manslaughter. Similarly one who handles a gun with gross negligence and thus causes another's death is guilty of this offence.[5] A further instance is afforded by the example of a workman throwing timber into a street which he ought to have known was crowded after no more precautions than shouting a warning.[6]

8.33 In determining whether he was guilty of criminal negligence,

---

1. (1925), 94 L.J.K.B. 791; *C. & J. Cases.*
2. *Ibid.*, *per* Lord Hewart, C.J., at p. 793.
3. [1937] A.C. 576, at p. 583; *C. & J. Cases.*
4. (1865), Le. & Ca. 567.
5. *Jones* (1874), 12 Cox C.C. 628; *C. & J. Cases.*
6. Para. 8.15a.

the jury may have to consider the state of the accused's knowledge at the material time. If A points a loaded gun at B with B's consent, thinking that it is safe for him to do so because the bullet is not in the chamber opposite the firing-pin, and B is accidentally killed, A can only be convicted of manslaughter on the basis of gross negligence if his belief was formed on grossly unreasonable grounds;[1] on the other hand, his conduct would almost certainly be held to be negligent had he known that the bullet was in the chamber opposite the firing-pin because he ought to have realised the danger that the trigger might be pressed accidentally. A similar allowance may have to be made for the limited capacities of the accused. If someone with no medical qualifications undertakes an operation in an emergency, it is obvious that a far lower standard will be demanded of him than of a fully qualified medical man but, even if he complies with the low standard demanded, he may yet be convicted of manslaughter by criminal negligence if, in the circumstances, it was grossly unreasonable of him to undertake the operation.

Conclusions on involuntary manslaughter

34 Similar problems are raised by each of the two types of involuntary manslaughter. Why should someone be liable to a maximum punishment of life imprisonment if he causes death by a common assault for which he could not receive more than a year's imprisonment if he had not caused death? Why should someone who causes death by gross negligence be liable to be convicted of manslaughter whereas, had he merely caused bodily harm, he would not have been guilty of any offence against the person and probably of no offence at all? No doubt these matters will be considered by the Criminal Law Revision Committee during their current examination of the law relating to offences against the person.

Infanticide[2]

35 Section 1 of the Infanticide Act 1938 provides that where a woman by any wilful act or omission causes the death of her child, being a child under the age of 12 months, in circumstances which *prima facie* amount to murder, but at the time of such act or omission the balance of her mind was disturbed by reason of her not having fully recovered from the effects of giving birth

---

1. *Lamb*, [1967] 2 Q.B. 981; [1967] 2 All E.R. 1282; *C. & J. Cases.*
2. Professor Seaborne Davies, *Modern Approach to Criminal Law*, pp. 301–343.

to the child, or by reason of the effect of lactation consequent upon the birth of the child, she is guilty of infanticide, an offence punishable in the same way as manslaughter. Where a woman is tried for the murder of a child under the age of 12 months, it is open to the jury to return a verdict of not guilty of murder but guilty of infanticide.[1]

The Infanticide Act 1938 thus enables a woman to plead as a defence to a charge of murder mental disturbance of such a nature as would not amount to insanity under the rule in *M'Naghten's Case*,[2] although it would now amount to diminished responsibility. Legally, infanticide is strictly limited to the conditions laid down in the Act, and the fact that the deceased child was less than 12 months old is not sufficient unless there is also evidence that the balance of the mother's mind was disturbed for one of the stated reasons.[3] Although the mother who raises infanticide as a defence on a murder charge must adduce evidence sufficient to raise the defence, the burden of disproving it rests on the Crown; infanticide differs from the defences of insanity and diminished responsibility where the burden of proving the defence is on the accused.[4] The Butler Committee on Mentally Abnormal Offenders[5] has recommended that the provisions concerning infanticide should be repealed since their purpose is now sufficiently covered by the defence of diminished responsibility. No practical difference would result from this proposal if the Committee's proposals concerning diminished responsibility[6] were implemented.

This offence has no application to unborn children, but only to those who attain an existence independent of the mother. It was originally created by the Infanticide Act 1922 in order to obviate the necessity of the judges sentencing the woman to death for the murder of her child when it was virtually certain that she would be reprieved by the Home Secretary. There were 13 convictions for infanticide in 1974.[7]

---

1. Infanticide Act 1938, s. 1.
2. Paras. 5.4–5.16.
3. *Soanes*, [1948] 1 All E.R. 289.
4. Para. 4.5.
5. Cmnd. 6244, paras. 19.22–19.27.
6. *Ibid.*, paras. 19.1–19.21.
7. *Criminal Statistics*, 1974, Cmnd. 6168.

Abortion and child destruction[1]

Abortion

36 Section 58 of the Offences against the Person Act 1861 provides the offence of attempting to procure a miscarriage, which is popularly known as abortion. The offence is punishable with a maximum of imprisonment for life and is committed in two cases:

a. Where a pregnant woman, with intent to procure her own miscarriage, unlawfully administers to herself any poison or noxious thing or unlawfully uses any instrument or other means; or
b. Where any other person, with the intent to procure the miscarriage of any woman, whether she is pregnant or not, unlawfully administers to her or causes to be taken by her any poison or noxious thing or unlawfully uses any instrument or other means.

In neither case is a miscarriage required to result from the accused's conduct. However, there are these distinctions between the woman who tries to procure her own miscarriage and any other persons who try to procure another's miscarriage:

a. A woman who administers poison etc. to herself can only be guilty if she is in fact pregnant; if she merely believes herself to be pregnant, but is not, she is not guilty under s. 58. If another person administers etc., it is irrelevant that the woman concerned was not in fact pregnant provided that the intent to procure a miscarriage can be proved.
b. A person other than the woman herself can commit the offence by causing to be taken by the woman any poison or noxious thing. This will occur where the woman administers the substance in question to herself on the directions of the accused (whether or not he is present at the time of administration).[2]

Section 58 is concerned with the unlawful administration of poison or a noxious thing or the use of an instrument or any other means with intent to procure a miscarriage. "Poison" means a recognised poison.[3] "Noxious thing" has been defined as something other than a recognised poison which is harmful in the dosage in which it was administered.[4] "Any other means"

1. See Glanville Williams, *The Sanctity of Life and the Criminal Law*, Ch. 6.
2. *Wilson* (1865), Dears. & B. 127.
3. *Cramp* (1880), 5 Q.B.D. 307.
4. *Cramp*; *Marlow* (1965), 49 Cr. App. Rep. 49.

is obviously a wide term, covering digital interference with a foetus among other things.[1] It is irrelevant, provided one of these things is administered or used, that unknown to the accused it was incapable of procuring a miscarriage.[2]

8.37 The word "unlawfully" in s. 58 must now be construed solely[3] in the light of the Abortion Act 1967. Under that Act an offence is not committed if a pregnancy is terminated by a registered medical practitioner provided that two such practitioners are of opinion formed in good faith that:

a. the continuance of the pregnancy would involve risk to the mother's life, or of injury to her physical or mental health or that of any existing children of her family, greater than if the pregnancy were terminated (a question in the determination of which account may be taken of the mother's actual or reasonably foreseeable environment); or
b. there is a substantial risk that if the child were born it would suffer from such physical or mental abnormalities as to be seriously handicapped.[4]

Whether the necessary opinions were formed in good faith is a question for the jury and the medical evidence although important is not conclusive.[5]

The abortion is lawful only if it is carried out in a National Health Service Hospital or other place approved by the Secretary of State for Social Services or the Home Secretary.[6] This limitation and the requirement for the opinion of two medical practitioners do not apply in an emergency where a medical practitioner performs an abortion, having formed the opinion in good faith that this is immediately necessary to save the mother's life or to prevent grave permanent injury to her physical or mental health.[7]

The Act refers to the termination of pregnancy but presumably, provided the various conditions are satisfied, it also applies where the thing administered or used to abort fails to procure a miscarriage or for some reason the operation is not completed.

Section 4 makes provision for conscientious objection, but s. 4 (2) provides that nothing shall affect any duty to participate in

---

1. *Spicer* (1955), 39 Cr. App. Rep. 189.
2. *Spicer*; *Marlow*.
3. Abortion Act 1967, s. 5 (2).
4. *Ibid.*, s. 1 (1) and (2).
5. *Smith*, [1974] 1 All E.R. 376.
6. Abortion Act 1967, s. 1 (3).
7. *Ibid*, s. 1 (4).

treatment which is necessary to save the life or to prevent grave permanent injury to the physical or mental health of a pregnant woman.

As was expected, the morality of the principles embodied in the Abortion Act remains controversial. The Act has also been criticised for fostering "inequality of opportunity" among women who wish to obtain an abortion. This may result from two main factors: the strain on the National Health Service in a particular area and a more or less restrictive view of the statutory criteria taken by doctors from place to place. The majority of women who are aborted are operated on in approved nursing homes or abortion clinics but this is not possible for poorer women. It is claimed that the Act has made a real contribution to the reduction of illegal and dangerous abortions by back-street abortionists. In recent years the number of operations performed under the Abortion Act has exceeded 100,000 annually. The working of the Act was reviewed recently by a departmental committee and found to be generally satisfactory.[1]

Child destruction

.38 Section I of the Infant Life (Preservation) Act 1929 provides that any person who, with intent to destroy the life of a child capable of being born alive, by any wilful act causes a child to die before it has an existence independent of its mother, is guilty of child destruction, also punishable with a maximum of imprisonment for life.

The Abortion Act 1967 does not apply to child destruction, but s. 1 of the 1929 Act contains a proviso that the prosecution must prove that the act which caused the death of the child was not done in good faith for the purpose only of preserving the life of the mother, which has been construed as including preserving the mother's physical or mental health.[2]

This offence was not originally intended to prevent late abortions but was introduced to fill in the gap between abortion and homicide by providing for the conviction of a person who destroys a child in the process of birth in circumstances where it could not be proved that the child had had an existence independent of the mother so as to be in law the object of murder.[3] However, as a result of the language used it became, and still is, unlawful for the termination of a pregnancy to be carried

1. Report of the (Lane) Committee on the Working of the Abortion Act, Cmnd. 5579.
2. *Bourne*, [1939] 1 K.B. 687; [1938] 3 All E.R. 615; *Newton and Stungo*, [1958] Crim. L. R. 469.
3. Para. 8.3.

out by a method which destroys a foetus capable of being born alive, even if its chances of survival are slight or non-existent.

The present offence can be distinguished from that under s. 58 of the Offences against the Person Act 1861 since it requires the actual destruction of the child while the latter offence is constituted by the act which attempts to procure a miscarriage. Another distinction is that child destruction can be committed only in respect of a child capable of being born alive. "Capable of being born alive" means capable of being born alive if delivered at the time when the act was done.[1] The fact that the pregnancy has lasted for 28 weeks is *prima facie* evidence that the child was capable of being born alive within the definition of child destruction.

8.39 In spite of these distinctions, there is an obvious overlap between child destruction and abortion. A successful abortion can be charged as child destruction if it can be proved that the child was capable of being born alive, and, except when the destruction occurs while the child is being born, all child destruction can be charged as abortion. In theory this overlap is unfortunate because the exemption from liability is much narrower in the case of child destruction and it is possible that a person could be convicted on a charge of child destruction although he would not under the Abortion Act 1967 have committed the offence of abortion. This injustice does not occur in practice for several reasons. First, the great majority of therapeutic abortions are performed in the early stages of pregnancy, at a time when the child is not capable of being born alive, in order to avoid or minimise the risk of the operation and the revulsion and distress (which are proportionately greater the later the operation) caused to the woman and the medical and nursing staff. Only in cases of great and sudden urgency is an abortion carried out after the twenty-fourth week of pregnancy. Secondly, in practice, abortion is charged when the pregnancy has not lasted for 28 weeks, and child destruction thereafter.

Upon an indictment for an offence against s. 58 of the Offences against the Person Act, the jury may bring in a verdict of child destruction and vice versa.[2] In 1974, there were 11 convictions for illegal abortion and none for child destruction.[3]

---

1. Williams, *The Sanctity of Life and the Criminal Law*, p. 25.
2. Infant Life (Preservation) Act 1929, s. 2 (2) and s. 2 (3).
3. *Criminal Statistics*, 1974, Cmnd. 6168.

Concealment of birth

8.40 Section 60 of the Offences against the Person Act 1861 provides that if any woman is delivered of a child, every person who, by any secret disposition of the dead body of that child, endeavours to conceal its birth is guilty of an offence punishable with a maximum of two years' imprisonment. It is irrelevant whether the child died before, at, or after its birth. A woman who cannot be convicted of homicide or child destruction, as the case may be, because an element of the offence (e.g. live birth in homicide) cannot be proved, may be convicted of this offence.

A stillborn child must have reached a sufficient state of maturity at the time of birth that, but for some accidental circumstances, it might have been born alive. The disposition of a foetus which is only a few months old is not an offence.[1]

Concealment means from the world at large, but this is not prevented by the fact that some of the woman's friends or confidants know of the birth. No offence is committed if she merely conceals the birth from a particular person, e.g. her father.[2] For the sake of completeness it should be mentioned that it is a common law offence to dispose of a corpse so as to prevent a coroner from holding an inquest when one ought to be held[3] and it is similarly an offence to prevent, without lawful excuse, the lawful and decent burial of a corpse.[4]

---

1. *Berriman* (1854), 6 Cox C.C. 388; *Hewitt and Smith* (1866), 4 F. & F. 1101. Contrast *Colmer* (1864), 9 Cox C.C. 506.
2. *Morris* (1848), 2 Cox C.C. 489.
3. *Price* (1884), 12 Q.B.D. 247.
4. *Hunter*, [1974] Q.B. 95; [1973] 3 All E.R. 286.

9

SEXUAL OFFENCES

9.1 While most sexual offences are protective in purpose, some raise the question of the extent to which the criminal law should enforce social morality.[1] Rape and buggery are common law offences but the other sexual offences are statutory, the principal statute now being the Sexual Offences Act 1956. Unless otherwise stated the maximum punishment for the offences mentioned in this chapter is provided by s. 37 of, and the Second Schedule to, that Act.

The definition of many of the offences refers to "sexual intercourse" which is defined as follows:

> "Where, on the trial of any offence under this Act, it is necessary to prove sexual intercourse (whether natural or unnatural), it shall not be necessary to prove completion of the intercourse by the emission of seed, but the intercourse shall be deemed complete upon proof of penetration only."[2]

Penetration is the entry of the penis into the vagina or the anus and the slightest degree is enough and where the intercourse is *per vaginam* the hymen need not be broken.[3] Boys under the age of 14 are irrebuttably presumed to be incapable of sexual intercourse and therefore cannot be convicted, as perpetrators, of any offence involving intercourse, although they may be convicted of indecent assault instead;[4] a boy under 14 may be convicted of aiding and abetting another of 14 or over.[5]

Many sexual offences can only be committed, as perpetrators, by males but even in the other offences the offenders are predominantly male.[6]

Rape

9.2 The offence of rape consists of a man having sexual intercourse *per vaginam* without the woman's consent with knowledge that she does not consent or reckless as to whether or not she consents[7] and is punishable with life imprisonment. The absence of

1. Paras. 2.15 to 2.23.
2. Sexual Offences Act 1956, s. 44.
3. *Hughes* (1841), 9 Car. & P. 752; *Lines*, (1844) 1 Car. & Kir. 393.
4. Para. 5.2.
5. Para. 19.2.
6. Walker, *Crime and Punishment in Britain*, 2nd ed., p. 22.
7. *Director of Public Prosecutions* v. *Morgan*, [1975] 2 All E.R. 347. The Report of the Advisory Group on the Law of Rape Cmnd. 6532 does not propose any change in matters dealt with in this book.

the woman's consent is an essential feature of the *actus reus* of rape. Thus, it is rape to have intercourse with a woman who is asleep[1] or otherwise unconscious[2] and therefore unable to give or withold consent. Moreover, an apparent consent is not a real consent, and rape is committed in the following cases:

a. Where submission is procured by threats of personal violence.[3]
b. Where the consent is obtained by fraud as to the nature of the act. Thus in *Williams*[4] a conviction for rape was upheld where a singing master had had sexual intercourse with a girl pupil by pretending that it was a method of training her voice. The girl made no resistance, as she believed him and did not know he was having sexual intercourse with her.
c. Where the consent is obtained by impersonating the woman's husband.[5]
d. Where the female is so mentally deficient[6] or young[7] or drunk[8] that her knowledge and understanding are such that she is not in a position to decide whether to consent or resist.

A wife is always presumed to consent to intercourse with her husband as long as they are not separated by an order of the court or a separation agreement,[9] or a decree *nisi* of divorce or nullity (in the case of a voidable marriage) has not been granted.[10]

If the accused mistakenly believes that the woman has consented his mistake is a defence even if it is not based on reasonable grounds.[11]

On an indictment for rape it is open to the jury, if rape is not proved, to bring in a verdict of attempted rape, or of an offence contrary to ss. 2, 3 or 4 of the Sexual Offences Act 1956, or of indecent assault.[12] The offence under s.4 is that of administering drugs to obtain or facilitate unlawful intercourse; the other offences are discussed later.[13]

---

1. *Mayers* (1872), 12 Cox C.C. 311.
2. *Camplin* (1845), 1 Den. 89; *Lang.* [1976] Crim. L.R. 65.
3. *Jones* (1861), 4 L.T. 154.
4. [1923] 1 K.B. 340.
5. Sexual Offences Act 1956, s. 1 (2).
6. *Barratt* (1873), L.R. 2 C.C.R. 81.
7. *Howard,* [1965] 3 All E.R. 684.
8. *Lang,* [1976] Crim. L.R. 65.
9. *Clarke,* [1949] 2 All E.R. 448; *Miller,* [1954] 2 Q.B. 282; [1954] 2 All E.R. 529.
10. *O'Brien,* [1974] 3 All E.R. 663.
11. *Director of Public Prosecutions* v. *Morgan,* [1975] 2 All E.R. 347.
12. Sexual Offences Act 1956, Sch. 2, as amended by Criminal Law Act 1967, Sch. 2.
13. Paras. 9.3 and 9.4.

Other offences involving sexual intercourse

9.3 Unless the contrary is stated, these other offences are punishable with two years' imprisonment. Generally, the intercourse is required to be "unlawful" which appears to mean "extra-marital".[1]

a. *Procuring unlawful sexual intercourse.*—The Sexual Offences Act 1956 contains a number of offences of this type, which may be committed by a man or a woman. "Procuring" means "persuading" so if the woman needed no persuading the accused has not committed an offence.[2] Liability for the full offence arises only when the intercourse has taken place: if it does not occur the accused can be charged with an attempt to procure.[3]

   Two examples of offences of procuring are those under ss. 2 and 3 of the Act. These provide, respectively, that it is an offence for a person to procure by threats or intimidation, or to procure by false representations, any woman to have unlawful intercourse (whether with himself[4] or another) in any part of the world. Apart from the element of procuring, these offences are distinguishable from rape in the following ways:

   i. Unlike rape, these offences are indictable even though the intercourse was committed abroad provided the procuring was done within the jurisdiction.
   ii. "Threats or intimidation" probably include threats not relating to physical violence. "False representation" is not limited to fraud which vitiates consent for the purposes of rape[5] but probably any false representation which induces a woman to give a consent which she would not otherwise have given will suffice.

   The rationale of these offences would seem to be to protect women whose consent, although not vitiated for the purposes of rape, is imperfect for one of the stated reasons.

b. *Unlawful sexual intercourse with a mental defective.*—Under s. 7 of the Sexual Offences Act 1956 it is an offence for a man to have unlawful intercourse with a mentally defective woman, her consent being no defence. It is a defence for the man to prove that he did not know, and had no reason to

---

1. *Chapman*, [1959] 1 Q.B. 100; [1958] 3 All E.R. 143.
2. *Christian* (1913), 78 J.P. 112.
3. *Johnston*, [1964] 2 Q.B. 404; [1963] 3 All E.R. 577.
4. *Williams* (1898), 62 J.P. 310.
5. *Williams*, [1923] 1 K.B. 340.

suspect, her to be a defective. Procuring a defective to have intercourse is also an offence, subject to a similar defence.[1] The rationale of these offences is to protect women who, while they understand the nature of the act, are easily open to persuasion and exploitation because of their mental defectiveness.

c. *Unlawful sexual intercourse with girls under 16.*—This is criminal for reasons similar to those just mentioned. Section 6 of the Act of 1956 provides that it is an offence for a man to have unlawful intercourse with a girl under the age of 16. Under s. 5 it is an offence punishable with life imprisonment for a man to have unlawful intercourse with a girl under 13.

Neither the girl's consent nor the accused's mistake concerning her age is a defence to a charge of unlawful intercourse, but there are two statutory defences which may be available to a man charged with unlawful intercourse with a girl who is under the age of 16. First, if a man has gone through a form of marriage with such a girl, it is a defence for him to prove that he believed and had reasonable cause to believe, that the girl was his wife.[2] Secondly, when a man who has not attained his twenty-fourth birthday is charged with this offence for the first time,[3] it is a defence for him to show that he believed and had reasonable cause to believe, that the girl was over the age of 16.[4]

d. *Incest.*—A man who has sexual intercourse with a woman whom he knows to be his granddaughter, daughter, sister or mother is guilty of incest, as is a woman of or above the age of 16 who with consent permits her grandfather, father, brother or son to have sexual intercourse with her.[5] Incest is punishable with seven years' imprisonment (or life if the other party is a girl under 13).

Consent is no defence to a charge of incest brought against a male; if the female did not consent, the man will be guilty of rape. The relationship of the persons having intercourse may be traced through the half-blood as well as through the whole blood and through illegitimate as well as legitimate channels. Apart from the act of intercourse and the fact of relationship, it is essential to prove that the accused had knowledge of the relationship. Incest cannot be committed

1. Sexual Offences Act 1956, s. 9.
2. *Ibid.*, s. 6 (2).
3. *Rider*, [1954] 1 All E.R. 5.
4. Sexual Offences Act 1956, s. 6 (3).
5. *Ibid.*, s. 10 (incest by a man); s. 11 (incest by a woman).

between persons whose relationship is merely that of adoption.

Indecency[1]

9.4 An indecent assault can be committed by a person of either sex. If it is committed against a girl under 13 or a male the maximum punishment is 5 and 10 years' imprisonment respectively, but otherwise it is 2 years.

An indecent assault is an assault or battery[2] accompanied by circumstances of indecency.[3] Thus, merely touching another or making a person apprehend this, without a valid consent on his part and in circumstances of indecency, constitutes an indecent assault. "Accompanied by circumstances of indecency" has not been defined, but it has been held that kissing a girl against her will with a suggestion of sexual activity will suffice.[4] On the other hand where an assault is accompanied by secret indecent purpose it is not accompanied by circumstances of indecency.[5]

Consent is no defence if the assault was of a kind to cause harm calculated to interfere with the victim's health or comfort,[6] nor if it was obtained by fraud concerning the nature of the transaction, as when the accused pretends that he is performing a medical operation.[7] In addition, the Act of 1956 provides that a female mental defective[8] or a person under 16[9] cannot give a valid consent. Thus, intercourse with a boy of 15 or petting a girl of 14 constitutes an indecent assault, even though the boy or girl was willing and encouraged it.[10] The accused's mistaken belief that the other party was over 16 (and thus able to give a valid consent) is no defence, even though it is reasonable.[11] It is illogical that a man under 24 should have a statutory defence based on his reasonable mistake about the girl's age if he is charged with unlawful intercourse, although he has no defence

1. Sexual Offences Act 1956, ss. 14 (indecent assault on a woman) and 15 (on a man).
2. *Rolfe* (1952), 36 Cr. App. Rep. 4.
3. *Leeson* (1968), 52 Cr. App. Rep. 185.
4. *Kilbourne*, [1972] 3 All E.R. 545.
5. *Ibid.*
6. *Donovan*; para. 7.2.a.
7. *Case* (1850), 1 Den. 580.
8. Sexual Offences Act 1956, s. 14 (4).
9. *Ibid.*, ss. 14 (2) and 15 (2).
10. *McCormack*, [1969] 2 Q.B. 442; [1969] 3 All E.R. 371. But see, in the case of the boy, *Mason* (1969), 53 Cr. App. Rep. 12, which would now seem to be wrong in the light of *McCormack*.
11. *Maughan* (1934), 24 Cr. App. Rep. 130.

either at common law or by statute if charged with an indecent assault based on exactly the same fact—the intercourse. However, the other defence available in unlawful intercourse, that the accused reasonably believed the girl was his wife because they have gone through a ceremony of marriage, also applies to indecent assault.[1] Where the other party is a defective woman the accused is only to be treated as guilty of indecent assault by reason of her incapacity to consent if he knew or had reason to suspect her to be a defective.[2]

Indecency with children

5 Since an assault is essential, an invitation to perform indecent acts is not an indecent assault unless accompanied by force or the threat of force.[3] To deal with such conduct in relation to children, the Indecency with Children Act 1960 was passed. It makes it an offence for a person of either sex to commit an act of gross indecency with or towards a child under 14 or to incite such a child to such an act with him or another, e.g. where the accused asks a child to touch his genitalia. The offence is punishable with two years' imprisonment.[4]

Indecent exposure

6 Under s. 4 of the Vagrancy Act 1824 it is an offence for a man wilfully and indecently to expose his penis,[5] whether in public or private, with intent to insult any female. This offence is punishable on summary conviction with three months' imprisonment.[6]

The indecent exposure of any part of the body, whether by a man or a woman, may in certain circumstances constitute the common law offence of outraging public decency. Indecent exposure is sometimes also punishable under local Acts and bylaws.[7]

Abduction

7 The abduction of women and girls is punished by ss. 17–21 of the Sexual Offences Act 1956. The offences specify a "taking"

1. Sexual Offences Act 1956, s. 14 (3).
2. *Ibid.*, s. 7 (2).
3. *Fairclough* v. *Whipp*, [1951] 2 All E.R. 834; *Burrows*, [1951] 1 All E.R. 58, n.
4. Indecency with Children Act 1960, s. 1 (1).
5. *Evans* v. *Ewels*, [1972] 2 All E.R. 22.
6. Vagrancy Act 1832, s. 4.
7. For proposals for reform of the law relating to indecent exposure, see the *Working Paper of the Working Party on Vagrancy and Street Offences* (1974).

but this does not have to be without the consent of the female.[1] If the girl is glad to go there will still be a "taking" if the accused has persuaded her, or assists her, to do so.[2] The first four offences of abduction about to be discussed require a taking out of the possession and against the will of her parent or guardian which means some conduct by the accused amounting to a substantial interference with the possessory relationship of parent and child. Thus, while permanent deprivation is not required, merely taking a girl for a short walk without her parent's permission, even though sexual misconduct occurs during the walk, does not constitute a taking out of parental possession for the purposes of these offences.[3] The offences of abduction are:

a. Taking, without lawful authority or excuse, an unmarried girl under 16 out of the possession of her parent or guardian against his will (s. 20). It is irrelevant that the accused reasonably believed that the girl was 16 or over,[4] but it must be proved that he knew she was in the possession of her parent or guardian.[5]
b. Taking an unmarried girl under 18 out of the possession of her parent or guardian against his will with intent that she shall have unlawful (i.e. extra-marital[6]) intercourse with men or a particular man (s. 19). As in the first offence the accused must know that the girl is in the possession of her parent or guardian but, although knowledge of the girl's age is not necessary, it is a defence for him to prove that he believed on reasonable grounds that the girl was 18 or over.[7]
c. Taking a woman who is a defective out of the possession of her parent or guardian against his will with intent that she shall have unlawful intercourse with men or a particular man (s. 21). Although the accused must know that the woman is in the possession of a parent or guardian he need not know that she is a defective; however, he has a defence if he proves that he neither knew nor had reason to suspect this.[8]

These three offences of abduction are punishable with two years' imprisonment.

1. *Mankletow* (1853), Dears. C.C. 159.
2. *Robins* (1844), 1 Car. & Kir. 456; *Jarvis* (1903), 20 Cox C.C. 249.
3. *Jones*, [1973] Crim. L.R. 621.
4. *Prince* (1875), L.R. 2 C.C.R. 154.
5. *Hibbert* (1869), L.R. 1 C.C.R. 184.
6. *Chapman*, [1959] 1 Q.B. 100; [1958] 3 All E.R. 143; *Jones*, [1973] Crim. L. R. 710.
7. Sexual Offences Act 1956, s. 19 (2).
8. *Ibid.*, s. 21 (2).

d. Taking or detaining a girl under 21 out of the possession of her parent or guardian against his will, if she has property or expectation of property and is so taken or detained by fraud and with intent that she shall marry or have unlawful intercourse with the accused or another (s. 18). The accused must know that the girl is in the possession of a parent or guardian but a belief that she is 21 or over, however reasonable, is no defence.[1]
e. Taking or detaining a woman of any age against her will with intent that she shall marry or have unlawful intercourse with the accused or another, if she is so taken or detained either by force or for the sake of her property or expectation of property (s. 17).

The offences under ss. 17 and 18 are punishable with 14 years' imprisonment.

Buggery

.8 The Sexual Offences Act 1956, s. 12, provides that it is an offence for a person to commit buggery with another person or an animal. Buggery is defined by the common law and consists of sexual intercourse between a man and a woman or another man *per anum* or between a man or woman and an animal *per anum* or *per vaginam*.[2] Unless one party is not a consenting party, both parties are criminally liable as perpetrators. Where the buggery is between two men the offence has been qualified by the Sexual Offences Act 1967 which was passed in consequence of the recommendations of the Wolfenden Committee.[3] Section 1 of that Act provides that it is not an offence for a man to commit buggery with another man if three conditions are satisfied:

a. The act must be done in private. Section 1 (2) states that an act is not done "in private" if more than two persons are present, or if it is done in a lavatory to which the public have access. Apart from this, the question of privacy is one of fact and the jury must answer it by considering all the surrounding circumstances, such as the time, the nature of the place and the likelihood of third parties coming upon the scene.[4]
b. Both parties must consent. A person suffering from severe mental subnormality is incapable of consenting, but the

1. *Prince* (1875), L.R. 2 C.C.R. 154.
2. Hale, 1, P.C., 669; Hawk, 1 P.C., c.4; East, 1 P.C. 480.
3. Cmnd. 247; see para. 2.19.
4. *Reakes*, [1974] Crim. L.R. 615.

absence of knowledge or reason to suspect that the other party was suffering from severe subnormality is a defence.

c. Both parties must have attained the age of 21. On its wording, and as long as *Prince*[1] stands, the Act's probable construction will be that a reasonable but mistaken belief that the other party is over 21 is no defence.

The prosecution has the burden of proving that one of the three factors did not exist. The provisions of s. 1 do not apply where the act takes place on a United Kingdom merchant ship between two members of the crew of such a ship or ships. Where a party to buggery is under 21, neither party may be prosecuted without the consent of the Director of Public Prosecutions.[2] It is an offence punishable with two years' imprisonment to procure[3] another to commit with a third person an act of buggery which is not an offence under the above provisions.[4]

Section 3 of the 1967 Act contains elaborate provisions with regard to the punishment of buggery which may in some cases be punished with imprisonment for life in those cases where it continues to be an offence.

Gross indecency

9.9 Section 13 of the Sexual Offences Act 1956 provides that it is an offence for a man:

a. to commit an act of gross indecency with another man; or
b. to be a party to the commission of an act of gross indecency with another man; or
c. to procure[5] the commission by a man of an act of gross indecency with another man (who may be the procurer).

By way of comparison it should be noted that lesbian conduct between women is not an offence unless one of them is under 16, in which case an indecent assault is committed.

The meaning of "gross indecency" is not clear but the phrase clearly covers conduct such as mutual masturbation. As in buggery the consent of the other party is no defence. If both parties consent they are each liable as perpetrators. Gross indecency falling within categories a. and b. above is not an offence if the three conditions mentioned in the Sexual Offences Act 1967 are satisfied. Moreover, if these three conditions are satisfied the

---

1. (1875), L.R. 2 C.C.R. 154. See para. 6.1.
2. Sexual Offences Act 1967, s. 8.
3. Para. 9.3.a.
4. Sexual Offences Act 1967, s. 4. (1).
5. Para. 9.3.a.

offence of procuring described in category c. is not committed if the indecency procured is with the procurer.[1]

The 1967 Act provides that the maximum punishment for gross indecency is normally two years' imprisonment, but if it took place between a man of or over 21 and a man under that age, the former is liable to five years'.[2]

Statistics

0 It is impossible to estimate how many sexual offences are committed or who commits them. The reason is that many sexual offences, especially homosexual offences, incest and unlawful sexual intercourse with girls, are unreported since both parties are often willing participants; alternatively offences such as rape or indecent assault may not be reported for fear of the embarrassment which a prosecution might cause to the victim. In addition many of the reported offences are not traced to the offender.

The number of the more common indictable sexual offences reported to the police in 1974 was:[3]

Rape	1,052
Indecent assault on females	12,417
Intercourse with girl under 16	5,050
Incest	337
Buggery	587
Indecency between men	1,769

Bigamy

1 The effect of s. 57 of the Offences against the Person Act 1861 is that whoever, being married, goes through a ceremony of marriage with any other person during the life of his or her spouse (wherever, in the case of a British subject who is a citizen of the United Kingdom and Colonies, the second ceremony takes place) is guilty of bigamy, subject to the statutory and other defences which are discussed below. Bigamy is punishable by a maximum of seven years' imprisonment.

The essential ingredients of bigamy are the existence of a valid marriage, its subsistence at the time of the second ceremony, and the second ceremony. If the first marriage was invalid and one of the parties goes through a second ceremony with a third person, no offence is committed, assuming that no false declaration was made in connection with the second ceremony.

1. Sexual Offences Act 1956, s. 4 (3).
2. *Ibid.*, s. 3.
3. *Criminal Statistics*, 1974, Cmnd. 6168.

The first marriage

9.12 The prosecution must prove that the accused went through a valid marriage ceremony with the first spouse. In the case of ceremonies celebrated in England, this is usually done by production of the marriage certificate and calling someone who was present at the ceremony to identify the parties. The accused's spouse is competent but not compellable to do so.

Once the parties are proved to have gone through a ceremony of marriage, there is a rebuttable presumption of law that it is valid, but if the defence can raise a doubt as to its validity, the accused is entitled to the benefit of that doubt.[1] In *Morrison*,[2] A married Mrs A in 1919 and in 1928 deserted her. She did not hear any news of him for 10 years. In 1939 she married B and, shortly afterwards, B went through a form of marriage with Miss C. B was charged with bigamy. It was necessary for the prosecution to prove that B was already married, which was done by proving the ceremony which he went through with Mrs A. B objected that it was the duty of the prosecution to prove not only the ceremony but also the validity of that marriage and that they could only do that by proving that A was dead. It was held that the prosecution need not prove that A was dead provided that *prima facie* B's marriage to Mrs A was valid but that it was open to the defence to call evidence tending to show that A was alive and that it was for the jury to decide on that evidence whether the validity of B's marriage to Mrs A was proved or whether there was a doubt. The jury convicted of bigamy.

A polygamous or potentially polygamous marriage is not a valid first marriage for the purposes of the offence of bigamy. However, a potentially polygamous marriage will become monogamous if the party entitled to marry again loses his entitlement, e.g. because he becomes domiciled in a country which only permits monogamy or because an amendment to the law of his country of domicile forbids polygamy, in which case the marriage will become a first marriage for the purposes of bigamy.[3]

The subsistence of the first marriage

9.13 The continuance of the first marriage is proved by evidence that the accused's spouse was alive at the time of the second cere-

---

1. *Willshire* (1881), 6 Q.B.D. 366.
2. [1938] 3 All E.R. 787; *C. & J. Cases*; cf. *Tweney* v. *Tweney*, [1946] P. 180; [1946] 1 All E.R. 564.
3. *Sagoo*, [1975] 2 All E.R. 926.

mony. Evidence that he or she was alive and well at an earlier date which is not too remote may suffice when no better evidence is available.

The second ceremony

14 If the celebration of a second ceremony "known to and recognised by the law" as being capable of producing a valid marriage is proved, it does not matter that the second ceremony would have been invalid for reasons other than that one of the parties was already married. Thus, if A, being married, goes through a form of marriage with a person within the prohibited degrees of relationship, he is guilty of bigamy, although that marriage would have been null and void in any case.[1] This would also be the case if the form of marriage through which the accused goes on the second occasion would have been invalid because he had not complied with the residential requirements of the law of the place of celebration.[2] It would be different if the second ceremony was celebrated by a layman without a licence in a private house because the ceremony could hardly be said to have been "known and recognised by the law" as capable apart from its bigamous nature of producing a valid marriage.

Defences

15 Apart from the adduction of evidence casting doubt on any of the above matters there are several defences open to a person charged with bigamy:

a. If a person who "marries" a second time can call evidence to show that his, or her, spouse has been continuously absent from him or her for seven years and has not been known by him or her to be living during that time, there is a complete defence.[3] But such absence for seven years merely provides a defence to a charge of bigamy and does not dissolve the first marriage so that, if the first spouse is alive, the second "marriage" is a complete nullity.
b. It is a defence that the accused believed on reasonable grounds that his or her spouse was dead, although there has not been absence for seven years,[4] or that the first marriage was void,[5] or that the first marriage had been dissolved.[6]

---

1. *Allen* (1872), L.R. 1 C.C.R. 367; *C. & J. Cases*.
2. *Robinson*, [1938] 1 All E.R. 301.
3. Offences against the Person Act 1861, s. 57 proviso.
4. *Tolson* (1889), 23 Q.B.D. 168; *C. & J. Cases*.
5. *King*, [1964] 1 Q.B. 285; [1963] 3 All E.R. 561; *C. & J. Cases*.
6. *Gould (No. 2)*, [1968] 2 Q.B. 65; [1968] 1 All E.R. 849; *C. & J. Cases*.

c. It is a good defence that the first marriage has been annulled by a court of competent jurisdiction or that, at the time the second marriage took place, the first had been dissolved.[1]

d. If the accused is not a British subject who is also a citizen of the United Kingdom and Colonies, of which the onus of proof rests on him,[2] he has a defence if the second ceremony took place abroad. Section 57 of the Offences against the Person Act 1861 expressly provides that the definition of bigamy shall not extend to persons who are not British subjects in cases where the second ceremony was celebrated abroad. It seems that, by virtue of s. 3 of the British Nationality Act 1948, British subjects who are not also citizens of the United Kingdom and Colonies but are, for instance, citizens of Australia, are likewise exempt from the English law of bigamy if the ceremony in respect of which they are charged took place abroad.

Bigamy is sometimes committed as a cloak for seduction or the obtaining of property and when this is so the propriety of severe punishment is not disputed. When this is not so the justification for punishing bigamy is that it endangers the sanctity of marriage by profaning the ceremony. Some people consider that the offence should not be heavily punishable, or even punishable at all when considered in this light[3] and in practice sentences are often very lenient.

Related offences

9.16 Under s. 3 of the Perjury Act 1911 it is an offence punishable with imprisonment for seven years wilfully to make false statements in order to procure a marriage or a certificate of marriage.

Various penalties are imposed by the Marriage Act 1949 on those who knowingly officiate at irregular marriage ceremonies.

1. Offences against the Person Act 1861, s. 57 proviso.
2. *Audley*, [1907] 1 K.B. 383.
3. 61 L.Q.R. 76.

10

OFFENCES AGAINST PROPERTY 1 THEFT

The elements

).1 A person is guilty of theft, an offence punishable with imprisonment for 10 years,[1] if he dishonestly appropriates property belonging to another with the intention of permanently depriving the other of it.[2]

For convenience in this chapter and the next we shall refer to the Theft Act 1968 as "the Act". Before the Act came into force on January 1, 1969, the law relating to offences involving dishonesty was extremely complicated, but it is fortunately unnecessary to say anything about it because the Act, which is based on the Eighth Report of the Criminal Law Revision Committee,[3] is an entirely new code and replaces all the previous common law and all previous statutes governing the subject.[4] The *actus reus* of theft is the appropriation of property belonging to another. The *mens rea* is dishonesty coupled with the further intention of permanently depriving the other of his property but before we discuss these matters it will be convenient to say something about ownership and possession, and to give illustrations of typical situations in which theft may be committed. Section 5 (1) of the Act provides that property belongs to any person having possession or control of it or having any proprietary right or interest in it, so that refined analyses of the concept of ownership and its transfer are largely irrelevant.

Ownership and possession

.2 Ownership of land, goods or money is the ultimate right to control. It lasts longer than any other right to control, but ownership or possession do not necessarily entail control. A's

---

1. Theft Act 1968, s. 7.
2. *Ibid.*, s. 1.
3. 8th Report of the Criminal Law Revision Committee 1966, Cmnd. 2977; Griew, *The Theft Act 1968*, 2nd ed.; Smith, *The Law of Theft*, 2nd ed.
4. Theft Act 1968, s. 32.

land may be leased to B for a thousand years, C may have hired his car to D for a day, and E's tenpenny piece may have been stolen by F who placed it in his pocket. A, C and E are still the owners of their land, goods and money respectively, although B, D and F have possession. Even if E's tenpenny piece were mixed with F's other money, E would remain its owner although he would probably not be able to identify it but F could make someone who gave value and received the tenpenny piece in good faith its owner. This is because money is negotiable; a thief can give a better title to it than he has got. Goods are not negotiable; hence, if G steals H's watch and sells it to J who acts in good faith, H remains the owner of the watch and can sue J for its return.

Possession is essentially physical control. A person who is not the owner of goods may have the right to possess them although he has not got actual possession of them. If A hires his car to B for a month and C steals it a day later, A is still the owner of the car, B has the right to possess it as against both A and C, while C has actual possession of it. Possession may mean something more than mere physical control; for example, a guest has not got possession of the cutlery with which he eats the meal provided by his host. Possession may also mean less than physical control; for example, a man possesses that which is in his house when he is at his office. When no one has physical control, or when physical control is disputed, the person with the right to possession is usually also said to have possession. If someone drops his wallet in the street, he continues to possess it until someone else assumes control.

10.3 In spite of the elaborations mentioned in the last paragraph, possession is essentially control, and ownership the right to possession and control. Ownership and possession are very often vested in the same person. When they are separated, allowance must be made for the fact that someone who is neither an owner nor a possessor may have a right to possession. That right may be good against the possessor, but not against the owner. A steals B's goods and sells them to C; D steals the goods from C. As against D, C has the right to possession, but he has no such right as against B. In law the ownership of goods is often spoken of as "the property in the goods". This use of the word "property" is confusing and it is simpler to use that word only in its other sense, namely to cover the tangible objects or intangible rights which may be the subject of ownership, such as land, goods, money or debts. It is in this latter sense that the word "property" is used in the Act and in the title to this chapter. Theft may take the form of a violation of ownership, or of a right to possession, or of bare possession or control which can even be the unlawful possession by a previous thief of the same thing.

Illustrations of theft

.4 The obvious example of a theft is a direct taking. If A takes money or other articles from B's pocket or house, he is guilty of theft if he dishonestly intends to permanently deprive B of the thing in question. Someone who extracts cigarettes from an automatic machine with the intention of smoking them is guilty of theft whether he achieves his object by brute force or by inserting a coin which he knows to be false. In addition, a person who is already in possession of property to which another is entitled is guilty of theft if he dishonestly appropriates it with intent to permanently deprive the other. Thus, theft by a trustee or other fiduciary owner, theft by a bailee and theft by a servant are possible. An example of fiduciary ownership is that of a stockbroker who receives a cheque from a client with instructions to buy shares with the proceeds. The broker is in law the owner of the cheque, as well as its proceeds, but he is guilty of theft if he dishonestly appropriates either of them with the intention of depriving his client.

A bailee is a person entrusted with the possession of goods who is under an obligation to return those goods to the person who entrusted him with them as when goods are hired, or to deliver them to a third party in accordance with that person's directions. If A delivers goods to B with instructions to keep them safely for him, or to carry them to C, B is a bailee of the goods. He is guilty of theft if he dishonestly appropriates them with the intention of permanently depriving A or C of them.

A servant is generally said to have custody or control, not possession, of goods entrusted to him by his master. The goods, of course, are owned by the master, and the servant is guilty of stealing them if he dishonestly appropriates them with the intention of permanently depriving the master of them. Similarly, if a master buys goods and sends his servant to collect them, the servant on receiving the goods is in possession or control of them, but the master is their owner. If the servant dishonestly appropriates the goods with the intention of permanently depriving the master of them, he is guilty of theft.

The foregoing illustrations of theft are no more than typical examples. No legal significance attaches to the differences between them, and the types are in no sense exhaustive of the possible situations covered by the definition of theft. There is one last but very important point. The student will get an entirely wrong picture of the offences created by the Act of 1968 which are discussed in this and the following chapter if he thinks of them as mutually exclusive. Although it is possible to point to conduct which falls within the definition of one offence and no other, many of the definitions overlap with the result that the same conduct very frequently constitutes more than one offence.

Actus reus of theft

Appropriation

10.5 The prosecution must prove that the accused appropriated property belonging to another. Section 3 (1) of the Act provides that any assumption by a person of the rights of an owner amounts to an appropriation, and this includes, where he has come by the property (innocently or not) without stealing it, any later assumption of a right to it by keeping or dealing with it as owner.

The person who takes property belonging to another from that other's person or premises, intending to keep it or sell it, clearly assumes the rights of an owner. If A takes B's property intending to return it to him, he does not steal it because he does not intend to deprive B permanently; but, if A later decides to keep the property or sells it, he is guilty of theft on account of his later assumption of a right to it by keeping or dealing with it (e.g. selling or destroying) as owner. If A had acquired the property entirely innocently as a bailee or fiduciary owner, he is likewise guilty of theft if without authority he keeps or sells or attempts to sell or otherwise to deal with it. In *Skipp*[1] A, by posing as a genuine haulage contractor, obtained instructions to collect two loads of oranges and one of onions in London and deliver them in Leicester. A collected the loads but made off with them. It was held that although A did not appropriate the goods when he collected them pursuant to his instructions, he did when he diverted them from their true destination because he was then assuming rights of ownership over them.

There are some unusual situations in which the accused is guilty of theft owing to the definition of "appropriates". One example is the sale or attempted sale of a chattel which the thief has never possessed. If A points to B's empty car drawn up out-

---

1. [1975] Crim. L. R. 114.

side A's house and says to C, "That car is mine, you can have it and drive it away at once", A is guilty of theft of the car for he appropriated it with the dishonest intention of depriving B through C permanently of the car. A further example of what would amount to theft without possession of the property by the thief would be when the accused, intending to deprive someone permanently of property belonging to him, destroys the property without touching it by, for example, throwing stones at a vase or shooting domestic animals. The right of destruction is one of the rights of the owner and it is therefore hard to escape the conclusion that there would be an appropriation within the meaning of the Theft Act, although the conduct would also constitute an offence under the Criminal Damage Act 1971. It has even been suggested that the pickpocket whose "theftuously outstretched hand is fortuitously grabbed by a convenient policeman"[1] could be convicted of theft, but it might well be held in such a case that an appropriation entails the disposal or retention of the prosecutor's property in which event the pickpocket's offence would be attempted theft.

Section 3 (2) of the Theft Act provides that "where property or a right or interest in property is or purports to be transferred for value to a person acting in good faith, no later assumption by him of rights which he believed himself to be acquiring shall, by reason of any defect in the transferor's title, amount to theft of the property". The effect of the subsection is that, if A steals goods from B and sells them to C who acts in good faith, the retention or disposal of the goods by C after his discovery of the theft is not theft from B. Although the retention in itself would be no offence, if C sold the goods this would amount to obtaining the purchase price by deception because of an implied representation that C was the owner of the goods. So far as the civil law is concerned, B's ownership would be unaffected and he could sue A or C or a purchaser from C in tort for the conversion of his goods.

Property

6 By s. 4 (1) of the Act "property" includes money and all other property, real or personal, including things in action and other intangible property. Although this definition includes all real and personal property, there are special provisions restricting the theft of land, whether freehold or leasehold, and things forming

1. Stuart, Law Reform and Reform of the Law of Theft, (1967) 30 M.L.R. 628.

part of it which are dealt with later.[1] Likewise there are special provisions restricting the theft of wild creatures.[2]

The expression "personal property" includes goods, a term defined by s. 34 (2) (b) as including money and every other description of property, except land, and including things severed from the land by stealing.

A "thing in action" is a right to sue, and its inclusion in the definition of property means that one who dishonestly assumes rights of ownership over a thing in action, such as a debt, a copyright or a trade mark, with the intention of permanently depriving the person entitled to it is guilty of theft. Thus, if A knowing that B owes C £100, forges an assignment of the debt and demands payment of it from B who pays him the £100, in addition to forgery A is guilty of theft of the debt and of obtaining the £100 from B by deception.

"Other intangible property" covers such things as gas stored in pipes which is undoubtedly capable of being owned. The phrase could on appropriate facts cover chemical formulae, but there are difficulties in bringing them within the law of theft, because the person who uses them can hardly be said to intend to deprive the owner permanently of them; his intention is rather to share them with his victim.

In spite of the broad definition of property in s. 4 (1) of the Act, there are some things, a few of them tangible, and more intangible, which do not or may not come within the definition of property and hence cannot be stolen. Traditionally a human corpse not preserved as an anatomical specimen is not property but there is no reason why not: on the analogy of *Hibbert* v. *McKiernan*[3] and *Woodman*[4] it should belong to the owner of the cemetery: before burial it should belong to the relatives, executors, police, coroner or mortuary. If A cuts off a girl's hair with the intention of making it into a wig or keeping it as a fetish or selling it there is no reason why he is not guilty of theft.

Electricity is not property, and cannot be stolen,[5] but under s. 13 of the Act it is an offence punishable with maxima of five years' imprisonment if tried on indictment, and three months' imprisonment if tried summarily, for a person to use dishonestly

---

1. Paras. 10.16 and 10.17.
2. Para. 10.18.
3. [1948] 2 K.B. 142; [1948] 1 All E.R. 860. See para. 10.20.
4. [1974] Q.B. 754; [1974] 2 All E.R. 955. See para. 10.7.
5. *Low* v. *Blease* (1975), 119 Sol. Jo. 695.

and without due authority, or cause to be wasted or diverted, any electricity. Although the wastage or diversion of electricity can no doubt constitute a serious offence, it is possible to think of many trivial examples. If A turns on B's torch so that the battery may run down with the result that B will have to go home in the dark, he commits an offence under s. 13 as does someone who inserts a false disc in an electrical weighing machine and weighs himself.

Someone who uses a private phone without authority and without intending to pay for the call is guilty of an offence under s. 13. This would also be so if the phone were public, but in that event it is more likely that the prosecution would be brought under s. 65A of the Post Office Act 1953 by which a person who uses a public telephone dishonestly with intent to avoid payment is guilty of an offence punishable on indictment with a maximum of two years' imprisonment.

Rides in cars, coaches or trains, services rendered and lodging for the night are not property but it is sometimes possible to prosecute those who obtain them under s. 16.[1]

Belonging to another

10.7 In ordinary language property is frequently said to belong to someone only when he owns it[2] but, under s. 5 (1) of the Act, property also belongs to someone who has possession or control of it, or a proprietary right or interest in it falling short of complete ownership. "Control" covers cases where a person has physical custody of property which is in the ownership and possession of another. For instance, a customer examining goods in a shop has control of them.

In *Woodman*[3] the accused took some scrap metal from a disused factory belonging to English China Clays. Originally there had been a substantial amount of scrap metal on the site. This had been sold to a company which removed the bulk of it but some was too inaccessible to be removed in such a way as to be attractive to the company: it was left on the site for perhaps a couple of years until the accused took it away. After the company had removed the bulk of the scrap, English China Clays erected a barbed wire fence and put up notices such as "Private Property, Keep Out" and "Trespassers will be prosecuted". The Court of Appeal held that there was ample evidence that English China Clays were in control of the site and therefore, in control

1. Paras. 11.23–11.29.
2. Para. 10.2.
3. [1974] Q.B. 754; [1974] 2 All E.R. 955.

of articles which were on the site, in spite of the fact that they were not aware of the existence of the scrap: control of a site by excluding others is *prima facie* control of the articles on the site as well.

An example of a proprietary right falling short of complete ownership is the interest which a beneficiary of a trust has in the trust fund or a legatee under a will.

The result of the definition of "belonging to another" is that the same property may "belong" to more than one person, and an owner may be guilty of stealing his own property as in *Turner (No. 2)*,[1] where someone whose car had been repaired was held guilty of theft when he took the car from outside the repairer's garage with the object of evading payment of the repairer's charges. The repairer had possession of the car.

A partner may likewise be held guilty of stealing partnership property for partners are co-owners of their property and each of them has a proprietary right in it.[2]

As we have just seen, an equitable owner, such as a beneficiary under a trust, has a proprietary right or interest under s. 5 (1), and therefore the trust property is regarded for the purposes of the Act as being owned by the legatee or beneficiary as well as by the trustees who are the legal owners. Thus, if A holds goods, money or shares in trust for B, A as trustee has the legal ownership of the goods, money or shares, but B has an equitable interest in them. Thus, A will be guilty of stealing if he dishonestly appropriates them with the intention of defeating the trust by permanently depriving B of them.

Section 5 (1) says that "proprietary right or interest" in the present context does not include "an equitable interest arising only from an agreement to transfer or grant an interest". This needs to be explained to those who have not yet encountered the rules of equity. When a person contracts to buy, for example, land or shares, he receives what is called an equitable interest in them although legally the person contracting to sell retains the legal ownership. The above words are designed to ensure that an owner who contracts to sell his property to A, and then contracts to sell it to B, does not steal it from A.

Spouses may be guilty of stealing each other's property although, in many instances their possession and in some instances their ownership, is joint; the leave of the Director of Public Prosecutions is required for proceedings for theft by one

1. [1971] 2 All E.R. 441; *C. & J. Cases.*
2. *Bonner*, [1970] 2 All E.R. 97.

spouse of the other's property, unless, by virtue of any judicial decree or order, the parties were not obliged to cohabit at the material time.[1] The reason for requiring the leave of the D.P.P. is that otherwise there is a danger of trivial marital quarrels coming into the criminal courts.

Special cases

10.8 There are some cases in which unless special provision were made theft would not be committed because at the material time the property would have belonged exclusively to the accused under s. 5 (1). In these cases, dealt with in s. 5 (2), s. 5 (3) and s. 5 (4), property which does not belong to the accused's victim within s. 5 (1) is deemed to belong to him as against the accused for the purposes of the definition of theft.

Trusts

10.9 As we have seen, property subject to a trust is deemed to belong to the beneficiaries, but there are many examples, mostly in charitable trusts, where the beneficiaries cannot be identified. Section 5 (2) provides that "where property is subject to a trust, the persons to whom it belongs shall be regarded as including any person having a right to enforce the trust, and an intention to defeat the trust shall be regarded accordingly as an intention to deprive of the property any person having that right". Therefore, if a trustee holds property on trust for charitable purposes, the Attorney-General, as a person who, though not a beneficiary, has the right to enforce the trust, is someone to whom the property "belongs", and the trustee is therefore guilty of theft if he dishonestly appropriates it.

Ownership on behalf of others

10.10 The Act recognises that the ownership of money or goods need not be absolute in the sense that the owner can do what he chooses with them for his own benefit or otherwise, but yet they are not subject to a trust in the strict sense of the term. Section 5 (3) provides that "where a person receives property from or on account of another, and is under an obligation to the other to retain and deal with that property or its proceeds in a particular way, the property or proceeds shall be regarded (as against him) as belonging to the other".

If a man collects subscriptions for a wreath to be placed on

1. Theft Act 1968, s. 30.

someone's grave and dishonestly appropriates them, he is guilty of theft because, although he is in law the owner of the money suscribed, he is guilty of stealing it because it "belongs" to the donors, and he would be guilty of stealing the wreath he purchased with the subscriptions if he took it away.

A man is the manager of a partnership: he receives cheques from customers payable to himself and his duty to the firm is to pay the cheques into the firm's bank account. If, instead of doing so, he endorses the cheques and cashes them through friends, making off with the proceeds, he is guilty of theft of the cheques and the proceeds from the partners in the firm because the cheques were received on their account and the same is true of the proceeds. That the distinction is difficult to draw is shown by *Hall*,[1] where a travel agent received money from clients as deposits and payments for air trips to America: in some instances a lump sum was paid by schoolmasters in respect of charter flights for their pupils; in other instances individuals made payments in respect of their own projected flights. In none of the seven cases covered by the charges did the flights materialise and in none was there any refund. The accused claimed to have paid into his firm's general trading account all sums received by him and asserted that those sums had become his own property and had been applied by him in the conduct of the firm's business; he submitted that he could not be convicted of theft just because the firm had not prospered and there was no money. He was acquitted. It is not an offence to fail in business. In the ordinary conduct of industry and commerce money paid in consideration of one thing is used for another purpose and the remedy of someone who does not get what he expected is to sue for breach of contract. In contrast, if someone pays his solicitors money for counsel's fees, the solicitors are under a legal obligation to pay the money into their client account until the time comes for counsel to be paid: it would be wrong for the solicitors to use the money for the ordinary purposes of carrying on their practice. In the judgment of the Court of Appeal in *Hall* it was not established that the clients of the firm expected the firm "to retain and deal with that property or its proceeds in a particular way". The Court of Appeal made it clear that each case turns on its own facts but emphasised that dishonesty must be proved to be present at the time of appropriation and dishonesty is for the jury to decide. It is not enough to prove dishonesty: the prosecution must go further and prove that there

1. [1973] Q.B. 126; [1972] 2 All E.R. 1009; *C. & J. Cases.*

was a legal[1] obligation on the part of the payee to retain and deal with the money in a particular way.

It is therefore essential if s. 5 (3) is to apply that property should have been received "from or on account of another". If a chauffeur plies for hire, against his employer's instructions in his employer's car, the fares are not received by him on account of his employer as they are not proceeds of the employer's property within the meaning of s. 5 (3). In that subsection, "proceeds" must mean the proceeds of a sale or other disposition of the property. The chauffeur's offence would be that of taking a conveyance.[2] A case where proceeds were held to belong to another under s. 5 (3) is *Meech*.[3] X fraudulently obtained a cheque for £1,450 from a finance company. He asked the accused to cash the cheque for him. The accused agreed and paid it into his own bank account. Two days later, having discovered X's fraud, the accused withdrew £1,410 from his account. This represented the £1,450 less a debt of £40 which X owed him. The accused had arranged with B and C to stage a fake robbery with him as victim, so that he could give an excuse for not returning the money to X, and this was carried out. The accused, B and C were convicted of the theft of the £1,410 and appealed unsuccessfully to the Court of Appeal, which held that at the time of the appropriation, which was when the money was divided up after the fake robbery, the money belonged to another, X, under s. 5 (3) because the accused had initially received the money from X under an obligation to retain and deal with it or its proceeds in a particular way. This obligation was not affected by the fact that X, having acquired the money illegally, could not have enforced it in a court.

Mistake

10.11 Section 5 (4) provides that, "where a person gets property by another's mistake, and is under an obligation to make restoration (in whole or in part) of the property or its proceeds or of the value thereof, then to the extent of that obligation the property or proceeds shall be regarded (as against him) as belonging to the person entitled to restoration, and an intention not to make restoration shall be regarded accordingly as an intention to deprive that person of the property or proceeds".

---

1. *Meech*, [1974] Q.B. 549; [1973] 3 All E.R. 939.
2. Paras. 11.8 to 11.12.
3. [1974] Q.B. 549; [1973] 3 All E.R. 939. Also see *Wakeman* v. *Farrar*, [1974] Crim. L. R. 136.

In some cases in which A becomes possessed of B's property in consequence of a mistake, B continues to be the owner of the property and it is quite unnecessary for the prosecution to invoke the aid of this subsection. For example, A lends or sells his bureau to B, forgetting that he has left an envelope containing £100 in a drawer; B, on discovering the envelope, knowing full well that it belongs to A, misappropriates its contents; B is guilty of theft by misappropriating money in which A has "a proprietary right" within the meaning of s. 5 (1). A enters B's shop disguised as one of B's trusted regular customers, and buys a quantity of goods on credit, a transaction into which B would never have entered had he known of the deception practised by A; as well as being guilty of obtaining property and a pecuniary advantage contrary to ss. 15 and 16 of the Act which are discussed later,[1] A is guilty of theft because the contract for the sale of the goods is void and B remains their owner. A purports to buy a bar of iron from B, and B purports to sell a bar of iron to A but the object is a bar of gold: the contract of sale is void, the bar still belongs to B, and A is guilty of theft if he appropriates the bar.

10.12 There may be, however, cases of mistake in which the transferor does not retain a proprietary right in that which is transferred, although the transferee is under an obligation to make restoration to him. For example, if an employer pays an employee a week's wages of £30 forgetting that he has already paid the employee £20 as an advance against wages, it is arguable that the employee becomes the owner of the £30 as the employer intended to pay the £30 to him: if this is so, thanks to s. 5 (4), the employee is guilty of theft if he appropriates the excess on becoming aware of the mistake.

Section 5 (4) was principally intended to cover the circumstances of *Moynes* v. *Coopper*[2] in which an employee had had an advance of most of his week's wages, but the employer forgot to tell the wages clerk who gave the employee an envelope containing the full wages without any deduction. The employee knew that he was not entitled to keep the contents of the envelope but decided to do so: the Divisional Court held that he committed no offence under the pre-1969 law because he had become the owner of the money and had his employer's consent. The fact remains that the employer's wages clerk had made a mistake

1. Paras. 11.13 to 11.29.
2. [1956] 1 Q.B. 439; [1956] 1 All E.R. 450.

of fact and the employee was under an obligation to make restoration. It was reasonable to assume that s. 5 (4) had disposed of this problem but it emerged again in an unexpected form in *Gilks*[1] who placed a bet with one of Ladbrokes' betting shops on a horse called *Fighting Scot*. This animal was unsuccessful but the relief manager of the betting shop made a mistake and paid the accused as if *Fighting Scot* had won. The accused knew that a mistake had been made but kept the money, his attitude being that it was Ladbrokes' hard lines. At first sight the case came within s. 5 (4) but as it was a gaming debt there was no legal obligation to make restoration and, as the Court of Appeal held that obligation means legal obligation, s. 5 (4) did not apply. The accused did not escape because the Court of Appeal held that when the manager paid the money the ownership was not affected and that it remained with Ladbrokes', so that the accused stole money "belonging to another". This appears to strain language and it seems that if a person who pays money by mistake still remains the owner there is little if any need for s. 5 (4). The subsection may, however, prove useful in cases in which there is a mistake concerning the amount of money or quantity of goods transferred. A intends to pay a debt of 50 pence to B by handing him 10 fivepenny pieces. He mistakenly hands him 11 fivepenny pieces. One of the fivepenny pieces received by B belongs to A and B could be convicted of stealing a fivepenny piece without recourse to s. 5 (4), but this subsection prevents B from raising any issue as to which of the 11 fivepenny pieces he misappropriated because he was under an obligation to restore one of the fivepenny pieces to A and, as against B, any one of the fivepenny pieces or its equivalent belonged to A; B's intention not to make restoration will be regarded as an intention to deprive A permanently of five pence, but on the authority of *Gilks* it can be argued cogently that A did not part with the ownership of five pence. In any event the subsection is there whether necessary or not.

10.13 There are cases in which a person gets property by another's mistake and in spite of s. 5 (4) is under no obligation to make restoration of the property or its proceeds or its value. If A were to make a gift of a book to B mistakenly believing that it was of little value when it was in fact a valuable first edition, B would be guilty of no offence by appropriating the book even if he were aware of A's mistake from the outset.

1. [1972] 3 All E.R. 280; *C. & J. Cases.*

If A induces B to sell him goods on credit by dishonestly saying that he is a very rich man, there is a sense in which A gets the goods by B's mistake, but it is very doubtful whether s. 5 (4) would be held to apply because A is not under an obligation to "make restoration of the property or its proceeds or of the value thereof". A's obligation is to pay the agreed purchase price. His offence is certainly obtaining the goods by deception; it is, as we shall see, an open question whether he would also be guilty of stealing the goods at this stage.[1] If B were to give A notice avoiding the contract of sale on account of A's fraud, the ownership of the goods would revert to B and they would clearly belong to him within s. 5 (1), and A would be guilty of theft by retaining or disposing of them.

Corporation sole

10.14 Section 5 (5) deals with a different kind of special case from those covered by s. 5 (2)–(4). It provides that the property of a corporation sole, examples of which are a bishop and the Treasury Solicitor, shall be regarded as belonging to the corporation notwithstanding a vacancy in the corporation. This is simply to guard against the possibility that for example the property of a bishopric might be regarded as belonging to no one, and therefore incapable of being stolen, during a vacancy in the see.

Employee handing goods over as a trap

10.15 One last question may be raised with regard to the meaning of "belonging to". If A incites B's employee to join with him in the theft of B's property and the employee informs B of the project, would A be guilty of theft if, on B's instructions, the employee actually handed the goods to him? The answer to this question is not expressly provided for by anything in s. 5 of the Theft Act. It depends on whether A became the owner of the goods the moment they were handed to him. This seems to depend on an arguable point in the civil law of contract; B certainly did not intend to make a gift to A, but he did know that A intended to deprive him permanently of the goods, and this might perhaps be enough to effect a transfer of ownership.

Land and things forming part of it

10.16 Subsections (2) and (3) of s. 4 of the Act provide:

"A person cannot steal land, or things forming part of land and

1. See para. 11.22.

severed from it by him or by his directions, except in the following cases, that is to say:

a. when he is a trustee or personal representative, or is authorised by power of attorney, or as liquidator of a company, or otherwise to sell or dispose of land belonging to another, and he appropriates the land or anything forming part of it by dealing with it in breach of the confidence reposed in him; or
b. when he is not in possession of the land and appropriates anything forming part of the land by severing it or causing it to be severed, or after it has been severed; or
c. when, being in possession of the land under a tenancy, he appropriates the whole or part of any fixture or structure let to be used with the land" (s. 4 (2)).

"A person who picks mushrooms growing wild on any land, or who picks flowers, fruit or foliage from a plant growing wild on any land, does not (although not in possession of the land) steal what he picks, unless he does it for reward or for sale or other commercial purpose" (s. 4 (3)).

These are the words of the Act and, whereas the majority of the sections in the Act are clear, s. 4 is not. The reason is that the Criminal Law Revision Committee drew back from making a fundamental change in legal tradition and chose to perpetuate the feudal customs which have always shrouded the law of land.

7 It comes to this:

a. Land as a whole cannot be stolen except where the appropriator is of a defined class and acts in a defined way. The class of appropriators comprises a trustee or personal representative or holder of a power of attorney or liquidator of a company or someone otherwise authorised to sell or dispose of land belonging to another. The defined mode of appropriation is dealing with the land in breach of the confidence reposed in him. The result is that a man cannot steal land as a whole by moving a boundary fence or by forging a conveyance or by occupying it as a squatter: if in moving the boundary fence he resorts to any deception, he can be prosecuted under s. 15 and for forging a conveyance he could be prosecuted for forgery, but as the law is at present he commits no offence by merely squatting although he would be guilty of conspiracy if he agreed to do so with others.[1]

---

1. Para. 17.12.

b. Things forming part of land, such as soil, bricks in a wall, plants and fixtures, can be stolen in three cases:
   i. As for land as a whole, by the defined persons in the defined ways.
   ii. Where a person not in possession of the land severs the thing, causes it to be severed or appropriates it after severance. If a trespasser digs gravel, removes tiles and bricks from a building, cuts turf, digs up flowers and other growing things or cuts down trees or saws off their branches, or causes such severance to be done, or appropriates such things (e.g. by selling them) after they have been severed he is guilty of theft.
   iii. When, being in possession of the land under a tenancy, he appropriates the whole or part of any fixture or structure let to be used with the land.[1]

   On the other hand it is not theft merely to pick wild mushrooms and other fungi, flowers, fruit or foliage from plants, including shrubs and trees, growing wild unless it is done for reward or for sale or other commercial purpose. It is a question of fact in each case whether the fungi and plants are wild or not, whether they are picked or severed, and whether there is a commercial purpose. For example, shortly before Christmas a florist and an electrician go out in their cars: both pick holly from a tree which is cultivated in a garden and both are guilty of theft because the tree is not wild. They continue and both pick holly from a tree which is wild: the florist is intending to sell it in his shop and is guilty of theft whereas the electrician is intending to decorate his home and is not guilty. Both dig up small fir trees growing wild and both are guilty of theft. The same principle applies to blackberries, heathers and other fruits and foliage.[2]

c. Generally, things forming part of land cannot be stolen by tenants but tenants can steal the whole or part of any fixture or structure let to be used with the land. A structure is a building of some kind such as a hut, a dam or a bridge: a fixture is an object, such as a washbasin or fireplace, which is attached to land in some way, other than by its own weight, and which by the ordinary law of land becomes part of the land.

Wild creatures

10.18 Section 4 (4) of the Act provides that wild creatures tamed or untamed are property. A person cannot steal a wild creature

1. Theft Act 1968, s. 4 (2).
2. But see the Conservation of Wild Creatures and Wild Plants Act 1975.

not tamed nor ordinarily kept in captivity, or the carcase of any such creature, unless either it has been reduced into possession by or on behalf of another person and possession of it has not since been lost or abandoned, or another person is in course of reducing it into possession.

While they are alive, wild creatures which are neither tamed nor ordinarily kept in captivity are not owned by anyone, but on being killed they become the property of the owner of the land on which they are killed or, if he has granted the sporting rights to someone else, the grantee of those rights.[1] This is why the Act specifically states that they shall be regarded as property. Section 4 (4) distinguishes two groups of wild creatures:

a. Wild creatures which have been tamed or are ordinarily kept in captivity can be stolen in the same ways as any other property. Thus a man may be guilty of theft by dishonestly appropriating a bear from a zoo.
b. Wild creatures neither tamed nor ordinarily kept in captivity. Such a creature or its carcase cannot normally be stolen but becomes "stealable" (i) if reduced into possession by or on behalf of another (in which case it remains "stealable" so long as possession has not subsequently been lost or abandoned), or (ii) if another person is in course of reducing it into possession. Thus it is not theft to poach game on another's land, unless for instance the game is taken from a trap set by another, even another poacher (because another is in the course of reducing into possession), or from a sack into which another has put the product of his own shooting (because there has been a reduction into possession by another). Poaching is subject to its own legislation.

The Eighth Report of the Criminal Law Revision Committee recommended that the whole law with regard to poaching should be considered by an appropriate committee.[2] In the meantime, certain provisions of the Larceny Act 1861 punishing the unlawful killing or taking of deer or fish have been transferred to the first schedule of the Act. They are all summary offences.

Mens rea of theft

19 It is immaterial that the appropriation is not made with a view to gain or is not made for the thief's own benefit (s. 1 (2)), but the appropriation must have been made dishonestly and with

1. *Blade* v. *Higgs* (1865), 11 H.L. Cas. 621.
2. *Op. cit.*, para. 53.

the intention of permanently depriving the person to whom the property belongs.

At common law it was essential that the accused should have acted "fraudulently" in order that he might be guilty of theft, and this requirement was incorporated in the definition of stealing contained in the Larceny Act 1861. It was said that "fraudulently" simply meant "dishonestly",[1] and it was settled at common law that the accused was guilty of theft although he may have been acting solely for the benefit of a friend by, for example, destroying the evidence of the friend's crime.[2] There is no doubt that s. 1 (2) of the Act of 1968 would support similar decisions.

Meaning of "dishonestly"

10.20 The question of dishonesty is one of fact for the jury and not of law for the judge, subject to the provisions of s. 2 of the Act which expressly and as a matter of law excludes some states of mind from being dishonest. It reads:

> "A person's appropriation of property belonging to another is not to be regarded as dishonest:
>
> a. if he appropriates the property in the belief that he has in law the right to deprive the other of it, on behalf of himself or of a third person;
>
> b. if he appropriates the property in the belief that he would have the other's consent if the other knew of the appropriation and the circumstances of it;
>
> c. (except where the property came to him as trustee or personal representative) if he appropriates the property in the belief that the person to whom the property belongs cannot be discovered by taking reasonable steps".[3]

Paragraph a. makes a claim of right a defence to theft as it is to other charges under the Act which means that a mistake of law may be a defence, as where a creditor seizes property belonging to his debtor intending to recoup himself thereby under the erroneous belief that the law permits debts to be recovered in this way. The concluding words of paragraph a. make it plain that someone who appropriates property in the belief that he is entitled to do so on behalf of, for example, the company by which he is employed, is not guilty of theft.

Paragraph b. would clearly cover the case of an undergraduate

---

1. *Rose* v. *Matt*, [1951] 1 K.B. 810, at p. 814.
2. *Cabbage* (1815), Russ. & Ry. 292.
3. Section 2 (1).

who takes a bottle of beer from a friend's room leaving the price behind him believing that his friend would have assented had he known of all the circumstances; clearly he would not be held to have acted dishonestly.

Paragraph c. aims at protecting the honest finder as long as he remains honest. There is no theft if, believing that the owner of goods or money found by him cannot be discovered by taking reasonable steps, the finder appropriates the goods or money during the currency of that belief. A finder who knows who the owner is or believes that he could be discovered by taking reasonable steps is guilty of theft if he appropriates what he finds with the intention of permanently depriving the owner for he will be acting dishonestly.

It is important to appreciate the extremely limited nature of the immunity conferred on the honest finder. In the first place property may, as we have seen, belong to more than one person for the purpose of the Act. Although someone who finds goods on or embedded in another's land may well believe that their owner, the loser, cannot be discovered by taking reasonable steps, the goods would probably be held to belong to the landowner on the ground that he has possession or control of them.[1] In *Hibbert* v. *McKiernan*[2] for instance it was held that golf balls which had been lost and abandoned by their owners were in the possession of the golf club on whose course they were lying in unknown numbers. Appropriation with knowledge of the landowner's rights would be theft. Secondly if, while he is in possession of the goods, the finder becomes aware of the person to whom they belong he is guilty of theft in consequence of any subsequent appropriation by keeping or disposing of the goods with the intention of permanently depriving that person. There is no equivalent to the protection of honest purchasers from thieves conferred by s. 3 (2) of the Act.[3]

10.21 In *Feely*[4] doubts about whether dishonesty is for the judge to decide as a matter of law or for the jury to decide as a matter of fact were resolved in favour of it being a matter of fact for the jury. Feely was employed by a firm of bookmakers as a manager of one of their branches in Liverpool. His employers sent a circular to all their managers stating that the practice of

1. Para. 10.7. See the civil cases cited in *Salmond on Torts*, 16th ed., 109–110.
2. [1948] 2 K.B. 142; [1948] 1 All E.R. 860.
3. Para. 10.5.
4. [1973] 1 Q.B. 530; [1973] 1 All E.R. 341.

borrowing from tills was to stop and after receiving that circular Feely knew that he had no right of any kind to take money from a till or safe for his own purposes, even though the practice is common and frequently tolerated by employers. The facts became complicated and the judge in his summing-up told the jury "... as a matter of law ... I am bound to direct you, even if he were prepared to pay back the following day and even if he were a millionaire, it makes no defence in law to this offence". The Court of Appeal held that this was wrong: it may happen that an employee is acting dishonestly when he removes money from a till but it is for the jury to decide. "We do not agree" said Lawton, L.J., "that judges should define what 'dishonestly' means".

10.22 It follows that the categories of innocence contained in s. 2 are not exhaustive of those in which the accused's conduct would not be dishonest, although all the other ingredients of theft were present; although s. 2 (1) caters for all ordinary cases there are some in which the question whether the accused's conduct was dishonest is one of fact for the jury. Subsection 2 (2) provides: "A person's appropriation of property belonging to another may be dishonest notwithstanding that he is willing to pay for the property". Someone who knows that the owner of a picture does not wish to sell it might well be held guilty of theft if he took the picture intending to deprive the owner permanently of it but leaving the price behind, whereas an undergraduate who takes a bottle of beer from a friend's room leaving the price might not be held to have acted dishonestly even if he did not believe that the owner would have consented to the appropriation, so that the case is not covered by the earlier provisions of s. 2.

10.23 As Lawton, L.J., observed in *Feely* the decision in that case is inconsistent with dicta in pre-1969 cases on the meaning of "fraudulently" in the old crime of larceny such as *Cockburn*[1] in which the following dictum of Lord Goddard, C.J., in an earlier case was disapproved:

> "It is one thing if a person with good credit and plenty of money uses somebody else's money which may be in his possession and which may have been entrusted to him or which he may have had

1. [1968] 1 All E.R. 466; also see *Williams*, [1953] 1 Q.B. 690; [1953] 1 All E.R. 1068.

the opportunity of taking, merely intending to use those coins instead of his own which he has only to go to his room or to his bank to obtain. No jury would then say there was any intent to defraud or any fraudulent taking. It is quite another matter if the person who takes the money is not in a position to replace it at the time but only has the hope or expectation that he will be able to do so in the future".[1]

We suggest that even before 1969 Lord Goddard was right and the disapproval was unjustified because the logical consequence of the view that it must always be fraudulent for someone to take another's property against his will, while substituting the equivalent, would be that someone who took a fivepenny piece out of another's pocket, replacing it with another fivepenny piece would inevitably be guilty of theft. Whether or not the decision in *Cockburn* was correct at the time it cannot now be said that an employee is inevitably guilty of theft if he takes money from his employer's till leaving a cheque for the amount in the till, even if this is contrary to orders. It is arguable that it may be dishonest to expose the owner of money, against his will, to the risk that a cheque will not be met, but it certainly does not follow that in all cases in which fungibles are substituted for fungibles without the owner's consent, real or supposed, the accused must have been acting dishonestly and, as the Court of Appeal decided in *Feely*, it is a matter for the jury to decide.

4 That the decision whether a person was acting dishonestly is, subject to s. 2 of the Act, a question of fact for the jury may be thought to be inconsistent with the rule that the ordinary meaning of statutory words is a question of law for the judge, but this is not so because the question whether conduct was dishonest turns on the application of the moral standards of the ordinary man. Juries frequently have to apply standards, although it may look as though they were interpreting statutory words; an obvious example is provided by the case of prosecutions for dangerous driving.

Intention of permanently depriving

5 The existence of an intention of permanently depriving the person to whom the property belongs is a question of fact. This gives rise to no difficulty in the ordinary case in which the accused is shown to have sold, or to have intended to sell, or to have intended to keep or to give away the property in ques-

1. Williams, [1953] 1 Q.B. 690, as reported in [1953] 1 All E.R., at p. 1070.

tion. Whenever it occurred, the appropriation, defined in s. 3 (1) as any assumption of the rights of an owner, would have entailed an intention of permanent deprival. The accused must mean that the person to whom the property belongs should lose it permanently; it is likely that direct intention is necessary and that oblique intention will not do.[1]

If the accused may have intended to return the actual property to his victim at some future date, the jury must acquit in the normal case.[2] They must also acquit if they conclude that the accused intended simply to examine the goods he took, and only to keep them if he considered it worth while to do so.[3]

In *Easom*,[4] the accused picked up a handbag which had been placed as a trap by a policewoman in front of the seat in which he was sitting in a cinema. He removed the bag to a lavatory where he opened it and examined its contents. He then closed the bag and replaced it with its contents intact on the floor of the cinema. His conviction for the theft of the bag and its contents was quashed on the ground that, although he had appropriated both, the appropriation was not accompanied by the intention of permanently depriving the owner of her property. It is therefore clear that it is not enough for the prosecution to prove a conditional intention to deprive the owner of any article which the accused decided was worth stealing.

Section 6 (1) of the Act extends the meaning of "intention of permanently depriving". It provides that a person appropriating property belonging to another without meaning the other permanently to lose it is nevertheless to be regarded as having the intention of permanently depriving the other if his intention is to treat the property as his own to dispose of regardless of the other's rights. This means, for instance, that someone who takes goods with the impudent intention of selling them back to the owner is guilty of theft.

Section 6 (1) also provides that a borrowing or lending of property may amount to treating it as the accused's own to dispose of if, but only if, for a period and in circumstances making it equivalent to an outright taking or disposal. A girl who borrows a dress for a dance and thereafter takes it to America well knowing that the owner would object might be guilty of theft notwithstanding her intention to return it when it was worn

1. Paras. 3.12–3.19.
2. *Warner* (1970), 55 Cr. App. Rep. 93.
3. *Easom* [1970] 2 Q.B. 315; [1971] 2 All E.R. 945; *C. & J. Cases.*
4. *Ibid.*

out. Under s. 6 (2) the unauthorised parting with property under a condition which he may not be able to fulfil amounts to the accused's treating it as his own to dispose of; this would cover the case of a man who takes another's property and pawns it, intending to return if it he wins a bet.

The requirement of an intention of permanent deprival excludes from the law of theft conduct such as the unauthorised taking, using and return of goods, which many think should be included, but this is a question of the proper sphere of the criminal law. Are people to be punished for simply being a nuisance to others? Is it wise to have prohibitory laws (and there are plenty of them as it is) which work only provided that there are no prosecutions in venial cases? Such offences of temporary deprival as exist are covered in paras. 11.7 to 11.12.

11

OFFENCES AGAINST PROPERTY 2 OFFENCES UNDER THE THEFT ACT OTHER THAN THEFT

11.1 In the last chapter we described the basic law of theft and the definitions necessary to it. In this chapter we have to deal with several offences which are related to theft in some way but which differ from it in one or more vital respects. One consequence of these differences is that the definitions contained in ss. 2–6 of the 1968 Act are not always relevant and so s. 1 (3) provides that those sections have effect only as regards the interpretation and operation of s. 1: if any of them is to apply to any other section in the Act special provision is made. For example, s. 8 defines robbery as stealing coupled with force or the threat of force: "steal" is defined in s. 1 which incorporates ss. 2–6 all of which are therefore relevant to s. 8. Section 9 defines burglary which does not necessarily involve stealing or any offence relating to property so that ss. 1–6 are irrelevant, but where s. 9 does relate to stealing, ss. 1–6 are relevant. Sections 11 and 12 create offences which not only do not contain the words "dishonestly", "appropriates", "property" or "belonging to another" but expressly provide that in essence there is no intention of permanently depriving the owner of what is taken so that ss. 1–6 are wholly irrelevant. Section 15 covers obtaining property by deception which, like theft, involves dishonesty and the intention of permanently depriving, but does not impose any limitation on the word "property" with the strange result that, although a person cannot steal land he can obtain it by deception. We have said enough to demonstrate that it is necessary to be very careful when applying the sections of the Act. There is at least one other possible source of confusion: not everyone would agree that the order and arrangement of the Act are the best which could be devised, but as experience has shown that the ideal is unattainable we have thought it least confusing to follow the order of the Act.

Robbery

.2 Section 8 of the Act provides that a person is guilty of robbery if he steals and, immediately before or at the time of doing so, and in order to do so, he uses force on any person or puts or seeks to put any person in fear of being then and there subjected to force. The maximum punishment for robbery and assault with intent to rob is imprisonment for life. Robbery is therefore theft aggravated by the use of force or the threat of force, so that the necessary ingredients of theft must be proved and all the defences are available,[1] but to constitute robbery the force must be used or threatened immediately before or at the time of the theft. It need not be used against the owner of the property stolen, so that if a gang uses force against a signalman only in order to stop and steal from a train, its members are guilty of robbery. Difficult questions of degree can arise. If the signalman were bound and gagged by force an hour before the stealing from the train, the gang having operated the signals in the meantime, it could be argued that the force was used immediately before the theft, but there must be some limit unless the word "immediately" becomes meaningless. Questions of degree are, however, difficult to avoid if the definition of robbery is not to be unduly wide.

It is clear that there is no robbery if the force is used after the theft. The thief who aims a blow at someone surprising him after he has taken the goods is guilty of robbery only if it can be established that the theft is still in progress, but here again there must be a limit. The force must be used "on" a person. The members of the Criminal Law Revision Committee did not regard the mere snatching of property, such as a handbag, from an unresisting woman as using force for the purpose of the definition of robbery, though they thought that it might be so if the owner resisted.[2]

Force used for the purpose of types of theft other than by direct taking suffice to render the person using it guilty of robbery. For example, if A finds B's watch and, having intended to return it to B, changes his mind when B discovers the whereabouts of his watch and calls upon A to return it, A is guilty of robbery if he accompanies his refusal to return the watch with force aimed at B. On the other hand, if A appropriates the watch before B asks for it, he has already stolen it and so his use of

---

1. *Skivington*, [1968] 1 Q.B. 166; [1967] 1 All E.R. 483.
2. Eighth Report of the Criminal Law Revision Committee, para. 65.

force in order to keep it does not make him guilty of robbery.[1]

Again the fact that robbery requires the use of force to be for the purpose of theft is restrictive of the scope of the offence, although the restrictions are perhaps of more theoretical than practical interest. A uses force against B for the purpose of temporarily taking B's car; C uses force against D who is seeking to prevent him from uttering deceitful words whereby he hopes to obtain a gift of money from a gullible old lady; E uses force against F who is preventing him from executing a fraudulent conveyance of the land of which he is trustee. Assuming that A, C and E accomplish their purposes, E alone is guilty of robbery. If their purposes are not accomplished, E alone is guilty of an assault with intent to rob, but it does not follow that those who for one reason or another escape a conviction for robbery avoid criminal liability altogether. Obviously, if force is used or threatened there is the possibility of a conviction for assault or one of the more serious offences against the person. In some cases there is the possibility of a conviction for blackmail. The man who demands the temporary possession of a car coupled with a threat of force is not guilty of robbery because there is no theft but he is guilty of blackmail.

Burglary and aggravated burglary

11.3 There are two separate offences of burglary.[2] Both are governed by s. 9 of the Act and are punishable with a maximum of 14 years' imprisonment.

The first offence is defined by s. 9 (1)(a), whose effect is that a person is guilty of burglary if he enters any building, which includes an inhabited vehicle or vessel,[3] or part of a building as a trespasser and with intent to steal anything in the building or part of a building in question, or to inflict grievous bodily harm on anyone therein, or to rape any woman therein, or to do unlawful damage to the building or anything therein. A person enters a building as a trespasser when he does so without a right by law or licence. Rights of entry are granted by statute to certain people for certain purposes. For instance a police officer entering premises with a search warrant authorised under some statute is not a trespasser; accordingly it is doubtful whether he would be guilty of burglary in the unlikely event of his entering with the intention of searching pursuant to such a warrant, but with the additional intention of raping some

1. See generally on this subject Andrews, Theft Bill: Robbery, [1966] Crim. L.R. 524.

2. *Hollis*, [1971] Crim. L. R. 525.

3. Theft Act 1968, s. 9 (3).

woman inside the premises. A licence means permission to enter given by the occupier or someone with his authority. A licence to enter does not necessarily permit entry into every part of the building. Thus, a person may lawfully enter a building, such as an hotel, shop or railway station, but trespass in the manager's office, stockroom or booking office: equally he may be a lawful guest at a meal in a private house but trespass in a bedroom. In certain circumstances a person may enter as a trespasser despite the fact that he has an apparent licence, e.g. where consent was given under a mistake as to his identity which normally will have been induced by fraud.

.4 Part of the *mens rea* required for burglary is that the accused must know that he is entering as a trespasser or be reckless as to this fact. This was established by the Court of Appeal in *Collins*.[1] About two o'clock early one morning in July a young lady of 18 went to bed. She wore no night apparel and the bed was very near the open lattice-type window of her room. She awoke about two hours later and saw in the moonlight a vague form crouched in the open window. She leapt to the conclusion that her boyfriend was paying her an ardent nocturnal visit: she sat up in bed, and (according to Collins) helped him to enter the room, after which they had full intercourse; then she realised that he was not her boyfriend but Collins, who was later convicted of burglary. The Court of Appeal, allowing Collins' appeal, held that the prosecution had to prove that Collins entered as a trespasser and knew it or was reckless as to this: on the basis that Collins had not entered the room before he was helped in by the young lady, it could hardly be suggested that his subsequent entry was accompanied by knowledge or suspicion on his part that he was entering as a trespasser.

The premises entered as a trespasser must be a building or inhabited vehicle such as a caravan or inhabited vessel such as a houseboat, (whether or not the person having a habitation in it is there at the time).[2] Someone who forces his way into a tent with the intention of committing one of the specified offences is not guilty of burglary: his only offence would be an attempt to commit the specified offence in question, and then only provided that his conduct was sufficiently proximate to the commission of that offence.[3]

.5 In addition to knowledge that he enters as a trespasser, the accused's entry must be accompanied by the further intent to

1. [1973] 1 Q.B. 100; [1972] 2 All E.R. 1105; *C. & J. Cases*.
2. Theft Act 1968, s. 9 (3).
3. Para. 17.26.

steal or to commit one of the other specified offences in the building, vehicle or vessel, or part of it, entered as a trespasser. If someone enters one house as a trespasser with the intention of thereby gaining access to and stealing from an adjoining house, he is not, thus far, guilty of burglary.

The punishment of burglary by entry with intent is a branch of preventive justice, like the punishment of attempts to commit crime. A further illustration of this kind of preventive justice is contained in s. 25.[1]

11.6 The second offence of burglary is defined by s. 9 (1)(b): "A person is guilty of burglary if, having entered any building or part of a building as a trespasser he steals or attempts to steal anything in the building or that part of it and inflicts or attempts to inflict on any person therein any grievous bodily harm". "Trespasser" and "building" have the same meanings as in the other offence of burglary. The important distinction is that this offence requires the accused, having entered the building or part as a trespasser, actually to have committed the offence of theft, or inflicting grievous bodily harm, or attempting these; on the other hand he is not required to have had the intent when he entered.

Both offences require a trespassory entry into a building. To be guilty of the first offence, it must be proved that, at the time of his trespassory entry, the accused intended to commit one of the specified offences. Someone who enters a building as a trespasser with the intention of going to sleep inside is not guilty of burglary of the first type if he subsequently forms the intention of stealing something from the premises, but if he actually steals or attempts to steal the thing in question, he is then guilty of burglary of the second type by virtue of the commission or attempted commission of theft on premises entered as a trespasser.

By s. 10 a person is guilty of aggravated burglary if he commits any burglary and at the time has with him any firearm or imitation firearm, any weapon of offence or any explosive. Aggravated burglary is punishable with a maximum of imprisonment for life.

Temporary deprivation

11.7 So far, we have considered offences in which, if property is involved, an intention of permanently depriving the owner

1. Para. 11.38.

must be proved. At this stage we deviate in order to consider those offences where an intention of temporarily depriving is enough. Section 11 (1) of the Theft Act provides that where the public have access to a building in order to view the building or part of it, or a collection or part of a collection housed in it, any person who without lawful authority removes from the building or its grounds the whole or part of any article displayed or kept for display to the public in the building or that part of it or in its grounds is guilty of an offence punishable with a maximum of five years' imprisonment.

In recommending the creation of this offence, the Criminal Law Revision Committee had in mind such eccentric behaviour as the removal of Goya's portrait of the Duke of Wellington from the National Gallery in which it was not clear beyond reasonable doubt that the taker intended to deprive the person to whom the property belonged permanently of it.

The offence under consideration covers removals only from non-commercial collections, but if the thing removed is there otherwise than as forming part of, or being on loan for exhibition with, a collection intended[1] for permanent exhibition, it must be removed on a day when the public has access to the building or grounds.[2] Thus, the offence is not committed if a painting is removed from a wholly temporary art exhibition in a church hall on a day when the hall is closed.

The accused's belief that he had lawful authority for the removal of the thing in question or that he would have it if the person in question knew of the removal and its circumstances is a defence. The belief does not have to have been a reasonable one as a matter of law, and the burden of proving it is not borne by the accused.[3]

Taking conveyances without authority

.8 Section 12 of the Act provides that a person is guilty of an offence punishable with a maximum of three years' imprisonment if, without having the consent of the owner or other lawful authority, he takes any conveyance for his own or another's use. Although a dictionary definition of a conveyance confines it to a vehicle or carriage, there is no reason for such limitation for the purposes of s. 12 which defines it as "any conveyance constructed or adapted for the carriage of a person or

1. *Durkin*, [1973] 1 Q.B. 786; [1973] 2 All E.R. 872.
2. Theft Act 1968, s. 11 (2).
3. *Ibid.*, s. 11 (3).

persons whether by land, water or air, except that it does not include a conveyance constructed or adapted for use only under the control of a person not carried in or on it". There is no need for it to have either wheels or engine, but it seems to be generally accepted that a horse is not a conveyance for this purpose because it is assumed that construction and adaptation must be by man and not by nature, although it would be enlightening to hear argument on the point. It is clear that a conveyance cannot include either a handcart or a trailer because, although passengers can be carried in them, they are not constructed or adapted for this purpose and anyway, even if they are, they are controlled by persons not carried in or on them. The same applies to perambulators and lawnmowers and pedestrian-controlled milkfloats, but a conveyance would undoubtedly include a lawnmower controlled by a person carried on it and an invalid carriage, whether powered or not, controlled by the occupant. There seems no reason why the definition should not include skates and skis but the extension to a pair of shoes might be resisted.

11.9 Where a person such as an employed lorry or coach driver is in lawful possession of a vehicle, it seems clear that some active use of it inconsistent with his employment must be proved. Unauthorised use by a person already in possession or control may amount to a taking. An employee who uses his employer's lorry for his own purposes after the expiry of the period for which he is authorised to use it, usually the working day, or during that period appropriates it to his own use in a manner which is inconsistent with the rights of the employer and shows that he has assumed control of it for his own purposes, may be held to take it. The first alternative covers the driver who has his employer's authority to leave the employer's car outside the driver's home for the night, but not to use it for his own purposes, and presents no difficulties.[1] Under the second alternative, a serious deviation from the employee's proper route may be a taking. In *McKnight* v. *Davies*[2] the accused crashed his employer's lorry while driving back to the depot after making some deliveries. Scared by this, he drove to a public house for a drink, then took three men to their houses, then drove to another public house for another drink, parked the lorry near his house and only on the following day returned it to the depot.

---

1. See, for instance, *Wibberley*, [1966] 2 Q.B. 214; [1965] 3 All E.R. 718.
2. [1974] Crim. L. R. 62.

The Divisional Court, upholding the accused's conviction under s. 12, said that not every brief unauthorised diversion from his proper route by an employed driver during the working day would necessarily involve a taking: it would if he appropriated the vehicle to his own use in a manner which repudiated the rights of the true owner and showed that he had assumed control of the vehicle for his own purposes, which he had done on leaving the first public house.

A similar principle applies to a bailee who takes a conveyance if he uses it for a purpose other than that for which he has been given permission or after the end of the bailment. In *Phipps and McGill*[1] the accused asked the owner of a car if he could borrow it to take the accused's wife to a London station. The owner agreed on the express condition that the accused returned the car immediately after dropping his wife, but apparently the accused brought his wife back because she had missed the train. Instead of returning the car, the accused drove it to Hastings and did not return it until two days later: the Court of Appeal held that the accused had taken the car as soon as he drove it outside the purpose or condition of the bailment.

Even where the accused is not in possession or control of the conveyance, the mere unauthorised assumption of possession was held in *Bogacki*[2] not to be enough to constitute a taking: some movement, however small, must take place. It had been thought that, whereas under the previous law[3] both taking and driving away had to be proved, the need to prove taking only did not imply the need for motion but the situation is almost the same as before.

The taking must be for the accused's use or that of another so that there would be no offence under s. 12 if someone as an act of spite were to push someone else's car off a quay into the sea but there would probably be a conviction for criminal damage.

10 The taking must be without the consent of the owner: unlike theft, the lack of consent is crucial. A consent obtained in consequence of the accused's misrepresentation about the type or duration of the journey for which he required the vehicle is valid. In *Peart*[4] the accused in Newcastle obtained the owner's consent to the loan of a van by falsely saying that if he were

1. (1970), 54 Cr. App. Rep. 301; *C. & J. Cases.*
2. [1973] Q.B. 832; [1973] 2 All E.R. 864.
3. Road Traffic Act 1960, s. 217.
4. [1970] 2 Q.B. 672; [1970] 2 All E.R. 823; *C. & J. Cases.*

not in Alnwick by 2.30 p.m. he would lose an important contract, whereas his actual intention was to drive to Burnley which is much further away. It was held that the initial taking was with the consent of the owner. Of course, as *Phipps and McGill*[1] shows, once the accused used the vehicle outside the terms of the bailment the taking became without consent.

It is an open question whether a more fundamental misrepresentation than in *Peart* would vitiate the consent for the purposes of the section. If A were to procure B's consent to his driving B's car by disguising himself as C, would he be guilty of taking the car without B's consent?

11.11 The conveyance must be taken without lawful authority. Taking is not without lawful authority where it is by police or local authority officers in the exercise of statutory powers to remove vehicles which constitute obstructions or are dangerous or where bailors of conveyances recover them under a term in the bailment. Not only is the actual consent of the owner or the actual existence of lawful authority a defence, but under s. 12 (6) also the belief in the existence of lawful authority, or belief that the owner would, if asked, have consented are defences.[2] As usual in the Act the belief is subjective and does not have to be reasonable; the burden of proving it is not borne by the accused.

Other offences under s. 12

11.12 Section 12 (1) contains the ancillary offence where the accused "knowing that any conveyance has been taken without [the owner's consent or other lawful authority], drives it or allows himself to be carried in or on it". A person may be guilty of driving or allowing himself to be carried in a conveyance which he knows to have been taken without authority if the conveyance has, to his knowledge, been stolen and not merely taken temporarily.[3]

The above offences do not apply to pedal cycles, but two similar offences, punishable with a fine of £50, apply to them.[4]

If on the trial of an indictment for theft the jury is not satisfied that the accused committed the theft, but it is proved that the accused committed an offence under s. 12 the jury may find him

1. (1970), 54 Cr. App. Rep. 300; *C. & J. Cases*
2. Theft Act 1968, s. 12 (6).
3. *Tolley* v. *Giddings*, [1964] 2 Q.B. 354; [1964] 1 All E.R. 201.
4. Theft Act 1968, s. 12 (5).

guilty of that offence.[1] Where a motor vehicle has been taken and driven away there can be a charge of stealing the petrol but this is extremely difficult to prove and usually the police rely on s. 12.

Deception

3 Until now we have described those offences in which an essential element is usually the appropriation by one person of the property of another unaccompanied by any attempt to influence the mind of the victim who often is unaware he is being deprived of his property. However, there are many cases in which the victim has been persuaded to part with the ownership, possession or control of his property only by some kind of deception without which he would not have acted as he did. A housewife puts the money for the week's milk in an envelope and leaves it outside the back door: a man who is not the milkman appropriates it and so commits theft. If the housewife keeps the money in her possession and the same man comes and says he is the milkman, whereupon she hands him the money, he has not appropriated the money as it had been given to him by the housewife because she was deceived. The ordinary sensible observer can see little or no difference, but our legal ancestors could. "Shall we indict one man for making a fool of another?" asked a judge rhetorically many years ago, and rightly or wrongly a distinction has been drawn between theft and obtaining property by deception which is difficult to justify logically but which must be observed in practice. Fortunately, the distinction has been blurred for many years and it has now been held[2] that there is no rigid line to be drawn and that the same course of conduct can constitute both appropriation and obtaining by deception at different stages.

There are two principal offences: the first is obtaining property by deception under s. 15, where the overlap with theft is very substantial[3] and the second is obtaining a pecuniary advantage by deception under s. 16 which comprises a variety of frauds and other actions which would be impossible to force into the definition of theft.

"Deception" means, for the purposes of the two offences, "any deception (whether deliberate or reckless) by words or

1. *Ibid.*, s. 12 (4).
2. *Lawrence* v. *Metropolitan Police Commissioner*, [1972] A.C. 626; [1971] 2 All E.R. 1253; *C. & J. Cases.*
3. Para. 11.20 onwards.

conduct as to fact or as to law, including a deception as to the present intentions of the person using the deception or any other person".[1] Five separate points emerge:

a. reckless deception;
b. deception by conduct;
c. deception concerning the law;
d. deception concerning a person's present intentions;
e. omission or concealment.

Recklessness

11.14 In this context "reckless" bears its subjective meaning[2] of the state of mind of someone who knows that there is a risk that his statement is false, but nonetheless makes it without caring whether it is true or false.[3] Suppose an accountant whose sole concern is to induce someone to pay him money for investment in a company makes a favourable report on the financial position of the company without checking certain accounts and knowing that there is a good chance that they would reveal a far less happy state of affairs. If the money were duly paid, the accountant might well be held guilty of dishonestly obtaining the payment by reckless deception. If the accountant had checked the accounts and believed his report to be true, however incompetently he may have acted, he would not be guilty of an offence under s. 15 of the Act because negligence does not constitute recklessness in the present context.[4]

Conduct

11.15 The inclusion of deception by conduct covers not only express misrepresentation by conduct, as where someone in Oxford who is not an Oxford undergraduate puts on a gown in order to convey the impression that he is,[5] but also implied representations, such as the representation that someone who sells property has a right to do so. That is why we said[6] that the disposal of stolen goods by way of sale by someone protected from a charge of theft by s. 3 (2) of the Act would amount to obtaining the price by deception. A common example of an implied deception concerns bouncing cheques. The law implies that the giver of a cheque represents that he has an account at the bank and that

1. Theft Act 1968, ss. 15 (4) and 16 (3).
2. See para. 3.21.
3. *Derry* v. *Peek* (1889), 14 App. Cas. 337; *Staines* (1975), 60 Cr. App. Rep. 160.
4. *Staines* (1975), 60 Cr. App. Rep. 160.
5. *Barnard* (1837), 7 C. & P. 784.
6. Para. 10.5.

the cheque will be honoured either because the account is in credit or because he has arranged or will arrange an overdraft.[1]

Law

6 Assuming that the other ingredients of the offence are present, it seems right that deception about the law should be enough, although it is not clear that a misrepresentation of law will found civil liability in the tort of deceit.[2]

Intention

7 Greatly to the detriment of the criminal law, it used to be held in the context of false pretences that a statement of intention was not a statement of fact. This meant that someone who made a promise with the intention of breaking it was not guilty of making a false pretence. The definition of deception makes it clear that the making of a false promise can amount to deception. The promise may of course be implied from the nature of the transaction in which the accused engages. A request for a loan of money implies a promise to repay, and a purchase of goods implies a promise to pay for them but, while it is true that an intention never to repay the loan or never to pay for the goods is one thing, to prove it is another.

Omission and concealment

8 Misrepresentation by omission or concealment is not mentioned in the definition of deception presently being considered. In *Director of Public Prosecutions* v. *Ray*,[3] the majority of the House of Lords held that if a representation is made which is true at the time but which subsequently becomes untrue there is a deception if the representor fails to inform the representee. In this case the accused ordered a meal in a restaurant thereby impliedly representing that he would pay for it, which was then his true intention. Having consumed the meal, the accused decided not to pay for it and sat inactively at his table until the waiter left the room, when he made his escape. The House upheld the accused's conviction for obtaining a pecuniary advantage by deception, his initial true representation having become false. It is uncertain to what extent other types of concealment may constitute a deception for present purposes, e.g. where A fails to point out to B who is selling something to him

---

1. See, for instance, *Page*, [1971] 2 Q.B. 330; [1971] 2 All E.R. 870.
2. *Winfield and Jolowicz on Tort*, 9th ed., 219–220.
3. [1974] A.C. 370; [1973] 3 All E.R. 131; para. 11.27.

under the impression that it is of little value that it is really very valuable.

Obtaining property by deception

11.19 Section 15 (1) of the Act of 1968 provides that a person who by any deception dishonestly obtains the ownership, possession or control of property belonging to another with the intention of permanently depriving him of it is guilty of an offence punishable with imprisonment for a maximum of 10 years.

In addition to proving deception, the prosecution must prove that:

a. the accused acted dishonestly;
b. his deception caused the victim to part with the ownership, possession or control of the property;[1] and
c. the accused intended to deprive his victim permanently of the property.

In some cases, no detailed direction to the jury about dishonesty is required because, if the accused did what he is alleged to have done his conduct could not fail to be dishonest, but, especially where the case is one of reckless deception, a careful direction on the subject of dishonesty is sometimes necessary.[2] The question of dishonesty is one of fact for the jury in each case.[3]

The normal way of proving that the property was obtained in consequence of the deception is to ask the prosecutor this very question, but the jury will sometimes be entitled to infer the requisite causation. The precise nature of the deception alleged against the accused is very relevant to the question whether it was the deception which caused the prosecutor to part with his property. Someone who buys a second-hand car in ignorance of the fact that the number plates have been altered may have been under the impression that the vendor was representing that the car was the original car to which that number was assigned, or he may merely have acted on the true implied representation that the vendor was the owner of the actual car which he was buying, in which latter case the purchase money will not have been obtained by deception.[4]

---

1. In Kovacs, [1974] 1 All E.R. 1236 it was held that the deception could be of one person as a result of which another was deprived of his property. There is now (January 1976) pending in the House of Lords in *Charles* (1975), *Times*, November 25) in which Kovacs may be reconsidered.
2. Potger (1969), 55 Cr. App. Rep. 42.
3. *Greenstein*, [1976] 1 All E.R. 1. Paras. 10.21–10.23.
4. *Laverty*, [1970] 3 All E.R. 432.

Section 15 (2) of the Act expressly provides that "obtain" includes obtaining for another or enabling another to obtain or retain. "Property" includes money and all other property, real or personal, including things in action and other intangible property.[1] Thus land may be the subject of this offence, although generally it cannot be stolen.

The extended meaning of "intention of permanently depriving" provided for by s. 6 of the Act in relation to the definition of theft[2] is applied to deception by s. 15 (3).

Theft and obtaining property by deception

20 As we have seen, there is a considerable overlap of theft and obtaining property by deception in the sense that the same conduct may constitute both offences. Someone who hires a car without any intention of returning it to the owner both steals the car (when he appropriates it) and obtains possession of it by deception (when he obtains it), but there is some uncertainty about the precise extent of the overlap. A very large number of cases of theft have nothing to do with obtaining property by deception for the simple reason that no deception was practised by the accused; within this category come all cases of theft by direct taking and all cases of theft of property the original receipt of which was entirely innocent, for example by a bailee or trustee. A very few cases of obtaining property by deception cannot possibly be theft because the property cannot be stolen; land and wild plants growing on it may be obtained by deception although there could not be a conviction of theft.[3] Subject to this very limited class of exception whenever possession or control, without ownership, of property is dishonestly obtained by deception with the intention of permanently depriving the person to whom it belongs, theft is also committed.

.21 Where a person gets ownership as well as possession of property by another's mistake which he induces by deception, and is under an obligation to make restoration of the property or its proceeds or of the value thereof, the offence is both obtaining property by deception and theft. This is because s. 5 (4) of the Act[4] expressly provides that, to the extent of the obligation to make restoration, the property or proceeds are regarded, as against the accused, as belonging to the person entitled to restoration, and an intention not to make restoration is regarded

---

1. Theft Act 1968, s. 34 (1) applies s. 4 (1) to s. 15.
2. Para. 10.25.
3. Paras. 10.16 and 10.17.
4. Paras. 10.11–10.13.

as an intention to deprive the person entitled to it permanently of the property. A servant who falsely informs his master that he has not received an advance of £20 on his weekly wage of £30 and thereby obtains the full £30 is guilty both of obtaining £20 by deception and of stealing that sum although he became the owner of the money on receiving it.

At this point dispute begins. Is s. 5 (4) confined to a very limited class of case of which it is difficult to think of examples other than a mistake as to the amount due, or does it cover all cases in which ownership is obtained in consequence of a mistake? If the latter view is correct, all cases of obtaining property by deception must necessarily be theft with the unimportant exception of cases in which land or wild plants are obtained. However, we have already seen that it is doubtful whether s. 5 (4) can be applied to such cases as the obtaining of a sale of goods on credit by deception because, unless and until the contract is avoided by the vendor, the purchaser is not under an obligation to make restoration to him of the property or its proceeds or value.[1]

This is not the end of the matter; it is arguable that, quite apart from s. 5 (4), all cases in which ownership is obtained by deception, apart from those of land and wild plants, are cases of theft. This raises the question whether someone can be said to "appropriate property belonging to another" when he dishonestly induces the transfer of ownership by deception. A offers to buy goods on credit from B without intending to pay for them: B accepts the offer and instantly delivers the goods. Can A be said to have "assumed the rights of an owner" within the meaning of s. 3 (1) of the Act while the property still belonged to B within the meaning of s. 5 (1), or did he merely obtain those rights from B within the meaning of s. 15?[2]

11.22 In *Lawrence* v. *Metropolitan Police Commissioner*,[3] an Italian student who spoke little English wanted to take a taxi from Victoria Station in London to Ladbroke Grove. The accused, a taxi driver, said it was a long way and very expensive, although the correct fare was only in the region of 50p. The student, holding open his wallet, gave a pound to the accused, and the accused took a further £6 from the wallet. He was charged with stealing this sum. He was convicted and unsuccessfully appealed to the

---

1. Para. 10.13.
2. Para. 11.20.
3. [1972] A.C. 626; [1971] 2 All E.R. 1253; *C. & J. Cases*.

Court of Appeal and House of Lords. The student did not consent to the appropriation because there was no evidence that he agreed to pay more than the correct fare, but Lord Dilhorne stressed that on a charge of theft the prosecution does not have to prove that appropriation was without the owner's consent. When the £6 was taken from the wallet, it belonged to the student. If the facts had been different it would have been possible to test the question of the extent of the overlap between theft and deception: if the taxi driver had stipulated for and obtained the payment of the excessive fare in advance and then driven off on receiving it, he would have been guilty of obtaining ownership of the money by deception because he never intended to carry out his part of the bargain, but would he also have been guilty of theft? There would have been no appropriation until the money was handed over, but on the handing over of the money it would have ceased to belong to the student. Lord Dilhorne's speech contained the following remark: "In some cases the facts may justify a charge under s. 1 (1) and also a charge under s. 15 (1). On the other hand there are cases which only come within s. 1 (1) and some which are only within s. 15 (1)". It is unlikely, although it is possible, that the concluding observation relates to the obtaining of land by deception, but another authoritative decision is required before it is possible for anyone to make a definitive statement about the precise extent of the overlap of theft and deception. In the meantime it must be regarded as an open question whether the offence would be obtaining ownership alone, or theft as well, when a sale of goods on credit, an advance payment for services to be rendered, or a loan of money is obtained by deception. The prudent course for the prosecution to adopt in cases of doubt is to charge deception or to charge theft and deception in the alternative.

Obtaining a pecuniary advantage by deception

23 Section 16 of the Theft Act provides that a person who by any deception dishonestly obtains for himself or another any pecuniary advantage commits an offence. The cases in which a pecuniary advantage within the meaning of the section is to be regarded as obtained for a person are those where:

a. "any debt or charge for which he makes himself liable or is or may become liable (including one not legally enforceable) is reduced or in whole or in part evaded or deferred; or
b. he is allowed to borrow by way of overdraft, or to take out any policy of insurance or annuity contract, or obtains an improvement of the terms on which he is allowed to do so; or

c. he is given the opportunity to earn remuneration or greater remuneration in an office or employment, or to win money by betting".[1]

This is the section which Edmund Davies, L.J., described as creating a judicial nightmare.[2] More recently, Lord Reid has said "... I would hope that ways can be found of drafting such provisions in a form which does not require elaborate and rarified analysis to discover their meaning.... No doubt any attempt to make such provisions readily intelligible would require them to be greatly expanded, but surely any disadvantage arising from that would be trifling in comparison with the advantage of making them intelligible to more than a minute proportion of Her Majesty's subjects to whom they are addressed".[3] No one therefore can say that he has not been warned. The offence is at present (January 1976) being reconsidered by the Criminal Law Revision Committee, which published provisional proposals for reform in May 1974.[4]

The section is designed to cover a wide range of situations where the accused has been both dishonest and deceitful but has not thereby obtained any property within the meaning of s. 4 (1), although he has gained some advantage which can be expressed in pecuniary terms as a result of his deception. A obtains employment by falsely stating that he has a degree; B engages a taxi driver to drive him from Reading to Birmingham having no intention to pay the fare, and makes off without doing so on arrival at his destination; both may be convicted under s. 16. We will deal in turn with the three different types of pecuniary advantage, one of which must be obtained as the result of the accused's deception.

In paragraph a. the deception must result in the evasion or reduction (in whole or in part) or deferment of a debt or charge (whether or not it is legally enforceable) for which the accused makes himself liable or is or may become liable. One open question is whether there is any difference between a debt and a charge and so far no one has succeeded in producing a convincing one. Charge has been defined[5] as whatsoever constitutes a burden on property as rents, taxes, liens, etc. whereas a debt is

1. Theft Act 1968, s. 16 (2).
2. *Royle*, [1971] 3 All E.R. 1359.
3. *Director of Public Prosecutions* v. *Turner*, [1974] A.C. 357, at p. 368; [1973] 3 All E.R. 124, at p. 129.
4. Criminal Law Revision Committee, Working Paper, *S. 16 of the Theft Act 1968*.
5. *Webster's New International Dictionary*.

defined as that which is due from one person to another whether money, goods or services. Until the point arises there is no advantage in speculating in the abstract.

24 Most of the nightmares in the offence have centred round the requirement of evasion, reduction or deferment of a debt or charge and these have lost some of their terror since the unanimous decision of the House of Lords in *Director of Public Prosecutions* v. *Turner*,[1] where a previous conflict in case law was resolved.

In *Turner* the accused employed two brothers to do some work in a house. At a certain point sums amounting to £24 and £14 had become due to them, but when one of them went to collect the money the accused told him that he did not have any ready cash and asked him to accept a cheque for £38 which was agreed. This cheque was dishonoured and the accused knew that it would be. There was therefore ample material from which the jury could infer that the accused was dishonest, had practised deception and that the deception had caused the cheque to be accepted, the brothers being deceived into believing that the debt had been paid. The House of Lords held that the accused had properly been convicted under s. 16 because, by deception, he had obtained the evasion of the debts for which he was liable. Lord Reid (with the concurrence of his brethren) said that a debt "is evaded if by some contrivance the debtor avoids or gets out of fulfilling or performing his obligation. In the days when such things happened a welshing bookmaker not only evaded his pursuers, he also evaded his obligations. Evasion does not necessarily mean permanent escape. If the bookmaker evaded his pursuers on Monday, the fact that he is caught and made to pay up on Tuesday does not alter the fact that he evaded his obligations on Monday. Unlike reducing and deferring an obligation, evading an obligation is a unilateral operation. It leaves the obligation untouched and does not connote any activity on the part of the creditor".[2] Another example of an evasion of a debt is provided by *Page*[3] where the accused gave cheques, knowing they would bounce, in payment of a deposit and of hire charges at the time of hiring a car. His conviction under s. 16 was upheld because by deception he had obtained the evasion of a debt for which he then had made himself liable.

---

1. [1974] A.C. 357; [1973] 3 All E.R. 124.
2. [1974] A.C., at pp. 365–366.
3. [1971] 2 Q.B. 330; [1971] 2 All E.R. 870; *C. & J. Cases.*

11.25 Deferment and reduction of a debt or charge, unlike evasion, are not unilateral and require the agreement of the creditor. In *Turner*, Lord Reid said that a debt "is deferred if creditor and debtor agree that the date of performance be postponed ... Deferment of the debt necessarily requires the consent of the creditor because it alters the obligation to pay"[1] and that a debt "is reduced if the creditor agrees with the debtor that the amount owed shall be reduced".[2]

There is a certain amount of overlap between evasion and deferment according to some of their Lordships (but not Lord Reid) in *Turner*. According to them a person obtains the deferment of a debt, as well as its evasion, if he induces a creditor to accept a cheque instead of cash. It would certainly be more natural to say that the debt in such a case had been deferred in consequence of deception. In *Page* the owner of the car would certainly not have given any credit for his fees or accepted a cheque as conditional payment had it not been for the deception. The same can be said of *Waterfall*,[3] where the accused induced a taxi driver to drive him from Southampton to London for £14 by falsely stating that he had the money to pay. He never paid the fare and was charged with and convicted of obtaining a pecuniary advantage by deception. The conviction was quashed on the ground that the jury had been misdirected on the question of dishonesty because of a suggestion that an unreasonable belief, even though honestly entertained, that he could get the money in London would not have afforded a defence to the accused, but the Court of Appeal said that the accused had obtained a pecuniary advantage because he had made himself liable for a debt which he had evaded. It would have been much more natural to have said that he had produced the deferment of a debt, i.e. the granting of credit by deception.

The following are clear illustrations of evasion: A owes B £100 and promises, in consideration of B's releasing the debt, to work for him. A never intended to keep his promise; a debt for which A is liable is evaded. An employee without authority or hope induces an hotelier to whom he owes money for board to look to his employer for payment; a debt for which the employee is liable has been evaded.[4] A has guaranteed B's overdraft but by deception he induces the bank to accept a substitute

1. [1974] A.C., at p. 365.
2. *Ibid.*
3. [1970] 1 Q.B. 148; [1969] 3 All E.R. 1048; *C. & J. Cases.*
4. *Nordeng* (1975), *Times*, December 2nd.

guarantor; a debt for which A may become liable has been evaded.

26 One nightmare at least which remains is the problem of obtaining reduced credit. Suppose that A, knowing that a taxi-driver carries pensioners at reduced rates, induces the driver to take him to Birmingham at a reduced rate by falsely saying that he is a pensioner; A has clearly obtained a reduced debt by deception, but can it be said that he has, by deception, obtained the reduction of a debt for which he makes himself liable? The better view is that it cannot since the only debt for which A makes himself liable is the reduced sum which the driver has agreed to charge. By deception A has made himself liable for a reduced debt but he has not, by deception, obtained the reduction of a debt for which he makes himself liable.[1]

27 One problem which has been engaging the attention of the Criminal Law Revision Committee in its consideration of s. 16 is that of restaurant and other bilkers.

In *Director of Public Prosecutions* v. *Ray*[2] the accused, who was a student, went into a restaurant with some others and ordered a meal, fully intending to pay. After he had eaten the meal, he decided not to pay for it and so became dishonest because there was nothing wrong with it. The Criminal Law Revision Committee point out that in *Ray* the mischief would have been as great but not criminal if the diner had run out of the restaurant immediately he decided not to pay the bill; because Ray purposely waited until the waiter had left the room and then ran out there was an element of deception and he was held guilty under s. 16 by the House of Lords by a majority of three to two on the basis that he had obtained the evasion of a debt by deception. In *Guildford* v. *Lockyer*[3] the accused went in a party of five to a restaurant and ordered a dish but it was not delivered and he complained about its non-delivery. He ate some portion of one of the dishes which had been delivered but he did not like it because it was cold and he left without paying anything and without practising any deception of any kind. He was acquitted on a charge under s. 16 on the ground not only that he had incurred no debt but that he had obtained no pecuniary advantage by deception. The difference is that in *Ray* there was held to

1. For two views on this problem, see Elliot, [1969] Crim. L. R. 339 and Smith, [1971] *ibid.* 448.
2. [1974] A.C. 370; [1973] 3 All E.R. 131. Para. 11.18.
3. (1975), 119 Sol. Jo. 353.

be continuing misrepresentation of intention to pay while the waiter remained in the room. The question arises whether the requirement for a trace of deception is not wholly unreal. The Criminal Law Revision Committee say:

"If a new offence is justified it should not be limited to restaurant bilking. Indeed, it must be very rare to be able to allege any deception of the waiter. Similar problems arise where a motorist fills the tank of his car with petrol at a self-service petrol station and then decides to leave without paying, or an hotel guest leaves without paying his bill. This suggests that the problem arises wherever the customer knows that he is expected to pay on the spot for goods supplied to him or services done for him. The question is whether, in such circumstances, it should be an offence dishonestly to go away without having paid and intending never to pay.

"While there may be a case for creating such an offence there are arguments the other way. The proposal can be represented as making it an offence to fail to pay a particular kind of debt and so producing a risk that the threat of prosecution will be used by creditors to enforce their claims. This argument applies in particular to the case of the lodger who leaves his lodgings without paying the outstanding rent. It would be possible to provide a specific exclusion for this case but can it be distinguished from the case of the guest who leaves an hotel without paying the bill? In many cases the hotel keeper is in a much stronger position to enforce his rights at civil law than is the proprietor of a restaurant or filling station, but there must be other cases where a civil claim against the dishonest guest is worthless. Clearly there is a case for keeping the hotel fraud within the proposed offence. While we are very conscious of the difficulties, we have come reluctantly to the conclusion that an offence on these lines may be needed. Of course, our views are provisional only and we are particularly anxious to receive comment on this proposal before we reach our final conclusions."

11.28 Paragraphs (b) and (c) of s. 16 (2) have so far not given rise to any problems.[1] The reason for inserting borrowing by way of overdraft is because it is not always possible to identify a particular sum or sums which have been obtained; this would be necessary for a conviction under s. 15 whereas paragraph b. enables a person to be prosecuted for obtaining permission to

1. In Kovacs, [1974] 1 All E.R. 1236 the point at issue was the causation between the deception and the pecuniary advantage and not whether the accused received a pecuniary advantage. There is now (January 1976) an appeal pending in the House of Lords in *Charles* (1975), (*Times*, November 25th) in which Kovacs may be reconsidered.

overdraw without actually making use of it. Equally, a person who makes a proposal for and is granted a life insurance policy without disclosing that he is suffering from some disease may not obtain any benefit because the deception may be discovered before any money is payable. Someone applying for employment may represent that he has experience which he has not whereby he is given employment. He commits an offence even if he is paid nothing and even if he does receive his wages he is not guilty of obtaining them by deception because the work he has done, not his deception, is the effective cause of his being paid.[1] The reference to winning money by betting appears to have been inserted purely in order to make it an offence to deceive someone into accepting a bet: in *Clucas*[2] it had been held that the accused could not be convicted of what is now obtaining property by deception because the winnings were paid to the accused as the result of his horse winning and not because the bookmaker would not have accepted the bet. There has been only one case in which it has been suggested that a charge under s. 16 (2) (c) would have been appropriate: in *Aston and Hadley*[3] the accused placed a bet in a betting shop but Aston counted out the notes very slowly and when it became clear that the dog they had backed was not going to win they retrieved the money and left. They were acquitted of evading the debt by deception but the Court of Appeal thought that by placing the bet they were falsely representing they were going to pay and so were given the opportunity to win money by betting.

29 Finally, in relation to the above types of pecuniary advantage, it must be stressed that the list in paragraphs (a) to (c) is exhaustive and that the words "... is to be regarded as obtained ..." mean that the accused need not be proved to have obtained any actual profit. The House of Lords in *Turner* held that this is the meaning of the words so that a penniless man who dishonestly evades a debt by deception may be convicted even though he had no money to pay with and would therefore have been in the same situation if he had not resorted to deception.

We assume that "dishonestly" is a question of fact to be decided by the jury.

Falsification

30 Sections 17–20 of the Theft Act 1968 define several offences dealing with false accounting, making false statements and procuring the execution or destruction of valuable securities, but

1. *Lewis* (1922), *Russell on Crime*, 12th ed., p. 1186n. Para. 11.19.
2. [1949] 2 K.B. 226; [1949] 2 All E.R. 40.
3. [1970] 3 All E.R. 1045.

they do not call for detailed discussion. Section 17 punishes the falsification of accounts with a view to gain or with intent to cause loss and is a very convenient section to use where there has been an elaborate and complicated system of fraud in which it is not easy to identify the particular sums of money and other property of which the owner has been deprived. This is one of those offences in which the definitions of gain and loss in s. 34, which are discussed in para. 11.32, are incorporated as well as dishonesty, so that temporary as well as permanent gain or loss is relevant. Under s. 18 the directors and secretaries of bodies corporate are liable for deception or falsification of accounts by those bodies[1] committed with their consent or connivance; s. 19 punishes the making of false statements by the officers of bodies corporate with intent to deceive, while s. 20 punishes the destruction, defacement or concealment of valuable securities and wills or the procuring of the execution of a valuable security provided, in each instance, that the accused acted dishonestly and with a view to gain for himself or another or with intent to cause loss to another.

Prevention of fraud in investments

11.31 Section 13 of the Prevention of Fraud (Investments) Act 1958 punishes with a maximum of seven years' imprisonment any person who, by any statement, promise or forecast which he knows to be misleading, false or deceptive, or by any dishonest concealment of material facts induces any person to enter into various transactions relating to the purchase or acquisition of stocks and shares, or the deposit of monies with industrial, building or provident societies. Many such offences are now covered by ss. 15 and 16 of the Theft Act 1968 but the overlap is not complete. First, on the preponderance of authority, a person can be reckless within the meaning of the Act of 1958 without being dishonest: all that the prosecution must prove is that the person making the statement knew of no real basis of fact (including what he had been told by other responsible persons) on which it could be founded[2] so that *mens rea* is objective, which is against the present current of judicial and parliamentary thought;[3] secondly, there can be cases in which an offence under the Act of 1958 is committed by someone who does not obtain any

1. Paras. 5.35 to 5.44.
2. Para. 3.27.
3. For example, Theft Act 1968 and *Director of Public Prosecutions* v. *Morgan*, [1975] 2 All E.R. 347.

property or pecuniary advantage within the meaning of the Theft Act; thirdly, mere concealment, if dishonest, suffices for an offence under the Act of 1958. The aim of that Act is to control investments generally. It contains a number of elaborate provisions which have nothing to do with the criminal law, and it does not call for further discussion here.

Blackmail

32 By s. 21 of the Theft Act a person is guilty of blackmail, an offence punishable with imprisonment for a maximum of 14 years, if, with a view to gain for himself or another or with intent to cause loss to another, he makes any unwarranted demand with menaces; and for this purpose a demand with menaces is unwarranted unless the person making it does so in the belief that he has reasonable grounds for making the demand, and that the use of the menaces is a proper means of reinforcing the demand.

The essence of the offence is a demand, so that a person may be guilty of blackmail if the other ingredients are present, and not merely of an attempt, if he obtains nothing. The nature of the act or omission demanded is immaterial[1] but, as it must be made with a view to material gain or intent to cause material loss, it usually takes the form of a demand for property; it can take the form of a demand that property, such as compromising letters, be destroyed or that the victim should submit to some indignity such as having his house daubed with paint, so long as the intent to cause material gain or loss can be proved. In *Treacy* v. *Director of Public Prosecutions*[2] the House of Lords held by a majority that a demand by letter is made where the letter is posted; it is therefore irrelevant that the letter is never delivered. More than in other offences under the Theft Act, it is possible for action to be taken partly within the jurisdiction of the English courts and partly outside. A demand may be in writing and posted outside the jurisdiction addressed to the victim within the jurisdiction or *vice versa*. We consider this subject more fully,[3] on the limits of criminal jurisdiction.

When the word was first used in this branch of the law, "menaces" meant threats of violence, but it has long since come to mean "threats of action detrimental to or unpleasant to the person addressed".[4] It is immaterial whether the menaces do or

1. Theft Act 1968, s. 21 (2).
2. [1971] A.C. 537; [1971] 1 All E.R. 110.
3. Para. 21.8.
4. *Thorne* v. *Motor Trade Association*, [1937] A.C. 797, at p. 817 *per* Lord Wright.

do not relate to action to be taken by the person making the demand.[1] The thug who says "Give me money or the boys will beat you up", and the man who says "Cancel the debt I owe you or my daughter will tell the world that you seduced her", are both as guilty of blackmail as the man who reinforces his demands with threats of action by himself.

If, on the facts known to the accused, his menace was such that the mind of an ordinary person of normal stability might be influenced so as to accede unwillingly to the demand, it does not matter that the addressee was not influenced by it.[2]

Under s. 34 (2) of the Act "gain" and "loss" are confined to money or other property but they may be temporary, which differentiates blackmail from most other offences under the Act. Hence girl A who tells girl B that A will reveal details of B's sexual aberrations to her fiancé unless B lends her a dress for a dance is guilty of blackmail. "Gain" includes a gain by keeping what one has, as well as getting what one has not; "loss" includes a loss by not getting what one might get, as well as losing what one has. A person presumably acts with a view to gain if he seeks to recover a debt, for he is endeavouring to get money which he has not got although it is legally due to him, but so long as the menaces go no further than the threat of legal proceedings no offence is committed since, as we shall see in the next paragraph, it is inconceivable that the demand with menaces would be found to be unwarranted.

The subjective nature of *mens rea* in the Act generally is particularly important in blackmail. Assuming the issue is raised by the accused, the prosecution must negative either the accused's belief that he had reasonable grounds for making the demand, or his belief that the use of the menaces was a proper means of enforcing it. It seems clear that the accused is to be judged according to his own moral standards, which is different from the defence of claim of right in its normal form because that consists of a belief on the part of the accused that he is legally entitled to act as he did[3] whereas in blackmail the accused's belief that his conduct is morally justified is a defence. It follows that the man whose moral standards are subnormal will be lucky, while the man whose moral standards are above normal will be unlucky because he will be liable to be convicted although the jury thinks that he acted reasonably.

---

1. Theft Act 1968, s. 21 (2).
2. *Clear*, [1968] 1 Q.B. 670; [1968] 1 All E.R. 74.
3. Para. 10.20.

For example, the mother of an illegitimate child by a rich and distinguished man demands a settlement of a large sum of money in excess of her legal rights for the benefit of the child against a threat to publish the facts in the press; the average Englishman might well consider the demand to be reasonable but the means of enforcing it to be improper; the woman must be acquitted unless the jury are satisfied that she did not believe her demand was reasonable or did not believe her means of enforcing it were proper.

Handling

33 By s. 22 of the Act a person handles stolen goods if (otherwise than in the course of the stealing) knowing or believing them to be stolen goods he dishonestly receives the goods, or dishonestly undertakes or assists in their retention, removal, disposal or realisation by or for the benefit of another person, or if he arranges to do so. Handling stolen goods is punishable with imprisonment for a maximum of 14 years.

There is considerable overlap between handling and theft. Some forms of handling involve appropriation by the handler who is therefore guilty of theft if the other conditions of s. 1 are fulfilled, but there are two reasons for having the separate offence of handling: one is that there are dealings with property which do not involve appropriation of property belonging to another and the other is that professional receivers of stolen property, or fences, are a serious menace and it is widely believed that without fences there would be fewer thieves so that handling is punishable more severely than theft.

The expression "goods" includes money and every other description of property, except land, and includes things severed from the land by stealing.[1] "Stolen goods" mean goods obtained in England or Wales or elsewhere by theft under s. 1, by deception under s. 15 or blackmail under s. 21 of the Act.[2] However, where goods were so obtained abroad the act by which they were stolen or obtained must also have been criminal by the law of the foreign country in question.[3] One vital limitation is that no goods which have been stolen are regarded as having continued to be stolen goods after one of the following events has occurred:[4]

a. After they have been restored to the person from whom they were stolen or to other lawful possession or custody; there-

---

1. Theft Act 1968, s. 34 (2) (b).
2. *Ibid.*, s. 24 (4).
3. *Ibid.*, s. 24 (1).
4. *Ibid.*, s. 24 (3).

fore, if the owner of goods which have been stolen resumes possession of them and then sets a trap for an intending receiver by passing them to him, the intending handler must be acquitted of handling.

It is often difficult to decide whether goods have been restored to lawful possession or custody, particularly when the police have traced the goods. In *Haughton* v. *Smith*,[1] it was admitted that the police had taken the goods into lawful custody; in *Attorney-General's Reference No. 1 of 1974*[2] (the first case in which use was made of the power conferred by s. 36 of the Criminal Justice Act 1972 to refer to the Court of Appeal a case where there has been an acquittal), it was held that it was for the jury to decide whether a police officer who had removed the rotor arm of a car containing goods about which the officer wished to question the driver had assumed control of the goods and reduced them into possession, or merely removed the rotor arm in order that the driver should not get away without interrogation. There are conflicting cases on this subject, both before and after the Act came into operation, and the only conclusion is that each case must be decided on its own facts.

b. After the person from whom they were stolen and any other person claiming through him have otherwise ceased as regards those goods to have any right to restitution in respect of the theft, so that if goods are obtained by deception and the original owner confirms the voidable title, he has lost his claim to restitution and the intending handler must be acquitted.

There is no escape merely because the goods or money stolen have been sold or used to buy goods as the case may be, because the proceeds of goods which have been stolen or obtained by blackmail or deception are deemed to be stolen goods and a person may be convicted of handling them.[3]

11.34 It has been calculated by Professor J. C. Smith[4] that there may be 18 different forms of handling but there is only one offence,[5] although the particulars in the indictment should be specific enough to enable the accused to know which form of handling is alleged. Receiving entails obtaining possession of the goods for the receiver's own benefit and this may occur by gift or sale.

1. [1973] 3 All E.R. 1109. See para. 17.22.
2. [1974] Q.B. 744; [1974] 2 All E.R. 899.
3. Theft Act 1968, s. 24 (4).
4. *The Law of Theft*, 2nd ed., para. 468.
5. *Griffiths* v. *Freeman*, [1970] 1 All E.R. 117.

The receiver need not have physical contact with the goods so long as he takes them under his control or an agent or servant does so acting under his orders, in which case the agent or servant is also a receiver if he has the necessary *mens rea*.[1] The other forms of handling which are set out in s. 22 (1) differ in one vital respect from receiving or arranging to receive in that all must be done "by or for the benefit of" a person other than the handler. Thus, one who assists in the removal of stolen goods must do so by or for the benefit of another, while one who undertakes their disposal must do so for the benefit of another. If the apparent handler is working solely for his own benefit he can only be charged with theft. It is necessary that the words "by or for the benefit of another" appear in the indictment where the case is not one of receiving.[2] A person assists in the retention of stolen goods by or for the benefit of another if he provides accommodation for them, but not if he merely fails to disclose their whereabouts to the police.[3] He assists in the retention of goods if he provides tarpaulins to protect them in someone else's warehouse; he undertakes their removal by lending the thief a lorry and assists in their disposal by putting the thief in touch with a possible buyer; he undertakes their realisation by selling them as the thief's agent; and arranges to assist in their removal by agreeing to send a van to collect them.

The phraseology of the definition of the offence is wide. The employee of a dishonest transport firm who believes that the goods he has been instructed to carry are stolen is in peril of a conviction for handling. Mere negotiation for the purchase of goods known to be stolen, without any further assistance, does not appear to constitute handling, although it is arguable that the prospective purchaser is assisting, or at least attempting to assist, in the disposal of the goods for the benefit of the thief as well as himself.

Mens rea

35 None of these various actions is enough to amount to handling unless the accused either knows or believes that the goods are stolen (in the extended meaning) when they are handled or at some time while the handling is taking place. It follows that, goods being received when they come into possession, subsequent knowledge by the person that they are stolen does

1. *Smith* (1855), Dears C.C. 559.
2. *Sloggett*, [1972] 1 Q.B. 430; [1971] 3 All E.R. 264.
3. *Brown*, [1970] 1 Q.B. 105; [1969] 3 All E.R. 198.

not make him a handler: if he received the goods as a gift and decides to keep them in spite of his knowledge, he appropriates them under s. 3 (1) and only if they were transferred to him for value in good faith is he protected by s. 3 (2).[1] A person knows that goods are stolen if the thief tells him so and presumably he believes they were stolen if he realises no other explanation is possible; the accused must be shown at least not only to have suspected that the goods were stolen but also to have deliberately shut his eyes to the obvious by refraining from inquiries the answers to which he would not have cared to have;[2] mere suspicion is not enough,[3] and still less is someone guilty of handling if he merely ought to have known that the goods were stolen, the test of knowledge being subjective.[4]

Knowledge or belief that the goods were stolen is not enough: the prosecution must also prove that the accused was dishonest so that a person would not be guilty of handling stolen goods, even if he knew them to be stolen, if he acquired them in order to return them to the owner, or to hand them over to the police. There would likewise be no handling if someone induced a thief to hand a stolen gun over to him in order to prevent the thief from committing suicide by shooting himself. In these cases the accused would not have been acting dishonestly.

11.36 The requirement that the handling must have been "otherwise than in the course of the stealing" means that the original thief is not guilty of handling so long as the stealing continues, nor is one of joint thieves, even in respect of the assistance he gives to the other or others. It is difficult to define exactly when the course of the stealing finishes. The thief is guilty of handling the goods he stole if he afterwards sells them to a receiver since he dishonestly undertakes their realisation for the benefit of another, and the receiver, in addition to being guilty of handling, is a thief by appropriating them or selling them to someone else. Where the prosecution has a choice of charging theft or handling, it is suggested that the wisest plan is to charge both in the alternative.

11.37 Section 23 of the Act punishes as a summary offence public advertisements of a reward for the return of stolen goods with statements to the effect that no questions will be asked or that the person returning them will be safe from inquiry or that

1. Para. 10.5.
2. *Grainge*, [1974] 1 All E.R. 928.
3. *Ibid.*
4. *Atwal* v. *Massey*, [1971] 3 All E.R. 881.

money spent on the goods will be returned. The printers and publishers are liable as well as the advertiser. The maximum punishment is a fine of £100.

Going equipped

38 Section 25 of the Act provides that a person is guilty of an offence punishable with a maximum of three years' imprisonment if, when not at his place of abode, he has with him any article for use in the course of or in connection with any burglary, theft, or deception under s. 15 or an offence under s. 12.

This offence, like burglary, is a form of preventive criminal law in that it penalises acts which are preparatory but which probably do not amount to attempts. Even so, it is still not an offence for a person to have at his place of abode articles which are for use in the course of any offence mentioned in s. 25, but if he is away from his place of abode he commits an offence if he has any such article with him. Some articles are specifically and clearly made or adapted for criminal use, and possession of these is rebuttable evidence that they are intended for such use,[1] but there must be very few of them. Most articles have both innocent and criminal uses and the prosecution must prove that such articles were intended for criminal use.

It is not necessary to prove that the accused intended the article to be used in the course of or in connection with any particular burglary, theft or cheat: it is enough to prove a general intention that it should be used for some burglary, theft or cheat. Nor is it necessary to prove that the accused intended to use the article himself, but it is not enough to prove that the article had been used before the accused came into possession of it.[2] Nor is it enough to prove that the articles were used to get a job which would give the opportunity to steal.[3]

A good example of going equipped to cheat is *Mandry and Wooster*[4] in which the accused, not being at their places of abode, had with them three magazines with false advertisements inserted therein. They were street traders who had inserted in a magazine an advertisement of Fame scent at two guineas a bottle. They then offered the scent at £1 for four bottles and displayed the magazine with the false advertisement, which was held to be an article for use in the course of and in connection with a cheat.

---

1. Theft Act 1968, s. 25 (3).
2. *Ellames*, [1974] 3 All E.R. 130.
3. *Mansfield*, [1975], Crim. L. R. 101.
4. [1973] 3 All E.R. 996.

12

OFFENCES AGAINST PROPERTY 3 OFFENCES OTHER THAN UNDER THE THEFT ACT

12.1 It is sometimes assumed that all offences against property consist in one form or another of depriving its owners of it. This is not so and in this chapter we gather together some offences which are usually concerned with property rather than with the person, although all may have important elements connected with the person.

Criminal damage

12.2 Section 1 (1) of the Criminal Damage Act 1971 provides that a person who without lawful excuse destroys or damages any property belonging to another, intending to destroy or damage such property, or being reckless as to whether any such property would be destroyed or damaged, is guilty of an offence punishable with imprisonment for a maximum of 10 years. If the destruction or damage is by fire, the offence is arson[1] and is punishable with a maximum of imprisonment for life.[2] By s. 1 (2) of the Act a person who without lawful excuse destroys or damages any property, whether belonging to himself or another a. intending to destroy or damage any property or being reckless as to whether any property would be destroyed or damaged; and b. intending by the destruction or damage to endanger the life of another or being reckless as to whether the life of another would be thereby endangered is guilty of an offence punishable with a maximum of imprisonment for life. Section 2 of the Criminal Damage Act punishes with a maximum of 10 years' imprisonment threats made without lawful excuse to destroy or damage property belonging to another or to a third person, if the person making the threats knows that the destruction or damage will endanger the life of the person threatened or a third

1. Criminal Damage Act 1971, s. 1 (3).
2. *Ibid.*, s. 4 (1).

person; a threat to destroy or damage his own property will suffice.

Section 3 punishes with a maximum of 10 years' imprisonment those who have anything in their custody or under their control intending, without lawful excuse, to use it or cause or permit another to use it a. to destroy or damage any property belonging to some other person; or b. to destroy or damage his own or the user's property in a way which he knows is likely to endanger the life of some other person.

"Property" means property of a tangible nature, whether real or personal, including money; it includes wild creatures which have been tamed or are ordinarily kept in captivity, and any other wild creatures or their carcases if, but only if, they have been reduced into possession which has not been lost or abandoned or are in the course of being reduced into possession.[1] "Property" does not include mushrooms or the flowers, fruits or foliage of plants growing wild on any land. Property "belongs" to any person who has the custody or control of it, or any right or proprietary interest in it (not being an equitable interest arising only from an agreement to grant or transfer an interest), or who has a charge on it.[2] Where one spouse damages the other's property proceedings for criminal damage may not be instituted without the consent of the Director of Public Prosecutions, unless, by virtue of any judicial decree or order, the spouses were not obliged to cohabit at the material time.[3]

Arson was the only offence of damage to property known to the common law. Section 11 (1) of the Act of 1971 abolished the common law offence. The preservation of arson as a separate offence may be justified by the exceptional danger to life and property involved in the use of fire for the destruction of or damaging of property. The current statutory offence is broader than the common law offence of arson which was confined to dwelling houses.

It may be assumed that "recklessness" means recklessness in the subjective sense of the deliberate taking of a foreseen and unjustified risk. If it is construed to mean gross negligence, the Act of 1971 will have extended the basis of criminal liability for damage to property for, under the Malicious Damage Act 1861, liability was based on "malice" which, in the context, meant intention to cause the kind of harm prohibited by the statute or foresight of the risk of such harm.[4]

---

1. Para. 10.18.
2. Criminal Damage Act 1971, s. 10. See para. 10.7.
3. Theft Act 1968, s. 30.
4. Paras. 3.23 and 3.24.

12.3 The inclusion in the Act of 1971 of the destruction of, or damage to, property with the intention of endangering life or with recklessness as to whether life is endangered has been criticised on the ground that such conduct should be dealt with in a statute dealing with offences against the person. Under the Criminal Damage Act 1971 a sharp distinction is drawn between offences involving an intention to endanger life or recklessness as to whether life is in danger and other offences. In the first place, it is only in the case of the former offences that the destruction by the accused of his own property renders him liable; secondly, the question whether the accused had a lawful excuse for acting as he did is dependent on the common law where the charge is based on the accused's knowledge that he was endangering the life of another, whereas there is by virtue of s. 5 of the Act of 1971 an additional statutory defence of lawful excuse where the charge is simply based on intention or recklessness with regard to the destruction of, or damage to, property. In these latter cases, the accused has a defence under s. 5 if he believed that the person entitled to consent to the destruction or damage would have consented, or if he acted in the honest belief that he was protecting property belonging to himself or another, whether that belief was well founded or not, provided he believed that the property was in immediate need of protection and that the means of protection adopted were reasonable in all the circumstances.

A few illustrations of the above distinctions may be helpful. A sets fire to his empty house with the intention of making a false claim in respect of its destruction against his insurance company. The house is remote from other houses, so there can be no question of A's having been reckless as to whether the lives of others would be endangered. The house being A's property, he has committed no offence under the Act of 1971, and it is doubtful whether he has committed any offence at all for it would probably be held that A's conduct was not sufficiently proximate to the main offence to constitute an attempt to obtain

money by deception.[1] Let it be assumed that the facts were as set out above, except that A's child was asleep in the house and A acted with reckless disregard for the life of the child. A would be guilty of arson, even if the child miraculously escaped unharmed. B is about to drive off in his car with a load of bombs to be used for terrorist purposes. C threatens to shoot at the car's tyres if B carries out his project. C knows that B's life would

1. *Robinson*, [1915] 2 K.B. 342; para. 17.26.

be endangered if the threat were carried out, but he would probably be held to have had a lawful excuse for the threat by s. 3 of the Criminal Law Act 1967.[1] D has the shooting rights over a piece of land. He shoots and kills E's dog which was chasing a hare on the land. D has a defence to a charge under s. 1 (1) of the Criminal Damage Act if he believed that the hare belonged to him, although this was not so in law, provided he also believed that the hare was in immediate danger and that the shooting of the dog was a reasonable means of preserving the hare. This is the effect of s. 5 of the Act of 1971 which may have varied the previous law.[2]

Section 5 (5) provides that the section is not to be construed as casting doubt on any defence recognised by law as a defence to criminal charges. In *Smith (D. R.)*[3] the accused became the tenant of a ground floor flat including a conservatory in which he installed some electric wiring for use with stereo equipment. With the landlord's permission he put up roofing material and asbestos wall panels and laid floor boards and there was no dispute that these articles became in law the property of the landlord. When the time came to leave the flat the accused damaged the roofing, wall panels and floor boards in order to gain access to and remove the wiring. He claimed that all were his own property. The Court of Appeal held that the honest though mistaken belief that the property was his own was a defence and, provided that the belief is honest, it is irrelevant to consider whether or not it is justifiable.

The Criminal Damage Act largely replaces the Malicious Damage Act 1861, but certain sections of the latter Act remain in force. These are sections dealing with conduct such as the obstruction of railways, the alteration of signals and the cutting away of buoys, which deal with conduct that does not involve the destruction of or damage to property;[4] they do not call for comment here.

Harassment, eviction and forcible entry

4 Whether it is more logical to classify this group of offences as against person or against property is arguable: they may be against both but because some kind of right to property or possession is always involved, it appears better to deal with them under property, although often an assault is involved. Although

1. Para. 18.11.
2. *Gott* v. *Measures*, [1948] 1 K.B. 234; [1947] 2 All E.R. 609.
3. [1974] Q.B. 354; [1974] 1 All E.R. 632.
4. Section 35; s. 36; s. 47.

the Statutes of Forcible Entry have been with us for nearly six centuries, only since 1965 have there been simple and effective provisions which entitle residential tenants to the protection of the criminal law.

Harassment

12.5 By s. 30 (2) of the Rent Act 1965 a landlord commits the offence of harassment if he does acts calculated to interfere with the peace or comfort of his tenant or his family or if he persistently withdraws or withholds services. Before the 1965 Act such things were either breaches of contract or torts but so widespread did they become during the period after 1957 that they were made criminal. Examples of harassment cited in the report which preceded the Act of 1965 were dumping on the floor of a tenant's room slimy cooked potatoes mixed with other filth and a dead rat, sprinkling itching powder on a tenant's bedding, damaging furniture and fittings, breaking a glass panel in a door, changing locks, removing wallpaper and putting snakes in a tenant's bathroom[1] but since the Act prosecutions have been rare: those which have been reported were based on allegations of withholding services and the summonses were dismissed.[2]

Unlawful eviction and unlawful re-entry

12.6 Whereas in the past a landlord who was lawfully entitled to possession of a residence was able to take possession of his own property so long as he did not contravene the Statutes of Forcible Entry, since the 1965 Act he must in every case, whether it is otherwise within the scope of the Rent Acts 1968–1974 or not, obtain a court order. If any person, whether or not he is the landlord, unlawfully deprives the residential occupier of any premises he is guilty of an offence under s. 30 (1) of the 1965 Act unless he proves that he believed with reasonable cause that the occupier had ceased to reside in the premises. Finally, it is an offence under s. 32 of that Act for a landlord to enforce a right to possession if the occupier continues to reside in the premises, unless he obtains a court order.

---

1. Report of the Committee on Housing in Greater London. Cmnd. 2605, p. 172.
2. *Abrol* (1972), 116 Sol. Jo. 177: *Westminster City Council* v. *Peart* (1968), 112 Sol. Jo. 543 and see *Norton* v. *Knowle*, [1969] 1 Q.B. 572; [1967] 3 All E.R. 1061.

Forcible entry or detainer[1]

7 A person who, without the authority of the law, violently and with menaces, force and arms, takes or keeps possession of lands or tenements, is guilty of forcible entry or detainer, an offence punishable by imprisonment and a fine. At common law, forcible entry was criminal only if effected by someone who had no title to the land. Statutes of the reign of Richard II which, as amended by a statute of 1429, are referred to as the Statutes of Forcible Entry, are still in force, make it an offence whether or not the entrant has any title to the land.

Force is necessary to constitute the offence. If the person with the right to possession of land can retake it peaceably there was nothing in the criminal law to prevent him doing so until 1965, but an entry may be forcible within the statutes if force is used against persons or things on land which has been entered peaceably. The breaking open of doors or windows, therefore, constitutes an offence. It is unnecessary for the prosecution to prove an intention to occupy the premises entirely.[2]

A person who unjustifiably seeks to retain possession of land by force is guilty of a forcible detainer. Therefore, if a lessor uses force to recover possession of land against a lessee who is holding over unlawfully and the lessee forcibly resists him, both parties may be guilty of an offence. The number of situations in which this can arise is very small, having regard to the large amount of legislation which protects tenants.

If someone enters a house peacefully and barricades himself in it, it is a question of degree whether the detainer is forcible.[3] There is no such thing as criminal trespass known to English law so that if premises are entered peacefully, no offence is committed by remaining there in circumstances not amounting to a forcible detainer. The creation of an offence of criminal trespass is sometimes advocated after sensational sit-ins; even if it is thought that such conduct should be punished, the offence would require careful definition to avoid the inclusion of much venial conduct which certainly ought not to be punished. If there is evidence of conspiracy to occupy then, as the law now stands, the conspiracy is punishable.[4]

---

1. For proposals for reform, see Law Commission Working Paper No 54, *Criminal Law Offences of Entering and Remaining on Property*.
2. *Brittain*, [1972] 1 Q.B. 357; [1972] 1 All E.R. 353.
3. [1971] Crim. L. R. 317, 330 and 342.
4. *Kamara* v. *Director of Public Prosecutions*, [1974] A.C. 104; [1973] 2 All E.R. 1242.

Forgery

12.8 Forgery is the making of a false document in order that it may be used as genuine,[1] or the counterfeiting of a seal or die, if committed with intent to deceive or defraud in the case of a public document but, in the case of a private document, there must be an intent to defraud. The punishment for forgery varies according to the nature of the document which is forged.

At common law forgery was a misdemeanour, but in practice the offence no longer depends on the common law and is now based on the Forgery Act 1913.[2] There are two types of forgery. First, the counterfeiting of a number of seals or dies with intent to deceive or defraud is punishable with terms of imprisonment for maximum periods varying from life to seven years by s. 5 of the Forgery Act. In this chapter we concentrate on the second and more common type of forgery, forgery of documents. Section 4 of that Act of 1913 provides that the maximum punishment for the forgery of documents which is not otherwise punishable shall be imprisonment for two years. Forgery in itself is no crime unless accompanied by the relevant intent to defraud or, in the case of a public document, to deceive or defraud. The term "public document" is not defined but, when dealing with a branch of the law of evidence in which a distinction is drawn between public and private documents, Lord Blackburn said that a public document is one that "is made by a public officer for the purpose of the public making use of it and being able to refer to it".[3]

A similar distinction appears to underly ss. 2 and 3 of the Act. Under the former the forging of wills, deeds, bonds and banknotes[4] is punishable with a maximum of imprisonment for life, while forgery of valuable securities, documents of title to land and goods, powers of attorney over public funds, registers of public funds, insurance policies and charter parties is punishable with imprisonment for a maximum of 14 years. These may all be regarded as private documents, and an intention to defraud must be proved. Section 3 mentions a large number of documents all of which can regarded as public. These include documents bearing the stamp or impression of the great seal, the privy seal and any royal seal, the forgery of which is punishable with a maximum of imprisonment for life. Under the same section it is an offence punishable with imprisonment for up to 14 years

1. Forgery Act 1913, s. 1 (1).
2. *Hopkins and Collins* (1957), 41 Cr. App. Rep. 231 at p. 235.
3. *Sturla* v. *Freccia* (1880), 5 App. Cas. 623, at p. 643.
4. This covers currency notes.

to forge registers of births, marriages or deaths, and the forgery of a number of records and certificates of a public nature is punishable with imprisonment for seven years. An intent to defraud or deceive suffices in cases covered by s. 3. There are three ingredients of the offence. These are a document, a false document and an intent to deceive or defraud.

A document

The term "document" is not defined in the Act, but basically it is a "writing", and that is what was required by several common law definitions of forgery. Difficulty has, however, been occasioned by the decisions of the Court of Crown Cases Reserved in *Closs* and *Smith*.

In *Closs*,[1] it was held to be no forgery for a dealer to sign the name of a well-known artist on a picture which had not been painted by that artist. In holding that the picture was not a document the court appears to have treated the signature as a mark of identification for the accused's own purposes and not as having been intended to convey the message that the picture was painted by the artist. When the accused came to sell the picture he would have been guilty of what is now obtaining money by means of deception, had there been evidence that the signature induced the purchaser to make the purchase.

In *Smith*,[2] it was held that the accused was not guilty of forgery when he caused a number of wrappers to be made in the same distinctive black and white form as those in which Borwick's Baking Powder was sold. This decision may be treated as having turned on the point that, although the wrappers were documents within the meaning of the law of forgery, they were not rendered false by the mere fact that the accused intended to use them for the improper purpose of passing off his own baking powder as that manufactured by Borwick;[3] but two of the judges held that the wrappers were not documents because, viewed apart from the use which the accused intended to make of the wrappers, the case was indistinguishable from one in which a person caused brown paper to be manufactured and this could not be said to be a forgery merely because other tradesmen sold their goods in brown paper. This ignores the distinction between a neutral article such as brown paper and a distinctive article such as a label on a tin of Borwick's Baking Powder which, though now less distinctive than it was when *Smith* was

1. (1857), Dears. & B. 460; *C. & J. Cases*.
2. (1858), Dears. & B. 566; *C. & J. Cases*.
3. Judgment of Bramwell, B.

decided, is still more distinctive than brown paper. Forgery or not, if the accused obtained money by selling his baking powder as Borwick's, he would be guilty of obtaining by deception because the wrappers would have been used to convey the message that the powder was Borwick's.

These decisions have led to the suggestion that, if the thing is intended to have utility apart from the fact that it conveys information or records a promise, it is not a document;[1] a document may be said, for the purpose of the law of forgery, to be a writing which is only intended to convey information or record a promise. If this is right, a signature on a blank piece of paper is or is not a forgery according to the circumstances. If it is the false signature of a famous person, intended to pass as that person's autograph, the person making the signature could be held guilty of forgery.

False document[2]

As the definition of forgery is the making of a false document in order that it may be used as genuine, two requirements result:

a. There must be a making of a false document, which includes the alteration of a genuine one. Section 1 (2) lays down a partial definition of what can amount to a false document. It lays down that a document is false within the meaning of the Act if the whole, or any material part thereof, purports to be made by, or on behalf, or on account of, a person who did not make it, nor authorise its making; or, if, though made by, or on behalf or on account of the person by whom, or by whose authority, it purports to have been made, the time or place of making where either is material or, in the case of a document identified by number or mark, the number or any distinguishing mark identifying the document is falsely stated therein. The subsection goes on to provide that in particular a document is false i. if any material alteration has been made therein whether by addition, insertion, obliteration, erasure, removal or otherwise; ii. if the whole or some material part of it purports to have been made by or on behalf of a fictitious or deceased person (merely using a false name creates a fictitious person);[3] iii. if, though made in the name of an existing person, it is made by him or by his authority with the inten-

1. Professor Williams, (1948) 11 M.L.R., at p. 160.
2. Gooderson, When is a document false in the law of forgery? (1952) 15 M.L.R. 11; Professor Williams, Forgery and falsity, [1974] Crim. L. R. 71.
3. *Gambling*, [1975] Q.B. 207; [1974] 3 All E.R. 479.

tion that it should pass as having been made by some person real or fictitious, other than the person who made or authorised it. These words are wide enough to cover most types of forgery but, as they are not an exhaustive definition,[1] any other falsification of documents which the human mind can invent can constitute forgery.

b. To be a forgery the document must have been made false in order that it may be used as genuine. These words were considered recently by the Court of Appeal in *Gambling*[2] in the course of which it was said:

> "We think that ['in order to be used as genuine'] also involve that the untrue statement in the document must be the reason or one of the reasons which results in the document being accepted as genuine when thereafter used by the maker. It is this concept which we think is sought to be expressed in the aphorism—as to the usefulness of which views may differ strongly—that the document must not only tell a lie, it must tell a lie about itself."

The aphorism referred to has its roots in the common law, the classic statement being contained in *Re Windsor*:[3]

> "Forgery is the false making of an instrument purporting to be that which it is not; it is not the making of an instrument which purports to be what it really is, but which contains false statements. Telling a lie does not become a forgery because it is reduced into writing."

As the Court of Appeal in *Gambling* recognised, its formulation quoted above requires the falsity to have been material; to adapt the aphorism, the document must tell a material lie about itself. A lie which the document tells about itself is immaterial where, for instance, the false date inserted in a document does not affect the validity or invalidity which it would have had if the true date had been inserted or where the identity of the person who signs a document in a false name is not a factor which bears on the mind of the person who accepts it as genuine.

These principles are well illustrated by *Gambling*. The accused opened five separate National Savings Bank accounts at different Post Offices in different names and filled in five declarations which were false in that he did not give his correct name. The Court of Appeal held that the declarations,

---

1. Criminal Justice Act 1925, s. 35 (1).
2. [1974] 3 All E.R. 479, at p. 482.
3. (1865), 10 Cox C.C. 118, at p. 123, *per* Blackburn, J.

which were clearly false documents telling lies about themselves (lies about the identity of their maker), would only be forgeries if having regard to all the circumstances of the transaction the identity of their maker was a material factor. It said that in many cases the materiality of the identity of the maker would be so obvious that evidence would be unnecessary, as where the document is a cheque and the purported signature of the drawer or endorser has been written by someone other than the person whose signature it purports to be. In other cases, such as that before it, evidence would be required and the question of the materiality of the identity of the maker would be a matter for the jury. The accused's appeal against conviction was allowed because the trial judge had failed to direct the jury to decide whether the Post Office if it had known that the accused was signing in a false name would have refused to open an account, in which case the identity of the person signing the declaration would have been material.

Another case where forgery was not proved is *Dodge and Harris*.[1] Harris falsely told G from whom he was borrowing money that he was owed money by Dodge; the latter signed bonds undertaking to pay £10,000 to Harris. It was held that the bonds were not forgeries because they simply contained false statements concerning Dodge's intentions; they did not tell lies about themselves. True, G was deceived into believing the bonds were valid but he could not be deceived into accepting the documents as genuine because they were genuine. On the other hand, provided he has the appropriate *mens rea*, a person who inserts a false date of execution in a document is guilty of forgery if the date is material, as it would be where priorities of mortgages were involved,[2] or where stamp duties or the right to claim relief from income tax[3] were affected.

A case which is difficult to explain is *Martin*.[4] The accused signed a cheque with a false forename in the presence of the prosecutor to whom he was well known. The accused handed the cheque to the prosecutor in payment for goods then delivered to him by the prosecutor. The cheque was dishonoured, and the accused knew that this would be so. At

1. [1972] 1 Q.B. 416; [1971] 2 All E.R. 1523.
2. *Ritson* (1869), L.R. 1 C.C.R. 200; *C. & J. Cases*.
3. *Wells*, [1939] 2 All E.R. 169.
4. (1879), 5 Q.B.D. 34; *C. & J. Cases*.

first sight this looks a straightforward case of forgery but it was held that, though the accused might have been convicted of obtaining goods by false pretences (now deception) had he been charged with that offence, he was not guilty of forgery. A possible explanation for this decision is that the cheque in the exceptional circumstances did not tell a material lie about itself because it was given and received as the cheque of the accused and the prosecutor would not have been misled about the identity of its maker.

An intent to deceive or defraud[1]

0 The third requirement of forgery is that at the time the document is made false there should be an intent to deceive or, in the case of private documents, an intent to defraud. The following statement of Buckley, J. is that which is usually relied on: "To deceive is, I apprehend, to induce a man to believe that a thing is true which is false and which the person practising the deceit knows or believes to be false. To defraud is to deprive by deceit; it is by deceit to induce a person to act to his injury. More tersely ... to deceive is by falsehood to induce a state of mind; to defraud is by deceit to induce a course of action."[2] As the greater includes the less an intent to deceive is included in an intent to defraud.

A person may be held to have had such an intention although at the time he forged or uttered a forged document he intended to make good any damage thereby occasioned and although he in fact made it good.[3] Similarly a person may have an intent to defraud although he could not in fact cause any injury to his intended victim because, for instance, the latter was aware of his plan.[4] There cannot, however, be an intent either to deceive or to defraud where the accused thinks that the belief which he induces in another is true, as where someone executes a document as agent under the honest though erroneous impression that he was entitled to do so.[5]

In *Bassey*,[6] the accused was held to have had the requisite intent to defraud when he obtained admission as a student of the

---

1. Gooderson, Prejudice as a test of intention to defraud (1960), *Cambridge Law Journal* 199; Hadden, Intent in Forgery (1965), 28 M.L.R. 154.
2. *Re London and Globe Finance Corporation, Ltd.*, [1903] 1 Ch. 728, at p. 732.
3. *Geach* (1840), 9 C. & P. 499; *C. & J. Cases.*
4. *Holden* (1810), Russ. & Ry. 154.
5. *Parish* (1837), 7 C. & P. 782.
6. (1931), 47 T.L.R. 222; followed in *Potter*, [1958] 2 All E.R. 51.

Inner Temple by means of forged certificates stating that he had passed an examination of an African University.

Bassey's case shows that a person may have an intention to defraud, although he does not intend to cause economic loss to anyone, and this has been confirmed by the House of Lords in *Welham* v. *Director of Public Prosecutions*.[1] Welham was held to have been rightly convicted of uttering forged documents with intent to defraud when he had witnessed false hire purchase agreements on the strength of which finance companies made advances in excess of the amount permitted by the relevant legislation. Welham did not intend to defraud the finance companies because he believed that they concurred in his plan to deceive the authorities into taking no action. It was held that this plan constituted an intent to defraud. The intention was to prejudice the rights of the Inland Revenue and impede its officials in the execution of their duties.

An example of a forgery with intent to deceive, but no intent to defraud, would be forging a birth certificate or an entry in a baptismal register merely in order to induce the belief that the forger came of a noble family. The documents in question being public, their maker could be convicted of forgery, although his intent was to do no more than induce a state of mind.

In *Hodgson*,[2] the accused was held not guilty of forgery when he altered a diploma of the Royal College of Surgeons so as to make it appear that it had been granted to him. There was not sufficient evidence that the accused intended anyone to act on the document, and the court took the view that it was not a public document. Although under s. 17 (2) of the Forgery Act 1913 it is unnecessary to allege an intent to defraud or deceive any particular person, and a corresponding statutory provision was in force when *Hodgson* was decided, such a case might be decided in the same way today, as it is doubtful whether the document in question comes within s. 3 of the Act of 1913, or whether it could be described as a "public document" within the meaning of s. 4.

Uttering

12.11 Under s. 6 of the Forgery Act 1913, a person who knowingly utters a forged document, seal or die is punishable to the same

---

1. [1961] A.C. 103; [1960] 1 All E.R. 805; *C. & J. Cases*; *cf. Manner-Astley*, [1967] 3 All E.R. 899. See also *Moon*, [1967] 3 All E.R. 962.
2. (1856), Dears. & B. 3.

extent as one who actually commits the forgery, provided he intends to deceive or, where this is necessary to make the forger liable, to defraud. A person utters a document if he uses, offers, publishes, delivers or disposes of it. The copying followed by the dispatch of a document amounts to a "using" although it is not clear that the mere copying and retention of the document would do so.[1]

Obtaining

12.12 Section 7 of the Forgery Act provides that it is an offence punishable with imprisonment for up to 14 years to demand, receive, obtain or endeavour to obtain any property, or cause it to be delivered to any person, with intent to defraud under or by virtue of a forged instrument.

A telegram has been held to be an instrument within the meaning of this section, so that a Post Office clerk who inserted a false time of dispatch on a telegram in which he placed a bet on a race of which he already knew the result, was held guilty of obtaining or endeavouring to obtain money under a forged instrument.[2] It is difficult to reconcile this case with others: the telegram did not purport to be anything except what it was but it did contain false information about the time of dispatch.

In *Hurford and Williams*,[3] the accused informed a firm of motor dealers that they wished to have a lorry on hire purchase. They were referred to a finance company and as he was not credit worthy Hurford signed a proposal form in a false name. This induced the finance company, after inquiry, to make the necessary advance to the dealers, and the lorry was released by them to the accused. It was held that the accused had been rightly convicted for obtaining the lorry "by virtue" of a forged instrument, because it was sufficient that they got the lorry by means of the existence of the forged proposal form. Although the proposal form did not purport to be anything except a proposal form, it did purport to be by someone other than Hurford and so could be said to tell a lie about itself.

There is a considerable overlap between s. 7 of the Forgery Act 1913 and s. 15 of the Theft Act 1968 which defines the offence of obtaining property by deception, but it has been held that a right to the property demanded is not a defence to a charge under the section, so that a creditor who forged a letter from

1. *Harris*, [1966] 1 Q.B. 184, [1965] 3 All E.R. 206.
2. *Riley*, [1896] 1 Q.B. 309; *C. & J. Cases.*
3. [1963] 2 Q.B. 398; [1963] 2 All E.R. 254.

the Admiralty to a sailor warning him to pay his debt has been convicted under the section.[1]

Possession

12.13 Sections 8–10 of the Forgery Act 1913 punish the possession or use of certain forged documents, seals and dies without lawful authority or excuse.

A person who intends to take a forged bank note to the police has such an excuse, even if he does not hand the note over at the earliest opportunity.[2]

The Law Commission's Report

12.14 A number of proposals for the reform of the law of forgery are made in Law Commission Report No. 55 published in 1973. Put very briefly they are as follows:

a. The Forgery Act 1913, together with other statutory provisions concerning offences akin to forgery should be repealed, and it should be declared that the common law of forgery is abolished.

b. To replace the offences of forgery in ss. 2–4 of the 1913 Act with two new offences: making a false instrument, and making a copy of a false instrument. An instrument would include written matter and any disc, tape or other device on which instructions or data are recorded or stored. An instrument would be characterised as false if it purported to be made in the terms in which it stands by a person who did not make it, or if it otherwise purported to be made in circumstances in which it was not made. The mental element in forgery should be an intention that the false instrument shall be used to induce someone to accept it as genuine and to act on it to his (or another's) prejudice. "Prejudice" would be defined so that any act or omission, if it occurred, would be to a person's prejudice if, and only if, it were to result in loss to that person in money or other property, or to take the form of giving another an opportunity to earn remuneration, or to be attributable to his having accepted the false instrument as genuine in connection with the performance by him of a duty.

c. There should be additional offences of using a false instrument, or a copy of such, knowing or believing it to be false, with intent to prejudice another, possessing false instruments

---

1. *Parker* (1910), 74 J.P. 208.
2. *Wuyts*, [1969] 2 Q.B. 474; [1969] 2 All E.R. 799.

without lawful authority or excuse, and making or possessing, without such authority, a counterfeit die for hallmarking or for denoting that stamp duty has been paid.

The Law Commission rejected the arguments made against the need for an offence of forgery in important articles in the Criminal Law Review.[1] The main point made in these articles is that, like the present law of forgery, the proposals of the Law Commission are based on the unproved assumption that the creation of a document or thing which tells a lie about itself is socially more dangerous than the creation of a document which simply contains lies. The latter is, in general, no offence until the document comes to be used for a dishonest purpose: why should the former be an offence before such a stage is reached?

We find this argument attractive, not least because it would be a step towards the rationalisation and simplification of our criminal law, and consider the Law Commission's rejection of it unfortunate. If adopted it would be necessary of course to preserve certain specific statutory forgeries, such as the forging of documents in order to obtain licences under the Road Traffic Acts.

Coinage

5 In conclusion, passing mention should be made of the Coinage Offences Act 1936 under which a variety of coinage offences are defined and punished.

---

1. Professor Griew, Forgery, [1970] Crim. L. R. 548; Glazebrook, Forgery, Some Further Comments, *ibid.*, 554.

Statistics

12.16 *Number of persons convicted in England and Wales of the offences against property mentioned in Chapters 10 to 12 in 1974.*

(Source: *Criminal Statistics*, 1974, Cmnd. 6168, Table IV)

Offence	Number of persons convicted	Percentage of total*
Theft	147,402	46
Robbery	2,767	1
Burglary	61,771	19
Aggravated burglary	137	†
Taking conveyance	33,636	10
Deception	13,319	4
Blackmail	258	†
Handling stolen goods	21,023	7
Going equipped for stealing	2,307	1
Arson	1,802	1
Criminal damage endangering life	46	†
Other criminal damage	34,038	11
Forgery and uttering	3,876	1
Other property offences	834	†
Total convictions for property offences	323,216	—
Total convictions for all offences (except motoring offences)	760,568	—

* Since percentages are given as whole numbers they do not total 100 per cent.
† Less than 0.5 per cent.

13

OFFENCES AGAINST THE ADMINISTRATION OF JUSTICE

Assisting offenders[1]

.1 Section 4 (1) of the Criminal Law Act 1967 provides that where a person has committed an arrestable offence, any other person who, knowing or believing him to be guilty of the offence, or of some other arrestable offence, does without lawful authority or reasonable excuse any act with intent to impede his apprehension or prosecution is guilty of an offence. The consent of the Director of Public Prosecutions is required before a person can be prosecuted for assisting offenders.[2] This offence replaces that of accessory after the fact to felony. It is limited to cases where the person assisted was guilty of an arrestable offence, although a person who assists someone guilty of a non-arrestable offence may be convicted of perverting the course of justice or, in some cases, obstructing a police officer.[3]

In order to succeed on a charge of assisting an offender, the prosecution must prove four things:

a. *The commission of an arrestable offence.*—The definition of an arrestable offence is given later.[4] Though the commission of the principal arrestable offence must be proved, no one need have been convicted of it and presumably even if there has been an acquittal that would not prevent a conviction for assisting the person acquitted at a separate trial on different evidence. The arrestable offence alleged to have been committed must be specified in the indictment for assisting an offender but if the principal offender was not guilty of the specified offence, the accused may still be convicted if the principal offender was guilty of another arrestable offence of which he might have been convicted on the indictment for

---

1. Professor Williams, Evading Justice, [1975] Crim. L. R. 430, 479, 608.
2. Criminal Law Act 1967, s. 4 (4).
3. Paras. 13.18 and 15.2 and 15.3.
4. Para. 22.7.

the specified offence under s. 6 (3) of the Criminal Law Act 1967.[1]

b. *The accused's knowledge or belief that the actual arrestable offence, or some other arrestable offence, was committed by the principal offender.*—It is not necessary for the prosecution to prove that the accused knew or believed the particular offence to be arrestable, or that he was aware of the identity of the person who committed it.[2]

c. *An act done by the accused with the intention of impeding the apprehension or prosecution of the principal offender.*—The principal offender need not actually be assisted (the definition of this offence as assisting offenders is somewhat inaccurate) but the accused must have done some act with intent to impede prosecution or apprehension of the principal offender. An omission to act even if accompanied by such intent will not suffice. Thus, failure to report the principal offender to the police or to arrest him does not constitute assisting an offender. Authorities on prosecutions of accessories after the fact suggest that the requisite intent is a direct one.[3] Mere foresight that the offender will be assisted is insufficient, if the only direct intent of the accused was the acquisition of money for himself or the protection of himself from prosecution.[4] The mere provision of accommodation in the ordinary way by the principal offender's family or landlord will not suffice, nor will mere efforts at persuasion not to prosecute. On the other hand, driving the principal offender away after the crime, hiding him from the police,[5] destroying fingerprints or other evidence of the crime or telling the police lies to put them off the scent do fall within the scope of the offence.[6]

d. *The absence of lawful authority or reasonable excuse for the act of assistance.*—There would be lawful authority for impeding the prosecution if action were taken in consequence of an executive decision not to prosecute. An example of a case in which, notwithstanding the intent to impede prosecution,

---

1. *Morgan*, [1972] 1 Q.B. 436; [1972] 1 All E.R. 348. S. 6 (3) is discussed in para. 23.14.c.
2. *Brindley and Long*, [1971] 2 Q.B. 300; [1971] 2 All E.R. 698; *C. & J. Cases.*
3. This view was also taken by the Criminal Law Revision Committee who drafted the offence. See its Seventh Report, *Felonies and Misdemeanours*, Cmnd. 2659, para. 30.
4. *Rose J* (1962), 46 Cr. App. Rep. 103; *Andrews and Craig*, [1962] 3 All E.R. 961.
5. *Morgan*, [1972] 1 Q.B. 436; [1972] 1 All E.R. 348.
6. *Brindley and Long*, [1971] 2 Q.B. 300; [1971] 2 All E.R. 698; *C. & J. Cases.*

there would be a lawful excuse would be one in which a forged cheque was destroyed in pursuance of a lawful agreement[1] not to prosecute in consideration of the making good of the loss caused by the forgery.[2]

Punishment

Punishment varies according to the nature of the principal offence. If the punishment for that crime is fixed by law, the maximum punishment for impeding its prosecution or the apprehension of the offender is 10 years' imprisonment; it is 7 years' imprisonment if the maximum punishment for the principal offence is 14 years' imprisonment, 5 years' when the maximum punishment for the principal offence is 10 years' imprisonment, and 3 years' imprisonment in all other cases.[3]

Assisting traitors

The Criminal Law Act 1967 retains treason as a separate category of offence.[4] Someone who, knowing a treason has been committed, assists the traitor with intent to impede his apprehension or trial or punishment is himself guilty of treason as a principal offender and is punishable with life imprisonment. He could alternatively be convicted of assisting the accused (treason being an arrestable offence), in which case he would be liable to a maximum of 10 years' imprisonment.

Concealing

.2 Section 5 (1) of the Criminal Law Act 1967 provides that where a person has committed an arrestable offence, any other person who, knowing or believing that the offence or some other arrestable offence has been committed, and that he has information which might be of assistance in securing the prosecution or conviction of an offender for it, accepts or agrees to accept for not disclosing that information any consideration other than the making good of loss or injury caused by the offence, or the making of reasonable compensation for that loss or injury, is guilty of an offence. The consent of the Director of Public Prosecutions is required for a prosecution for this offence.[5] The present offence replaces, with a considerably

1. Para. 13.2.
2. Seventh Report of the Criminal Law Revision Committee, Cmnd. 2659, para. 28.
3. Criminal Law Act 1967, s. 4 (3).
4. Para. 2.26.
5. Criminal Law Act 1967, s. 5 (3).

limited scope, the offences of misprision of felony (failing to report a felony to the police) and compounding a felony (agreement not to prosecute, or to impede prosecution of, a felony). It is far less serious than assisting offenders, the maximum punishment being 2 years' imprisonment.[1]

The prosecution must prove three things:

a. The commission of an arrestable offence.
b. The accused's knowledge that it, or some other arrestable offence has been committed and that he has information which might assist the prosecution.
c. The acceptance by the accused of, or agreement by him to accept, some consideration, e.g. money or goods, other than the making good of loss or injury caused by the offence. Merely failing to inform the police of an arrestable offence is not an offence. The sole exception is failure to report a treason which still survives as the common law offence of misprision of treason, with a maximum punishment of life imprisonment. It is expressly provided by s. 5 (5) of the Criminal Law Act 1967 that compounding an offence other than treason shall not be an offence save under s. 5 (1). The acceptance of any consideration for not reporting or prosecuting a non-arrestable offence is therefore no offence. We described earlier the related offence of advertising rewards for the return of stolen or lost goods with the promise that no questions will be asked etc.[2]

Causing wasteful employment of the police

13.3 It is a summary offence to cause the wasteful employment of the police by knowingly making a false report tending to show that an offence has been committed or that the informant has information material to any police inquiry, or giving rise to apprehension for the safety of persons or property.[3] There is no corresponding statutory provision concerning the wasteful employment of the fire, ambulance and similar services.

Perjury

13.4 Section 1 (1) of the Perjury Act 1911 provides that perjury is committed by a person who, lawfully sworn as a witness or interpreter in a judicial proceeding, wilfully makes a statement material in that proceeding which he knows to be false or does

1. Criminal Law Act 1967, s. 5 (1).
2. Para. 11.35.
3. Criminal Law Act 1967 s. 5 (2).

not believe to be true. The maximum punishment is 7 years' imprisonment. The following matters require further explanation:

a. *Lawfully sworn in a judicial proceeding.*—A person is "lawfully sworn" within the meaning of the Act if he gives his evidence on oath, affirmation or solemn declaration.[1] The term "judicial proceeding" includes a proceeding before any court, tribunal or person having by law power to hear, receive and examine evidence on oath, and a statement made for the purposes of a judicial proceeding before a person authorised to administer oaths may be treated as made in a judicial proceeding.[2] A person may therefore be guilty of perjury if he wilfully makes a false statement in an affidavit which is sworn for the purpose of judicial proceedings, such as an affidavit in support of a summons.

   If the accused is charged with having made a false statement in a judicial proceeding it must have been made before the relevant tribunal. Therefore, in *Lloyd*,[3] when, after a person had been duly sworn in bankruptcy proceedings, the registrar left the court, it was held that no charge of perjury could be made in respect of false answers given to questions put to the witness in the registrar's absence.

b. *Material statement.*—The statement must have been material to the judicial proceeding. Whether it was so or not, is a question of law for the judge.[4] In *Baker*,[5] the accused was charged with selling beer without a licence and denied that on a previous occasion he had instructed his solicitor to plead guilty to a similar charge. It was held that this denial was material to the proceedings because it affected his credit as a witness and might affect the sentence. In *Sweet-Escott*,[6] on the other hand, it was held that the accused's answers to questions put to him in committal proceedings in which he had been a witness concerning previous convictions which were 20 years old were not material on the issue of credibility because a truthful admission of those convictions, instead of the false denial which was given, could not have affected the magistrates' decision.

c. *Mens rea.*—The false statement must have been made wilfully. Mere inadvertence is not enough. Therefore, if the

---

1. Perjury Act 1911, s. 15.
2. *Ibid.*, s. 1 (2), (3).
3. (1887), 19 Q.B.D. 213.
4. Perjury Act 1911, s. 1 (6).
5. [1895] 1 Q.B. 797.
6. (1971), 55 Cr. App. Rep. 316; see also *Holden* (1872), 12 Cox C.C. 166.

deponent to an affidavit made in a judicial proceeding is told, and believes, that everything is in order and proceeds to swear it without due consideration he cannot be convicted of perjury. A person may be guilty of perjury although the statement which he makes is true, because the definition of the offence includes statements which are made wilfully and which are not believed to be true even though they are.

Subornation of perjury

13.5 Section 7 (1) of the Perjury Act 1911, provides that a person who "aids, abets, counsels, procures or suborns [i.e. procures by bribery or other corrupt means]" another to commit perjury is liable for perjury "as if he were a principal offender". This offence is redundant since it adds nothing to the criminal liability which would otherwise be imposed under the principles of aiding and abetting.[1]

Other offences under the Perjury Act

13.6 Under the Perjury Act 1911, certain offences are punishable in the same way as perjury. These are the making of false statements on oath when required by law, otherwise than in a judicial proceeding, or in an affidavit made for the purposes of the Bills of Sale Acts,[2] the making of a false statement in relation to the registration of a marriage,[3] and the making of false statements in relation to the registration of births or deaths.[4]

The making of a false statutory declaration or of a false statement in a document required by any public general Act of Parliament or in an oral answer required to be made to any question in pursuance of such an Act of Parliament is punishable with imprisonment for two years,[5] and the making of a false statement to procure a certificate in relation to a professional calling is punishable with imprisonment for one year.[6]

Proof

13.7 No one can be convicted of perjury, subornation of perjury, or any other offence under the Act of 1911, unless there is corroborative evidence of the falsity of the statement with which the

---

1. Paras. 19.1–19.23.
2. Perjury Act 1911, s. 2.
3. *Ibid.*, s. 3.
4. *Ibid.*, s. 4.
5. *Ibid.*, s. 5.
6. *Ibid.*, s. 6.

accused is charged.[1] Evidence of statements made by the accused when he was not on oath contradictory to the statements made by him when he was on oath may suffice. Thus, in *Hook*,[2] the accused had sworn in a judicial proceeding that he did not see anyone leave a certain public house after 11 o'clock on a particular night. Three witnesses gave evidence that the accused had told them that he had seen four men leave the public house after 11 o'clock on that night. Other witnesses proved that four men did leave the house. A conviction for perjury was upheld.

The mere fact that a person has made two wholly inconsistent statements, even when both are on oath, does not establish perjury because it is not enough for the prosecution to show that one of the two sworn statements must be false; the falsity of the statement charged in the indictment must be established. It is not unheard of for a witness at a trial on indictment to make a statement on oath completely inconsistent with his statement, likewise on oath, at the committal proceedings. Many people deplore the fact that this can happen and that the witness can yet remain unpunished. However, when the subject was considered by the Criminal Law Revision Committee in their sixth report, they recommended no change in the existing law of perjury mainly on the ground that a witness who had once made a false statement on oath would be discouraged from telling the truth if the consequence of his doing so were to be a possible prosecution for perjury.

The issues involved are put in a nutshell in the following extract from the committee's report:

> "The paramount purpose of the law should be to obtain true evidence at the trial. If it is a choice between having true evidence at the trial and having the satisfaction of prosecuting a perjurer afterwards, it is better to have the truth and forgo the satisfaction".[3]

Proposals for reform

.8 In proposals published provisionally in 1970[4] and confirmed with amendments in 1975[5] the Law Commission advocates the repeal of the Perjury Act 1911 together with a number of other

---

1. *Ibid.*, s. 13. The 11th Report of the Criminal Law Revision Committee (Cmnd. 4991) proposes that the requirement of corroboration should be confined to perjury in judicial proceedings.
2. (1858), Dears. & B. 606.
3. *Perjury and the Attendance of Witnesses*, Cmnd. 2465, para. 22 *ad fin.*
4. Law Commission Working Paper No. 33, *Perjury and Kindred Offences.*
5. Law Commission Working Paper No. 62, *Offences Relating to the Administration of Justice*, paras. 38–59.

statutory provisions, and the substitution of simpler legislation. It is suggested that this should provide for four classes of offence:

a. perjury in judicial proceedings, punishable with seven years' imprisonment as a maximum, to consist only of statements which are in fact false;
b false statements in statutory declarations or certificates which are admissible in judicial proceedings;
c. false statements or representations in relation to births, marriages and deaths, to be punishable with a maximum of five years' imprisonment; and
d. false statements made
   (i) on oath otherwise than in judicial proceedings; or
   (ii) in a statutory declaration; or
   (iii) in any oral or written statement required or authorised by, under, or in pursuance of any Act of Parliament, to be punishable with three years' imprisonment.

It is further suggested that the mental element of the offence should, in each instance, be an intention that the statement should be taken as true coupled with knowledge of its falsity or an absence of belief in its truth.

Contempt of Court[1]

13.9 Contempt of court was examined recently by the Phillimore Committee[2] some of whose recommendations are mentioned later. We are not concerned with civil contempt of court which consists in the disobedience of orders of the court such as an injunction restraining some act or a direction to one parent to allow the other to have access to their child; civil contempt may result in imprisonment for an indefinite period until the contempt is purged.

Criminal contempt of court, a common law misdemeanour punishable at the discretion of the court, involves conduct which tends to obstruct, prejudice or abuse the administration of justice either in relation to a particular case (whether criminal or civil) or generally. There are six principal categories of criminal contempt.

13.10 *Contempt in the face of the court.*—This is concerned with words or actions in the presence of the court which interfere, or are liable to do so, with the course of justice in a case being, or about

---

1. See Borrie and Lowe, *The Law of Contempt.*
2. Report of the Committee on Contempt of Court, Cmnd. 5794 (1974). For comment, see Borrie, [1975] Crim. L. R. 127.

to be, tried, such as throwing a tomato at the judge, breaking up the trial (as where students, striving to preserve its use, chanted the Welsh language in court),[1] and the refusal of a witness to be sworn or to answer a lawful question[2] or to leave court when ordered to do so.[3]

11 *Scandalising the court.*—"Judges and courts are alike open to criticism, and if reasonable argument or expostulation is offered against any judicial act as contrary to law or the public good no court could or would treat that as a contempt of court."[4] Broadly speaking what is prohibited is scurrilous abuse of a judge as a judge or of a court,[5] or attacks upon the impartiality of a judge or court. Thus, an allegation that a fair trial of someone who held certain views could not be obtained from a named judge constitutes contempt.[6] Proceedings for scandalising the court are rare. The Phillimore Committee proposes that this branch of the law of contempt should be replaced by an indictable offence of defaming a judge in such a way as to bring the administration of justice into disrepute, because summary contempt proceedings are inappropriate, "scandalising" not normally requiring to be dealt with urgently. It proposes that it should be a defence to show that the allegations were true and that publication was for the public benefit.[7]

12 *Reprisals against jurors and witnesses.*—It has long been established that it is a contempt to threaten or punish a juror in relation to his part in legal proceedings which have ended[8] and more recently, in *Re Attorney-General's Application, A. G.* v. *Butterworth*,[9] the Court of Appeal held that it was contempt to take reprisals against a witness who has given evidence in legal pro-

---

1. *Morris* v. *Crown Office*, [1970] 2 Q.B. 114; [1970] 1 All E.R. 1079.
2. *Ex parte Fernandez* (1861), 10 C.B.N.S. 3.
3. *Chandler* v. *Herne* (1842), 2 Mood. & R. 423.
4. *Gray*, [1900] 2 Q.B. 36, at p. 40, *per* Lord Russell, C.J.; *Ambard* v. *A.-G. for Trinidad and Tobago*, [1936] A.C. 322; [1936] 1 All E.R. 704; *Metropolitan Police Commissioner, Ex parte Blackburn* (No. 2), [1968] 2 Q.B. 150; [1968] 2 All E.R. 319.
5. *McLeod* v. *St. Aubyn*, [1899] A.C. 549, at p. 561, *per* Lord Morris.
6. *New Statesman Editor, Ex parte Director of Public Prosecutions* (1928), 44 T.L.R. 301.
7. *Op. cit.*, paras. 159–167.
8. *Martin* (1848), 5 Cox C.C. 356.
9. [1963] 1 Q.B. 696; [1962] 3 All E.R. 326. See also *Chapman* v. *Honig*, [1963] 2 Q.B. 502; [1963] 2 All E.R. 513; *Moore* v. *Clerk of Assize (Bristol)*, [1972] 1 All E.R. 58.

ceedings. In this case a man who had appeared as a witness in proceedings involving his trade union was deprived of office as treasurer and as a delegate of a branch of the union because his colleagues thought that in giving evidence he had acted against the interests of the union. The Court of Appeal held that, although clearly the proceedings themselves were no longer capable of being affected, there was no doubt that reprisals of this kind could interfere with the administration of justice since a witness might be deterred from giving evidence by the fear of reprisals even if he had not been threatened before the proceedings, and since other witnesses in future cases might be deterred if reprisals were not punishable. It stressed that in this type of contempt the accused's purpose of punishing was important in determining whether his conduct tended to interfere with the administration of justice.

For similar reasons to those given in *Butterworth's* case it was held recently that it is a contempt to publish the names of witnesses who have been the victims of blackmail in defiance of a request for anonymity made by the judge at the blackmail trial.[1]

The Phillimore Committee proposes that taking or threatening" but that such conduct should be made an indictable offence, tempt for the same reasons as apply to its proposal on "scandalising" but that such conduct should be made an indictable offence; with provision for the victim to recover compensation for any loss or damage suffered.

13.13 *Obstructing officers of the court.*—It is a contempt to obstruct such an officer when he is carrying out his duties.[2]

13.14 *Conduct liable to prejudice the fair trial or conduct of pending or imminent proceedings.*—Actual prejudice need not be proved here but the words or action must be likely to prejudice a fair trial, or intended to do so.

This category of contempt covers offering bribes or threats to witnesses or jurors to distort or suppress their evidence or reach a corrupt verdict, as the case may be. However, this type of contempt usually takes the form of comments or statements in a newspaper or television programme[3] which create a serious risk

1. *Socialist Worker Printers and Publishers, Ltd., Ex parte A.-G.*, [1975] 1 All E.R. 142.
2. *Williams* v. *Johns* (1773), 1 Mer. 303, n. See also *Re Johnson* (1887), 20 Q.B.D. 68.
3. *A.-G.* v. *London Weekend Television*, [1972] 3 All E.R. 1146.

of prejudice to the fair trial of pending or imminent proceedings. To suggest that an accused person is guilty of the offence charged[1] or to refer to the character of a party to the proceedings, if it may prejudice the trial,[2] constitutes a contempt, as do publications tending to deter or influence witnesses.

Contempt of court in a civil action is not restricted to conduct likely to prejudice a fair trial. It extends also to conduct which may deter or inhibit parties from having their legal rights determined by the courts, by holding them up to public obloquy or disparagement for doing so.[3] On the other hand, fair and temperate public criticism of a party which is intended to cause him to compromise or discontinue an action and which does not prejudge the issues involved is not a contempt[4] Clearly private persuasion in the form of fair and temperate criticism, as opposed to intimidation, does not constitute a contempt.

Prejudicial conduct of the types mentioned above must relate to legal proceedings which are pending or (at least in the case of criminal proceedings[5]) imminent. "Imminent proceedings" remains undefined but it would seem that proceedings are imminent if at the date of the prejudicial conduct it is obvious that the suspect is about to be arrested.[6] Criminal proceedings are pending from the moment that the accused is arrested and in custody[7] and continue to be so until an appeal to the Court of Appeal has been determined or time for appeal has run out.[8] Civil proceedings are pending when the writ has been issued[9] and probably remain so until an appeal is determined or time for appeal has expired. The Phillimore Committee thought that conduct relating to proceedings which have not started could hardly be regarded as a contempt of court and, in addition, that "imminent proceedings" engendered uncertainty.[10]

Where a publication is intended or likely to prejudice the conduct or fair trial of proceedings, a contempt may be committed by any person responsible for that publication, such as the editor,

---

1. *Hutchinson, Ex parte McMahon*, [1936] 2 All E.R. 1514.
2. *Higgins* v. *Richards* (1912), 28 T.L.R. 202.
3. *A.-G.* v. *Times Newspapers, Ltd.*, [1974] A.C. 273; [1973] 3 All E.R. 54.
4. *Ibid.*
5. *Savundranayaga*, [1968] 3 All E.R. 439, at p. 441, *per* Salmon, L.J.
6. *Ibid.*
7. *Clarke, Ex parte Crippen* (1910), 27 T.L.R. 32.
8. *Davies, Ex parte Delbert Evans*, [1945] K.B. 435; *Duffy, Ex parte Nash*, [1960] 2 Q.B. 188; [1960] 2 All E.R. 891.
9. *Dunn* v. *Bevan*, [1922] 1 Ch. 276.
10. *Op. cit.*, paras. 70 to 72 and 115 to 129.

the reporter and a distributor.[1] Generally, it is irrelevant that the alleged contemnor was ignorant of the contents of the publication or did not know of, or intend to prejudice, the proceedings.[2] However, s. 11 (1) of the Administration of Justice Act 1960 provides that a person is not guilty of contempt of court on the ground that he published any matter calculated to interfere with any pending or imminent proceedings if he proves that, having taken all reasonable care, he did not know, and had no reason to suspect, that the proceedings were imminent. Section 11 (2) provides a defence for a distributor of such matter if he proves that, at the time of distribution, having taken all reasonable care, he did not know that it contained such matter and had no reason to suspect that it was likely to do so.

13.15 *Publications which prejudge issues in pending proceedings.*— Where there is a jury, which is rare in civil proceedings, prejudgment is a contempt under the previous category. On the other hand, in a trial by a judge alone, only in very rare cases can prejudgment be held to constitute such a contempt because it is accepted that judges are capable of remaining uninfluenced by prejudicial matter in deciding a case.[3] However, it is now clear that prejudging the issues, as opposed to simply setting out the facts and issues, in a case to be tried by a judge alone constitutes a contempt, irrespective of the effect, or likely effect on the particular proceedings, on the ground that "trial by newspaper" is a usurpation of the proper function of the court. This was authoritatively established by the House of Lords in *A.-G.* v. *Times Newspapers, Ltd.*[4] where it was held that the publication of an article in a Sunday newspaper, which set out in some detail evidence and argument tending to show that the manufacturers of the drug thalidomide had not exercised due care in its manufacture, would constitute a contempt because it prejudged one of the things at issue in pending litigation between the manufacturers of thalidomide and parents of children alleged to be deformed by the maternal use of it during pregnancy.

---

1. *Evening Standard*, [1954] 1 Q.B. 578; [1954] 1 All E.R. 1026; *Griffiths, Ex parte A.-G.*, [1957] 2 Q.B. 192; [1957] 2 All E.R. 379.
2. *Odhams Press Ltd., Ex parte A.-G.*, [1957] 1 Q.B. 73; [1956] 3 All E.R. 494; *Griffiths, Ex parte A.-G.*
3. *Re William Thomas Shipping Co. Ltd.*, [1930] 2 Ch. 368, at p. 373; *Vine Products, Ltd.* v. *Mackenzie*, [1966] Ch. 484, at p. 496; [1965] 3 All E.R. 58, at p. 62.
4. [1974] A.C. 273; [1973] 3 All E.R. 54.

Trial

6 Criminal contempt of court is triable at common law on indictment but this procedure has fallen into disuse, and the usual method of dealing with criminal contempt is by summary process without a jury. This summary power to commit to prison, being arbitrary and unlimited, should be exercised with great caution.[1] A number of limits on this process should be noted:

a. Magistrates' courts have no direct power to punish for contempt, but in the case of disorderly conduct in the face of the court or obstruction of court officers in the execution of their duty, magistrates can order a person to find sureties to guarantee his good behaviour and imprison him in default of finding sureties.
b. County courts have no common law powers to punish for a contempt in relation to their proceedings[2] but s. 157 of the County Courts Act 1959 empowers a County Court judge to imprison for a maximum of one month, or fine, any person who wilfully insults him or any juror, witness or officer of the court, during his attendance in court, or in going to or returning from the court, or who wilfully interrupts or otherwise misbehaves in court.
c. A judge of the Crown Court or of the High Court or Court of Appeal has jurisdiction to punish a person of his own motion[3] (i.e. without any notice of formal institution of proceedings by another) whenever there has been a gross interference with the course of justice in a case being, or about to be, tried or, possibly, just over[4] This power is normally confined to contempts in the face of the court but can be used in a proper case where the contempt is reported to the judge.[5] It should only be exercised where it is urgent and imperative for the judge to act immediately to prevent justice being obstructed or undermined.[6]
d. A High Court judge may punish for a contempt committed in connection with any civil proceedings in the High Court. The Court of Appeal (Civil Division) has similar powers over contempts relating to civil proceedings in that court.[7]

---

1. *Davies*, [1906] 1 K.B. 32.
2. *Lefroy* (1873), L.R. 8 Q.B. 134.
3. R.S.C., O. 52, r. 5; Courts Act 1971, s. 4 (8).
4. *Balogh* v. *Crown Court at St. Albans*, [1975] Q.B. 73; [1974] 3 All E.R. 283.
5. *Ibid.*
6. *Ibid.*
7. R.S.C., O. 52, r. 1.

Proceedings are instituted by the Attorney-General or a private person.

e. A Divisional Court of the Queen's Bench Division has sole jurisdiction to punish:
   i. a contempt in connection with any proceedings before it;
   ii. a contempt of a Magistrates' Court;
   iii. a contempt of a County Court or Crown Court which those courts do not have power to punish under b. and c. above;
   iv. a contempt committed otherwise than in connection with any proceedings (viz. scandalising any court other than the Court of Appeal, which itself has jurisdiction if either of its Divisions is scandalised);[1]
   v. a contempt, other than scandalising, of the Court of Appeal (Criminal Division).[2]

Proceedings are normally instituted by the Attorney-General.

Proposals for reform

13.17 In addition to the proposal already mentioned, the Phillimore Committee recommends that any conduct, including a publication creating the risk of serious prejudice, which is intended to pervert or obstruct the course of justice in particular proceedings should continue to be capable of being dealt with as a contempt, provided proceedings have started and not been finally settled or concluded. Such conduct should normally be dealt with as perversion of the course of justice or some similar offence, unless there are compelling reasons requiring it to be dealt with as a matter of urgency by means of summary contempt proceedings, or the offending act does not fall within the definition of any other offence.

However, as an exception to the general rule that an intention to affect the course of justice would be required, the committee proposes that strict liability should still apply to publications (including broadcasts) to the public at large which create a risk that the course of justice will be seriously impeded or prejudiced. Strict liability for publication would only apply in relation to criminal proceedings where the accused has been charged or a summons served, and in relation to civil proceedings where the

1. *Metropolitan Police Commissioner, Ex parte Blackburn (No. 2)*, [1968] 2 Q.B. 150; [1968] 2 All E.R. 319.
2. R.S.C., O.52, r. 1.

case has been set down for trial, and would cease to operate where a verdict has been returned and sentence pronounced, or judgment has been given. The defences of innocent publication and distribution would be retained with necessary amendments and it would be a defence that the publication, although it incidentally but unintentionally caused a risk of serious prejudice in particular proceedings, formed part of a legitimate discussion of matters of general public interest.[1]

Perverting the course of justice[2]

18 This offence, which is also known by other titles, such as obstructing the administration of justice or attempting to defeat the due course of justice, is a common law misdemeanour punishable at the discretion of the court. Like contempt of court, this offence has a more general application than offences such as perjury. It has never been precisely defined by the courts, but, broadly speaking, the offence penalises any conduct which wrongly interferes, directly or indirectly, with the initiation, progress or outcome of any criminal or civil proceedings, including arbitration proceedings, accompanied by a direct intention to do so.

The following types of conduct are among those which have been held to constitute perverting the course of justice:

a. Interference with witnesses. A person who threatens or seeks to persuade a witness or potential witness[3] not to give evidence[4] or to give evidence of a particular character[5] is guilty of perversion of the course of justice, whether or not the proceedings in question have been instituted at the time.[6] It is irrelevant that the threat is to do an otherwise lawful act, such as to sue for damages or to expose misconduct.[7] The offence is not committed by a person who seeks by reasoned argument to persuade a witness to tell the truth.[8] The dissuasion of a person from bringing a civil suit or from notifying the police of a crime does not constitute perverting the course of justice.[9]

b. Making or using false statements to officers of justice with a view to perverting the course of, or preventing, judicial proceedings constitutes perverting the course of justice.[10]

---

1. *Op. cit.*, paras. 73 to 154.
2. Professor Williams, Evading Justice, [1975] Crim. L. R. 430, 479, 608.
3. *Grimes*, [1968] 3 All E.R. 179n.; *Panayiotou*, [1973] 3 All E.R. 112.
4. *Panayiotou*; *Kellett*, [1975] 3 All E.R. 468.
5. *Greenberg* (1919), 26 Cox C.C. 466.
6. *Panayiotou*.
7. *Kellett*.
8. *Ibid*.
9. *Panayiotou*.
10. *Andrews*, [1973] 1 Q.B. 422; [1973] 1 All E.R. 857.

Such conduct may also amount to the statutory offence of obstructing a constable in the execution of his duty[1] or assisting offenders.[2]

c. Fabrication of false evidence for the purpose of misleading a tribunal constitutes perverting the course of justice, even though the evidence was never tendered.[3]

Various types of conduct which fall within the broad offence of perverting the course of justice are alternatively punishable as specific common law misdemeanours, punishable at the discretion of the court. Embracery, which consists of an attempt to influence jurors, such as by a bribe,[4] is an example of such a specific offence.

Conduct of the above type involving two or more persons is often penalised as conspiracy to pervert the course of justice or, before the decision in *Withers* v. *Director of Public Prosecutions*,[5] as a conspiracy to effect a public mischief. Where a person agrees with a surety for bail[6] that the surety will be indemnified if the conditions of bail are broken and the surety is required to pay, the offence of perverting the course of justice is not committed unless there was an intent to defeat justice, nor is any other offence. However, such an agreement has been indicted as conspiracy to effect a public mischief[7] and, while this course is no longer possible,[8] the House of Lords in *Withers* appears to have accepted that an agreement to indemnify bail is indictable as a conspiracy to pervert the course of justice even where there is no intention to defeat justice. To deal with the uncertainty engendered by this case, the Law Commission[9] has provisionally proposed a statutory offence of agreeing to indemnify bail.

Proposals for reform

13.19 A major criticism of the law relating to offences against the administration of justice is the overlap which exists between the various offences. For instance, interference with witnesses,

1. Para. 15.2.
2. Para. 13.1.
3. *Vreones*, [1891] 1 Q.B. 360. Also see *Smalley*, [1959] Crim. L. R. 587.
4. Hawkins, 1 Pleas of the Crown, c. 85.
5. [1974] 3 All E.R. 984.
6. Paras. 22.12 and 22.13.
7. *Porter*, [1910] 1 K.B. 369.
8. Para. 17.14.
9. Law Commission Working Paper No. 62, *Offences Relating to the Administration of Justice*, para. 110.

parties, jurors and officers of the court may be punishable either as a contempt of court or as a perversion of the course of justice or, possibly, as one of the more specific common law offences. The overlap between contempt and perversion of the course of justice would be restricted if the Phillimore Committee's recommendation[1] is adopted, that contempt proceedings in the case of conduct intended to pervert justice should be limited to conduct relating to proceedings which have started but not been completed.

The offence of the perversion of the course of justice and the related specific common law offences need rationalisation, not only because they overlap but more particularly because of their imprecise nature, which is open to extension by judicial interpretation, with the uncertainty which this entails. The provisional proposal of the Law Commission[2] to abolish these offences and to replace them with a simplified series of statutory offences as precisely defined as possible would be an improvement.

---

1. *Op. cit.*, para. 72.
2. Law Commission Working Paper No. 62.

14

POLITICAL OFFENCES

Treason

14.1 It is unlikely that in any future conflict, whether it is called war or not, the Treason Act 1351, which is nearly incomprehensible, written in Norman-French, open to many interpretations, distorted by the doctrine of constructive treason and amended many times, would be the basis for any criminal proceedings. It is necessary to mention it only for the sake of completeness and because some of the case law illuminates a few dark corners in the criminal law at large.

With these reservations the following acts among others constitute the offence of treason for which the only punishment is death:

a. Compassing the death of the King, the Queen, or their eldest son and heir.
b. Levying war against the King in his realm.
c. Adhering to the King's enemies in his realm, giving them aid and comfort in the realm, or elsewhere.

14.2 During the sixteenth and seventeenth centuries certain acts were held by judicial construction to be treasons under the Act of 1351. The Treason Act 1795 confirmed that these constructive treasons were treasons, but in the Treason Felony Act 1848 all but one were made treason felonies punishable with life imprisonment. In such cases, however, it is still theoretically possible to prosecute for treason under the Act of 1351.

By judicial construction, "compassing the King's death" came to include compassing the end of his political existence. It might, therefore, be committed by someone who promoted a revolt in a colony,[1] or by inciting friendly aliens to invade the kingdom.[2] These acts would not always be covered by the second and third heads, because the levying of war must be within the realm, and the enemies adhered to must already be at war with the sovereign.

1. *Maclane* (1797), 26 State Tr. 721.
2. *Hensey* (1758), 1 Burr. 642.

Compassing the bodily harm or restraint of the sovereign, originally constructive treason, remains a statutory treason under the Act of 1795.

.3 In relation to the second head the doctrine of constructive treason was most fully developed. "Levying war against the King in his realm" has been held to include any attack on a general class of his subjects, such as the incitement of a mob to wreck the meeting houses of dissenters,[1] or the instigation of anti-papist riots.[2]

It was also held to include any armed organisation for the purpose of changing the policy of the government.[3] Levying war against the Queen or attempting to intimidate Parliament for such general political purposes was made a treason felony by the Act of 1848. A riot or plot to assassinate ministers of the Crown which does not have the general object of effecting a change of policy is neither treason nor treason felony.

4 Under the third head of treason, in *Ahlers*[4] it was held that a British subject who, as German consul in Sunderland, had assisted Germans of military age to return to Germany immediately after the declaration of the war of 1914–18, was entitled to be acquitted on a charge of high treason because the jury had not been directed that it was a defence for him to rebut the presumption that he intended the natural consequences of his acts by showing that he had not got "the evil purpose" of "adhering to and comforting the King's enemies" within the Act. The accused said that he simply meant to fulfil what he conceived to be his obligation under international law of facilitating the return of enemy subjects after the outbreak of war. Although the decision was criticised by the late Professor Kenny,[5] it seems to embody a principle similar to that upon which the court acted in *Steane*.[6] The direct intent of "adhering" to the enemies by giving them "aid and comfort" had to be proved and the fact that the accused did acts which were likely to be of assistance to the enemy was only evidence upon which the jury might find

1. *Damaree* (1709), Foster 213.
2. *Lord George Gordon's case* (1781), 21 State Tr. 485.
3. *Thistlewood* (1820), 33 State Tr. 681.
4. [1915] 1 K.B. 616; *C. & J. Cases*.
5. Kenny, Intention and Purpose (1915), 31 L.Q.R. 299.
6. Para. 3.17.

that he intended to assist them. They were not obliged to do so, and ought not to have done so if they entertained a reasonable doubt on the matter after hearing all the evidence. This accords with s. 8 of the Criminal Justice Act 1967.[1]

During the Boer War in *Lynch*,[2] it was held that there was an adherence to the enemy within the Act of 1351 when a British subject became a naturalised subject of an enemy state in time of war. Both the adherence, and the giving of aid and comfort to the enemy, may take place outside the realm. In *Casement*,[3] a British subject was held guilty of treason when he incited British prisoners of war to join the enemy forces and to participate in an expedition in a submarine which had as its object the landing of arms in Ireland.

14.5 These two decisions must now be read in the light of s. 3 of the British Nationality Act 1948 under which a British subject who is not also a citizen of the United Kingdom and Colonies is not amenable to the jurisdiction of the English courts in respect of acts done in a foreign country (which expression includes the Republic of Ireland and Commonwealth countries), unless he would have been subject to their jurisdiction if he had been an alien. Accordingly, on facts such as those of *Lynch* and *Casement*, the accused could not now be tried in England if they were for example, Canadian citizens, or citizens of Eire, unless they owed allegiance to the Crown, either on the principle of *Joyce* v. *Director of Public Prosecutions*,[4] or by virtue of the resolution of 1707, each of which is mentioned in the next paragraph.

Joyce, an American citizen, obtained a British passport by falsely representing that he was a British subject, and he caused this to be renewed shortly before the outbreak of the 1939–45 war, when he went to Germany where after hostilities had begun he broadcast for, and thus adhered to, the enemy. He was convicted of treason because he owed local allegiance to the Crown on account of his continuing use of a British passport. There never has been any doubt that an alien owes local allegiance, and is therefore subject to the law of treason, so long as he resides in Her Majesty's Dominions with the express or

1. Para. 4.10.
2. [1903] 1 K.B. 444.
3. [1917] 1 K.B. 98.
4. [1946] A.C. 347; [1946] 1 All E.R. 186; Lauterpacht, Allegiance, Diplomatic Protection and Criminal Jurisdiction over Aliens (1947), 9 *Cambridge Law Journal* 330; Williams, The Correlation of Allegiance and Protection (1948), 10 *ibid.*, 54.

implied permission of the sovereign. Moreover, a resolution of the judges in 1707[1] declared that an alien, who had once settled here under the protection of the Crown, could be dealt with as a traitor if he returned to his native country and adhered to the enemy leaving his family and effects behind him, for they would still enjoy the protection of the Crown. It is not clear how far this extends. Would it cover a case in which the alien left only effects behind him? In any event, the decision under discussion is a considerable extension underlying the resolution, for Joyce did not leave either family or effects in this country. The question naturally arises whether a person who has any kind of British passport bearing Her Majesty's Arms owes allegiance within the meaning of the law of treason.[2] If so, theoretically there may be many cases in which a British subject who is not a citizen of the United Kingdom and Colonies would be guilty of treason committed abroad notwithstanding the provisions of s. 3 of the British Nationality Act 1948.

Sedition

6 Sedition, a common law misdemeanour punishable with a fine and imprisonment at the discretion of the court, is committed by anyone who publishes a seditious writing or utters seditious words with a seditious intention.

Under the provisions of Fox's Libel Act of 1792, the judge has to determine whether the words of the accused are capable of bearing a seditious meaning, leaving the jury to decide, after a proper direction, whether the accused was guilty of sedition. The following statement by Sir James Stephen concerning the meaning of a seditious intention was adopted by Cave, J., in his direction to the jury in *Burns*:[3]

> "a seditious intention is an intention to bring into hatred or contempt or to excite disaffection against the person of Her Majesty, her heirs or successors, or the government and constitution of the United Kingdom as by law established, or either House of Parliament, or the administration of justice, or to excite Her Majesty's subjects to attempt, otherwise than by lawful means, the alteration of any matter in Church or State by law established, or to raise discontent or disaffection among Her Majesty's subjects, or to promote feelings of illwill and hostility between different classes of her subjects."

---

1. Foster, *Crown Law* 183.
2. Parry, *British Nationality* 87.
3. (1886), 16 Cox C.C. 355.

It follows from this that reasonable criticism is perfectly lawful, and that it is entirely a question of degree to distinguish such reasonable criticism from seditious utterances. Everything depends upon the particular facts with which the judge and jury are concerned, but generally speaking it is wrong for a jury to infer that the accused was acting with a seditious intent if he drew attention to what he regarded as blemishes in the existing system of government, and urged their removal by constitutional means, however strong the words used might be. Similarly, one who complains that a class of persons enjoys a monopoly, or that if a particular class continues to behave in a certain way it may encounter violence,[1] would not be guilty of sedition. On the other hand, one who glorifies a recent assassination and implies that the assassin's conduct might be emulated by others, runs a risk of being convicted of sedition.[2]

Official secrets[3]

14.7 Section 1 of the Official Secrets Act 1911[4] provides that a person who for any purpose prejudicial to the safety or interests of the State:

a. approaches, inspects, passes over or is in the neighbourhood of or enters any prohibited place; or
b. makes any sketch, plan, model or note which is calculated to be or might be or is intended to be directly or indirectly useful to any enemy (including a potential enemy);[5] or
c. obtains, collects, records, or publishes or communicates to any other person any secret official code word or pass word or any sketch, plan, model, article or note, or other document or information which is calculated to be or might be or is intended to be directly or indirectly useful to an enemy;

is guilty of an offence punishable by imprisonment for a maximum of 14 years.

A "prohibited place" includes defence works, arsenals, dockyards and many other places occupied by or on behalf of Her Majesty and any other place which is declared to be a prohibited place.

The above offences are not confined to espionage, but the accused must have acted with a purpose prejudicial to the safety

---

1. (1948) 64 L.Q.R. 203.
2. *Aldred* (1909), 74 J.P. 55.
3. D. G. T. Williams, *Not in the Public Interest.*
4. As amended by Official Secrets Act 1920.
5. *Parrott* (1913), 8 Cr. App. Rep. 186.

and interests of the State. The prosecution may endeavour to prove the existence of such a purpose by leading evidence of the accused's character, a course which is prohibited in most other criminal cases. In *Chandler* v. *Director of Public Prosecutions*[1] the accused were held to have acted with a purpose prejudicial to the safety and interests of the State when they impeded the operation of an airfield. Their object was to demonstrate against nuclear armament, but they were not allowed to give evidence of the disadvantages which would accrue to the State in consequence of such armament, as their short-term purpose was held to be clearly prejudicial to the safety and interests of the State because it impeded the efficient running of the airfield.

14.8 Section 2 of the Official Secrets Acts 1911[2] provides that a person who has in his control any information, etc., mentioned in paragraph (c) of s. 1 of the Official Secrets Act 1911[3] which relates to a prohibited place or has been obtained in contravention of the Official Secrets Acts or has been entrusted in confidence to him by any person holding office under Her Majesty or which he has obtained as a result of service under a contract with Her Majesty, and

a. communicates the information to an unauthorised person; or
b. uses the information for the benefit of any foreign power or in any manner prejudicial to the safety of the State; or
c. retains a document, etc., in his possession when he has no right to do so; or
d. fails to take reasonable care of such a document, etc.;

is guilty of an offence punishable with a maximum of two years' imprisonment.

These less serious offences, with one exception, do not require proof of a purpose prejudicial to the safety and interest of the State. They too are in no way confined to espionage and cover a wide variety of cases in which the accused possesses himself of, or discloses, official information. In *Crisp and Homewood*,[4] for instance, a clerk in the War Office gave to a director of a firm of tailors details of contracts between the War Office and manufacturers of officers' clothing. It was held that the clerk, having obtained information owing to his position in the War Office and having communicated it to a person to whom he was

1. [1964] A.C. 763; [1962] 3 All E.R. 142.
2. As amended by Official Secrets Act 1920.
3. Para. 14.7.
4. (1919), 83 J.P. 121.

not authorised to communicate it, was guilty of an offence under s. 2 of the Act of 1911.

A Departmental Committee has recommended that s. 2 should be repealed and replaced by an Official Information Act, which would make it an offence to leak classified information whose disclosure would affect such matters as defence, internal security, foreign relations, currency and the reserves, and the maintenance of law and order.[1]

14.9 Where a chief officer of police is satisfied that there are reasonable grounds for suspecting that an offence under s. 1 of the Official Secrets Act 1911 has been committed and for believing that any person is able to furnish information as to such offence, he may apply to the Home Secretary for permission to authorise a superintendent of police to require such person to give any information in his power relating to such offence. Failure to comply with such a requirement is an offence and in cases of emergency the permission of the Home Secretary may be dispensed with subject to the police officer's duty to report.[2] The general rule is that no one commits an offence by refusing to answer questions put to him by the police, and the above provisions constitute an exception to that rule. On the application of the prosecution the court may exclude the public from a trial under the Acts, but the passing of sentence must be in public. The leave of the Attorney-General is required before a prosecution can be brought under the Official Secrets Act 1911.[3]

---

1. Departmental Committee on s. 2 of the Official Secrets Act 1911 (Franks), Cmnd. 5104 (1972).
2. Official Secrets Act 1920, s. 6, as substituted by Official Secrets Act 1939.
3. Official Secrets Act 1911, s. 8.

15

PUBLIC ORDER AND DECENCY

1 All criminal offences in some degree are contrary to public order or decency, which is the reason why they are put in the category of crime, but there are some which have as almost their sole characteristic a threat to public order or decency. As we saw in the previous chapter, there are actions which are unmistakably treasonable or seditious but there are others which merge imperceptibly into actions which are merely conducive to disorder and it is the purpose of this chapter to gather together the principal offences concerned with order and decency.

Obstructing the police

2 Under s. 51 (3) of the Police Act 1964, a person who resists or wilfully obstructs a constable in the execution of his duty, or a person assisting a constable in the execution of his duty, is guilty of an offence punishable by a maximum of one month's imprisonment or a fine of £20 or both.

We have already seen that it is an aggravated assault to assault a constable in the execution of his duty[1] and what is now said about "in the execution of his duty" is equally applicable to that offence. A constable is acting in the execution of his duty as long as he is performing some legal duty imposed on him by virtue of his position. Examples of such duties are the protection of life and property, the prevention, detection and investigation of crime and keeping the peace.[2] However, a constable is not acting in the execution of such a duty if his action becomes or is unlawful.[3] Thus, where a constable purports to be performing one of his duties the question immediately arises of whether he is exceeding his powers because, if he is, his action is unlawful and he is no longer acting in the execution of his duty. The

1. Para. 7.9.d.
2. *Rice* v. *Connolly*, [1966] 2 All E.R. 649, at p. 651; *C. & J. Cases*; *Haynes* v. *Harwood*, [1935] 1 K.B. 146.
3. *Waterfield*, [1964] 1 Q.B. 164; [1963] 3 All E.R. 659.

powers of a constable are derived partly from the common law and partly from statutes, both general and local.

The question of lawful action can give rise to fine distinctions. It has been held that a constable, like any other member of the public, has an implied licence to enter the drive or approach to a private house and knock on the door if on lawful business. A constable entering a house in this way for the purpose of inquiring about an offence is acting in the execution of his duty until he has been told to leave and a reasonable time has been allowed for him to go:[1] if a constable remains on the premises after an implied licence has been revoked his presence is unlawful and he is not acting in the execution of his duty.[2] It has also been held on a charge of assaulting a constable in the execution of his duty that, as he has no right to detain a person for questioning without making an arrest, he is acting unlawfully and not in the execution of his duty, if he seeks to enforce such a right. The result is that he may be guilty of assault himself, and the person he seeks to detain may use reasonable force in self-defence.[3] On the other hand, a constable is acting lawfully and in the execution of his duty if he merely taps a person on the shoulder to stop him in order to speak to him.[4]

Apart from the powers of arrest and search which are set out in paras. 22.4 and 22.6, other powers of a constable which are particularly relevant to the present offences are:

a. where the constable has reasonable grounds to apprehend a breach of the peace, to forbid a meeting or to enter premises and remain there despite a request to leave. Reference will be made in para. 15.12 to the case of *Duncan* v. *Jones*,[5] in which it was held to be the duty of the police to prevent any action likely to result in a breach of the peace and that a person who persists in doing something which the police forbid on that ground is guilty of obstructing the police. The duty of the police to restrain breaches of the peace is not confined to public places in the strict sense. In *Thomas* v. *Sawkins*,[6] a public meeting was advertised to be held in a hall to which the public were invited. The police had reasonable grounds for apprehending that seditious speeches might be made or

1. *Robson* v. *Hallett*, [1967] 2 Q.B. 939; [1967] 2 All E.R. 407.
2. *Davis* v. *Lisle*, [1936] 2 K.B. 434; [1936] 2 All E.R. 213.
3. *Kenlin* v. *Gardiner*, [1967] 2 Q.B. 510; [1966] 3 All E.R. 931; *C. & J. Cases*.
4. *Donnelly* v. *Jackman*, [1970] 1 All E.R. 987.
5. [1936] 1 K.B. 218; *C. & J. Cases*.
6. [1935] 2 K.B. 249; *C. & J. Cases*; Goodhart, Thomas v. Sawkins; A Constitutional Innovation, (1936) 6 Cambridge Law Journal 22.

a breach of the peace might be occasioned and two police officers entered the hall and sat among the audience. It was held that it is part of the preventive duty of the police, where there are such reasonable grounds of apprehension as were found to exist in fact, to enter and remain on private premises. The action was one for assault against a police officer which failed for the reasons indicated and the case is important in relation to constitutional law, as it places further difficulties in the way of a complete acceptance of Dicey's theory of freedom of public meeting. In cases of this sort it is essential that the court should find that there were reasonable grounds for the apprehension on the part of the police of a breach of the peace; an officer's statement that he expected such a breach will not suffice;[1]

b. where the constable has reasonable grounds to apprehend a breach of the peace, to use reasonable force to prevent it;[2]
c. to direct traffic, where this is necessary either to protect life or property[3] or to make a motorist take part in a traffic census;[4]
d. to require a specimen of breath under the breathalyser legislation;[5]
e. to remove a motor vehicle which is causing an obstruction.[6]

The offence of obstructing a constable may be committed without anything in the nature of an assault. In general, any act which hampers the police in the execution of their duty amounts to obstructing them, whether they are hampered themselves, e.g. in making an arrest, or whether the escape of an offender is thereby facilitated. The refusal, when requested by the police, to remove an obstruction from the highway may constitute the offence,[7] but, as there is in general no duty to answer questions by the police, a refusal to answer such questions does not constitute a wilful obstruction.[8] On the other hand, any positive act making it more difficult for the police to carry out their

1. *Piddington* v. *Bates*, [1960] 3 All E.R. 660.
2. *King* v. *Hodges*, [1974] Crim. L. R. 424.
3. *Johnson* v. *Phillips* (1975), 119 Sol. Jo. 645; *Hoffman* v. *Thomas*, [1974] 2 All E.R. 238 (note the actual decision in this case is now no longer law).
4. Road Traffic Act 1974, s. 6.
5. Para. 16.32.
6. Removal and Disposal of Vehicles Regulations 1968 (S.I. 1968 No. 43), made in pursuance of the Road Traffic Regulations Act 1967, as amended.
7. *Tynan* v. *Balmer*, [1967] 1 Q.B. 91; [1966] 2 All E.R. 133; and see paras. 15.7 and 15.8 on picketing.
8. *Rice* v. *Connolly*, [1966] 2 Q.B. 414; [1966] 2 All E.R. 649; *C. & J. Cases*.

duties, such as deliberate lying or the consumption of further alcohol in order to avoid a valid breath test under the Road Traffic Act 1972,[1] constitutes wilful obstruction.

15.3 It does not amount to obstruction for one person to prevent another from committing an offence. In *Bastable* v. *Little*[2] two police officers established a police trap to catch motorists exceeding the speed limit. The accused gave warning of the existence of the trap to approaching cars, but there was no evidence that, at the time when the warning was given, any of the cars was exceeding the speed limit and the case was dismissed. On the other hand, in *Betts* v. *Stevens*,[3] there was a similar police trap of which the accused gave warning to approaching motorists. In this case, however, there was evidence that at the time when the warning was given the motorists concerned were actually exceeding the limit and thus were committing an offence. The accused was convicted. In the former case the accused merely warned an innocent person not to commit an offence, while in the latter the offence was being committed and the acts of the accused were directed towards preventing the detection of the offence. The police are under a duty to enter licensed premises in order to ascertain whether the licensing legislation is being observed. Accordingly someone who impedes their entry into a public house is guilty of obstructing the police.[4]

Words or behaviour causing a breach of the peace

15.4 By s. 5 of the Public Order Act 1936[5] any person who, in any public place or at any public meeting:

a. uses threatening, abusive or insulting words or behaviour, with intent to provoke a breach of the peace or whereby a breach of the peace is likely to be occasioned; or
b. distributes or displays any writing, sign or visible representation which is threatening, abusive or insulting;

is guilty of an offence punishable summarily with a maximum of imprisonment for three months, or a fine of £100 or both, and, on indictment, with imprisonment for 12 months or a fine of £500 or both.

Acts constituting the offences defined by s. 5 of the Public

1. *Ingleton* v. *Dibble*, [1972] 1 Q.B. 480; [1972] 1 All E.R. 275; *C. & J. Cases*.
2. [1907] 1 K.B. 59.
3. [1910] 1 K.B. 1.
4. *Hinchliffe* v. *Sheldon*, [1955] 3 All E.R. 406; *C. & J. Cases*.
5. As amended by the Public Order Act 1963, and substituted by the Race Relations Act 1965, s. 7.

Order Act 1936, also sometimes constitute the graver offence of sedition.[1] It is important to note that s. 5 covers a variety of offences. In particular, there is a distinction between the use of insulting words or behaviour with intent to provoke a breach of the peace, and the use of such words or behaviour when they are "likely to occasion a breach of the peace". A speaker must take his audience as he finds it. If he uses insulting words at a meeting, he is liable if they are likely to occasion a breach of the peace by the particular audience he is addressing, even if the words might not have caused a hypothetical reasonable man to break the peace.[2]

As an offence against s. 5 of the Act of 1936 has to be committed in a public place, it is not an infringement of the statute for a man standing on his own private premises to insult his next door neighbour standing on his own private premises,[3] but it is an offence under s. 5 for a man standing in the street to insult another who is standing on his own adjoining property,[4] and it is probably an offence for a man in his house to insult another who is in the street, provided in each instance that there is a likelihood of or an intention to cause a breach of the peace. Section 5 is not confined to conduct at public meetings.

By s. 33 of the Criminal Justice Act 1972, "public place" includes "any highway or any other premises or place to which at the material time the public have or are permitted to have access whether on payment or otherwise".

The common law offence of blasphemy has fallen into disuse: if blasphemous words are uttered, the probability is that there would be a prosecution only if they were uttered in such circumstances or in such terms that they are likely to cause such resentment as is likely to lead to a breach of the peace and thus come within s. 5 of the Public Order Act 1936 or local Acts and bye-laws.

Related offences

.5 Any person who at a lawful public meeting acts in a disorderly manner for the purpose of preventing the transaction of the business for which the meeting was called together is guilty of an offence punishable in the same way as the offences dealt with in the previous paragraph.[5] If the offence is committed at an

1. Para. 14.6.
2. *Jordan* v. *Burgoyne*, [1963] 2 Q.B. 744; [1963] 2 All E.R. 225.
3. *Wilson* v. *Skeock* (1949), 113 J.P. 294.
4. *Ward* v. *Holman*, [1964] 2 Q.B. 580; [1964] 2 All E.R. 729.
5. Public Meeting Act 1908, s. 1 as amended by Public Order Act 1936.

election meeting between the issue of the writ and the date for the return to the writ to be made, he is guilty of an illegal practice under the Corrupt and Illegal Practices Prevention Act 1883.

The difficult problem of race relations within Great Britain is tackled by the Race Relations Acts of 1965 and 1968. After considerable hesitation, it was decided not to apply the criminal sanction to racial discrimination in general. Provision is made for conciliation procedure through the medium of the Race Relations Board. If this fails, the Board has power to refer the matter to a specially constituted County Court, but the procedure is entirely civil.

The exception to the non-applicability of the criminal sanction is to be found in s. 6 of the Race Relations Act 1965, under which a person commits an offence punishable with up to two years' imprisonment if, with intent to stir up racial hatred against any section of the public in Great Britain distinguished by colour, race, or ethnic or national origins, he:

a. publishes or distributes written matter which is threatening, abusive or insulting; or
b. uses in any public place or at any public meeting words which are threatening, abusive or insulting being matter or words likely to stir up hatred against that section on grounds of colour, race, or ethnic or national origins.

The leave of the Attorney-General is required before a prosecution can be brought under the section. In *Britton*,[1] the accused deposited some pamphlets at the door of the house of a Member of Parliament. The pamphlets contained the words "Blacks not wanted here" in large type. It was held however that, notwithstanding the presence of members of the householder's family in addition to himself, there had been no distribution or publication within the meaning of the Act. It was also held, on the facts, that there was no intention to stir up racial hatred. In the absence of any other authority, there does not seem to be much point in an attempt to analyse the expressions used in s. 6, although words like "threatening", "abusive" and "insulting" may, like the corresponding words of s. 5 of the Public Order Act 1936, summarised in para. 15.4, give rise to difficult problems.

Local statutes and bye-laws

15.6 In addition to the above provisions which are of general application, there are in most parts of the country local Acts and byelaws in force which deal with this subject. For example, in Liver-

1. [1967] 2 Q.B. 51; [1967] 1 All E.R. 486.

pool and in the Metropolitan Police District, there are Acts which strengthen very considerably both the substantive law and also the power of the police in connection with the maintenance of public order. It is the usual practice to prosecute under these local Acts and bye-laws and not under the Public Order Act. A typical example is s. 54 of the Metropolitan Police Act 1839[1] which punishes threatening, abusive or insulting words or behaviour in a thoroughfare or public place with intent to provoke a breach of the peace or whereby such a breach may be occasioned with a maximum fine of £10.

Picketing[2]

7 It is lawful for one or more persons in contemplation or furtherance of a trade dispute to attend at or near

a. a place where another person works or carries on business; or
b. any other place where another person happens to be, not being a place where he resides;

for the purpose only of peacefully obtaining or communicating information, or peacefully persuading any person to work or abstain from working.[3] A trade dispute means a dispute between employers and workers, or between workers and workers which is connected with a wide range of subjects which are exhaustively defined in s. 29 of the Trade Union and Labour Relations Act 1974. In *Kavanagh* v. *Hiscock*[4] it was held that s. 134 of the (now repealed) Industrial Relations Act 1971 did not confer on a picket a positive right to picket but merely to confer in specified circumstances an immunity from prosecution or civil proceedings to which the picket might otherwise be liable. Section 15 of the Act of 1974 appears to change this because it specifically enacts that "it is lawful" to picket. It therefore follows that, whereas in *Kavanagh* v. *Hiscock* it was held that by preventing pickets from approaching a coach the police were not infringing any legal right, now there is a right to approach a coach for the purpose of peaceful picketing and a police officer who attempts to interfere with that right is not acting in the execution of his duty. If therefore a picket were to persist in exercising his right so that he committed an assault on the police there would be no offence of assaulting a police officer in the execution of his duty under the Police Act 1964 s. 51.[5]

1. As amended by the Criminal Justice Act 1967.
2. For a review of the subject see Kidner, [1975] Crim. L. R. 256.
3. Trade Union and Labour Relations Act 1974, s. 15.
4. [1974] Q.B. 600; [1974] 2 All E.R. 177.
5. See para. 7.9.d.

15.8 The Act of 1974 may also have changed the law on the lawful use of the highway. In *Broome* v. *Director of Public Prosecutions*,[1] the accused was convicted of wilfully obstructing the highway without lawful authority or excuse contrary to s. 121 of the Highways Act 1959. He stood in front of a lorry but there were no angry words or violent actions. A police officer told the accused that if he did not move, he would be arrested and, as he did not move, he was arrested. It is possible that the positive words of s. 15 might be interpreted so as to legalise obstruction of the highway but it seems likely that as it is possible to picket without doing more than technically obstruct the highway the law has not been changed, and this was the view of Lords Reid and Dilhorne in *Broome*.[2] The situation has been explained by Bridge, J. in this way:

> "At common law, the use of the highway for picketing is illegal as it is a use not responsive to the purposes for which the highway was dedicated. It is, therefore, at least a trespass. It may also be an unreasonable use of the highway and therefore a common law nuisance.... As picketing is a use of the highway wholly unconnected with the purposes of dedication and is, in fact, designed to interfere with the rights of an adjoining owner to have unimpeded access from the highway, it is likely to be found to be an unreasonable user unless it is so fleeting and insubstantial that it can be ignored under the de minimis rule. By statute picketing on the highway is legal so long as it is in contemplation or furtherance of a trade dispute and satisfies the other provisions of s. 15 of the Trade Union and Labour Relations Act 1974. Put shortly, therefore, the use of the highway for picketing is illegal unless (1) it is in contemplation or furtherance of a trade dispute in the circumstances set out in the statute or (2) it is found to be insubstantial in the sense I have mentioned."[3]

Public processions

15.9 Section 3 of the Public Order Act 1936 contains the following provisions concerning public processions. If a chief officer of police has reasonable ground for apprehending that a proposed procession may occasion serious public disorder, he may impose conditions upon its conduct. If a chief officer of police is of opinion that the foregoing power is not sufficient, he may apply for an order prohibiting all public processions or any class

---

1. [1974] A.C. 587; [1974] 1 All E.R. 314.
2. *Ibid.*, at pages 317 and 322.
3. *Hubbard* v. *Pitt*, [1975] 1 All E.R. 1056, at p. 1068.

thereof to the district council which may, with the permission of the Home Secretary, make such an order.

A person who fails to comply with any such order or conditions is guilty of an offence whose maximum punishment is imprisonment for three months or a fine of £50.

In the areas of the City of London Police and of the Metropolitan Police, orders prohibiting processions are made by the respective Commissioners with the consent of the Home Secretary.

Unlawful assembly[1]

0 Where three or more persons gather together for the common purpose of committing an offence involving the use of violence, or engage in concerted action in order to carry out a lawful or unlawful purpose in such a way as to lead to the apprehension by a reasonable person of a breach of the peace as a direct result of their conduct, they are guilty of unlawful assembly which is a common law misdemeanour and punishable with a fine and imprisonment. An unlawful assembly in such a manner as to disturb the peace can occur inside a building, in which case it is not necessary to prove that fear was engendered in persons beyond the bounds of the building.[2]

All those who participate in the assembly in any way are guilty of the offence, but it is questionable whether mere presence amounts to participation.[3] The gist of the offence is conduct which will, or may, lead to a breach of the peace. A meeting of 60,000 is not in itself enough to make an assembly unlawful. "You must look to the purpose for which they meet, you must look to the manner in which they come, you must look to the means which they are using."[4] But "the moment when persons in a crowd, however peaceful their original intention, commence to act for some shared common purpose, supporting each other in such a way that reasonable citizens fear a breach of the peace, the assembly becomes unlawful".[5]

11 The tendency to lead to a breach of the peace is easily proved

---

1. Goodhart, Public Meetings and Processions, (1937) 6 *Cambridge Law Journal*, 161–175; Wade, Police Powers and Public Meetings, *ibid.* 175–181.
2. *Kamara* v. *Director of Public Prosecutions*, [1974] A.C. 104; [1973] 2 All E.R. 1242.
3. *Coney* (1882), 8 Q.B.D. 534; *C. & J. Cases.*
4. *Hunt* (1820), 1 State Tr. N. S. 171, *per* Bayley, J.
5. *Caird* (1970), 54 Cr. App. Rep. 499, *per* Sachs, L.J.

if the assembly was aimed at promoting an unlawful purpose the execution of which would involve open violence. Three or more participants in a meeting in a private house convened to conduct a prize fight would be guilty of the offence even if the fight never took place. Conversely, although the purpose of the assembly may be unlawful, the offence is not committed if no breach of the peace would be likely to result if the purpose were carried out. The participants in a private meeting to effect the commission of coinage offences would presumably not be guilty of an unlawful assembly although they would be guilty of a criminal conspiracy.

It is true that the commission of most offences may involve violence or lead to a breach of the peace, and any three or more persons who meet together in order to execute a criminal purpose technically guilty of an unlawful assembly, wherever and however they meet, but it is unusual for proceedings to be brought. Far more difficult questions arise when the purpose of the meeting is lawful, and it then becomes a pure matter of fact whether the conduct of the accused was likely to lead directly to the reasonable apprehension of a breach of the peace by those who witnessed it.

The word "directly" is necessary in order to allow for the decision in *Beatty* v. *Gillbanks*,[1] in which members of the Salvation Army meeting in Weston-super-Mare were held to be not guilty of an unlawful assembly, in spite of the fact that previous meetings had led to breaches of the peace caused by a rival organisation called the Skeleton Army.

In *Wise* v. *Dunning*,[2] a Protestant lecturer, together with some supporters, used language and gestures in the streets of Liverpool which were insulting to the Roman Catholic religion. He was bound over to keep the peace under a local statute, but his meeting may well have constituted an unlawful assembly because it was its conduct, as much as that of the Roman Catholics, which led to an apprehension of a breach of the peace.

15.12 The problems raised by *Beatty* v. *Gillbanks* and *Wise* v. *Dunning* were considered again in *Duncan* v. *Jones*.[3] It is the duty of the police to preserve the peace. If an event is about to take place as a result of which the police reasonably apprehend that

---

1. (1882), 9 Q.B.D. 308; *C. & J. Cases*.
2. [1902] 1 K.B. 167; *C. & J. Cases*.
3. [1936] 1 K.B. 218; *C. & J. Cases*. See an article by Daintith in [1966] *Public Law* 248.

there is likely to be a breach of the peace, the police are under an obligation to prevent that event taking place although it may not constitute an unlawful assembly nor be illegal for any other reason. If, although the police forbid the event to take place, the persons responsible continue their actions, they are guilty of obstructing the police in the execution of their duty. The facts of *Duncan* v. *Jones* were that an open-air meeting was about to begin when a police officer told the accused that she could not hold it at that particular place on the ground that on a previous occasion the accused at the same place had addressed a meeting which had been followed by a breach of the peace. There being a reasonable cause to apprehend a breach of the peace, it was held that the police were entitled to forbid the meeting and that the accused, by persisting in continuing with it, was guilty of obstructing the police. While the specific point has not been decided, it may be that, as the members of the Salvation Army were forbidden to hold their procession and persisted in doing so, they would now have been guilty of obstructing the police though not of unlawful assembly.

These questions are important in relation to constitutional law, because A. V. Dicey, the famous constitutional lawyer of the nineteenth and early twentieth centuries, argued that the Englishman's freedom of public meeting is limited only by such negative duties as that of not participating in an unlawful assembly.[1] Limitations on the freedom of public meeting as a result of the law of public nuisance and trespass, restrictions imposed by local statutes and bye-laws, and the magistrates' powers of binding over militate against Dicey's argument. The argument becomes even more difficult to maintain if a person may be guilty of obstructing the police when he does not refrain from or cease holding a public meeting upon orders from the police. Nevertheless, such orders are lawful only if the police are held, as a matter of fact, to apprehend on reasonable grounds that a breach of the peace will be committed. Furthermore, such apprehension does not make the meeting an unlawful assembly if the breach is exclusively caused by the previous unlawful conduct of others.

A number of statutes prohibit meetings in particular places. An example is the Seditious Meetings Act 1817 which declares a meeting of more than 50 persons within a mile of Westminster Hall on any day on which Parliament or the Law Courts are

1. Dicey, *Introduction to the Study of the Law of the Constitution*, 10th ed., Chapter 7.

sitting to be an unlawful assembly if its purpose is to consider an address to the Crown or both or either of the Houses of Parliament for the alteration of matters of Church or State.

Rout

15.13 Where persons gathered in an assembly which is unlawful because its object is unlawful move towards the achievement of such object, they are guilty of rout, a common law misdemeanour punishable with fine and imprisonment. When the assembly which had met to arrange a prize fight moves to the scene of the fight it becomes a rout and therefore an unlawful assembly on the move.

Riot

15.14 When persons who have been gathered in an assembly which is unlawful because of its purpose are actually carrying out such purpose with violence or an intention to use violence, so as to cause alarm, they are guilty of riot, a common law misdemeanour punishable with fine and imprisonment. It is commonly said that there are five elements necessary to constitute a riot:

a. There must be three or more persons present,
b. who have a common purpose and
c. have begun to execute such purpose,
d. intending to help one another by force if necessary and
e. they must display such violence as to alarm at least one person of reasonable firmness and courage.

If one of these elements is not present there is authority for the view that there is no riot, but the fifth requirement—that at least one person must be alarmed—is modern and has been questioned.[1] It is probably enough to prove that the circumstances were such that reasonable people might have been alarmed, or it may only be necessary for the prosecution to prove the first four elements of the offence.

In *Field* v. *Metropolitan Police Receiver*,[2] a number of youths exceeding three were assembled together and were engaged in demolishing a wall, which they ultimately succeeded in doing. On the face of it, all the essential elements of a riot were present except the intention to help one another by force if necessary, and the display of violence sufficient to alarm one person of reasonable firmness and courage. Not only was there no evi-

1. *Sharp, Johnson*, [1957] 1 Q.B. 552; [1957] 1 All E.R. 577; *C. & J. Cases.*
2. [1907] 2 K.B. 853; *C. & J. Cases.*

dence of their violence alarming anyone but it was proved that as soon as the caretaker of the premises appeared the youths dispersed. It was therefore held that there was no riot. In *Ford* v. *Receiver of Metropolitan Police*,[1] a crowd of people exceeding three were assembled together to celebrate Peace Night, 1919. They lit a bonfire and in order to get fuel for it broke into an empty house. The owner of the house next door gave evidence that he made no attempt to prevent the crowd from damaging the empty house because he was afraid that if he did so he would be injured. There was some evidence of an intent to assist one another by force and so it was held that there was a riot.

Riot (Damages) Act

15 Under the Riot (Damages) Act 1886 compensation may be claimed out of the police rate in respect of damage done by rioters to a house, shop or building or any property therein whether or not the rioters have been prosecuted. In order that there shall be recovery under the Act of 1886, three or more persons must have been "tumultuously" as well as "riotously" assembled. Accordingly there can be no recovery if four people enter a shop, and rob its owner without attracting external attention.[2] The right conferred by the Act is supplemental to civil actions which the owner of the damaged property may bring against the rioters themselves and to compensation orders made on conviction and there are provisions preventing him from being compensated twice.

There is a separate common law misdemeanour of riotous assembly. An unlawful assembly becomes a riotous assembly when alarming force or violence begins to be used.[3]

Affray

16 If two or more persons fight or show force to the terror of the Queen's subjects, they are guilty of an affray, a common law misdemeanour punishable with fine and imprisonment.

An affray may take place on private premises,[4] as well as in a public place.[5]

1. [1921] 2 K.B. 344; *C. & J. Cases*, followed in *Munday* v. *Metropolitan Police District Receiver*, [1949] 1 All E.R. 337.
2. *J. W. Dwyer, Ltd.* v. *Metropolitan Police District Receiver*, [1967] 2 Q.B. 970; [1967] 2 All E.R. 1051.
3. *Caird* (1970), 54 Cr. App. Rep. 499.
4. *Button* v. *Director of Public Prosecutions*, [1966] A.C. 591, at p. 626; *C. & J. Cases*.
5. *Scarrow* (1968), 52 Cr. App. Rep. 521, cited in [1972] Crim. L. R. 635; *Jones*, [1974] I.C.R. 310.

The distinction between a fight which at most gives rise to cross charges of assault and an affray is that the latter is a fight which is likely to cause alarm; it is enough to constitute an affray if a reasonable person might have been frightened by the conduct of the accused. It is not necessary to show that a member of the public was in fact alarmed, nor, in the case of a fight in a public place, that any bystander was present or within earshot,[1] but a fight on private premises cannot be an affray unless there is at least one bystander.[2] Someone who was acting in self-defence cannot be guilty of an affray by fighting[3] but, where only one person is fighting unlawfully because, for instance, his victims acted in self-defence, he can be convicted of an affray on his own, provided all the other ingredients of an affray are present.[4]

Obscenity

15.17 Obscene publications are governed by the Obscene Publications Act 1959, which has superseded the common law misdemeanour of obscene libel.[5] The performance of obscene plays, the showing of obscene films (other than those exhibited in private dwelling houses to which the public are not admitted) and obscene broadcasts are not dealt with by the Act,[6] but special statutory provisions, outside the scope of this book, apply to theatres, cinemas, and television and sound broadcasting. Obscene films in unlicensed private premises to which the public are admitted and obscene performances, such as "live sex shows", fall outside these special provisions; however, such conduct may be dealt with by a prosecution for conspiracy to corrupt public morals or conspiracy to outrage public decency.[7] These conspiracies may also be charged in the case of obscene publications in addition to, or instead of, the statutory offences involving such publications.

---

1. *Mapstone*, [1963] 3 All E.R. 930. Contrast Lord Reid in *Taylor* v. *Director of Public Prosecutions*, [1973] 2 All E.R. 1108, at pp. 1114–1115.
2. *Button, loc. cit.*
3. *Sharp, Johnson*, [1957] 1 Q.B. 552; [1957] 1 All E.R. 577; *C. & J. Cases.*
4. *Taylor* v. *Director of Public Prosecutions*, [1973] A.C. 964; [1973] 2 All E.R. 1108.
5. Obscene Publications Act 1959, s. 2 (4).
6. *Ibid.*, s. 1 (3).
7. For law reform proposals in relation to these matters see Law Commission Working Paper No. 57, *Conspiracies Relating to Morals and Decency.*

Section 2 (1) of the 1959 Act provides that a person who publishes, whether for gain or not, an obscene article is, subject to the defences of excusable ignorance and public good, guilty of an offence punishable with a maximum of three years' imprisonment. The terms "article", "publish" and "obscene" are defined in s. 1.

An article means any article containing or embodying matter to be read or looked at or both, any sound record, and any film.

Publishing means distributing, circulating, selling, lending, giving, hiring and offering for sale or hire, or additionally, in the case of a record or film, playing it or projecting it, provided that the projection is in a private dwelling house to which the public are not admitted.

8 An article is deemed to be obscene if its effect, or the effect of any one of its items, is, taken as a whole, such as to tend to deprave and corrupt persons who are likely, having regard to all the circumstances, to read, see or hear the matter contained in it. Though a novel may be considered as a whole, a magazine must be considered item by item and, if any one of the items is obscene, the accused is guilty. "A novelist who writes a complete novel and who cannot cut out particular passages without destroying the theme of the novel is entitled to have his work judged as a whole, but a magazine publisher who has a far wider discretion as to what he will and will not insert by way of items is to be judged under the 1959 Act on what we call the item to item basis."[1]

Obscenity is not confined to that which has a tendency to corrupt sexual morals; the Act has been applied to a book depicting the career of a drug addict.[2]

"Deprave and corrupt" are strong words; to lead morally astray is not necessarily to deprave and corrupt.[3] An article is obscene even though it is directed only to persons who are already depraved; it is sufficient that it increases or maintains a state of corruption.[4] "Deprave and corrupt" refer to the effect

1. *Anderson*, [1972] 1 Q.B. 304, at p. 313; [1971] 3 All E.R. 1152, at p. 1158, *per* Lord Widgery, C.J.
2. *John Calder (Publications) Ltd.* v. *Powell*, [1965] 1 Q.B. 509; [1965] 1 All E.R. 159.
3. *Knuller, Ltd.* v. *Director of Public Prosecutions*, [1973] A.C. 435, at pp. 456–457 and 491, *per* Lords Reid and Simon.
4. *Director of Public Prosecutions* v. *Whyte*, [1972] A.C. 849; [1972] 3 All E.R. 12.

of the articles on the mind, including the emotions, and it is not necessary that any overt activity, such as sexual acitivity, should result.[1] Expert evidence is inadmissible on the issue of whether an article tends to deprave and corrupt persons likely to read, see or hear the matter in question.[2] The sole exception is where the alleged obscene matter is directed at very young children, in which case the evidence of child psychiatrists is admissible on the issue of tendency to deprave and corrupt.[3]

The meaning of "obscene" in the 1959 Act is specialised. The word is used in other statutes without any definition. For example, s. 11 of the Post Office Act 1953 punishes the posting of an "obscene" article. In these contexts the word bears its ordinary meaning of "filthy, loathsome or lewd".[4]

Defences

15.19 Section 2 (5) gives the accused a defence if he can show that he had not examined the article in question, and had no reasonable cause to suspect that it was obscene. Under s. 4, it is a defence for the accused to show that the publication was for the public good, on the ground that it was in the interests of science, literature, art or learning, or other objects of general concern. Under s. 4 (2) the opinion of experts is admissible on the issue of the scientific or other merits of the article.

Possession of obscene articles

15.20 Section 2 (1) of the 1959 Act provides that it is an offence for a person to have an obscene article for publication for gain (whether gain to himself or to another). A person is deemed to have an article for publication for gain if with a view to such publication he has the article in his ownership, possession or control.[5] The maximum punishment is the same as for the offence of publication and "publication," "article" and "obscene" bear the same meaning as in that offence. The defences of excusable ignorance[6] and public good are available.

Forfeiture[7]

15.21 "Obscene articles" kept on premises for "publication for gain" may be seized under a search warrant. The user of such

1. *Ibid.*
2. *Anderson.*
3. *Ibid.*; *Director of Public Prosecutions* v. *A. and B.C. Chewing Gum, Ltd.*, [1968] 1 Q.B. 159; [1967] 2 All E.R. 504.
4. *Anderson.*
5. Obscene Publications Act 1964, s. 1 (2).
6. As amended by s. 1 (3) of the 1964 Act.
7. Obscene Publications Act 1959, s. 3.

premises may be summoned to show cause why the articles should not be forfeited and the owner, author or maker of the article, or anyone who dealt with it before seizure, may also show cause why it should not be forfeited. The defence of public good is available in forfeiture proceedings.

Firearms and offensive weapons

2 An escape from lawful custody, or the assistance of such an escape, is a common law misdemeanour, but the common law has been strengthened by several statutory provisions of which one of the most important is s. 17 of the Firearms Act 1968[1] which provides that a person who makes or attempts to make any use whatsoever of a firearm or imitation firearm, with intent to resist or prevent the lawful arrest or detention of himself or any other person, commits an offence punishable with a maximum of imprisonment for life. Such punishment may be additional to that imposed for any offence for which the accused was being arrested.

3 Under s. 17 (2) of the Firearms Act 1968[2] a person who, at the time of committing or being arrested for any of the offences specified in the first schedule to that Act has in his possession a firearm or imitation firearm may be sentenced to up to 14 years' imprisonment in addition to the penalty for the specified offence unless he shows that his possession of the firearm was for a lawful purpose.

The offences mentioned in the first schedule to the Act include those defined by the Offences against the Person Act 1861 and the Theft Act 1968. Where the case is one of possession at the time of arrest the accused's apprehension must have been in respect of one of these offences actually committed by him before he can be liable under s. 17.[3]

Many other important provisions concerning the control of firearms are contained in the Firearms Act 1968. Under s. 16, for example, it is an offence punishable with life imprisonment to be in possession of a firearm with intent to endanger life. Under s. 18 (1) it is an offence punishable with 14 years' imprisonment for a person to have with him a firearm with intent to commit an indictable offence or to resist his own or another's arrest. Section 2 punishes the possession of shotguns without a

---

1. Also see 6th Schedule as amended by Criminal Justice Act 1972 s. 28.
2. *Ibid.*
3. *Baker*, [1961] 2 Q.B. 530; [1961] 3 All E.R. 703.

certificate, while s. 24 punishes the supply of firearms to minors of varying ages and even makes the recipients guilty of an offence.

Offensive weapons

15.24 Section 1 of the Prevention of Crime Act 1953 provides that any person who without lawful authority or reasonable excuse, the proof whereof shall lie on him, has with him in any public place any offensive weapon is guilty of an offence punishable on summary conviction with up to three months' imprisonment, a fine of £50 or both, and on indictment with up to two years' imprisonment, a fine of £100 or both.[1]

The Prevention of Crime Act 1953 is aimed against the trouble-maker who arms himself with an offensive weapon as a prelude to creating a disturbance in a public place. It provides the police with some opportunity of suppressing crime before it has taken place.

The Crown must prove that the accused was in a public place, in possession of an offensive weapon, and that he was aware of such possession. The burden then lies on the accused to prove some lawful authority or reasonable excuse for his possession.

A "public place" is any highway, or other public premises or place to which the public is permitted to have access.

An "offensive weapon" is any article either made or adapted for use for causing injury to the person, or intended by the person having it with him for such use by him. There are thus two classes of offensive weapons—those which may be described as offensive *per se*, such as a revolver, and those which are only rendered offensive by the use intended for them by the accused. A razor would come into the second category.[2] When the weapon comes into the second category, the jury must be directed to consider whether the particular accused did intend to use it in order to injure someone or, if he was acting in concert, whether an intent to injure was the concerted purpose. It is not necessarily enough that he intended to frighten people with the weapon.[3]

The definitions of "public place" and "offensive weapon" come from s. 1 (4) of the Act. The Act does not expressly require proof of guilty knowledge against the accused, but it has been

---

1. Ian Brownlie, The Prevention of Crime Act 1953, [1961] Crim. L. R. 19.
2. *Petrie*, [1961] 1 All E.R. 466.
3. *Edmonds*, [1963] 2 Q.B. 142; [1963] 1 All E.R. 828; *Allamby and Medford*, [1974] 3 All E.R. 126.

held that the word "knowingly" must be read into it; accordingly, someone who has a cosh thrust into his pocket by a stranger, or who is not shown to have been aware of the presence of revolvers in his van would not be guilty of an offence under the Act.[1]

5 The fact that a weapon was used for an unlawful purpose does not necessarily bring its possessor within the statute. A man may have a lawful excuse for possessing a weapon, such as an air rifle handed to him in a shooting gallery so that he could fire it at the proper target, although he unlawfully fires it at his companion.[2]

Section 4 of the Public Order Act 1936 prohibits the carrying of an offensive weapon at a public meeting, otherwise than in pursuance of lawful authority. The construction of this section does not appear to have attracted any substantial body of case law.

---

1. *Cugullere*, [1961] 2 All E.R. 343.
2. *Jura*, [1954] 1 Q.B. 503; [1954] 1 All E.R. 696; *Ohlson* v. *Hylton*, [1975] 2 All E.R. 490.

16

ECONOMIC AND ENVIRONMENTAL OFFENCES

16.1 A century ago there was very much less criminal law than there is today and it could be said that the majority of crimes even in the widest sense involved either violence or dishonesty. Acts or omissions which caused unintended damage to the property of individuals or corporate bodies were left to be dealt with by the civil courts: potentially harmful acts were at the most restrained by injunctions but the principal initiative lay with individuals and, where it was impossible to identify an individual who was actually or potentially harmed, the number of cases in which a public authority would take criminal or quasi-criminal proceedings was strictly limited. One example which can be traced back for many centuries is public nuisance: it has been defined as an act not warranted by law, or the omission to discharge a legal duty which obstructs or causes inconvenience or damage to the public in the exercise of rights common to all Her Majesty's subjects.[1] Typical examples are the obstruction of the highway or the emission of noise or smells in such a way and to such an extent as to cause serious inconvenience or worse to the neighbourhood. Again, the contamination of food and false weights and measures have for a very long time been regarded as matters which are more than private disputes between one citizen and another.

16.2 It is not difficult to discover the reasons for the vast increase in criminal law, using that term in its widest sense, during the past century, among which are:

a. The rise in standards which has been brought about by a combination of direct action and pressures by the workers in industry and agriculture and of persuasion and propaganda by altruists. The public conscience has been educated and made aware of working conditions which used to be accepted as part of the pattern of life.

1. Stephen, *Digest of Criminal Law*, 9th ed., 179.

b. The increase of mechanisation which has made production and distribution more dangerous. This has produced over many years Acts of Parliament which have culminated in the Health and Safety at Work etc. Act 1974 and other protective legislation. Although the Highways Act 1835 contained some provisions relating to the regulation of traffic, they were insufficient to deal with motor vehicles and it is surprising that no comprehensive Act was passed until the Road Traffic Act 1930, which although amended on many occasions and supplemented by voluminous delegated legislation, is still the basis of the law consolidated in the Road Traffic Act 1972.

c. Mechanisation and new processes have brought with them not only danger to workers but also the hazards to the people at large of pollution of land and water by industrial waste. Again a long succession of Acts, earlier in the simple form of the Public Health Act 1848 and very recently in the Control of Pollution Act 1974, have been passed in order to deal with this situation but every year brings with it new problems with which legislation has to deal.

d. The need to protect consumers which emerges from the previous three reasons and the case for which was well explained by the Molony Report[1] in these words:

> "... the old-established balance between buyer and seller has been seriously disturbed in recent years by the emergence of radically different methods of manufacture, of distribution and of merchandising ... the consumer of 50 years ago needed only a reasonable modicum of skill and knowledge to recognise the composition of the goods on offer and their manner of production, and to assess their quality and fitness for his particular purpose, the consumer of today finds it difficult if not impossible to do so because of the development of complicated production techniques ... the ordinary consumer now spends a good deal of money on appliances and equipment of types unknown, or known only to a favoured few, 30 years ago. His car or his motor scooter, his radio or television set, his vacuum cleaner, washing machine or refrigerator are relatively expensive and complicated assemblies of components, the precise working of which is imperfectly understood by the vast majority of buyers. ... In such a maze, the contention runs, the consumer finds it beyond his power to make a wise and informed choice and is vulnerable to exploitation and deception."

---

1. *Final Report of the Committee on Consumer Protection* (1962), Cmnd. 1781, Paras. 40–43.

The traditional law of contract and tort is inadequate to cope with this major social problem of protecting the consumer and so in the past 20 years there has been a steady flow of legislation designed to protect the consumers of goods and services as distinct from trade purchasers: much of this legislation is enforced by criminal sanctions.

e. The United Kingdom is overpopulated: too many people try to live, work and enjoy themselves in a country which is limited with the result that land has to be rationed and controlled by the Town and Country Planning Acts 1971–74, accompanied by an enormous amount of delegated legislation, all of which in the end is enforced by criminal penalties.

f. Finally for the purposes of this short survey, although the list of reasons has not been exhausted, is the fact that new threats to health, both of the individual and of the community, emerge from time to time. Alcohol in the past has been and still is such a threat although the laws which are supposed to deal with it do no more than impose control and do little to eradicate the evil. For the past quarter century the threat has been drugs: neither violence nor dishonesty are directly involved and the harmful effect of some controlled drugs may be less than that of alcohol, tobacco or gambling.

16.3 These and other allied developments have an important effect on the contents of this book. In most works, even those which are elementary, on other branches of the law it is possible to mention almost everything on the subject. In a book on the law of torts, most torts can be covered at least superficially, but in a student's book on criminal law it is possible to mention only a few of the full number of offences so that necessarily we are selective: others will dissent from our selection but we have based it on the various reasons for the growth in this field which we have summarised.[1]

Pollution

16.4 Pollution is making something impure, unclean, foul or filthy. In ordinary language it applies to land, water and air but for legal purposes it is extended to peace and quiet. All these in varying degrees were in the past the subject of civil proceedings only, except when they could be brought under the vague heading of public nuisance, but over the last century much legislation has been passed, particularly in successive Public Health Acts, to subject pollution to criminal prosecution and

1. Para. 16.2.

penalties. We now have in the Control of Pollution Act 1974 the first substantial move towards a comprehensive code. It is far from complete: the pollution of food is still dealt with in the Food and Drugs Act 1955 and is likely to remain so: pollution of air is dealt with only partially in the 1974 Act, most of the law being contained in the Clean Air Act 1956. It is convenient to deal in order with the subjects covered by the 1974 Act, adding references to other legislation where relevant. Not all the provisions of the Act were in force in January 1976 and it is necessary to look at the relevant commencement orders.[1]

Land

5 Part I of the 1974 Act deals with the disposal of controlled waste which is household, industrial and commercial waste, including scrap material, an effluent or other unwanted surplus substance arising from the application of any process and any substance or article which requires to be disposed of as being broken, worn out, contaminated or otherwise spoiled: explosives are dealt with by the Explosives Act 1875. For this purpose therefore waste need not pollute in the narrow sense. In general it is an offence to deposit controlled waste on any land or cause or knowingly permit controlled waste to be deposited on any land, or to use any plant or equipment for disposing of controlled waste, without a licence from the county council in England or the district council in Wales. The penalty is a maximum fine of £400 on summary conviction, or on indictment imprisonment for a maximum of two years or an unlimited fine or both. If the waste is poisonous, noxious or polluting, and its presence is likely to give rise to an environmental hazard, and it may reasonably be assumed that whoever deposited it there abandoned it or brought it for the purpose of being disposed of as waste, the maximum term of imprisonment increases to five years.

Where a person is charged with permitting, *mens rea* is expressly required to be proved, but it is likely that *mens rea* need not be proved on a charge of depositing or of causing to be deposited and that mistake is no defence.[2]

The 1974 Act follows the beneficial new fashion of providing a number of statutory defences. It is a defence for the accused to prove:

a. that he took care to inform himself, from persons who were

1. By February 1, 1976 the following commencement orders had been made in relation to England and Wales: S.I. 1974 No. 2039; S.I. 1974 No. 2169; S.I. 1975 No. 2118.
2. *Alphacell, Ltd.* v. *Woodward*, [1972] A.C. 824; [1972] 2 All E.R. 475; *C. & J. Cases.*

in a position to provide that information, as to whether the deposit would contravene s. 3 (1) and did not know and had no reason to suppose that the information given to him was false or misleading; or

b. that he acted under instructions from his employer and neither knew nor had reason to suppose that the deposit contravened s. 3 (1); or

c. where conditions in a licence are contravened that he took all steps reasonably open to him to ensure that the conditions were complied with; or

d. that the acts were done in an emergency in order to avoid danger to the public.[1]

These defences are novel in recognising ignorance of the law, superior orders and necessity as defences to prosecutions under the Act. Finally s. 3 (3) recognises that five years' imprisonment is an appropriate maximum penalty for poisoning land which takes the offence outside the category of economic and regulatory.

Water

16.6 Part II of the 1974 Act deals with the control of the entry of polluting matter and effluents into water. It is an offence for a person to cause (which does not require proof of *mens rea*[2]) or knowingly permit any poisonous, noxious or polluting matters to enter any stream, river, watercourse or inland water or the sea within three miles of low water mark or specified underground water: this applies also to any matter which tends to impede the proper flow of the water so as to aggravate pollution or to any solid waste matter. A licence by the Secretary of State for the Environment or a water authority can legalise what otherwise would be illegal, and in any case there is a defence for good agricultural practice and emergency.[3] It is also an offence to cause or knowingly permit any trade effluent or sewage effluent to be discharged into relevant waters.[4]

Noise

16.7 Part III of the 1974 Act replaces the Noise Abatement Act 1960 which is repealed. Offences relating to noise and/or vibration amounting to a nuisance are among those where no prose-

1. Control of Pollution Act 1974, s. 3 (4).
2. *Alphacell, Ltd.* v. *Woodward*, [1972] A.C. 824; [1972] 2 All E.R. 475.
3. Control of Pollution Act 1974, s. 31.
4. For examples of actions aimed at by this and similar Acts see *Alphacell, Ltd.* v. *Woodward*, [1972] A.C. 824; [1972] 2 All E.R. 475; *Price* v. *Cromack*, [1975] 2 All E.R. 113.

cution can be brought until notice is served on the person responsible for the nuisance or, if that person cannot be found or the nuisance has not yet occurred, on the owner or occupier of the premises from which the noise is emitted or would be emitted.[1] If a person on whom a notice is served without reasonable excuse contravenes any requirement of the notice, only then is it possible to prosecute him. If the noise is caused in the course of a trade or business, it is a defence for the accused to prove that the best practicable means have been used for preventing or for counteracting the effect of the noise. The word "practicable" means reasonably practicable having regard among other things to local conditions and circumstances, to the current state of technical knowledge and to the financial implications: the means include the design, installation, maintenance and manner and periods of operation of plant and machinery and the design, construction and maintenance of buildings and acoustic structures. It is clear from these details that offences relating to noise and vibration can be described as qualified offences because, possibly to a greater degree than in any other offence, liability depends on the surrounding circumstances. We observed in Chapter 3 that conduct is seldom, if ever, prohibited by the criminal law in all circumstances but it is unusual for liability to be a matter of degree to this extent.

.8 An obvious problem arises on construction sites where a level of noise must be accepted temporarily which is usually far above the ordinary tolerable limit. Local authorities are faced with the task of serving notices imposing requirements as to the way in which works are to be carried out and among other things must have regard to any code of practice. It seems that a contractor who is determined to get on with the work irrespective of what the local authority may do has ample opportunity for delay and argument whereas amenable contractors do not need the sanction of the criminal law.[2] Easier to apply in our opinion is s. 62 which prohibits loudspeakers in streets between nine at night and eight the following morning for any purpose or at any other time for advertising any entertainment, trade or business: the exemptions, such as the use of loudspeakers for police, fire brigade or ambulance, are reasonably clear.

A local authority may by order confirmed by the Secretary of State for the Environment designate all or any part of its area

1. Control of Pollution Act 1974, s. 58.
2. *Ibid.*, ss. 60 and 61.

a noise abatement zone[1] and in due course serve a noise reduction notice, contravention of which is an offence.[2]

Atmosphere

16.9 The main part of the law relating to the pollution of the atmosphere is in the Clean Air Act 1956 to which the 1974 Act has made some additions and amendments. By s. 1 of the 1956 Act the occupier of a building is guilty of an offence if dark smoke is emitted from a chimney of that building, but several defences are available such as the failure of a furnace or that suitable fuel was unobtainable. The definition of dark smoke is by reference to a highly technical chart known as the Ringelmann Chart with which it is unlikely that most magistrates are familiar, but s. 34 (2) of the Act goes on to say that the court may be satisfied that smoke is or is not dark smoke even if there has been no actual comparison with such a chart and in addition the Secretary of State for the Environment may prescribe methods of ascertaining whether smoke is or is not dark smoke, the results of any such test being sufficient evidence.

16.10 As the emission of dark smoke is normally an industrial practice when it occurs, s. 1 does not affect smoke from domestic fires, and in order to deal with the widespread pollution resulting from them as well as from non-domestic fires it is open to any district council by order confirmed by the Secretary of State to declare the whole or any part of its area to be a smoke control area.[3] Subject to a variety of exemptions and limitations, the occupier of a building in that area commits an offence if smoke is emitted from a chimney of that building. It is important to remember that the emission must be from a chimney so that a bonfire in the open air is not affected unless it can be brought within the definition of a public nuisance at common law or a statutory nuisance under the Public Health Acts. Smoke is not statutorily defined and thus must be regarded as the gaseous products of burning organic materials such as wood and coal, and by statute[4] it includes soot, ash, grit and gritty particles emitted in it. It is a defence to prove that the emission of smoke was not caused by the use of any fuel other than an authorised fuel.[5]

---

1. Control of Pollution Act 1974, s. 63.
2. *Ibid.*, s. 66.
3. Clean Air Act 1956, s. 11.
4. *Ibid.*, s. 34 (1).
5. *Ibid.*, s. 11 (2).

Food

1 Chronologically it would have been sensible to begin this chapter with the pollution or contamination of food, because long before the dangers of pollution of the earth and air became apparent, and possibly even before the dangers of polluting water were recognised, food poisoning and similar evils were regarded as too important to be left to private remedies in contract and in tort but as fit subjects for the full apparatus of inspection, prosecution and penalty, irrespective of the harm done to individuals and their willingness or ability or otherwise to exercise their legal rights. A further forceful argument in favour of criminal sanctions is that it is possible for a public authority to act not only when no one has actually been injured but also preventively before anyone is at risk.

The present law is contained in the Food and Drugs Act 1955 as amended and in a vast number of detailed regulations which are far beyond the scope of this book and occupy the whole or a large part of the time of specialists. It is possible only to extract from the Act a few of its more important provisions, to explain some of the defences available to those who are prosecuted and so far as possible to put this vital branch of criminal law into perspective. Although the Act at present covers the adulteration of drugs and protects purchasers of drugs, we confine our remarks to food because when the relevant parts of the Medicines Act 1968 come into force drugs will cease to be dealt with by the Act of 1955.

.2 Section 1 (1) of the 1955 Act forbids a person to add any substance to food, to use any substance in the preparation of food, to abstract any constituent from food or to subject food to any other process or treatment so as to render the food injurious to health, with intent that the food shall be sold for human consumption in that state. Under s. 1 (3) it is an offence to sell, or expose or possess for sale, for human consumption any food rendered injurious to health in one of the above ways. It seems clear from a long line of authorities that no *mens rea* as to the adulteration or injuriousness of the food is required and that mistake is no defence.[1] Subsection (5) provides that in determining whether an article of food is injurious to health regard must be had not only to the probable effect of that article on the health of a person consuming it, but also to the probable cumulative

---

1. Chapter 6; *Betts* v. *Armstead* (1888), 20 Q.B.D. 771.

effect of articles of substantially the same composition on the health of a person consuming such articles in ordinary quantities.

16.13 Section 2 is frequently used in prosecutions and provides that if a person sells to the prejudice of a purchaser any food or drug which is not of the nature, or not of the substance, or not of the quality, of the food or drug demanded by the purchaser, he is guilty of an offence. In view of the fact that many prosecutions under this section are founded on test purchases by officers of local authorities, it is expressly provided in s. 2 (2) that it is not a defence to allege that the purchaser bought for analysis or examination and therefore was not prejudiced. "Nature" means that what is sold is something different from the article asked for:[1] "substance" seems to include adulteration and "quality" means commercial quality. There have been many prosecutions under s. 2 and its predecessors which can fairly be described as substantial such as *Lindley* v. *George W. Horner & Co., Ltd.*[2] in which a nail was found in a sweet: there have been others which can be equally fairly described as trivial such as *Smedleys, Ltd.* v. *Breed.*[3]

16.14 Section 3 provides a number of defences in relation to the offence under s. 2, the most important of which is that, in respect of any food containing an extraneous matter, it is a defence for the accused to prove that the presence of that matter was an unavoidable consequence of the process of collection or preparation. This defence was considered in *Smedleys, Ltd.* v. *Breed* in which a customer at a supermarket bought a tin of peas containing, in addition to the peas, a caterpillar which was of similar density, diameter and weight to the peas so that it escaped Smedleys' elaborate mechanical screening process. Because it was of a similar colour to the peas, it had passed unnoticed by the visual inspectors. The House of Lords held that the defence mentioned above did not apply because the caterpillar was there not in consequence of but despite the process. There are three significant points about this case which apply in varying degrees to many prosecutions. First, the caterpillar was harmless. Secondly, the fine was only £25. Thirdly, Viscount Dilhorne criticised the taking of proceedings.[4]

---

1. *Knight* v. *Bowers* (1885), 14 Q.B.D. 845.
2. [1950] 1 All E.R. 234.
3. [1974] A.C. 839; [1974] 2 All E.R. 21.
4. Para. 21.5.

A third party defence, described in para. 6.10, is available on charges under ss. 1 and 2 and also in relation to other offences under the Act.[1]

Trade descriptions and allied subjects[2]

5 The Trade Descriptions Acts 1968 and 1972 are outstanding examples of this new kind of criminal legislation and without delving into the details of the 1968 Act (the 1972 Act being a very short amending Act which is not important for our present purposes), it is of interest to analyse the purposes of the Act and the changes which it has made. It does three principal things:

a. It re-enacts and strengthens some earlier criminal legislation contained mainly in the Merchandise Marks Acts 1887–1953, so that in this respect it does no more than continue a trend in criminal law which had existed for many years.
b. It makes criminal some breaches of contract for which until the Act came into operation the normal remedy would have been only a civil action, although in extreme cases it might have been possible to prove fraud on which to found a criminal prosecution.
c. The Act makes criminal certain actions which for many years have been regarded as undesirable but which gave rise to no legal remedy either civil or criminal. One other material change took place in 1973 which has eased the task of those who have suffered loss by some breach of the 1968 Act: s. 1 of the Criminal Justice Act 1972 (now s. 35 of the Powers of Criminal Courts Act 1973) enabled all criminal courts to make compensation orders so that a person who has suffered loss need no longer bring a separate civil action if a conviction is recorded.[3]

Goods

6 Section 1 of the 1968 Act provides that any person who, in the course of a trade or business,

a. applies a false trade description to any goods; or
b. supplies or offers to supply any goods to which a false trade description is applied;

is guilty of an offence.

---

1. Food and Drugs Act 1955, s. 113. See also s. 115.
2. For a very full survey of the whole subject see O'Keefe, *The Law Relating to Trade Descriptions*. Also see *A Review of the Trade Descriptions Act* (1975) Office of Fair Trading.
3. Professor Street, Offences taken into consideration, compensation orders and the Trade Descriptions Act, [1974] Crim. L. R. 345.

One thing is clear: the transaction must be in the course of a trade or business so that a transaction in which neither party is acting in the course of a trade or business is not covered. A solicitor who sells his private car to an individual private purchaser is not affected but if he sells one of his office typewriters he is.

16.17 The expression "trade description" is very carefully and comprehensively defined in s. 2 of the Act while s. 3 requires that to be false it must be so to a material degree. So far no decided cases have turned on these words: the reason is probably that it is understood to be the policy of consumer protection departments not to prosecute in trivial cases.[1] It is enough if a description, although not positively false, is misleading in the sense that it is likely to be taken for an indication of any of the matters specified in s. 2 as would be false to a material degree, in which case it is deemed to be a false trade description. It is possible to apply a false trade description to goods in a variety of ways, including using it in any manner likely to be taken as referring to the goods. The description may be oral as well as written, and it must be applied either at the time of supply or have been applied in the course of negotiations leading to such supply.[2]

So far, it appears that the law is very heavily weighted against the person who applies the description but he can disclaim it in whole or in part so long as he does so before a contract is entered into. Provided that the parties are not in some special category, any disclaimer to be effective must be as bold, precise and compelling as the trade description itself and must be as effectively brought to the notice of any person to whom the goods may be supplied.

16.18 Section 1 (1) of the Act is not limited to false trade descriptions applied by a seller of goods. A person who, in the course of a trade or business, applies a false trade description to goods which he is buying is guilty of an offence. In *Fletcher* v. *Budgan*[3] a dealer in motor cars said of a car which he was contemplating buying that there was "no possibility of repairing" the car, that "repairs would not make the car safe" and that "the only possible course of action with this car would be for the car to be scrapped" and

1. Compare the remarks of Viscount Dilhorne in *Smedleys, Ltd.* v. *Breed*, [1974] 2 All E.R. at p. 32.
2. *Norman* v. *Bennett*, [1974] 3 All E.R. 351.
3. [1974] 2 All E.R. 1243.

on the strength of these statements bought the car for £2 as scrap value. The magistrates found that these statements were false and the Divisional Court upheld his conviction.

9 Finally on this topic, one of the most remarkable examples of extended legal definition is in s. 6, which simply provides that a person not only exposing goods for supply but even having goods in his possession for supply is deemed to offer to supply them: we have seen that it is an offence under s. 1 to offer to supply goods to which a false trade description is applied, so that a shopkeeper who has in his storeroom a pair of shoes marked "Leather soles. Made in England" when they were made in Hong Kong and their soles are of synthetic rubber is at first sight committing an offence even though no prospective purchaser has seen them. As we shall see later the shopkeeper may have a statutory defence and it is a welcome development in much recent legislation that Parliament has not simply ignored the question of fault and left its relevance to the courts' interpretation of the statute but has gone further and enacted exactly what constitute defences.[1]

Prices

0 Section 11 of the 1968 Act provides that if any person offering to supply goods of any description gives, by whatever means, any false indication to the effect that the price at which the goods are offered is equal to or less than:

a. a recommended price; or
b. the price at which the goods or goods of the same description were previously offered by him;

or is less than such a price by a specified amount he is guilty of an offence. If a supplier of goods gives, by whatever means, any indication likely to be taken as an indication that the goods are being offered at a price less than that at which they are in fact being offered he is guilty of an offence.

21 These provisions are directed against the practices of some shopkeepers who have been known to tempt customers into their shops by advertising goods for sale at bargain prices. If the goods on sale are not at bargain prices or if there are no goods at bargain prices on sale an offence is committed. If a person is persuaded to buy something because he thinks he is getting

1. For other examples see Food and Drugs Act 1955 ss. 3, 113 and 115 and Misuse of Drugs Act 1971 s. 28. Para. 16.37.

it cheaply when he is not, it is true that apart from the 1968 Act there might be a remedy in contract but certainly there would be none in criminal law unless the prosecution could prove that the misstatement was deliberate: when a shopkeeper puts a notice outside his shop advertising goods at cut prices and none are there, none of the customers has any legal remedy, civil or criminal, apart from s. 11 of the 1968 Act. The best known case arising from this section is *Tesco Supermarkets, Ltd.* v. *Nattrass*[1] in which a packet of detergent reached the House of Lords. It was admitted that posters were displayed in a Tesco supermarket advertising that Radiant washing powder was on sale at 2s. 11d. per pack instead of 3s. 11d., but there were none in stock at the lower price.

No one suggested that Tesco had acted deliberately, but even if they had there would have been no remedy apart from the 1968 Act: as we have seen it was all an unfortunate mistake, and Tesco were able to rely on s. 24,[2] but there is no doubt that there was a contravention of s. 11.

In *Doble* v. *David Greig, Ltd.*[3] the Divisional Court held that, where a bottle of fruit juice in a self-service store had on the label "the deposit on the bottle is 4d. refundable on return" but no refund was payable, the label amounted to an indication likely to be taken as an indication that the bottle was being offered at a price less than that at which it was in fact being offered.

Services and accommodation

16.22 The 1968 Act makes a significant departure in extending the principle of false statements from goods to services and accommodation. We have seen that while it is not possible to steal a night's lodging, it is possible to steal breakfast. This is illogical and the draftsman of the Trade Descriptions Act did not leave out lodging. Section 14 makes it an offence for any person in the course of any trade or business:

a. to make a statement which he knows to be false; or
b. recklessly to make a statement which is false, as to the provision of services, accommodation or facilities, their nature, the time at which, the manner in which or persons by whom they are provided, their examination, approval or evaluation, their location or the amenities of any accommodation.

---

1. [1972] A.C. 153; [1971] 2 All E.R. 127; *C. & J. Cases.*
2. Para. 16.23. See also para. 5.43.
3. [1972] 2 All E.R. 195.

It is not surprising that the great majority of the cases which have come before the courts arising out of this section have related to holidays.

There is one vital point which distinguishes offences under this section from those we have already dealt with: *mens rea* is required. The accused must know the statement to be false or make it recklessly which is defined as making it regardless of whether it is true or false and whether or not the person making it had reasons for believing that it might be false.[1]

In *Beckett* v. *Cohen*[2] it was held that although it seems that a builder who erects a building for another is providing a service within the meaning of s. 14, an undertaking by him to complete the work in 10 days is not a trade description because, if a person makes a promise as to what he will do and that promise does not relate to an existing fact, nobody can say at the date when the statement is made that it is either true or false. Lord Widgery, C.J. said: "In my judgment Parliament never intended or contemplated for a moment that the Act should be used . . . to make a criminal offence out of what is really a breach of warranty."

In *Sunair Holidays, Ltd*[3] the accused company advertised in their 1970 summer brochure holidays at a hotel in Spain. The description read: ". . . swimming pool. Modern restaurant: the food is good, with English dishes also available—as well as special meals for children . . . pushchairs for hire." A family booked in January but when they arrived at the hotel in May they found no swimming pool, no English dishes, no special meals for children and no pushchairs. The Court of Appeal held that s. 14 deals only with statements of fact, past or present, and not with promises about the future which the court held these statements were. Obviously, every case has to be judged on its own facts and it is not difficult to think of cases where a hotel brochure contains a statement which is clearly one of present fact, but the courts appear to be leaning against any interpretation for this section which might make criminal a mere breach of contract.[4]

---

1. See further *M.F.I. Warehouses, Ltd.* v. *Nattrass*, [1973] 1 All E.R. 762.
2. [1973] 1 All E.R. 120.
3. [1973] 2 All E.R. 1233.
4. But in *British Airways Board* v. *Taylor*, [1976] 1 All E.R. 65, the House of Lords held that:
   a. a letter confirming a reservation on a flight two weeks ahead could be taken by the passenger as a statement of fact that he had a definite and certain booking on a particular flight; and
   b. the statement was false within s. 14 (1) since, in view of the overbooking policy the passenger's booking was exposed to the risk that he might not be able to obtain a seat on the aircraft.

16.23 We have already mentioned in paragraph 6.9 that the Act provides some defences similar to those which exist under other legislation. Section 24 provides that in any proceedings for an offence under the Act is a defence for the person charged to prove:

a. that the commission of the offence was due to a mistake or to reliance on information supplied to him or to the act or default of another person, an accident or some other cause beyond his control; and
b. that he took all reasonable precautions and exercised all due diligence to avoid the commission of such an offence by himself or any person under his control.

16.24 Section 23 of the Act enables the commission of an act which would be an offence but for the operation of s. 24 to be charged against the person whose act or default really caused it in addition to or instead of the person who apparently caused it. For example, in *Nattrass* v. *Timpson Shops Ltd.* and Another[1] the manager of a branch of a company owning multiple shoe shops was convicted under s. 23, a summons against the company under s. 24 having been dismissed on the principle of *Tesco Supermarkets Limited* v. *Nattrass.*[2] The operation of s. 23 is very strictly limited and an accused person who perpetuates an error which has been committed by someone else cannot blame that other person. In *Tarleton Engineering Co., Ltd.* v. *Nattrass*[3] a company of car dealers (Thornton) was summoned under s. 1 (1) (b) for offering to supply a car to which a false trade description had been applied in that the mileage recorded on the mileometer was under 24,000 whereas the actual mileage exceeded 40,000. The car had been sold to Thornton by another company of car dealers (Tarleton) when the mileometer was already reading under 24,000. It was not alleged that the mileometer had been altered while the car was in the possession of either Tarleton or Thornton. Tarleton was summoned under s. 23 on the ground that the commission of the offence by Thornton was due to the act or default of Tarleton, but the Divisional Court held that the commission of the offence by Thornton was quite independent of and unrelated to anything done or omitted by Tarleton, which itself could have been charged under s. 1 (1) (b) in relation

1. [1973] Crim. L. R. 197.
2. [1971] 2 All E.R. 127.
3. [1973] 3 All E.R. 699.

to the sale to Thornton. Likewise in *Cadbury* v. *Halliday*[1] a packet of chocolate was marked "extra value" by the manufacturer. Although on the particular facts it was held that the words were not a trade description, the court considered that if they had been the question of comparative value is one to be determined by looking at the weight, price and quality of the chocolate and therefore a matter which lies within the powers of the retailer. Although it is true that the retailer can initiate proceedings against his vendor in respect of the sale to him, the retailer is responsible for a trade description attached to the goods when he offers them.

Consumer Credit

5 For a long time there has been legislation designed to protect borrowers of money and others who receive financial credit in one form or another from oppression by their creditors and their equivalents. The Consumer Credit Act 1974, Little[2] of which in January 1976 had been brought into operation, is designed to provide a comprehensive code of law relating to the whole subject. Whereas much legislation in the past has relied on civil remedies, the 1974 Act contains 35 criminal offences which range from knowingly or recklessly giving false information to the Director-General of Fair Trading, carrying a maximum punishment of two years' imprisonment and an unlimited fine[3] to the failure to supply a debtor with a statement of the amount required to discharge an agreement which carries a maximum fine of £50.[4] Examples are:

a. A person who engages in any activities for which a licence is required under Part III of the Act where he is not a licensee or a licensee under a standard licence or who carries on business under a name not specified in the licence commits an offence.[5] A licence is required by any person, except a local authority or a body corporate empowered by a public general Act to carry on a consumer credit business or a consumer hire business.[6]
b. If an advertisement to which Part IV of the Act applies con-

1. [1975] 2 All E.R. 226.
2. Days had been appointed by S.I. 1975, No. 2123 for the purposes of ss. 21 (1), 35, 36, and 148 (1).
3. Consumer Credit Act 1974, s. 7.
4. *Ibid.*, s. 97 (3).
5. *Ibid.*, s. 39.
6. *Ibid.*, s. 21.

veys information which in a material respect is false or misleading the advertiser commits an offence. The advertisements which are affected by Part IV are those published for the purposes of a business carried on by the advertiser, indicating that he is willing to provide credit or to enter into an agreement for the bailment of goods by him, but there are several exceptions.[1]

c. A person who solicits another to enter into a consumer credit agreement which is regulated within the meaning of the Act away from trade premises commits an offence.[2]

d. It is an offence to send to a minor, with a view to financial gain, any document inviting the minor to borrow money, to obtain goods on credit or on hire, to obtain services on credit or to apply for information or advice on borrowing money or otherwise obtaining credit, or hiring goods, but it is a defence for the accused to prove that he did not know, and had no reasonable cause to believe, that the recipient was a minor.[3]

e. It is an offence to give a person a credit token, which is a card, cheque, voucher, coupon, stamp, form or booklet, which entitles the holder to cash, goods or services on credit, if he has not asked for it. When one bears in mind that a reputable bank did this only a few years ago it is surprising to find that this offence is one of those punishable with a maximum of two years' imprisonment and an unlimited fine. This can be described as an extreme example of social non-conformity unaccompanied by moral blame which is punishable as severely as gross indecency with or towards a child under the age of 14.

16.26 The curious or involved may see a list of all 35 offences in Schedule 1 of the 1974 Act which, in addition to this and other useful innovations, contains in s. 168 an express general defence in any proceedings under the Act instead, as has happened in the past,[4] of leaving the courts to speculate on the intentions of Parliament. It provides that it is a defence for the accused to prove that his act or omission was due to a mistake, or to reliance on information supplied to him, or to an act or omission by another person, or to an accident or some other cause beyond

1. Consumer Credit Act 1974, s. 46.
2. *Ibid.*, s. 49.
3. *Ibid.*, s. 50.
4. See for example the Licensing Act 1964; para. 6.4.

his control and that he took all reasonable precautions and exercised all due diligence to avoid such an act or omission by himself or any person under his control. We welcome this further example of a trend which has been visible in legislation during the past few years, one disadvantage of which is that it deprives teachers of law of problems with which to plague their students.

Road traffic

7 Offences connected with vehicles are not entirely a product of motor vehicles. For example, the Highways Act 1835 contains several provisions relating to vehicles and under s. 35 of the Offences against the Person Act 1861 it is an offence punishable with imprisonment for two years to cause bodily harm by the wanton driving of a vehicle, but the overwhelming majority of prosecutions in this field are brought under the Road Traffic Acts 1972 and 1974 and the regulations made thereunder. The 1972 Act is the principal statute, although some of its provisions have been amended by the 1974 Act. A very large number of these offences are purely regulatory and involve no moral blame, but some can fairly be regarded as coming within the ambit of criminal law in its strict and traditional sense: it is difficult to know where to draw the line and standards vary.

8 It is convenient to make these five preliminary observations before dealing with a small number of the offences contained in the Acts:

a. Before a person can be convicted of several offences, notably those of dangerous and careless driving and speeding, one important condition must be fulfilled unless, at the time of the offence or immediately thereafter, an accident occurs owing to the presence on a road of the vehicle in respect of which the offence is committed. The condition is that either the accused must have been warned, at the time the offence was committed, that the question of prosecuting him would be taken into consideration, or within 14 days after the offence the summons must be served on him or, if this is not done, a notice of intended prosecution must have been served by registered post on the accused or the person registered as owner of the vehicle. If this condition is not fulfilled, the court may nevertheless convict if satisfied that the name and address of the accused or registered owner could not have been ascertained in time with reasonable diligence, or that the accused himself contributed to the failure.[1]

b. A person who is alleged to have committed the offences of dangerous or careless driving is guilty of an offence if he refuses to give his name and address, or gives a false name and address, on being required to do so by a person who has reasonable grounds for asking for it.[2] A constable may arrest without warrant the driver of any motor vehicle who, within his view, commits the offences of dangerous or careless driving, unless the driver gives his name and address or produces his driving licence.[3]

c. An offence is usually committed by those who refuse to give information leading to the identification of the driver of a vehicle who is alleged to have contravened one of the provisions of the Acts.[4]

d. If personal injury or damage is caused in a motor accident to any person, vehicle, (including bicycle) or animal (including horses, cattle, sheep, pigs, goats or dogs), or to any property constructed on, fixed to, growing in or otherwise forming part of the road, such as a lamp-post or bollard, the driver of the vehicle or vehicles concerned must stop and give his name and address to any person reasonably requiring it. If for any reason the driver does not give his name and address, he must report the accident as soon as possible at a police station or to a police constable and in any case within 24 hours.[5] It has been held to be a defence if the accused was excusably ignorant of the fact that there had been an accident.[6]

e. The court has the power and in some cases the obligation to order the accused's licence to be endorsed with particulars of the conviction or to be suspended.[7] Unless there are special reasons for not doing so disqualification must be ordered on a conviction for causing death by dangerous driving or driving with excess alcohol in the body and in certain other cases. "Special reasons" are reasons special to the offence and not to the offender[8] so that for example the fact that the offender

---

1. Road Traffic Act 1972, s. 179, as amended by Road Traffic Act 1974, Sch. 6, para. 22.
2. *Ibid.*, s. 164 (1).
3. *Ibid.*, s. 164 (2).
4. *Ibid.*, s. 168.
5. *Ibid.*, s. 25, as amended by Road Traffic Act 1974, Sch. 6, para. 12.
6. *Harding* v. *Price*, [1948] 1 K.B. 695; [1948] 1 All E.R. 283; *C. & J. Cases.*
7. Road Traffic Act, 1972, Sch. 4, Part I.
8. *Whittall* v. *Kirby*, [1947] K.B. 194; [1946] 2 All E.R. 552.

is a professional driver is not a reason for not disqualifying him. An example of such a special reason on a conviction for driving with excess alcohol is the fact that the offender was going to an emergency and had no alternative but to drive, provided his alcohol content was not far in excess of the statutory limit.[1]

Dangerous driving

9 Section 2 provides that if any person drives a motor vehicle on a road recklessly, or at a speed or in a manner which is dangerous to the public having regard to all the circumstances of the case, including the nature, condition and use of the road, and the amount of the traffic which is actually at the time or which might reasonably be expected to be on the road, he is liable to a fine and imprisonment for two years or both if convicted on indictment, and to a fine of £400 or imprisonment for four months or both if convicted summarily. A person who drives a bicycle, or tricycle as aforesaid is liable to a fine of £30 for the first offence or three months' imprisonment or such a fine on a subsequent conviction.[2]

To support a conviction for reckless driving, it is presumably necessary for the prosecution to prove that the accused was either guilty of recklessness in the subjective sense of that term discussed in paras. 3.21 and 3.22 or else that he was guilty of gross negligence, also sometimes called "recklessness". The recklessness must relate to some consequence of the driving but need not presumably concern danger to life; danger to some other vehicle or the condition of the road is enough. A person may be convicted of driving at a speed or in a manner dangerous to the public if his driving was potentially dangerous to users of the road, although no one was in fact endangered.[3]

The question whether a particular piece of driving was dangerous is one of fact. The jury or magistrates trying the case have to ask themselves whether, if they had been present, they would have said "that driving is dangerous to the public". It has been said that if a man adopts a manner of driving which the jury think was dangerous to other road users, "it matters not whether he was deliberately reckless, careless, momentarily inattentive or even doing his incompetent best".[4] The reference

---

1. *Taylor* v. *Rajan*, [1974] Q.B. 424; [1974] 1 All E.R. 1087.
2. Road Traffic Act, 1972, s. 17.
3. *Bracegirdle* v. *Oxley*, [1947] K.B. 349; [1947] 1 All E.R. 126.
4. *Evans*, [1963] 1 Q.B. 412; [1962] 3 All E.R. 1086.

to "incompetent best" implies a requirement of fault,[1] although the fault may take the form of negligence in the sense of a failure to comply with the standard of a competent driver.

If, through no fault of his, the accused gets into a state of automatism while driving he has a defence,[2] and he also has a defence by reason of a mechanical defect in his car of which, without negligence on his part, he was unaware,[3] although he would probably be guilty of contravening one of the Motor Vehicles (Construction and Use) Regulations.

The courts have shown a tendency to construe the words "driving in a manner dangerous to the public" as including "driving in a condition dangerous to the public". Thus, it has been said that a motorist would be driving in a manner dangerous to the public if he continued to drive while feeling drowsy, and it has been held that the fact that the accused had taken enough drink to affect his driving is relevant on a charge of dangerous driving, although it was not alleged that the accused was unfit to drive through drink.[4]

Causing death by dangerous driving

16.30 The offence of causing death by dangerous driving, which is provided by s. 1 of the 1972 Act, is punishable with up to five years' imprisonment. It was created on account of the reluctance of juries to convict in cases of so-called "motor manslaughter". In addition to establishing a case of dangerous driving, the prosecution must prove that the driving was a substantial cause of the death in question; it need not necessarily have been the sole cause.[5] If the jury are not satisfied that the accused caused death, they may convict of dangerous driving. There is no power to convict of causing death by dangerous driving on a charge of manslaughter.[6]

Careless driving

16.31 By s. 3 of the 1972 Act, if any person drives a motor vehicle on a road without due care and attention, or without reasonable consideration for other persons using the road, he is liable to a fine of £200 for the first offence and to such a fine, or impri-

1. *Gosney*, [1971] 2 Q.B. 674; [1971] 3 All E.R. 220.
2. *Hill* v. *Baxter*, [1958] 1 Q.B. 277; [1958] 1 All E.R. 193.
3. *Spurge*, [1961] 2 Q.B. 205; [1961] 2 All E.R. 688.
4. *McBride*, [1962] 1 Q.B. 167; [1961] 3 All E.R. 6.
5. *Curphey* (1957), 41 Cr. App. Rep. 78.
6. The Committee on The Distribution of Criminal Business between the Crown Court and magistrates' courts (Cmnd. 6323) recommend that the offence of causing death by dangerous driving be abolished. See Appendix.

sonment for three months, or both for a subsequent offence. Anyone who drives a bicycle or tricycle as aforesaid is liable to a fine of £10 or £20 on a subsequent conviction.[1]

Section 3 creates two separate offences. An information which charged a person with driving "a motor car without due care and attention or without reasonable consideration for other persons using the road" was therefore held bad for duplicity.[2]

When someone is charged with driving without due care and attention, the question is whether he was exercising that degree of care and attention which a reasonable and prudent driver would have exercised in the circumstances, and it makes no difference whether his failure to do so was due to an error of judgment or any other cause.[3] A person drives without reasonable consideration for other persons using the road if he causes alarm to his own passenger.[4]

In many cases, the accused will have been driving in a manner dangerous to the public owing either to want of care and attention or else to lack of reasonable consideration for other road users, but there are many other cases in which, though no jury would say that the driving was dangerous to the public, the accused was at the same time not exercising due care or driving without adequate consideration for others. The difference between offences under s. 2 and s. 3 of the Act seems therefore simply one of the degree of danger of the driving in question, although there are divergencies of opinion.

Drinking and driving

32 Section 5 of the Road Traffic Act 1972 provides that any person who, when driving or attempting to drive a motor vehicle on a road or other public place, is unfit to drive through drink or drugs is liable to a fine or imprisonment for two years or both if convicted on indictment, and to a fine of £400 or imprisonment for four months if convicted summarily. Anyone who drives a bicycle or tricycle as aforesaid is liable to a fine of £30.[5] Under s. 6 it is an offence subject to the same punishment to drive or attempt to drive a motor vehicle on a road or other public place with a proportion of alcohol in the blood exceeding the prescribed limit.

---

1. Road Traffic Act 1972, s. 18.
2. *Surrey Justices, Ex parte Witherick*, [1932] 1 K.B. 450; *cf. Clow*, [1965] 1 Q.B. 598; [1963] 2 All E.R. 216.
3. *Simpson* v. *Peat*, [1952] 2 Q.B. 24; [1952] 1 All E.R. 447.
4. *Pawley* v. *Wharldall*, [1966] 1 Q.B. 373; [1965] 2 All E.R. 757.
5. Road Traffic Act 1972, s. 19.

Under ss. 5 (2) and 6 (2) it is an offence for a person to be in charge of a motor vehicle when unfit to drive through drink or drugs or with an excess alcohol content. By sub-s. (3) of the respective sections a person has a defence if he proves that at the material time the circumstances were such that there was no likelihood of his driving as long as he remained unfit or as long as there was any probability of him having excess alcohol in his blood, as the case may be.

It is the almost invariable practice at present to prosecute in those cases under s. 6 rather than under s. 5 because, in spite of the many technical rules which must be observed under s. 6, it lays down an objective test whereas under s. 5 it is necessary to prove that the accused's ability to drive properly is for the time being impaired which is a question of fact for the jury or magistrates. Juries are reputed to be sympathetic to motorists and in the same way as their reluctance to convict of motor manslaughter led to the creation of the offence of causing death by dangerous driving, so the high rate of acquittals on charges of driving under the influence of drink led to the passing of s. 1 of the Road Safety Act 1967, which is now s. 6 of the Road Traffic Act 1972.

The prescribed limit under s. 6 is at present 80 milligrams of alcohol to 100 millilitres of blood. The excessive proportion of alcohol in the accused's blood can be proved only by the laboratory tests prescribed by the statute. Moreover, it must have been in the accused's blood when he was driving or attempting to drive. Accordingly, if someone who has been involved in an accident takes drink before the test can be applied he cannot be convicted, even if there is expert evidence to show that the drink taken after driving was insufficient to account for the excessive quantity of alcohol in the blood;[1] the deliberate consumption of alcohol to avoid a proper test constitutes a wilful obstruction of the police.[2]

Under s. 8 of the 1972 Act a constable in uniform may require any person driving or attempting to drive a motor vehicle on a road or other public place to provide a specimen of breath for a breath test there or nearby if he has reasonable cause to suspect him of having alcohol in his body, or of having committed a traffic offence while the vehicle was in motion. In addition if an accident occurs on a road or other public place, a constable in uniform may require any person who he has reasonable cause to believe was driving, or attempting to, at the time of the acci-

---

1. *Rowlands* v. *Hamilton*, [1971] 1 All E.R. 1089.

2. Para. 15.2.

dent to provide a specimen of breath. There are special provisions where the victim of an accident has been removed to hospital. Failure without reasonable excuse to comply with the request is an offence, and the constable may arrest someone who fails to provide a specimen of breath, as well as someone whose test proves positive. The words "driving or attempting to drive" have been strictly construed. Thus it has been held that someone who was stopped by a police officer, got out of his car, discussed a detect in the rear light for some time, and was then suspected by the officer of having alcohol in his blood, was not driving or attempting to drive with the result that the breath test which proved positive has been invalidly administered.[1]

After arrest, the driver is taken to a police station where he must be given an opportunity to provide a specimen of breath for a second test. If this second test is positive or the driver does not take it, the driver is required to provide a specimen of blood or of urine for a laboratory test and if he fails without reasonable excuse to do so is guilty of an offence,[2] punishable with imprisonment for two years and disqualification if he was driving or attempting to drive, or with imprisonment for one year and disqualification if he was only in charge of the vehicle and not driving.

There cannot be a conviction for a breathalyser offence unless the arrest was valid and certain of other procedural requirements, some of which have been outlined, have been complied with[3] but this rule is at present the subject of an appeal to the House of Lords.[4] The breath test must be carried out with a breathalyser approved by the Home Secretary, but it was held in *Director of Public Prosecutions* v. *Carey*[5] that failure by the constable to comply with the instructions relating to the administration of the test does not prevent a conviction if the constable was genuinely trying to comply with them.

In *Carey* the House of Lords was primarily concerned with the manufacturer's instruction that a period of 20 minutes should be allowed to elapse between the occasion on which the suspect

---

1. *Pinner* v. *Everett*, [1969] 3 All E.R. 257; but see *Sakhuja* v. *Allen*, [1973] A.C. 152; [1972] 2 All E.R. 311.
2. Road Traffic Act 1972, s. 9. See *Metropolitan Police Commissioner* v. *Curran* [1976] 1 All E.R. 162, for a bizarre result of this provision.
3. *Scott* v. *Baker*, [1969] 1 Q.B. 659; [1968] 2 All E.R. 993.
4. *Spicer* v. *Holt* (1975), *Times*, 5th December.
5. [1970] A. C. 1072; [1969] 3 All E.R. 1662. See further *Attorney-General's Reference (No. 2 of 1974)*, [1975] 1 All E.R. 658.

last had an alcoholic drink and the moment when the test is administered.

The Act has produced a vast body of technical cases, of which we have given the effect of the more important.

Uninsured use

16.33 Subject to the defence provided by s. 143 (2) of the Road Traffic Act 1972 any person commits an offence if he uses, or causes or permits any other person to use, a motor vehicle on a road unless there is in force in relation to the use of the vehicle by that person or that other person, as the case may be, such a policy of insurance or such a security in respect of third party risks as complies with the Road Traffic Acts.

The prohibition against using or permitting or causing the use of an uninsured motor vehicle is absolute in the sense that it is no defence for the accused to show that he was ignorant of the fact that he, or the person allowed to drive, had not got the requisite policy[1] but under s. 143 (2) of the 1972 Act it is a defence for the accused to prove that the vehicle did not belong to him and was not in his possession under a contract of hiring or loan and that he was using the vehicle in the course of his employment and neither knew nor had reason to believe that it was not properly insured.

Misuse of drugs[2]

16.34 The Misuse of Drugs Act 1971, which replaced earlier legislation, seeks to achieve the two broad objectives of the control of dangerous or otherwise harmful drugs and the prevention of their abuse. Provision is made for the supervision of the problem of drug misuse by the Advisory Council on the Misuse of Drugs which has been established under s. 1 of the Act. The Council consists of members of the medical and allied professions and of persons experienced in the social problems to which the misuse of drugs can give rise. Its functions are to advise the Home Secretary or other Ministers on measures to prevent drug misuse and measures to deal with the social problems of misuse. It must also be consulted before the Home Secretary makes any regulations under the Act, e.g. regulations concerning the possession and supply of drugs by doctors and pharmacists or requiring

---

1. *Lyons* v. *May*, [1948] 2 All E.R. 1062; *Baugh* v. *Crago*, [1976] Crim. L. R. 72.
2. See Card, The Misuse of Drugs Act 1971, [1972] Crim. L. R. 744; Bean, *The Social Control of Drugs*.

the notification of addicts to a central authority. The bulk of the regulations made so far are contained in the Misuse of Drugs Regulations 1973.[1]

The drugs subject to the Act (the "controlled drugs") are specified in its second schedule. There are three classes: Class A includes cocaine, LSD, heroin, mescaline and opium; Class B includes amphetamine, cannabis and codeine; Class C includes benzphetamine and pemoline. One of the points of the classification is that it affects the maximum punishment of some of the offences under the Act. Variations in the list of controlled drugs can be made by Order in Council, as can variations of the classification.

Production and supply

35 The Act provides a number of offences involving controlled drugs, several of which provide that an activity is unlawful unless authorised by regulations. Under these, the offences of producing, supplying (which includes administering or prescribing) or offering to supply a controlled drug, or being concerned in such,[2] are not committed by a person who is licensed for this purpose by the Home Secretary, or by a doctor, pharmacist, public analyst or a person in certain other occupations, acting in his capacity as such, provided in the case of supply that the recipient is a person who may lawfully possess that drug.[3] These offences are punishable with a fine and/or up to 14 years' imprisonment in the case of Class A and B drugs and five years in the case of Class C drugs.[4]

Possession

36 There are two offences involving possession of a controlled drug:

a. Unauthorised possession,[5] punishable with a fine and/or imprisonment for up to seven, five or two years according to whether the drug belongs to Class A, B or C.[6] Those persons who have authority to produce or supply controlled drugs are also authorised to possess them. In addition certain persons, e.g. constables acting in the course of their duty and persons engaged in the business of a carrier when acting in

1. S.I. 1973 No. 797.
2. Misuse of Drugs Act 1971, s. 4.
3. Misuse of Drugs Regulations 1973, regs. 5, 8 and 9.
4. Misuse of Drugs Act 1971, Sch. 4.
5. *Ibid.*, s. 5 (1) and (2).
6. *Ibid.*, Sch. 4.

the course of it, have a general authority to possess any controlled drug. Lastly, a person in possession of a controlled drug for medical, dental or veterinary purposes in accordance with the direction of a doctor, dentist or "vet" is not in unauthorised possession unless, in the case of supply by or on behalf of a doctor, that person has failed to disclose to him that he was then being supplied with a controlled drug by another doctor or a statement false in a material particular has been made on his behalf by another.[1]

b. Possession (whether authorised or not) with intent to supply the drug unlawfully to another.[2] This is punishable more severely than a., the maximum being a fine and/or 14 years' imprisonment unless the drug is in Class C, in which case it is five years',[3] and is aimed at those who peddle drugs.

Physical custody of the drug is not necessary for possession but control over it is.[4] In addition, possession cannot begin until the person with control is aware that the thing is under his control: if a drug is slipped into a person's pocket, or left in his room, and he does not have the vaguest idea that it is there he is not in possession of it; nor is he in possession of tablets of controlled drugs contained in a parcel which he has received, believing it contains handkerchiefs, since he does not know the general nature of what is under his control, although he is in possession of the drugs if he believed the parcel contained aspirin tablets.[5] However, possession once begun continues as long as the thing is in the person's control although he has forgotten about it or mistakenly believes it has been destroyed or disposed of.[6]

16.37 The offences mentioned so far do not require proof of guilty knowledge that what the accused was supplying, possessing etc. was a controlled drug. However, s. 28 provides the accused with a defence if he can prove that he did not believe that the substance in question was any kind of controlled drug and that he neither suspected nor had reason to suspect that this was so. It is not a defence that the accused mistakenly believed the substance was

---

1. Misuse of Drugs Regulations 1973, regs. 5, 6 and 10.
2. Misuse of Drugs Act 1971, s. 5 (3).
3. *Ibid.*, Sch. 4.
4. *Lockyer* v. *Gibb*, [1967] 2 Q.B. 243; [1966] 2 All E.R. 653; Misuse of Drugs Act 1971, s. 37 (3).
5. *Warner* v. *Metropolitan Police Commissioner*, [1969] 2 A.C. 256; [1968] 2 All E.R. 356; *C. & J. Cases*. Also see *Wright* (1975), 119 Sol. Jo. 825, C. A.
6. *Buswell*, [1972] 1 All E.R. 75.

a different kind of controlled drug unless he mistakenly believed that the drug was one which he was authorised to produce, supply or possess as the case may be; even so he must have had no reason to suspect that it was a controlled drug of the type alleged. Of course, ignorance of the criminal law being no defence,[1] it is no defence for the accused to prove that while he knew etc. that he was in possession of LSD he did not believe or have reason to suspect that LSD was a controlled drug. Additional defences are provided for the offence of unauthorised possession, viz., that the accused took possession of the controlled drug in order to prevent the commission of an offence in connection with it by another and that as soon as possible thereafter he took reasonable steps to destroy it or to deliver it into lawful custody, or that he took possession of it for the purpose of delivering it into lawful custody and that as soon as possible afterwards he took reasonable steps to do so.[2] The accused has the onus of proving these defences.

Misuse on premises

38 The last offences we describe are those of being the occupier or a person concerned in the management of any premises, knowingly permitting or suffering the unauthorised production or supply of a controlled drug, or the preparation of opium for smoking, or the smoking of cannabis resin or prepared opium, to take place on those premises.[3] These offences are punishable with a fine and/or a maximum of 14 years' imprisonment where a Class A or B drug is involved and 5 years' if a Class C drug. Unlike the offences of production, supply and possession, these offences require proof of *mens rea* since the word "knowingly" is used in their definition.

All the offences which we have mentioned are triable on indictment or summarily. The punishments which have been mentioned are applicable in cases of conviction on indictment. Naturally, the maximum penalties on summary conviction are much lower and at the most are 12 months' imprisonment and/or a fine of £400.

.39 The application of the criminal sanction in the control of drugs is a controversial matter, especially with regard to the so-called "soft" drugs. The severity of the penalties for drug

1. Para. 3.34.
2. Misuse of Drugs Act 1971, s. 5 (4).
3. *Ibid.*, s. 8.

offences means that these offences cannot strictly be called regulatory and is an indication of the extreme seriousness with which the social problem constituted by drug taking is viewed by Parliament. The maximum penalty for possession with intent to supply is generally the same as for burglary while unauthorised possession of a Class A drug has a greater maximum penalty than an offence under s. 20 of the Offences against the Person Act 1861. It might be thought that the penalties are unduly severe. Another indication of the official view of the gravity of drug misuse is s. 23 (2) of the Act: "If a constable has reasonable grounds to suspect that any person is in possession of a controlled drug in contravention of this Act... [he] may search that person and detain him for the purpose of searching him." The unlawful possession of drugs is thus equated with the unlawful possession of firearms, for generally a constable has got an equivalent power of search only when he suspects that someone is in unlawful possession of a firearm.

17

INCHOATE OFFENCES

1 The common law offences of incitement, conspiracy and attempt are known as inchoate offences since they may be committed notwithstanding that the substantive offence to which they relate is not committed. Indeed, if the substantive offence is committed, no question of attempt normally arises, and where there has been incitement the person inciting becomes a party as an accomplice to the substantive offence and is not normally proceeded against for incitement. Conspiracy differs from the other two offences, in that even where the conspirators committed the substantive offence there are circumstances in which a charge of conspiracy is appropriate, although appellate courts have discouraged the practice.[1]

Incitement

2 It is an indictable offence to incite another person to commit any offence, including a summary one,[2] whether or not that offence is committed. The existence of the offence of incitement was established in *Higgins*,[3] where a conviction for inciting a servant to steal his master's property was upheld. Incitement requires a definite act of solicitation; the mere expression of a desire that someone should die, for instance, does not suffice but the encouragement or persuasion of another to kill him does. The solicitation must come to the notice of the person intended to act on it though it need not be effective in any way.[4] If the solicitation does not reach the mind of another because, for instance, the letter soliciting the commission of an offence never arrived, the person making it may be guilty of an attempt to incite.[5] The solicitation need not be directed to a particular person. In *Most*,[6] it was held that the accused, who had published

1. Para. 17.18.
2. *Curr*, [1968] 2 Q.B. 944; [1967] 1 All E.R. 478.
3. (1801), 2 East 5.
4. *Krause* (1902), 18 T.L.R. 238, at p. 243.
5. *Ransford* (1874), 13 Cox C.C. 9.
6. (1881), 7 Q.B.D. 244.

an article in a revolutionary newspaper exulting in the recent murder of the Emperor of Russia and commending it as an example to revolutionists throughout the world, could be convicted of incitement to murder.

17.3 The general principles of criminal liability suggest that incitement requires an intention or, at least, recklessness (in its subjective sense) that the offence incited should be committed and that the inciter knew of all the circumstances which would make the act incited criminal. In *Curr*,[1] the Court of Appeal imposed an additional requirement which related to the mental element of the person incited. The accused was acquitted of inciting women to commit offences under the Family Allowances Act 1945 because the prosecution had failed to prove that the women, who had done the acts incited, had the *mens rea* required for such offences. It is difficult to see why the mental element of the person incited should be relevant to liability for incitement since liability for that offence does not depend on the incited offence being committed or even attempted by the person incited.

17.4 An incitement is criminal even if it is to commit an offence which could not be committed at the time, as when someone incites a pregnant woman to kill her child when it is born or incites another to receive goods to be stolen in the future.[2] It is irrelevant that the offence incited cannot be committed by the means suggested,[3] as would be so if A encourages B to use a pill, which is in fact harmless, to kill C by poisoning; of course, if the inciter knows that the offence cannot be committed by the suggested means he is not guilty of incitement since he lacks the necessary *mens rea*.[4]

17.5 As common law misdemeanours, incitement and attempted incitement are punishable with imprisonment at the discretion of the court if they are prosecuted on indictment,[5] but it is not likely that an incitement or attempted incitement would be punished more severely than is possible for the offence to which the incitement relates. Incitements to commit those indictable offences which are triable summarily with the accused's consent

1. [1968] 2 Q.B. 944; [1967] 1 All E.R. 478.
2. *Shephard*, [1919] 2 K.B. 125.
3. *McDonough* (1962), 47 Cr. App. Rep. 37.
4. *Brown* (1899), 63 J.P. 790.
5. Para. 2.2.

are themselves triable summarily with his consent,[1] when the magistrates can impose a maximum punishment of six months' imprisonment,[2] as are incitements to commit a summary offence,[3] when the incitement cannot be punished more severely than is possible for the offence incited.[4] In some cases a special penalty is imposed by statute. Under s. 4 of the Offences against the Person Act 1861, for instance, incitement to murder is punishable with a maximum of 10 years' imprisonment.

Conspiracy

6 Conspiracy, which is a common law misdemeanour, is an agreement between two or more people to commit an offence or do certain other acts. Joint planning and joint action are frequently preliminaries to crime, but it would be inaccurate to regard conspiracy simply as an inchoate offence since it is also committed by those who conspire to commit certain types of non-criminal acts.

Actus reus—agreement[5]

7 There cannot be a conspiracy unless there is a concluded agreement for an "unlawful" object.[6] The offence is complete as soon as the parties agree and it is immaterial that they never begin to put it into effect[7] or that it is subject to a proviso, such as "if it is possible or propitious"[8], or that the details remain to be agreed.[9] It is not necessary that all the parties to the agreement should have evinced their consent at the same time, nor that they should all have been in communication with each other, provided they entertained a common purpose, communicated to at least one other party, expressly or tacitly, in relation to the object of the conspiracy.[10] This would be so for instance with members of a society who had each worked for the same end under some common superior but had never communicated with each other.[11]

---

1. Magistrates' Courts Act 1952, Sch. 1.
2. *Ibid.*, s. 19 (6).
3. *Ibid.*, Sch. 1.
4. *Ibid.*, s. 19 (8).
5. Orchard, "Agreement" in Criminal Conspiracy, [1974] Crim. L. R. 297, 335.
6. *Jones* (1832), 4 B. & Ad. 345, at p. 349, *per* Denman, C.J.
7. *Poulterer's Case* (1610), 9 Co. Rep. 55b.
8. *Mills* (1962), 47 Cr. App. Rep. 49, at pp. 54–55.
9. *Gill and Henry* (1818), 2 B. & Ald. 257.
10. *Ardalan*, [1972] 2 All E.R. 257.
11. See summing up of Fitzgerald, J., in *Parnell* (1881), 14 Cox C.C. 508, at p. 516. See also *Meyrick and Ribuffi* (1929), 21 Cr. App. Rep. 94.

Although conspiracy is committed as soon as the agreement for the "unlawful" object is made, it is clear that conspiracy is a continuing offence and is committed not only when agreement is first reached. The conspiracy continues as long as the agreement to effect the unlawful object continues.[1] The most important result of this is that a number of persons may be held parties to the same conspiracy although they joined it at different times[2] and may not have been parties to the agreement at the same time as each other.[3]

The fact that there must be two or more parties to constitute an agreement produces two interesting consequences:

a. A director who is the "one man" of a "one man" company cannot be convicted of conspiring with the company in spite of the fact that a company can be held guilty of conspiracy and is in law a separate entity from its directors.[4] This is because, in order that there should be a conspiracy, there must be an agreement between two minds, and the director's mind is that of the company only in a purely artificial sense. A company can be convicted of conspiring with several of its directors, but presumably the rule with regard to the one man company would prevent two companies with the same "one man" from being convicted of conspiring together.
b. A husband and wife who are the only parties to an agreement cannot be guilty of conspiracy.[5] The basis of this rule is the fiction that a husband and wife are considered in law for limited purposes to be one person.[6] This fiction has been eroded elsewhere in our law and the present rule should be abolished. It remains undecided whether the rule applies to a husband and wife whose marriage is of a type which is actually or potentially polygamous.[7] It certainly seems odd that if a husband and wife agree between themselves to commit an offence they cannot be convicted of conspiracy, whereas if the substantive offence is committed they can both be convicted of that offence. Moreover, the fact that a husband and wife can be convicted of conspiring together with a third

---

1. *Director of Public Prosecutions* v. *Doot*, [1973] A.C. 807; [1973] 1 All E.R. 940.
2. *Murphy* (1837), 8 C. & P. 297, at p. 311; *Sweetland* (1957), 42 Cr. App. Rep. 62, at p. 67.
3. *Simmonds* (1967), 51 Cr. App. Rep. 317, at p. 332.
4. *McDonnell*, [1966] 1 Q.B. 233; [1966] 1 All E.R. 193; *C. & J. Cases.*
5. *Mawji* v. *R.*, [1957] A.C. 126; [1957] 1 All E.R. 385.
6. *Ibid.*
7. This point was left open in *Mawji.*

party[1] is inconsistent with the principle of marital unity, since, if a husband and wife, being one, cannot make an agreement, how can they be a party to one agreement?

Actus reus—the unlawful object

8 The extent of the unlawful objects of an agreement which make it a conspiracy is a question which has been before the House of Lords on a number of occasions recently. For convenience these objects can be divided into five groups:

a. to commit a criminal offence;
b. to pervert the course of justice;
c. to defraud;
d. to commit a tort;
e. to corrupt and outrage morals or decency.

.9 *To commit a criminal offence.*—The offence may be indictable or summary.[2] All conspiracies must be tried on indictment and it is objectionable that a conspiracy to commit a summary offence should, unlike incitement to commit a summary offence,[3] always be tried by a higher court than that which tries the substantive summary offence, particularly when the sentence for conspiracy is unlimited,[4] whereas that for summary offences is severely restricted. In the Law Commission Working Paper on Inchoate Offences[5] the view is taken that criminal liability for conspiracy to commit summary crime should be restricted to conspiracies to commit such offences on a wide scale. It is proposed that, in relation to summary offences, a conspiracy should only be criminal if its object is to commit more than one summary offence of the same nature, such a conspiracy being triable only on indictment. It may be questioned whether a conspiracy limited to the commission of two or three offences can be said to involve crime on a large scale. As frequently happens in law reform, it is difficult to know where to draw the line.

It is immaterial that the offence which the accused persons conspired to commit is one for which one of them is not liable to prosecution. For instance if a man and woman conspire to

1. *Whitehouse* (1852), 6 Cox C.C. 38.
2. *Blamires Transport Ltd.*, [1964] 1 Q.B. 278; [1963] 3 All E.R. 170.
3. Para. 17.5.
4. Para. 2.2.
5. Law Commission Working Paper No. 50, *Inchoate Offences: Conspiracy, Incitement and Attempt*, paras. 103–110 and 122–124. For a discussion of the Working Paper's proposals concerning conspiracy, see Card, [1973] Crim. L. R. 674.

administer a drug to her to procure an abortion, although she is not pregnant, both the man[1] and the woman[2] can be convicted of conspiracy although the woman could not be convicted of attempting to procure a miscarriage (abortion).[3] It is, however, essential that the alleged conspirators should be proved to have agreed to act in contravention of the existing English law and not merely to have intended to break any future law which might come into effect.[4]

A conspiracy in England or Wales to do acts in a foreign country which infringe the criminal law of that country is not indictable in this country unless the contemplated offence itself, if committed in a foreign country, is one for which an indictment would lie here.[5] English criminal law does not generally extend to extraterritorial crime but notable exceptions are murder and bigamy by a citizen of the United Kingdom and Colonies.[6] Thus, if such a citizen agreed in England to murder a person in France the conspiracy is indictable in England.

A conspiracy abroad to commit an offence in England or Wales is indictable here if the parties perform acts here in furtherance of the conspiracy.[7] It remains undecided whether the conspiracy is indictable here if the parties enter this country but do not take steps to implement the conspiracy here. The continuing nature of conspiracy suggests that if parties to a conspiracy made abroad enter this country agreeing to implement it the conspiracy is committed in England and Wales.[8]

17.10 *To pervert the course of justice.*—Generally, this type of unlawful object adds nothing to the previous one since the object of such conspiracies would, when consummated, constitute an offence such as perjury or perverting the course of justice. However, an agreement to indemnify bail without any intent to pervert justice is an indictable conspiracy of this type, even though the

---

1. *Duguid* (1906), 75 L.J.K.B. 470.
2. *Whitchurch* (1890), 24 Q.B.D. 420; *C. & J. Cases.*
3. Para. 8.36.
4. *West*, [1948] 1 K.B. 709; [1948] 1 All E.R. 718.
5. *Board of Trade* v. *Owen*, [1957] A.C. 602; [1957] 1 All E.R. 411. See also *Cox*, [1968] 1 All E.R. 410.
6. Para. 21.8.
7. *Director of Public Prosecutions* v. *Doot*, [1973] A.C. 807; [1973] 1 All E.R. 940.
8. This was the view taken by Lords Dilhorne and Salmon in *Director of Public Prosecutions* v. *Doot*, [1973] AC. 807, at pp. 823 and 835 respectively.

indemnification of bail is not itself a substantive offence unless there is a corrupt intent.[1]

1 *To defraud.*—Many conspiracies to defraud are aimed at the commission of some offence of fraud but the fraudulent object need not be criminal or even tortious. In *Scott* v. *Metropolitan Police Commissioner*[2] the House of Lords held that there may be a conspiracy to defraud without deceit. The appellant agreed with the employees of cinema owners temporarily to abstract films, without the permission of the cinema owners and in return for payment to the employees so that, without the consent of the owners of the copyright and distribution rights in such films, he could make copies and distribute them commercially. His conviction for conspiracy to defraud was upheld by the House of Lords which held that on such a charge it was not necessary for the Crown to prove an agreement to deprive the owners of their property by deception. It was sufficient to prove an agreement "to deprive a person dishonestly of something to which he is or would or might, but for the perpetration of the fraud, be entitled".[3]

Where the intended victim of the conspiracy to defraud is a person performing public duties (which phrase does not include bank managers and the like[4]) as distinct from a private individual, there can be a conspiracy to defraud even though the purpose does not involve causing economic loss to anyone. It is sufficient if the purpose of the agreement is to cause such a person to act contrary to his duty (e.g. in granting a licence or giving information), and the intended means of achieving that purpose are dishonest.[5] There is authority that this type of defrauding requires an element of deception.[6]

12 *To commit a tort.*—An agreement to commit a tort amounts to an indictable conspiracy only if the execution of the agree-

---

1. Para. 13.18.
2. [1974] 3 All E.R. 1032.
3. *Ibid.*, at p. 1038, *per* Lord Dilhorne with whose speech the other Lords of Appeal agreed.
4. *Director of Public Prosecutions* v. *Withers*, [1974] 3 All E.R. 984, at p. 1009 *per* Lord Kilbrandon.
5. *Scott* v. *Metropolitan Police Commissioner*, [1974] 3 All E.R. 1032, see especially Lord Diplock at p. 1040; *Director of Public Prosecutions* v. *Withers*, pp. 1004–1005 and 1009 *per* Lords Simon and Kilbrandon respectively.
6. *Board of Trade* v. *Owen*, [1957] A.C. 603, at p. 622, *per* Lord Tucker; *Director of Public Prosecutions* v. *Withers*, at p. 1009, *per* Lord Kilbrandon.

ment has as its object either a. invasion of the "public domain" or b. the infliction on its victim of injury and damage which is more than nominal. This was held by the House of Lords in *Kamara* v. *Director of Public Prosecutions.*[1] Students from Sierra Leone agreed to occupy, and did occupy, the London premises of the Sierra Leone High Commission in order to draw attention to grievances which they had. The House of Lords dismissed the students' appeals against conviction for conspiracy to trespass because the execution of the tort of trespass invaded the public domain, the building being the High Commission of a friendly state. Other examples offered of "public domain" in the context of trespass were embassies and publicly owned buildings, although presumably the term would not extend as far as council houses, but what constitutes an invasion of the "public domain" in the context of other torts is uncertain. The alternative object is clearly satisfied by those who agree to squat or sit-in since if an owner is prevented, permanently or temporarily, from enjoying his property he suffers damage which is more than nominal.[2]

To corrupt and outrage morals and decency.—

17.13 a. *To corrupt public morals.*—In *Shaw* v. *Director of Public Prosecutions,*[3] the majority of the House of Lords recognised the continued existence of the offence of conspiracy to corrupt public morals. They accordingly upheld Shaw's conviction for this offence, arising out of his agreement with others for the publication of a "Ladies' Directory", giving the names, addresses and practices of prostitutes. *Shaw* was followed by the majority of the House of Lords in *Knuller* v. *Director of Public Prosecutions,*[4] where further explanation was given of conspiracy to corrupt public morals. The House held that an agreement to publish advertisements soliciting homosexual acts between consenting adults in private was a conspiracy to corrupt public morals, even though such conduct is no longer an offence.[5] Lords Reid and Simon said that "corrupt" was a strong word and that "corrupt public morals" meant more than "lead morally astray". Lord Reid thought that "corrupt" was synonymous with "deprave",[6] while Lord Simon said that what was required was conduct which "a

1. [1974] A.C. 104; [1973] 2 All E.R. 142.
2. [1974] A.C. at p. 130, *per* Lord Hailsham, L.C. and see para. 12.7.
3. [1962] A.C. 220; [1961] 2 All E.R. 446; *C. & J. Cases.*
4. [1973] A.C. 435; [1972] 2 All E.R. 898; *C. & J. Cases.*
5. Para. 9.8.
6. [1973] A.C. at p. 456.

jury might find to be destructive of the very fabric of society".[1] Lord Reid thought that conspiracy to corrupt public morals was something of a misnomer. "It really means to corrupt the morals of such members of the public as may be influenced by the matter published by the accused".[2] Although, of course, the judge must initially rule on whether there is evidence on which the jury can find the case proved, it is for the jury to find whether a particular object is corrupting of public morals and they should do this by applying the current standards of ordinary decent people.[3] This leads to considerable uncertainty about the conduct penalised by the criminal law.

b. *To outrage public decency*.—In *Knuller* v. *Director of Public Prosecutions* the accused had also been convicted of conspiracy to outrage public decency. The majority of the House of Lords held that there was a common law crime of outraging public decency and thus a conspiracy to outrage public decency was an offence, but the accused's appeals against conviction were allowed because the jury had not been properly directed on the relevant principles. The substantive offence, and therefore the object of the conspiracy, must be committed in a public place, in the sense that the circumstances must be such that the alleged outrageously indecent matter or conduct could have been seen by more than one person, although not necessarily simultaneously, even if in fact no more than one did see it. Thus it is not a defence that the indecent matter is contained in a book or newspaper sold in public. Moreover, it would not necessarily negative liability if an indecent act or exhibit is superficially hidden from view if the public is expressly or impliedly invited to penetrate the cover. Thus, public touting for outrageously indecent exhibitions in private would not escape. "Outrage" like "corrupt" is a strong word. "Outraging public decency" goes beyond offending the susceptibilities of, or even shocking, reasonable people. The offence is concerned with protecting the recognised minimum contemporary standards of decency and whether there is an "outrage" of such standards is a question for the jury.[4]

---

1. *Ibid.*, at p. 491.
2. *Ibid.*, at p. 456.
3. *Shaw* v. *Director of Public Prosecutions*, [1962] A.C. 220; [1961] 2 All E.R. 446; *Knuller* v. *Director of Public Prosecutions*, [1973] A.C. 435; [1972] 2 All E.R. 898.
4. See, in particular, the speech of Lord Simon with whom Lord Kilbrandon agreed.

Are there other types of unlawful object?

17.14 In a number of cases convictions for conspiracy to effect a public mischief have been upheld. In *Porter*,[1] it was held that an agreement by a person who was charged with an offence to indemnify sureties who went bail for him was a conspiracy to effect a public mischief, because it was in the public interest that a surety should have an interest in seeing that the accused person stood trial. In *Bassey*,[2] the appellant was held to have been rightly convicted of conspiracy to effect a public mischief where he had agreed to a course of action by which he gained admission to one of the Inns of Court on the basis of forged certificates because the public had an interest in the efficiency of those who intend to become barristers. *Dicta* in such cases suggested that there could be a criminal conspiracy even though the object in question did not constitute one of the types mentioned above. Thus the scope of "public mischief" was uncertain and this gave rise to the risk of the judicial extension of criminal conspiracy to new areas.

However, in *Director of Public Prosecutions* v. *Withers*[3] the House of Lords held that there was no such separate type of unlawful object as "public mischief". The appellants were private investigators, whose activities included making for clients reports about the status and financial standing of third parties. Inquiries were made of banks, building societies, government departments and local authorities, usually by telephone. To induce officers of the various bodies to part with information which they would not normally have given, lies were constantly told and as a result confidential information was obtained. The House of Lords quashed the appellants' convictions for conspiring to effect a public mischief, holding that there was no such separate object of a criminal conspiracy and that, while the conspiracy to induce public officers to give confidential information might have constituted a conspiracy to defraud, the conviction on the count involving these officers could not be upheld on this ground since the judge's summing-up had emphasised the aspect of public mischief rather than that of fraud.

This decision will not result in any significant diminution of the criminal law because, as the House recognised, an indictment for conspiracy to commit an offence or conspiracy to pervert the course of justice or conspiracy to defraud would have lain

1. [1910] 1 K.B. 369.
2. (1931), 22 Cr. App. Rep. 160.
3. [1974] 3 All E.R. 984.

in most, if not all, the cases where convictions for conspiracy to effect a public mischief have been upheld. However, the decision does prevent the expansion of the offence of conspiracy through the medium of the public mischief conspiracy.

15 Recent cases have shown that no new types of unlawful object can be created by the courts. In *Shaw* v. *Director of Public Prosecutions*,[1] the view taken by the House of Lords was that there remains in the courts as custodians of public morals a residual power, where no statute has yet intervened to supersede the common law, to superintend those offences which are prejudicial to the public welfare. In *Director of Public Prosecutions* v. *Bhagwan*,[2] it was held by the House of Lords that a conspiracy to defeat the purpose of a statute without in any way infringing its express provisions is not a criminal offence. Lord Diplock said that he did not understand any of the speeches in *Shaw's* case as having asserted that it is still open to courts to enlarge the number of categories of purposes which are so contrary to public policy that those who act in concert to achieve them are guilty of a criminal offence at common law. All that the case decided was that acting in concert for the purpose of corrupting public morals by encouraging prostitution was punishable at common law.[3] Similarly, in *Knuller* v. *Director of Public Prosecutions*[4] it was emphasised that the decision in *Shaw* was not to be taken as affirming or lending support to the doctrine that the courts have some residual power to create new offences or so to widen existing offences as to make punishable conduct of a type not hitherto subject to punishment. This view was repeated in *Director of Public Prosecutions* v. *Withers*.[5] Nevertheless, the existence of the wide general offence of conspiracy to corrupt public morals effectively gives the courts such a residual power in the field of morality that it remains possible that such a conspiracy might be extended to cover agreements to further lesbianism or fornication or adultery.

Proposals for reform

16 Even after the decision in *Withers*, the imprecision and width of the non-criminal objects of conspiracy are major criticisms of that offence, and it is not obvious why, if a particular act is

1. [1962] A.C. 220; [1961] 2 All E.R. 446: *C. & J. Cases.*
2. [1972] A.C. 60; [1970] 3 All E.R. 97.
3. [1972] A.C. at p. 80.
4. [1973] A.C. 435; [1972] 2 All E.R. 898; *C. & J. Cases.*
5. [1974] 3 All E.R. 984.

not criminal when done, an agreement to do it should be criminal. In the Law Commission Working Paper mentioned above it is proposed that criminal conspiracy should be limited to agreements to commit criminal offences.[1] Although outraging public decency is, and corrupting public morals may be, a common law offence, it is proposed that conspiracy to effect these objects should be abolished, along with the substantive offences since both these closely related objects are equally objectionable. The abolition of the non-criminal objects of a conspiracy would leave gaps in the law and three Working Papers have subsequently been published proposing specific substantive offences to fill these lacunae.[2]

Mens rea[3]

17.17 A person cannot be guilty of conspiracy unless he knows what the unlawful object is,[4] knows of the participation of other parties, and intends that the unlawful object shall be achieved. There is authority that there can be no liability at all for conspiracy where one of two alleged conspirators lacks the requisite knowledge and intention.[5] There would seem to be no logical reason why the conspirator with *mens rea* should not be convicted.[6]

a. *Knowledge of the unlawful object.*—This includes knowledge of any circumstances by reason of which the object is unlawful. Thus in the case of a conspiracy to trespass whose execution necessarily involves more than nominal damage it is a defence that the accused believed in a state of facts which would give rise to an enforceable right of way, or neither intended nor knew that it would inflict more than nominal damage.[7] The leading authority on the necessity of guilty knowledge is *Churchill* v. *Walton*,[8] which shows that the requirement applies even where the unlawful object is an offence of strict liability.

The appellant and others agreed to sell gas oil for use on the roads. This is an offence unless the oil has borne full cus-

---

1. *Op. cit.*, paras. 8–32.
2. Law Commission Working Papers Nos. 56, 57 and 63.
3. Orchard, "Agreement" in Criminal Conspiracy, [1974] Crim. L. R. 335.
4. *Pollman* (1809), 2 Camp. 230.
5. *Curr*, [1968] 2 Q.B. 944; [1967] 1 All E.R. 478.
6. Fridman, *Mens Rea* in Conspiracy, (1956) 19 M.L.R. 379.
7. *Kamara* v. *Director of Public Prosecutions*, [1974] A.C. 104, at p. 130.
8. [1967] A.C. 224; [1967] 1 All E.R. 497; *C. & J. Cases*.

toms duty, and the oil in question had not borne such duty. Had the appellant sold the oil for use on the roads, his ignorance of the fact that it had not borne full duty would not have been a defence to a charge of the substantive offence because the offence is one of strict liability. It was nevertheless held that he could not be convicted of conspiracy if guilty knowledge was not proved against him.

> "If what they agreed to do was on the facts known to them an unlawful act, they are guilty of conspiracy and cannot excuse themselves by saying that, owing to their ignorance of the law, they did not realise that such an act was a crime. If, on the facts known to them what they agreed to do was lawful, they are not rendered artificially guilty by the existence of other facts, not known to them, giving a different and criminal quality to the act agreed on".[1]

b. *Knowledge of other parties.*—A person may conspire with another although he does not know his identity and is not in direct communication with him, but he must at least know or believe that there is another who agrees with him otherwise he would be ignorant of the existence of the alleged agreement.[2] Where the number of conspirators exceeds two it need only be proved that a particular conspirator knew there were other parties; it is not necessary that he knew the full extent of the scheme "to which he attaches himself".[3]

c. *Intention that the unlawful object be achieved.*—For a person to become a conspirator, it is not necessary that it is intended that he should personally do anything to further the unlawful object.[4] On the other hand, it has been held that an accused who may have intended all along to resile from the agreement and only ostensibly entered into it in order to placate or lay a trap for the other party ought to be acquitted.[5] This suggests that a party is not a conspirator even though he expresses his agreement to an unlawful object, unless he intends that the object be achieved. The intention required here is a direct and not, despite one case to the contrary,[6] an oblique intent since something which is only obliquely intended can hardly be said to be the object of an agreement.

---

1. At p. 503, *per* Lord Dilhorne.
2. *O'Conner* (1843), 4 State Tr. N.S. 935, at pp. 1205–1206.
3. *Griffiths*, [1966] 1 Q.B. 589; [1965] 2 All E.R. 448.
4. *Gurney* (1869), 11 Cox C.C. 414, at pp. 436–438.
5. *Thomson* (1965), 50 Cr. App. Rep. 1; *C. & J. Cases.*
6. *Hunter*, [1974] Q.B. 95; [1973] 3 All E.R. 286.

Where the substantive offence has been committed

17.18 A conspiracy to commit an offence does not merge with the substantive offence when the latter is committed but as a general rule where there is an effective and sufficient charge of a substantive offence, the addition of a charge for conspiracy is undesirable because it tends to prolong and complicate the trial.[1] Exceptionally, as in complicated cases in which the interests of justice can be served only by presenting to the jury an overall picture and in which that cannot be done by counts charging substantive offences, a conspiracy count may be appropriate but it should not be included with counts charging substantive offences if this would result in unfairness to the defence.[2]

Acquittal of all save one

17.19 If the conspiracy is charged as being between two or more named persons and a person or persons unknown, dead or simply not charged, the acquittal of all but one of the named persons does not automatically result in the acquittal of that one.[3] However, complications arise where two or more persons are charged in the same indictment with conspiring together but not with others, and all but one are acquitted. In *Director of Public Prosecutions* v. *Shannon*,[4] the House of Lords held that if the conspirators are tried separately it is possible for one of them to be convicted despite the acquittal of the others. The House made statements, *obiter*, on the position where the conspirators are jointly tried and all but one is acquitted. Traditionally, the rule has been that the remaining person cannot be convicted.[5] Lords Simon and Dilhorne took the view that where the evidence against individual conspirators is significantly different one conspirator could properly be convicted although the others were acquitted. Lord Salmon thought this would only be possible in the most exceptional cases, while Lords Reid and Morris thought that the traditional rule should prevail. The validity of the traditional rule is left doubtful as the result of *Shannon* but we think it likely that it will be abandoned when it next comes directly

---

1. *Verrier* v. *Director of Public Prosecutions*, [1967] 2 A.C. 195, at pp. 223–224; [1966] 3 All E.R. 568, at p. 575.
2. *Simmonds*, [1969] 1 Q.B. 685, at pp. 689–690; *Jones*, [1974] I.C.R. 310.
3. *Anthony*, [1965] 2 Q.B. 189; [1965] 1 All E.R. 440; *Nichols*, (1742), cited in 13 East 412n.; *Cooke* (1826), 5 B. & C. 538.
4. [1974] 2 All E.R. 1009.
5. *Thompson* (1851), 16 Q.B. 832.

before the appellate courts. The objections to it centre on its illogicality in allowing a person to escape whom the evidence proves guilty, merely because the other named persons have to be acquitted on the ground that the evidence against them is inadmissible or less strong. Moreover, now that verdicts against jointly indicted but separately tried conspirators may be different it is unwise to persist with a rule requiring verdicts against jointly tried conspirators to be the same. Whether or not A can be convicted of conspiring with B although B is acquitted should not depend on whether he was tried jointly with B or separately. The Law Commission Working Paper on Inchoate Crimes proposes the abolition of the traditional rule.[1]

Punishment

20 Except in conspiracy to murder, which by statute is punishable with a maximum of 10 years' imprisonment,[2] any conspiracy, being a common law misdemeanour, is punishable at the discretion of the judge. However, a heavier punishment for conspiracy to commit an offence than could be imposed for the substantive offence should only be imposed in very exceptional circumstances,[3] e.g. where the element of conspiracy has transformed what might otherwise be considered as a relatively minor offence.[4] There is no moral justification for regarding a conspiracy to commit an offence as more serious than the substantive offence, at least where it is limited to the commission of one offence, and the proposal of the Law Commission Working Party that the maximum punishment for conspiracies to commit a single indictable offence should be that provided for the substantive offence is clearly right.[5]

Possible abuses

21 In the eighteenth and nineteenth centuries the law of conspiracy was applied somewhat harshly to industrial and political disputes. This led a famous Irish judge to say:

---

1. *Op. cit.*, paras. 59–61.
2. Offences against the Person Act 1861, s. 4.
3. *Verrier* v. *Director of Public Prosecutions*, [1967] 2 A.C. 195; [1966] 3 All E.R. 568; *C. & J. Cases*.
4. *Cooper*, [1974] Crim. L. R. 673.
5. *Op. cit.*, 117, 118 and 121–124. These paragraphs also contain other proposals relating to the punishment of conspiracies to commit more than one offence.

"The law of conspiracy is a branch of our jurisprudence to be narrowly watched, to be jealously regarded, and never to be pressed beyond its true limits".[1]

Since 1875 a conspiracy to do an act in contemplation or furtherance of a trade dispute is no longer an offence unless the act itself is criminal[2] and there is no modern instance of an oppressive use of the law of conspiracy on a purely political charge. All the same, it is sometimes used in circumstances in which it appears to give the prosecution an advantage, either in the admissibility of evidence,[3] or in the evasion of such a procedural rule as that of a time limit on prosecutions for the substantive offence, which limit does not bar a prosecution for conspiracy to commit that offence.[4] There is also the danger that conspiracy to corrupt public morals or conspiracy to outrage public decency will be charged in relation to pornographic books in order to circumvent the defence of public good which is available where the statutory offence of obscene publication, or conspiracy to commit it, is charged.[5] However, an undertaking was given to the House of Commons in 1964 that conspiracy to corrupt public morals would not be charged so as to circumvent that defence.[6]

Attempt[7]

17.22 An attempt to commit an indictable[8] offence is a common law misdemeanour normally punishable at the discretion of the court,[9] although a sentence greater than the maximum allowed for the offence attempted may not be imposed.[10] The maximum punishment for attempts to commit some offences is laid down by statute; thus attempted rape is subject to a statutory maximum of seven years' imprisonment[11] although imprisonment for life is the maximum punishment for rape itself. There is little

1. Fitzgerald, J.
2. Conspiracy and Protection of Property Act 1875, s. 3.
3. *Shaw* v. *Director of Public Prosecutions*, [1962] A.C. 220; [1961] 2 All E.R. 446. But see *West*, [1948] 1 K.B. 709, at p. 720; [1948] 1 All E.R. 718, at pp. 822–823; *Griffiths*, [1966] 1 Q.B. 589; [1965] 2 All E.R. 448.
4. *Simmonds*, [1969] 1 Q.B. 685; [1967] 2 All E.R. 399n.
5. Para. 15.19.
6. The effect of this undertaking was discussed by Lord Diplock in *Knuller* v. *Director of Public Prosecutions*, [1973] A.C. 435, at p. 480.
7. Turner, *Modern Approach to Criminal Law*, Vol. II, p. 224.
8. Stephen, *History of the Criminal Law*, Vol. II, p. 224.
9. *Higgins*, [1952] 1 K.B. 7; [1951] 2 All E.R. 758.
10. Powers of Criminal Courts Act 1973, s. 18 (2).
11. Sexual Offences Act 1956, Sch. II, Part 1.

else than the authority of Sir James Stephen[1] for the proposition that a person cannot be indicted at common law of an attempt to commit a summary offence. It is likely that, when the question comes to be decided, it will be held that such an attempt, like incitement to commit a summary offence[2] is indictable at common law. The Law Commission Working Party has provisionally concluded that attempts to commit summary offences should be criminal.[3] Ample provision is made by statute for attempts to commit particular summary offences. An attempt to commit an indictable offence triable summarily with the accused's consent[4] can be tried summarily with his consent,[5] as can an attempt to commit an offence which is both an indictable and a summary offence[6] but in this case the penalty inflicted must not be greater than that for which the offender would have been liable if he had been summarily convicted of the completed offence.[7]

In order that a person may be convicted of an attempt to commit an offence, he must be proved first to have had an intention to commit that offence,[8] and secondly to have done an act which constitutes the *actus reus* of a criminal attempt. Of these two elements, the first is the more important because a particular act may or may not be a criminal attempt depending on the intent with which it is done.[9]

Mens rea

3 An intent to commit the offence attempted exists where the accused intends to commit an act of the type necessary to constitute that offence. In addition, where the definition of that offence requires that some consequence be brought about by the accused's conduct, it must be proved that the accused intended that consequence.[10] Thus, it is not always sufficient for the

---

1. *Loc. cit.*
2. Para. 17.2.
3. Law Commission Working Paper No. 50, *Inchoate Offences: Conspiracy, Attempt and Incitement*, para. 110. For a discussion of the Working Party's proposals concerning attempt, see Buxton, [1973] Crim. L. R. 656.
4. Para. 23.18.
5. Magistrates' Courts Act 1952, Sch. 1.
6. *Ibid.*
7. Magistrates' Courts Act 1952, s. 19 (9).
8. *Laitwood* (1910), 4 Cr. App. Rep. 248; *Davey* v. *Lee*, [1968] 1 Q.B. 366; [1967] 2 All E.R. 423; *Haughton* v. *Smith*, [1975] A.C. at p. 476; [1973] 3 All E.R. 1109, at p. 1114, *per* Lord Hailsham, L.C.
9. *Schofield* (1784), Cald. Mag. Cas. 397.
10. *Doody* (1854), 6 Cox C.C. 463; *Mohan*, [1975] 2 All E.R. 193.

accused to have had the *mens rea* which would have rendered him guilty of the offence attempted if it had been completed. A person may be guilty of murder if he kills someone when intending merely to cause grievous bodily harm but, where the consequences of the accused's act are not fatal, the jury must be satisfied that he intended to kill his victim if he is to be convicted of attempted murder.[1]

Nothing short of a direct intent to bring about the consequence required for the offence attempted suffices for an attempt.[2] Thus, if A plants a bomb in his house, realising that B, an occupant, will almost certainly be killed, so that he can claim the insurance money on the house, A cannot be convicted of the attempted murder of B if B miraculously escapes injury.

17.24 It is uncertain what state of mind an attempter must have in relation to the circumstances of the *actus reus* of the offence attempted. Clearly, if that offence requires knowledge of its circumstances there can be no conviction of an attempt to commit it unless the accused knew them, although wilful blindness may be enough if it suffices for the completed offence. The situation where the offence attempted does not require guilty knowledge as to a circumstance is more doubtful. In *Gardner* v. *Akeroyd*,[3] there are dicta which suggest that knowledge of such a circumstance is required for an attempt even though the offence attempted is one of strict liability. On the other hand, the decision in *Collier*[4] tacitly envisages strict liability in attempts, since it was held that a statutory "no negligence" defence which was available on a charge of the full offence (which was otherwise one of strict liability) was available on a charge of attempting that offence. The present uncertainty can be illustrated in this way: a man may be guilty of abducting a girl under 16 although he believes on reasonable grounds that she is 16 or over,[5] but whether on a charge of attempting to abduct a girl under 16 there could be a conviction in the absence of actual knowledge of her age and an intent to abduct her is far from clear.[6] The Law Commission Working Party proposes that a person should be guilty of an attempt only when he has knowledge of or,

1. *Whybrow* (1951), 35 Cr. App. Rep. 141; Edwards, (1952) 15 M.L.R. 345.
2. *Mohan*.
3. [1952] 2 Q.B. 734, at pp. 747 and 751.
4. [1960] Crim. L. R. 204.
5. Para. 9.7.a.
6. Smith, Two Problems in Criminal Attempts Re-examined, [1962] Crim. L. R. 135.

where recklessness is all that the full offence requires, is reckless as to the existence of any circumstances of the *actus reus* of the full offence.[1]

5 As *mens rea* is an essential ingredient in a criminal attempt, a person cannot be liable for unauthorised attempts at infringing an absolute duty by those to whom he has delegated its performance, although he would be liable if they succeeded in breaking the duty.[2] It is sometimes suggested that the mental element required for an attempt should simply be the same as the mental element (here to be taken to include negligence) required for the offence alleged to have been attempted, but this would have the drastic result that a chemist who made up a prescription with such a high degree of negligence that he would be guilty of involuntary manslaughter if his customer died, could be convicted of attempted manslaughter if his customer survived.[3]

Actus reus[4]

6 We have suggested that in attempts the basis of the accused's liability is his *mens rea*. The function of the requirement of *actus reus* is to regulate the point at which acts in furtherance of the accused's intention incur criminal liability.

Throughout the cases runs the common theme originating in *Eagleton*[5] that before there can be an attempt there must be a step towards the commission of a specific offence which is immediately and not remotely connected with its commission. This is often termed the distinction between acts of perpetration and acts of preparation.

Though the jury must ultimately decide on the sufficiency of the *actus reus*[6] the judge must decide whether the accused's conduct is in law capable of constituting an attempt. This has led to difficulty because of the need to distinguish between acts which are merely preparatory to the commission of a crime, and those which are sufficiently proximate to it to amount to an attempt to commit it. If a man buys a box of matches he cannot be convicted of attempted arson, however clearly it may be proved that he intended to set fire to a haystack at the time of the purchase. Nor can he be convicted of this offence if he

---

1. *Op. cit.*, para. 89.
2. *Gardner* v. *Akeroyd*, [1952] 2 Q.B. 743; [1952] 2 All E.R. 306.
3. Stuart, *Mens Rea*, Negligence and Attempts, [1968] Crim. L. R. 647.
4. Stuart, The *Actus Reus* in Attempts, [1970] Crim. L. R. 505.
5. (1855), Dears. C.C. 376 and 515.
6. *Cook* (1963), 48 Cr. App. Rep. 98; *C. & J. Cases.*

approaches the stack with the matches in his pocket, but if he bends down near the stack and lights a match which he extinguishes on perceiving that he is being watched he may be guilty of an attempt to burn it.[1]

The narrow borderlines between mere acts of preparation and acts amounting to an attempt can be illustrated by comparing the cases of *Robinson*[2] and *Button*.[3] In *Robinson*, a jeweller hid his stock, tied himself up, pretended that his shop had been broken into and caused the police to be summoned. His intention, as he subsequently admitted, was to make a claim against his insurance company, but he was held not guilty of an attempt to obtain money by false pretences. On the other hand, in *Button* it was held that a man could be convicted of attempting to obtain prize money by false pretences where he had entered handicap races under the name of another and misrepresented his past prowess with intent to defraud. *Robinson* is distinguishable from *Button* because in the latter the accused had done all he could to influence the minds of the organisers of the race. It would, of course, have been different in *Robinson* if the accused had actually made a claim against his insurance company and in any case it does not follow that Robinson would be acquitted today.

17.27 Whether a particular act is immediately connected with the commission of the specific offence whose attempt is charged raises the question of how the specific offence is isolated. In *Davey* v. *Lee*,[4] the Divisional Court adopted a paragraph in *Archbold's Criminal Pleading, Evidence and Practice*[5] which not only read: "An attempt is complete if the prisoner does an act which is a step towards the commission of the specific crime, which is immediately and not merely remotely connected with the commission of it," but went on to say: "and the doing of which cannot reasonably be regarded as having any other purpose than the commission of the specific crime". In this case, the accused were held to have been rightly convicted of attempting to steal copper from the Electricity Board when they had cut the wire fence surrounding premises belonging to the Board near the place in which the copper was stored and had been interrupted when attempting to climb through the fence.

---

1. *Taylor* (1859), 1 F. & F. 511.
2. [1915] 2 K.B. 342; *C. & J. Cases*; see also *Comer* v. *Bloomfield* (1971), 55 Cr. App. Rep. 305.
3. [1900] 2 Q.B. 597; *C. & J. Cases*.
4. [1968] 1 Q.B. 366; [1967] 2 All E.R. 423; *C. & J. Cases*.
5. 36th ed., para. 4104.

Some greeted this decision with dismay since they thought that whether an act could not reasonably be regarded as having any other purpose than the commission of the specific offence had to be answered by reference only to the acts themselves, ignoring any statement of intention, contemporaneous or subsequent. These fears that there could be no conviction of attempt unless the accused's acts themselves pointed unequivocally to the specific offence attempted were dispelled in *Jones* v. *Brooks*,[1] where it was held that two questions had to be asked:

a. Does the act, looked at in conjunction with evidence of the expressed intention of the accused, show that it was directed to the commission of the specific offence whose attempt is charged?
b. If so, was it sufficiently proximate to the commission of the specific offence?

In *Jones* v. *Brooks*, the accused had been seen trying to open car doors; they admitted that they had intended to drive home in one of the cars. On appeal, the Divisional Court remitted the case to the magistrates with a direction to convict of attempting to take and drive away a motor vehicle. Purporting to apply the "unequivocal act" test, it held that trying to open a car door was equivocal in the sense that it might have been a step towards the offence of taking and driving away, theft of the car or its contents, or the innocent purpose of going to sleep in it. However, it refused to accept that the equivocal nature of the accuseds' act meant that they could not be convicted or that their expressed intention could not be taken into account in deciding whether they had committed the *actus reus* of attempt. Lord Parker, C.J., said:

> "The intention is relevant when the act concerned is equivocal in order to see towards what the act is directed. Once that is decided, then it still remains for the prosecution to show that the act itself is sufficiently proximate to amount to an attempt to commit the crime which it was the intention of the accused to commit. Looked at in this way, I have no doubt that the specific crime being isolated by the expressed intention as one to take and drive away, the insertion of the key into the door and seeking to open the door of the car was an act sufficiently proximate."[2]

28 Even when the purpose of the act has been determined, the problem of proximity remains. The distinction between acts

1. (1968), 52 Cr. App. Rep. 614; *C. & J. Cases.*
2. *Ibid.*, at p. 617.

which are proximate and those which are too remote is arbitrary and in no way indicates any quality which would determine on which side of the line a case falls. Only one thing can be said with certainty, that an act is sufficiently proximate when the accused has done the last act which it is necessary for him to do in order to commit the specific offence attempted, although something more remains to be done by another.[1] Thus, one who puts poison in another's drink, intending him to drink it and be killed in consequence, is guilty of attempted murder. The "last act" test is useful in that it determines many cases in a clear cut fashion, but it must be emphasised that it is merely a sufficient and not a necessary criterion, for otherwise offences like attempted rape could never be committed.

Apart from the "last act" test the jury must answer the question whether the accused's acts were immediately or merely remotely connected with the commission of the specific offence attempted on the basis of common sense.[3] The requirement of an act immediately connected with the commission of the specific offence is presumably based on the view that a time comes when a change of heart is so improbable that the punishment of criminal intent is justified because it would almost certainly be carried out and it may be relevant to consider whether the accused has reached a stage where the chances of repentance are slight.[3]

17.29 The problem of distinguishing between attempts and acts of preparation loses much of its practical importance if there is a separate common law misdemeanour of procuring instruments with intent to commit a particular offence. There is very little authority but some support for its existence is provided by *Gurmit Singh*[4] where the indictment which was upheld alleged that the accused unlawfully procured a rubber stamp bearing the words "Magistrate first class Jullundur" with intent to use the same and by means thereof to defraud and to forge a document. It has been said that there seems to be no difference between this case and, for example, "procuring ... an axe with intent to commit malicious damage, a screwdriver with intent to commit burglary, pen and paper with intent to obtain by

---

1. *Eagleton* (1855), Dears. C.C. 376 and 515, at p. 538 *per* Parke, B.; *Ransford* (1874), 13 Cox C.C. 9.
2. *Davey* v. *Lee*, [1967] 2 All E.R. 423, at p. 425 *per* Diplock, L.J.
3. *Hope* v. *Brown*, [1954] 1 All E.R. 330; *C. & J. Cases.*
4. [1966] 2 Q.B. 53; [1965] 3 All E.R. 384.

deception, a wedding ring with intent to commit bigamy...".[1] However, if there is a common law misdemeanour of procuring the instruments of crime with intent to use them, it may be confined to such instruments the possession of which can only be reasonably referable to the commission of the offence alleged to have been intended.

Proposals for reform

0 The Law Commission Working Party on Inchoate Offences[2] thought that the offence of attempt should be retained because it is just as important to prevent the commission of offences as to punish those who commit them, but that, while the mere intention in a serious case constituted a social danger, intervention was not justifiable until some act was done which sufficiently manifested the social danger present in the intent. In the light of this approach the Working Party rejected the existing tests because, by concentrating too fully on the accused's actions, they failed adequately to serve the law's purpose of crime prevention and failed to impose liability in cases like *Robinson* where the majority of people would probably feel it should be imposed.

The Working Party proposes the "substantial step" test which would cast very much more widely the net by which acts preceding the commission of an offence are brought within the law of attempt. Like the present tests, the "substantial step" test is not intrinsically clear and it is suggested that it should be given content by the provision of examples in the relevant legislation. Proposed examples include: committing an assault for the purpose of the intended offence; lying in wait for, searching out or following the contemplated victim or object of the intended offence; reconnoitring the place contemplated for the commission of the intended offence; acquiring, preparing or equipping oneself with materials to be employed in the commission of the offence, which are specially designed for such unlawful use or which have no lawful purpose in the circumstances; and preparing or acting a falsehood for the purpose of an offence of fraud or deception.

Abandonment of attempt

31 Although no argument of deterrence, reformation or prevention seems to require the punishment of one who abandons his attempt before he has done any harm, being truly repentant,

---

1. Smith and Hogan, *Criminal Law*, 3rd ed., 195.
2. *Op. cit.*, paras. 63–87.

once the accused has committed the *actus reus* of an attempt with the necessary *mens rea* he cannot escape liability by abandoning the attempt, however genuine and voluntary his repentance.[1]

Attempts to do the impossible

17.32 *Relative impossibility.*—This category is concerned with attempts to commit a specific offence which, at the time of the acts constituting the attempt, is capable of commission although, unknown to the accused, the particular attempt cannot succeed because of ineptitude, inefficiency, insufficient means or some supervening event. A person is guilty of attempted murder if he places a small quantity of poison in a glass of lemonade which he expects his intended victim to drink although, contrary to his belief, the dose of poison is not lethal.[2] Similarly, a person is guilty of an attempt where he tries to force a window to burgle a house with a jemmy which is not strong enough (attempted burglary), or to shoot and kill a person who moves at the critical moment or is out of range of his gun (attempted murder) or to obtain money from a person who sees through the deception when he receives the fraudulent begging letter (attempted obtaining property by deception).[3]

17.33 *Absolute impossibility.*—This category is concerned with attempts to commit a specific offence which, at the time of the acts constituting the attempt and unknown to the accused, is incapable of commission by him or anyone else whatever means are adopted. In *Ring, Atkin and Jackson*,[4] it was held that someone who puts his hand into an empty pocket intending to steal therefrom, might be convicted of attempted theft. No reasons were given for this decision, and it was difficult to say how far it went. However, in *Haughton* v. *Smith*,[5] the House of Lords, overruling *Ring*, held that attempts falling within the present category are not criminal. Thus the accused is not guilty of an attempt where he walks into an empty room intending to steal a specific diamond ring and finds that the ring is no longer there having been removed by its owner to the bank; or he shoots at a bolster in

1. *Lankford*, [1959] Crim. L. R. 209; *Haughton* v. *Smith*, [1973] 3 All E.R. 1109, at p. 1115, *per* Lord Hailsham, L.C.
2. *White*, [1910] 2 K.B. 124; *C. & J. Cases.*
3. Lords Hailsham and Reid in *Haughton* v. *Smith*, [1973] 3 All E.R. 1109. With regard to the last example see the decision in *Hensler* (1870), 22 L.T. 691.
4. (1892), 61 L.J.M.C. 116; *C. & J. Cases.*
5. [1973] 3 All E.R. 1109.

a bed, mistakenly believing it is B whom he intends to kill; or he sends a false begging letter to one who is dead.[1]

4 *Legal impossibility.*—In this category the accused has efficiently done or is able to do every act which he set out to do and has achieved, or could have achieved, his object in physical terms, but owing to some mistake on his part his conduct does not after all amount in law to an offence. Before *Haughton* v. *Smith* there was a division of opinion on whether such an accused could be convicted of attempting to commit the offence he intended to commit.[2] The accused in that case assisted in the removal of goods believing them to be stolen; in fact they had ceased to be stolen on coming into the custody of the police[3] who let him have the goods in order to set a trap. The House of Lords held that he could not be convicted of an attempt to handle stolen goods. Similarly someone who believed the girl he abducted to be under the age of 16 would not be guilty of an attempt to abduct a girl under 16 contrary to s. 20 of the Sexual Offences Act 1956 if she turned out to be 18. Again, a man who takes his own umbrella from a club, thinking it is the property of another, cannot be convicted of attempted theft.

Proposals for reform

5 The Law Commission Working Party has proposed that:

"(i) A person may be guilty of an attempt to commit a crime notwithstanding that the means by which the crime is intended to be commited would in fact be inadequate for the commission of the crime.

(ii) A person may be guilty of an attempt to commit a crime notwithstanding that—

a. the person in respect of whom the crime is intended to be committed is dead, does not exist or does not possess a characteristic which the person believes him to possess (necessary for the crime);

b. the property in respect of which the crime is intended to be

---

1. These, and other examples, were given by their Lordships in *Haughton* v. *Smith*. See also *Partington* v. *Williams* (1975), *Times*, December 19.
2. Contrast *Millar and Page* (1965), 49 Cr. App. Rep. 241, and *Curbishley and Crispin* (1970), 55 Cr. App. Rep. 310 (could be conviction for attempt) with *Percy Dalton (London) Ltd.*, [1949] L.J.R. 1626; *C. & J. Cases*: *per* Birkett, J. (no conviction for attempt). Also see Smith, Two Problems in Criminal Attempts Re-Examined, [1962] Crim. L. R. 212 and Williams, Criminal Attempt—A Reply, [1962] Crim. L. R. 300.
3. Para. 11.33.

committed does not exist or does not possess a characteristic which the person believes it to possess (necessary for the crime).

(iii) Save as aforesaid a person is not guilty of an attempt to commit the crime if he could not commit the crime contemplated owing to the non-existence of an element required by the law for that crime."[1]

These proposals would involve a considerable reversal of the present law. They are welcome in that they recognise that the accused's moral guilt is the basis of his liability for attempt, and also in that they remove the significance of the artificial distinction between relative and absolute impossibility.

Offences which cannot be attempted

17.36 There are some offences in respect of which a person cannot be convicted of an attempt.[2] It has been said that there cannot be a conviction for an attempt to demand money with menaces because the case is one of all or nothing: either there is or is not a demand.[3] This is doubtful where a demand is by post since, the demand being made when posted,[4] there is the possibility of an attempt to post. There could hardly be a conviction for an attempt to commit an offence, such as failure to report an accident, the *actus reus* of which consists in an omission; nor could there be a conviction for an attempt to commit involuntary manslaughter, for in such a case the deceased's death must have been unintended.[5] On the other hand, there is no reason in principle why a person who intends to kill, but would have had the defence of provocation or diminished responsibility if he had killed, should not be guilty of attempted voluntary manslaughter, as opposed to attempted murder, if his attempt is unsuccessful. However, such authority as there is denies that this is possible.[6]

Successful attempts

17.37 Where a person is charged on indictment with attempting to commit an offence he may, by virtue of s. 6 (4) of the Criminal Law Act 1967, be convicted of the attempt notwithstanding that he is shown to be guilty of the completed offence. *Rogers* v.

1. Paras. 126–136.
2. Stephen, *History of the Criminal Law*, Vol. II, p. 227.
3. *Moran*, [1952] 1 All E.R. 803, n.
4. Paras. 11.32 and 21.8.
5. Paras. 8.28 and 8.29.
6. *Bruzas*, [1972] Crim. L. R. 367.

Arnott[1] suggests the possibility that, at a summary trial for an attempt, the impertinent defence that the attempt was successful might succeed; the point was not argued, and the decision may be explicable on the ground that the particular offence charged to have been attempted, theft as a bailee, belongs to the category of offences that cannot be attempted. There cannot be a conviction for the full offence on a charge of attempt to commit it, but by virtue of s. 6 (3) and (4) of the Criminal Law Act 1967 there can be a conviction on indictment for an attempt on a charge of the main offence. If the case is tried summarily, however, the magistrates may not convict of an attempt if the completed offence is charged.[2]

1. [1960] 2 Q.B. 244; [1960] 2 All E.R. 417.
2. *Pender* v. *Smith*, [1959] 2 Q.B. 84, at p. 88; [1959] 2 All E.R. 360, at pp. 360–361; *Lawrence* v. *Same*, [1968] 2 Q.B. 93; [1968] 1 All E.R. 1191.

18

DURESS AND NECESSITY

Duress[1]

18.1 Duress is pressure by people: necessity is pressure by events. We have already seen that if someone is made to act by an external physical force the act is regarded as involuntary, cannot be imputed to him and cannot involve him in criminal liability.[2] Thus, if someone is made to stab another by superior physical force exerted on his arm, it is not his act which does the stabbing, but that of the person who forces him. We are now concerned with a different question—the extent to which threats which do not have the effect of making the act of the accused involuntary can afford a defence.

An account of the defence of duress, whose existence was affirmed in 1975 by the House of Lords in *Lynch* v. *Director of Public Prosecutions for Northern Ireland*,[3] requires the discussion of three separate issues:

a. the nature of the threat;
b. the "unavoidable dilemma" principle; and
c. the extent of the defence.

The nature of the threat

18.2 The threat, which may be express or implicit, must be of death or serious bodily harm.[4] In *Singh*[5] the Court of Appeal held that a threat to expose immorality could not give rise to the defence of duress and in *M'Growther*[6] it was ruled that the threat of harm to property was no excuse. In *Steane*[7] Lord Goddard stated that

1. Edwards, Compulsion, Coercion and Criminal Responsibility, (1951) 14 M.L.R. 297.
2. Para. 5.21.
3. [1975] 1 All E.R. 913.
4. *Hudson and Taylor*, [1971] 2 Q.B. 202; [1971] 2 All E.R. 244; *C. & J. Cases*; *Lynch* v. *Director of Public Prosecutions for Northern Ireland*, [1975] 1 All E.R. 913; Blackstone, IV Comm. 29; Stephen, *Digest*, 1st ed., 18.
5. [1973] 1 All E.R. 122.
6. (1746), Fost. 13.
7. [1947] K.B. 997; [1947] 1 All E.R. 813; *C. & J. Cases*.

a threat of "violence or imprisonment" would suffice. This statement was an *obiter dictum* and the reference to threats of imprisonment should be treated with reserve in view of the more restricted approach of the other cases. It is uncertain whether a threat to kill or seriously harm a person other than the accused is enough. In the Australian case of *Hurley*[1] the Supreme Court of Victoria held that threats to kill or seriously injure the accused's common law wife could amount to duress. We hope that when an English court is faced with the question it will extend the defence of duress to include threats to harm the accused's spouse, children and other persons with whom he has a special relationship since many a man who treats his own safety as of little consequence will be subjected to the most extreme mental stress if confronted with a threat to harm seriously one who is dear to him. Where a threat is insufficient to give rise to the defence of duress it may nevertheless mitigate the punishment which is imposed.

The "unavoidable dilemma"

3 The accused has the defence of duress only if, throughout the period from the making of the threat to the commission of the offence, he was faced by a dilemma between committing the offence or allowing the threatened harm to occur and had no safe third avenue of escape. In *Gill*[2] the accused was convicted of stealing his employer's lorry. He had raised the defence of duress at his trial, in that personal violence had been threatened against him and his wife if he did not steal the lorry. The Court of Criminal Appeal stated, *obiter*, that it was very doubtful whether the defence of duress was open to the accused since there was a time, after he had been left outside his employer's yard to get the lorry, when he could have raised the alarm and wrecked the whole enterprise. The Court referred approvingly to Professor Perkins' statement that: "The excuse [of duress] is not available to someone who had an obviously safe avenue of escape before committing the prohibited act."[3]

4 The case of *Hudson and Taylor*[4] shows that a third avenue of escape must be reasonably open to the accused in order to be regarded as safe. Two girls aged 19 and 17 admitted having

1. [1967] V.R. 526.
2. [1963] 2 All E.R. 688; *C. & J. Cases.*
3. Perkins, *Criminal Law*, 2nd ed., p. 347.
4. [1971] 2 Q.B. 202; [1971] 2 All E.R. 244; *C. & J. Cases.*

given false evidence at a former trial before which they had been approached by someone who had threatened to "cut them up" if they did not do so. The trial judge held that duress was no defence because the accused had not been subject to the threat of immediate physical violence when they gave the false evidence. The accused were convicted but appealed successfully to the Court of Appeal. One of the grounds on which the Crown relied in support of the conviction was that the accused should have removed the effect of the threat by seeking police protection either before or at the time of the former trial at which they had made the false statements. The Court of Appeal agreed that the defence of duress could not be relied on if an accused person failed to take an opportunity which was reasonably open to him to render the threat ineffective. However, in deciding whether such an opportunity was reasonably open to the accused, the jury should have regard to his age and the circumstances of the case and any risks which might be involved. Factors such as the period of time between the threat and the commission of the offence and the effectiveness of the protection which the police might be able to give would be relevant.

18.5 The defence of duress can only arise if the threat was operative at the time the offence was committed. Thus the accused is not excused if the threat has ceased when he commits the offence.[1] However, it was held in *Hudson and Taylor* that, when there is no opportunity for delaying tactics and the accused must make a decision whether or not to commit the offence, the existence at that moment of a relevant threat should provide him with a defence even though the harm threatened might not follow immediately but after an interval. The Court of Appeal said that the threats of violence were likely to be no less compelling because they could not be effected in the court room when the perjury was committed, if they could be carried out in the streets the same night. As might be expected duress is not a defence if the accused commits a criminal act which the compulsion does not oblige him to.[2]

Extent of the defence

18.6 The defence of duress applies to all offences "except possibly treason or murder as a principal".[3] With regard to murder, the

---

1. *Stratton* (1779), 21 State Tr. 1231, *per* Lord Mansfield, C.J.; *Hudson and Taylor*.
2. *Stratton*; *Hudson and Taylor*.
3. *Hudson and Taylor*, [1971] 2 Q.B. 202, *per* Widgery, L.J.

majority of the House of Lords in *Lynch* v. *Director of Public Prosecutions for Northern Ireland*[1] held that the defence of duress was open to a person charged as an accomplice to murder who had acted under the threat of death or serious injury. The accused, allegedly under duress, had driven three gunmen to and from a garage where they had killed a policeman. The trial judge, with whom the Court of Criminal Appeal in Northern Ireland agreed, withdrew the issue of duress from the jury on the ground that that defence was not available to a person charged as an accomplice to murder. The House of Lords (Lords Simon of Glaisdale and Kilbrandon dissenting), having held that this was wrong, ordered a re-trial, as is possible under Northern Irish legislation wherever it appears to the appellate court "that the interests of justice so require".[2] Those Lords in the majority refrained from reaching any conclusions on whether duress could afford a defence to the perpetrator of murder, but the scanty authority which is available indicates that duress is no defence.[3] There is of course no logical reason why the defence should not be open to such a person. If it is not, the following anomalous result will occur. Acting under duress, A strikes B with an iron bar. He is charged with causing B grievous bodily harm with intent and is acquitted on the ground that he was acting under duress. B then dies of the injury received. If duress is not a defence to any form of murder as perpetrator, A may now be convicted of murder, so that the act which was previously held to be excusable has now been rendered retrospectively inexcusable by B's death.[4] It would be unfortunate if, in the application of the defence, a distinction were drawn between perpetrators and accomplices of murder since the contribution of an accomplice to the death may be no less significant than that of the perpetrator.

It seems that duress can be a defence to some, if not all, types of treason. Lord Goddard, C.J., took a contrary view in *Steane*[5] but he must have overlooked cases such as *M'Growther*,[6] *Oldcastle's Case*,[7] *Stratton*[8] and *Purdy*[9] where the applicability of

1. [1975] 1 All E.R. 913.
2. See para. 24.6 for the more restricted power of the English Court of Appeal (Criminal Division) to order a re-trial.
3. *Tyler* (1838), 8 C. & P. 816; *A.-G.* v. *Whelan*, [1934] I.R. 518; *Brown*, [1968] S.A.S.R. 467. But see (1972) 30 *Cambridge Law Journal* 202.
4. Professor Smith, A Note on Duress, [1974] Crim. L. R. 347.
5. [1947] K.B. 997; [1947] 1 All E.R. 813.
6. (1746), Fost. 13.
7. (1419), 1 Hale P.C. 50.
8. (1779), 21 State Tr. 1045.
9. *Purdy* (1946), 10 *Journal of Criminal Law*, 182.

duress to treason was recognised. It seems from these cases that only a threat of death will suffice, but the decision in *Lynch* suggests that if the point arose today a threat of serious bodily injury would be held sufficient.

Proposals for reform

18.7 In 1974 a Law Commission Working Party examining the general principles of the criminal law with a view to codification made, *inter alia*, the following proposals concerning duress. The threat should be of death or serious bodily harm, either to the accused himself or to any third party. The defence should be available in cases where the accused himself is threatened by immediate harm, or where the threat of harm is not immediate if he has had no reasonable opportunity of seeking police protection; in cases where a third person is threatened, the defence should be available if execution of the threat is avoidable only by compliance with the demand made of the accused. The defence should be capable of being raised on a charge of any offence, but should not be available where the accused has joined an association or conspiracy which was of such a character that he was aware he might be compelled to participate in an offence of the type with which he is charged.[1]

Marital coercion

18.8 Before the Criminal Justice Act 1925 came into force, there was a rebuttable presumption of law that a felony, other than treason or murder, committed by a wife in the presence of her husband was committed under coercion. Accordingly, the prosecution bore the burden of negativing coercion. The presumption has been abolished by s. 47 of the Criminal Justice Act 1925 but this section provides that it shall be a defence on a charge of any offence, other than treason or murder, for a wife to prove that she committed the alleged offence in the presence of, and under the coercion of, her husband. The defence of marital coercion is rarely pleaded and, because s. 47 has not yet received authoritative judicial interpretation, may give rise to difficulty in the future, both because the nature of the threats covered by marital coercion is not certain, although they are probably not limited to threats of personal violence,[2] and because the word "presence" may require elucidation. It is, for instance, impossible to

1. Law Commission Working Paper No. 56, *General Principles: Defences of General Application*.
2. Hansard, House of Commons (1925) Vol. 188, Col. 873 *et seq.*

say whether s. 47 would cover a case in which a husband induced his wife to enter a house for the purpose of stealing something, by threatening to leave her if she did not comply with his wishes, while he remained outside and kept watch. The section places the burden of proving coercion on the wife, whereas in duress the accused merely bears an evidential burden.[1] The Law Commission Working Party referred to above has recommended the abolition of the defence of marital coercion on the grounds that it is not appropriate to modern conditions.

General

.9 There are two general points concerning the defences of duress and coercion.

a. Although the defences may be available to the person who actually performed the criminal act, the one who made the threats is under some form of criminal liability. There is no doubt on this point, but we shall see in the next chapter that the methods by which the result can be reached vary and have been made the subject of controversy.
b. There is doubt about the basis of exemption in cases in which duress or coercion is successfully pleaded. Reference has been made in a number of cases[2] to the will of a person who acts under duress being "overborne" and in *Bourne*[3] this appears to have been treated as negativing the existence of *mens rea*. The accused compelled his wife to allow a dog to have intercourse with her. Although his wife was not charged with an offence, he was convicted as a principal in the second degree to the buggery. When delivering the judgment of the Court of Criminal Appeal affirming the conviction, Lord Goddard, C.J., said: "If this woman had been charged herself with committing the offence, she could have set up the plea of duress, not as showing that no offence had been committed but as showing that she had no *mens rea* because her will was overborne by threats of imprisonment or violence so that she would be excused from punishment". However, the theory that as a result of his will being overborne the accused never forms the *mens rea* necessary to constitute the crime charged was rejected in *Lynch* v. *Director of Public Prosecutions for*

---

1. *Gill*, [1963] 2 All E.R. 688; *C. & J. Cases*.
2. *Bourne* (1952), 36 Cr. App. Rep. 125; *C. & J. Cases*; *Hudson and Taylor*.
3. (1952), 36 Cr. App. Rep. 125; *C. & J. Cases*; Edwards, Duress and Aiding and Abetting (1953) 69 L.Q.R. 226, reply by Cross, (1953) 69 L.Q.R. 354.

Northern Ireland;[1] in that case the House of Lords held that the defence of duress is something superimposed on the other ingredients of the offence, *actus reus* and *mens rea*, which by themselves would make up an offence. The person who acts under duress completes the act with the *mens rea* required but the element of duress prevents what he has done from being criminal in law.

Bourne can also be criticised on the ground that the passage cited above suggests, on one construction, that duress is a matter which affects punishment rather than liability, a view which conflicts with the well-established principle that where duress applies it must lead to an acquittal unless disproved. Any doubts engendered on this score by *Bourne* have been resolved by the House of Lords in *Lynch*, where it was affirmed that duress is a defence rather than a circumstance of mitigation. We will return to *Bourne* in the next chapter.[2]

Finally, someone who successfully pleads duress is not liable because he had no real choice when he did the prohibited act, although he was in control of his bodily movements, was aware of the relevant facts and foresaw the relevant consequences of his conduct. Duress is an excuse because the law recognises that the average man can only endure a limited amount of pressure from others.

Necessity

18.10 There are two types of case in which necessity can be raised as a defence. First, there are cases in which the accused alleges that he did the prohibited act when defending himself or his property or in order to prevent the commission of a crime of violence against someone else. Second, there are cases in which the accused commits what would otherwise be an offence against an innocent person in order to prevent harm to himself or to that person or another. Except in the first situation there is no clear authority on the extent to which necessity is a general defence to a criminal charge.

Self-defence and prevention of crime

18.11 Section 3 of the Criminal Law Act 1967 provides that a person may use such force as is reasonable in the circumstances in the prevention of crime, or in effecting or assisting in the lawful arrest of offenders or suspected offenders or of persons un-

1. [1975] 1 All E.R. 913.
2. Para. 19.12.

lawfully at large. It is expressly provided that the section replaces the rules of the common law on the question when force used for one of the purposes mentioned is justified by that purpose. A person acting in self-defence is invariably engaged in the prevention of crime, but the section may be confined to the prevention of crime against persons other than the accused. It was not directly applied in two of the cases on self-defence reported since the Act came into force.[1] However, those cases suggest that the test of reasonableness will be applied to the exclusion of some of the supposed old rules such as that the person attacked must retreat as far as he can before resorting to force; all that he need do is to manifest unwillingness to fight. Even if the Act does not apply to defence of property, it seems probable that the test of reasonableness will be applied by analogy to the exclusion of the old rules which can be deduced from some of the cases,[2] such as the rule that lethal force may always be used against a burgular, or against someone seeking to evict a householder unlawfully and forcibly.

12 There are two problems which are not covered by the Act:

a. If A believes that B is about to commit a crime of violence against him or some third person, what is his position if he attacks or kills B although it subsequently appears that his belief was ill founded? Must he adduce evidence of reasonable grounds for the belief?
b. If he fails to do so, and kills B, is he guilty of murder as opposed to manslaughter?

Case law answers each of these questions in the affirmative.[3] The conclusions are in accordance with the law governing the defence of mistake[4] but it is difficult to be satisfied with a rule according to which a person may be held guilty of murder if he killed someone in the belief, however irrational it may have been, that circumstances existed which justified his action. As an exception, a drunken mistaken belief in attack can be a defence, even though a drunken mistake cannot be described as reasonable.[5]

---

1. *Julien*, [1969] 2 All E.R. 856; *McInnes*, [1971] 3 All E.R. 295. See Harlow, Self-Defence: Public Right or Private Privilege, [1974] Crim. L. R. 528.
2. Lanham, Defence of Property in the Criminal Law, [1966] Crim. L. R. 368, 426.
3. *Rose* (1884), 15 Cox C.C. 540; *C. & J. Cases*; *Chisam* (1963), 47 Cr. App. Rep. 130.
4. Paras. 3.34 and 4.14–4.17.
5. *Gamlen* (1858), 1 F. & F. 90.

Necessity *stricto sensu*

18.13 As with self-defence and prevention of crime we are concerned here with situations in which the accused is faced with a choice between two courses, either to allow some harm to occur to him, to another or to property, or to prevent that harm by committing what would otherwise be an offence, and he chooses the second course thereby averting a greater evil. The difference between this situation on the one hand and self defence and the prevention of crime on the other is that the harm averted in this situation is not itself criminal and the person against whom, or against whose property, the otherwise criminal conduct is committed is an innocent party.

In the definition of many statutory offences allowance is made expressly or impliedly for the case where the accused has acted under the stress of necessity. One example of the express justification of what would otherwise be criminal is the offence of child destruction under the definition of which the prosecution must prove that the accused was not acting in good faith in order to preserve the life of the mother.[1] Some statutes provide defences which cover necessity. For example, s. 79 of the Road Traffic Regulation Act 1967 dispenses with the need for fire engines, police vehicles and ambulances to observe the speed limit in certain circumstances.[2] An implied allowance for necessity, as well as other circumstances, would seem to be made where the statutory definition uses words such as "without lawful excuse" or "dishonestly". If someone destroys inflammable material belonging to another in order to prevent a fire spreading, he would not be guilty of theft because he would not be acting dishonestly; if charged with the destruction of the property he would have the defence of lawful excuse under s. 5 of the Criminal Damage Act 1971.[3] It would presumably be a defence on a charge of abducting a girl of under sixteen "without lawful authority or excuse" that she had been taken to prevent the repetition of an offence such as incest.[4]

18.14 It is debatable whether there is a general defence of necessity which applies to common law offences or statutory offences

1. Infant Life Preservation Act 1929, s. 1; see para. 8.38.
2. Cf. Fire Services Act 1947, s. 30; see also Antarctic Treaty Act 1967, s. 2 (2).
3. Para. 12.3.
4. See the judgment of Denman, J., in *Prince* (1875), L.R. 2 C.C.R. 154; *C. & J. Cases*.

whose definition does not appear to make allowance for necessity.[1] We think it likely that such a defence exists, although its extent is uncertain. A defence of necessity was recognised by many writers of authority[2] and in most of the reported cases on the point it has been held that necessity can be a defence,[3] although, with one exception[4] no court has expressly recognised the existence of a general defence of necessity. For example, in *Vantandillo* it was said that the necessity for a mother to carry her infected child through the streets to seek medical attention "might have been given in evidence as a matter of defence" to a charge of exposing a person with a contagious disease on the public highway. In 1971, the Court of Appeal expressly recognised that "The plea of necessity may in certain cases afford a defence."[5] If there is a general defence of necessity, the questions arise of its nature and of its extent. Its nature is largely a matter of conjecture. It seems that there must be an "urgent situation of great peril"[6] and that the defence exists only if the accused had no alternative but to commit the offence and thereby prevent a considerably greater harm occurring or to allow that harm to occur.

15 It seems clear that necessity cannot be a defence in some offences. For instance, it has been accepted *obiter* by the Court of Appeal that necessity cannot justify the statutory offence of failing to obey traffic lights[7] and no doubt the same conclusion would be reached in some other offences. The dispute over the extent of the defence has traditionally centred on murder.

By analogy with *Lynch* v. *Director of Public Prosecutions for Northern Ireland*,[8] it seems that the defence of necessity is open to an accomplice to murder, but in relation to the perpetrator we must turn to the only English authority where the point was directly raised, *Dudley and Stephens*.[9] The accused were two shipwrecked seamen who had been adrift in an open boat with practically no food for twenty days, after which they killed

1. Compare Williams, *Criminal Law*, 2nd ed., p. 724 *et seq.*, with Glazebrook, *The Necessity Plea in English Criminal Law*, (1972A) 30 Camb. L. J. 87.
2. E.g., Hale, 1 P.C. 54.
3. *Vantandillo* (1815), 4 M. & S. 73; *Stratton* (1779), 21 State Tr. 1045.
4. *Southwark London Borough Council* v. *Williams*, [1971] Ch. 734; [1971] 2 All E.R. 175.
5. *Ibid.*, at pp. 743–744, 745–746.
6. *Ibid.*, at p. 746.
7. *Buckoke* v. *Greater London Council*, [1971] Ch. 655; [1971] 2 All E.R. 254.
8. [1975] 1 All E.R. 913.
9. (1884), 14 Q.B.D. 273.

and ate the cabin boy who was with them. Four days later they were picked up, and when they got back to England they were tried and convicted of murder, although sentence of death was later commuted to six months' imprisonment. The tenor of Lord Coleridge's judgment suggests that necessity can never be a defence to a charge of murder, but the case is not conclusive on the point, because in their special verdict the jury merely found that the accused probably would not have survived to be rescued if they had not killed the boy. Thus, the decision may not deny the application of necessity to a murder charge but simply deny the application of that defence to the facts. Lord Coleridge's judgment prompts reflection concerning the proper sphere of the criminal law.[1] Is it right for the law to impose a higher standard than that to be expected of the average member of society? It can only be justified in the most exceptional cases, but *Dudley and Stephens* was just such a case. If ever any form of mercy killing were to be countenanced by English law, recourse might perhaps be had to the doctrine of necessity,[2] but it is worth repeating that the exact scope of the defence is almost entirely a matter of speculation.

18.16 The scarcity of cases on the general defence of necessity may be due to the fact that although the conduct may be technically criminal it will not occur to the victim to report it because it has averted a greater harm, or to the fact that the police may decide not to prosecute because of the extenuating circumstances. The existence of the power, on conviction of an offence whose sentence is not fixed by law, to grant an absolute discharge may also provide some explanation for the scarcity of case law since the courts may regard it as the most practical way of dealing with cases involving necessity.

18.17 The Law Commission Working Party has proposed that there should be a general defence of necessity, available in any offence, however serious. It should be available where the accused himself believes that his conduct is necessary to avoid some greater harm which is otherwise likely to occur. In addition, the harm which the accused thought he was avoiding must, judged objectively, be found to be out of all proportion to the harm caused by his conduct.[3]

1. Paras. 2.15–2.23.
2. Williams, *Sanctity of Life and the Criminal Law*, 284.
3. Law Commission Working Paper No. 56, *General Principles: Defences of General Application*.

Superior orders

18 There is no clear English decision on the extent to which it is a defence for a person to show that he did the act with which he is charged under orders from his official superior. It is impossible to say much more on this matter than Willes, J., did in the course of the argument in *Keighley* v. *Bell*:[1] "The better opinion is that an officer or soldier acting under the orders of his superior not being necessarily or manifestly illegal would be justified by his orders." This view has been adopted in South Africa,[2] although a stricter opinion appears to prevail in the United States of America. According to that opinion, it is not enough that the soldier should believe the order to be lawful; it must be lawful in fact.

The order of a superior may bring other rules of law into play, and thus indirectly provide the accused with a defence. In some offences, such as criminal damage and theft, a person lacks *mens rea* if he believes that he has a legal right to act as he does, and in a servant such a belief may be brought about by the orders of his superior.[3] Moreover, in offences were negligence suffices for liability, a superior's orders may operate to shield a servant by showing that he was acting reasonably.[4]

---

1. (1866), 4 F. & F. 763, at p. 790.
2. *Smith* (1900), 17 S.C.R. 561; cited in Turner and Armitage, *Cases on Criminal Law*, 3rd ed., p. 68.
3. *James* (1837), 8 C. & P. 131.
4. *Trainer* (1864), 4 F. & F. 105.

19

PARTICIPATION

Aiding and abetting

19.1 A person who aids, abets, counsels or procures the commission of an offence (an accomplice) is liable to be tried and punished for that offence as a principal offender.[1]

19.2 Before we discuss the liability of an accomplice, we should say something about the perpetrator of an offence, otherwise known as the principal. Normally, it is clear who is the perpetrator; he is the one who, with the relevant *mens rea*, fires the fatal shot in murder, or has sexual intercourse in rape, or appropriates the property in theft. Of course, there can be more than one perpetrator, as where two men by their joint and aggregate violence kill another.[2] If a person makes use of an innocent agent in order to procure the commission of an offence, not the innocent agent, is the perpetrator, even though he is not present at the scene of the crime and does nothing with his own hands. An innocent agent is one who commits the *actus reus* of an offence but is himself devoid of responsibility, either by reason of incapacity (e.g., infancy) or because he lacks *mens rea* or has a defence such as duress. A striking example of innocent agency is where a mother gave her daughter some powder, instructing her to give it to her father to relieve his cold. Unknown to the daughter it was a poison and the father died. It was held that the mother was the principal of the crime of murder since the daughter, lacking *mens rea*, was an innocent agent by means of whom the mother had committed the crime. Of course if, as the report notes, the daughter had known that the powder was poison she would have been guilty as principal and the mother as an accomplice.[3]

19.3 Two other introductory points may be made:

1. Accessories and Abettors Act 1861, s. 8; Magistrates' Courts Act 1952, s. 35.
2. *Macklin and Murphy's Case* (1838), 2 Lew. C.C. 225.
3. *Anon* (1665), Kel. 53. Also see *Manley* (1844), 1 Cox C.C. 104.

a. For the purpose of following the old cases, until the Criminal Law Act 1967 those who aided and abetted the commission of a felony were described as "principals in the second degree" if they were present when it was committed, or as "accessories before the fact" if absent. In either event they were properly described as "principals" in offences other than felonies.
b. A number of participants may also be guilty of criminal conspiracy, a separate offence which has been discussed.[1]

4 In order that a person may be convicted as an accomplice, it is not necessary that the perpetrator should have been brought to trial or convicted, or even that his identity should be known, but it is necessary for the prosecution to prove:

a. that the accused assisted or encouraged the commission of the principal offence;
b. that the principal offence was in fact committed; and
c. that he had the intent to aid its commission.

Assistance or encouragement

5 "Aiding" and "abetting", which terms are synonymous,[2] are used to describe the activity of a person who assists or encourages the perpetrator to commit the principal offence, whether or not he is present at the time of commission.[3] "Counsel", which means encourage, does not add anything strictly but is used to describe encouragement before the commission of the principal offence. A person "procures" the commission of an offence not only where he assists or encourages it before its commission but also where he sets out to see that it is committed and takes appropriate steps to produce its commission. This was stated by the Court of Appeal in *Attorney-General's Reference under s. 36 of the Criminal Justice Act 1972 (No. 1 of 1975)*,[4] where it was also held that, whereas aiding, abetting and counselling "almost inevitably" involve a shared intention between the accomplice and the perpetrator that the principal offence should be committed, this is less likely to be so in the case of procuring. The importance of this decision is illustrated by the facts on which it was based.

---

1. Paras. 17.6–17.21.
2. *Lynch* v. *Director of Public Prosecutions for Northern Ireland*, [1975] 1 All E.R. 913, at pp. 924 and 941, *per* Lords Morris of Borth-y-Gest and Simon of Glaisdale.
3. *National Coal Board* v. *Gamble*, [1959] 1 Q.B. 11; [1958] 3 All E.R. 203; *C. & J. Cases*; *Thambiah* v. *R.*, [1966] A.C. 37; [1965] 3 All E.R. 661; *C. & J. Cases.*
4. [1975] 2 All E.R. 684.

A laced the drink of B, unknown to B, who was later convicted of the offence of strict liability of driving with an excess of alcohol. In holding that A could be convicted as an accomplice to this offence, Lord Widgery, C.J. said: "[The principal offence] has been procured because, unknown to the driver and without his collaboration, he has been put in a position in which in fact he has committed an offence which he would never have committed otherwise."[1]

For convenience, aiding and abetting will be used generally in this chapter to describe the conduct of an accomplice.

19.6 The encouragement or assistance must be given before, or at the time of, the commission of the principal offence. Someone who assists the perpetrator after the commission of the principal offence is not liable as a party to it, but one who assists the perpetrator to escape detection or arrest may be guilty of the statutory offence of assisting offenders.[2]

19.7 The encouragement or assistance of the principal offender which must be proved against a person charged with aiding and abetting may take a variety of forms. It may consist of active participation in the criminal act, short of actually committing it, such as holding a woman down while she is raped[3] or keeping watch.[4] Alternatively encouragement or assistance in the preparation of an offence even at an early stage suffices as where the accused opens a bank account with the intention of facilitating the paying in of forged cheques by the principal offender[5] Supplying the instrument for an offence or anything essential to its commission constitutes assistance in its commission.[6] A thing is supplied if it is given, lent or sold or a right of property in it is otherwise transferred.[7] A man who gives up to another for use in an offence a weapon of which the latter is owner aids in the commission of that offence as much as if he had sold or lent the weapon, but such conduct does not constitute aiding and abetting.[8] This has been explained on the basis that, although the

1. [1975] 2 All E.R. 684, at p. 687.
2. Para. 13.1.
3. *Clarkson*, [1971] 3 All E.R. 344.
4. *Betts and Ridley* (1930), 22 Cr. App. Rep. 148.
5. *Thambiah* v. *R.*, [1966] A.C. 37; [1965] 3 All E.R. 661; *C. & J. Cases.*
6. *National Coal Board* v. *Gamble*, [1959] 1 Q.B. 11; [1958] 3 All E.R. 203; *C. & J. Cases.*
7. *Ibid.*
8. *Lomas* (1913), 110 L.T. 239, as explained in *Bullock*, [1955] 1 All E.R. 15.

man who surrenders the weapon to its owner is physically performing a positive act, he is in law simply refraining from committing the civil wrong of detinue. It is unlikely that an action for the wrongful detention of a jemmy brought by a would-be burglar who owned it would succeed. If A lends a gun to B, and later drags his wife before B, shouting "Return my gun, I am going to kill this woman instantly with it", is it really the law that B incurs no liability, as accomplice, in respect of the murder of the wife if he meekly returns the gun with which she is instantly shot?

8 Normally, an act of assistance or encouragement is required. Thus, mere abstention from preventing an offence generally is not enough,[1] but a failure to prevent the commission of an offence constitutes aiding and abetting if the accused has the right of control over the perpetrator but deliberately refrains from exercising it. In *Tuck* v. *Robson*[2] a publican who deliberately made no effort to induce customers to leave his premises after closing time was held properly convicted of aiding and abetting their consumption of liquor out of hours because of his failure to exercise his right of control. Similarly, the owner of a car who sits in the passenger seat while another drives it dangerously can be convicted of aiding and abetting the dangerous driving if he deliberately fails to prevent it.[3]

9 Difficulties can arise where the accused is present at the scene of the crime but there is no evidence of overt assistance or encouragement. Clearly, if a person is present and there is such evidence, as by cheering and clapping an unlawful theatrical performance,[4] he is aiding and abetting it, but mere presence without evidence of assistance or encouragement is not necessarily enough. It will never suffice if the presence is accidental but if the presence is deliberate it is *prima facie*, but not conclusive, evidence that the accused by his presence was encouraging the commission of the offence.[5]

The principal offence

10 Although the commission of the principal offence must be proved, proof that the accused's aiding and abetting was a cause

---

1. *Coney* (1882), 8 Q.B.D. 534; *C. & J. Cases*.
2. [1970] 1 All E.R. 1171.
3. *Du Cros* v. *Lambourne*, [1907] 1 K.B. 40.
4. *Wilcox* v. *Jeffery*, [1951] 1 All E.R. 464; *C. & J. Cases*.
5. *Coney* (1882), 8 Q.B.D. 534; *C. & J. Cases*; *Allan*, [1965] 1 Q.B. 130; [1963] 2 All E.R. 897. *Clarkson* [1971] 3 All E.R. 344; *Wilcox* v. *Jeffery*.

of it is generally not required, but if the allegation against him is necessarily one of procuring, a causal link must be established. As was said in *Attorney-General's Reference (No. 1 of 1975)*: "You cannot procure an offence unless there is a causal link between what you do and the commission of the offence, and here we are told that in consequence of the addition of this alcohol the driver, when he drove home, drove with an excess quantity of alcohol in his body".[1]

19.11 The need for proof that the principal offence has been committed is shown by *Thornton* v. *Mitchell*.[2] The driver of a bus had to reverse it. In order to do so, he relied on the signals of the conductor. The conductor gave the driver a signal to reverse, which he did, and two pedestrians were knocked down. The driver was summoned for driving without due care and attention and the conductor for aiding and abetting him. The case against the driver was dismissed and it was held that the conductor could not be convicted of aiding and abetting an offence which had not been committed.

19.12 Where the principal offence is proved, it is immaterial that it is one which the accomplice could not have committed as principal so that a woman[3] or a boy under fourteen[4] may be guilty of aiding and abetting rape. Difficulties arise in cases where the *actus reus* of an offence is performed, with another's assistance or encouragement, by someone to whom a defence is available. As we have seen,[5] normally it is possible to treat the person who does the act as the innocent agent of the other and to convict the latter as perpetrator, but this is difficult, if not impossible, where the offence is one which cannot be perpetrated personally by the one who assists or encourages or procures. For example, if a bachelor exercises duress to induce a woman to go through a ceremony of marriage with him, logic might seem to require that he should be acquitted on a charge of aiding and abetting bigamy because, the woman being entitled to an acquittal on the ground of duress, there is no perpetrator; and that, as a bachelor, not "being married", cannot perpetrate bigamy, he should be acquitted on a charge of perpetrating bigamy through an innocent agent. However, there is authority against both of these suppositions. *Bourne*[6] shows that the man can be convicted

1. [1975] 2 All E.R. 684, at p. 687, *per* Lord Widgery, C.J.
2. [1940] 1 All E.R. 339. Also see *Morris* v. *Tolman*, [1923] 1 K.B. 166.
3. *Ram and Ram* (1893), 17 Cox C.C. 609.
4. *Eldershaw* (1828), 3 C. and P. 396.
5. Para. 19.2.
6. Para 18.9.

as an accomplice despite the fact that there is no perpetrator. However, it was held in *Cogan*[1] that a husband, who was cohabiting with his wife and therefore could not have been convicted of personally perpetrating the offence of rape against her,[2] could be convicted as the perpetrator of the rape of her through an innocent agent who lacked the necessary *mens rea* for rape and was acquitted. The reasoning in *Bourne* is preferable to that in *Cogan* since the latter case involves convicting a man as a perpetrator for something which he could not be convicted had he done it personally. *Bourne* shows that if A intends that the *actus reus* should be performed by B and induces B to perform it, but B has some defence such as duress or lack of *mens rea*, A's *mens rea* may be added to B's *actus reus* so as to make A liable as an accomplice when he cannot be liable as perpetrator. This assumes, of course, that the definition of the offence admits of such a solution. The problem posed by *Thornton* v. *Mitchell* cannot be solved in this way because a bus driver who is not negligent in following his conductor's signals is not failing to exercise due care and attention and there is thus no *actus reus* to which the conductor could be regarded as accomplice.

3 As we have just seen the acquittal of the alleged principal does not mean that another person cannot be convicted as accomplice. If A is charged with aiding and abetting the commission of an offence by B, with whom he is put up for trial, it would of course be logically absurd for A to be convicted and B acquitted if the evidence against each was identical. Nevertheless it sometimes happens that there is stronger evidence against A than against B, or that B has a defence, or that evidence which is admissible against A is inadmissible against B and, in such an event, the conviction of A is not logically incompatible with the acquittal of B.[3]

Intent to aid or encourage

4 Where the aiding and abetting consists of overt encouragement an intent to encourage must be proved. Normally this intent is easily inferable from the act of encouragement, but the inference is less easily drawn where the accused is merely voluntarily present at the scene of the crime; such presence merely provides some evidence that he was there with the intention of encouraging the principal offence.[4] Where the aiding and abet-

---

1. [1975] 2 All E.R. 1059.
2. See para. 9.2.
3. *Humphreys and Turner*, [1965] 3 All E.R. 689.
4. *Coney*; *Clarkson*.

ting consists of assistance, e.g. supplying an instrument for a crime or driving a murderer to the scene of the crime, an intent to aid is required. These intents are established by proof that the assistance or encouragement was voluntarily given, in the sense of a conscious action, with knowledge of the offence which is being committed, or is likely to be committed, by the perpetrator.[1] The accomplice need not desire that the principal offence should be committed. In *National Coal Board* v. *Gamble*,[2] Devlin, J, said:

> "... an indifference to the result of the crime does not of itself negative abetting. If one man deliberately sells to another a gun to be used for murdering a third, he may be indifferent about whether the third lives or dies and interested only in the cash profit to be made out of the sale, but he can still be an aider and abettor."

This approach was affirmed by the House of Lords in *Lynch* v. *Director of Public Prosecutions for Northern Ireland*,[3] where it was held that willingness to participate in the offence did not have to be established. In consequence a person who knows of another's criminal purpose and voluntarily aids him in it can be held to have aided and abetted even though he regretted the plan or indeed was horrified by it. Of course, if he was acting under compulsion sufficient to give rise to the defence of duress he would be not guilty on that ground. The knowledge required of an accomplice can be constituted by wilful blindness.[4]

19.15 The above requirements of *mens rea* apply even though the offence which the accused is alleged to have aided and abetted is one of strict liability. Thus a person charged as an accomplice to an offence of strict liability can be convicted of it only if he is proved to have known the facts essential to constitute the offence, even though such knowledge is not necessary so far as the perpetrator is concerned.[5]

19.16 How much must the accused know? This question is particularly important where the accused accomplice is not present when the offence is committed. He must know the essential facts which constitute the offence[6] although, of course, he need not

1. *National Coal Board* v. *Gamble*, [1959] 1 Q.B. 11; [1958] 3 All E.R. 203; *C. & J. Cases*; *Lynch* v. *Director of Public Prosecutions for Northern Ireland*, [1975] 1 All E.R. 913.
2. [1959] 1 Q.B. at p. 23.
3. [1975] 1 All E.R. 913.
4. *Poultry World* v. *Conder*, [1957] Crim. L. R. 803; *Carter* v. *Richardson*, [1974] R.T.R. 314.
5. *Johnson* v. *Youden*, [1950] 1 K.B. 544; [1950] 1 All E.R. 300.
6. *Ibid.*

know that those facts constitute an offence.[1] He need not know the details of the offence; it is enough that he knows facts sufficient to indicate the particular kind of offence intended and which is later committed.[2] Thus, if someone supplies another with a jemmy with knowledge that it will be used in a burglary (i.e. knowing the particular kind of offence), he is guilty of aiding and abetting a burglary committed with the jemmy and it makes no difference that he did not know which premises were going to be burgled or when the burglary was to take place. In *Bainbridge*[3] the accused supplied thieves with oxygen cutting equipment purchased by him six weeks earlier. The equipment was used for breaking into a bank, and it was held that the accused was an accomplice to this offence if he knew, when supplying the equipment, that it was to be used for a "breaking" offence. He would not have been an accomplice to the bank breaking if he had merely known that the equipment was to be used for some criminal purpose. A question left unresolved is whether Bainbridge would have been liable, as accomplice, for a large number of breaking offences committed over a considerable period of time with the equipment.

7 What we have just said must be qualified by adding that sometimes an accomplice can be liable for the unforeseen consequences of the perpetrator's acts. When two people embark on a joint enterprise, each is liable for the other's acts done in pursuance of that enterprise to the same extent as the other, and this includes liability for unusual consequences if they accidentally result from the execution of the agreed purpose.[4] Normally of course neither the perpetrator nor the accomplice is liable for an unforeseen consequence of the unlawful enterprise because they lack *mens rea* regarding it. However, some offences do not require the accused to foresee their necessary consequence and it is to these offences, examples of which are manslaughter and causing death by dangerous driving, that the present principle applies. As has been seen[5] a person is guilty of manslaughter if death results from the commission by him of an unlawful act likely to harm another even though he did not foresee that death

---

1. *Ibid.*
2. *Bainbridge*, [1960] 1 Q.B. 129; [1959] 3 All E.R. 200; *C. & J. Cases.*
3. [1960] 1 Q.B. 129.
4. *Anderson and Morris*, [1966] 2 Q.B. 110; [1966] 2 All E.R. 644; *C. & J. Cases.*
5. Para. 8.29.

was likely to occur. The principle that both perpetrator and accomplice are liable to the same extent for the accidental consequences of the unlawful enterprise produces the following results. If two people agree to assault a man with fists, and he dies in consequence of blows received from one of them, they are each guilty of manslaughter.[1] Similarly, someone who arranges for a criminal abortion to be performed is, like the perpetrator, guilty of manslaughter if the operation results in death.[2]

Cases of accidental departure from the unlawful enterprise must be sharply distinguished from those where the perpetrator deliberately goes beyond what was expressly or tacitly agreed. His accomplice is not liable for acts done by him outside the joint enterprise. If A and B agree to attack C with their fists and, unknown to A, B has a knife with which he kills C, A is not guilty of aiding and abetting murder, nor can he be convicted of manslaughter.[3]

19.18 Sometimes the perpetrator and the accomplice can be convicted of offences of a different degree:

a. a person who performs the *actus reus* of murder may have the defence of diminished responsibility which reduces his liability to manslaughter, but one who encourages or assists such a person to kill can be convicted of murder as an aider and abettor;[4]
b. some crimes, such as murder and manslaughter, and wounding with intent and unlawful wounding contrary to ss. 18 and 20 of the Offences against the Person Act 1861, share a common *actus reus* but are distinguished by the fact that a different state of mind is specified for each offence. If A is encouraged by B to assault C which he does, thereby killing C, A is guilty of murder if, knowing that C had an egg-shell skull, he intended the assault to kill C; B is guilty of only manslaughter if, not knowing of C's weakness, he did not foresee the risk of death or grievous bodily harm to C.[5] Conversely, an accomplice may be convicted of a greater offence than the perpetrator if he had a greater degree of

1. Para. 8.29.
2. *Creamer*, [1966] 1 Q.B. 72; [1965] 3 All E.R. 257; *Buck* (1960), 44 Cr. App. Rep. 213; *C. & J. Cases.*
3. *Anderson and Morris*, [1966] 2 Q.B. 110, [1966] 2 All E.R. 644.
4. Homicide Act 1957, s. 2 (4). Also see para. 8.19.
5. *Murtagh and Kennedy*, [1955] Crim. L.R. 315.

mens rea, provided he was present when the offence was committed.[1]

Victims as aiders and abettors.

9 It has been held that a girl under sixteen cannot be convicted of aiding and abetting a man to have unlawful intercourse with her,[2] but this does not mean that the victim of an offence can never be convicted of aiding and abetting its commission since the immunity from liability seems to extend only to the victims of offences which are designed to protect them against exploitation to which they are peculiarly open because of youth, poverty or the like.[3] Thus a woman can be convicted as an accomplice to the commission of an unlawful abortion on herself.[4] The immunity from liability seems to apply mainly to those sexual offences which are concerned with protecting young or mentally defective persons.

Entrapment and agents provocateurs

) Two issues must be considered. First, a law enforcement officer or some other person may participate in a criminal enterprise solely in order to entrap the other party or parties. Is such a person guilty as an accomplice if the offence is committed? The answer seems to be that a law enforcement officer or his agent is probably not liable[5] and is certainly not liable if his participation goes no further than pretending to concur with the other parties.[6] However, if a private citizen instigates an offence independently of the police in order to entrap a criminal he can be convicted as a party to the offence which the other commits,[7] but it is thought that he is not liable if he merely pretends to concur with other parties in order to entrap them.

Secondly, whereas in the United States the accused has a defence if he commits a crime as the result of the instigation of law enforcement officers and not as a result of his own initiative,[8]

---

1. *Richards*, [1974] Q.B. 776; [1973] 3 All E.R. 1088.
2. *Tyrrell*, [1894] 1 Q.B. 710; *C. & J. Cases.*
3. See articles by Professors Hogan and Williams respectively, [1962] Crim. L. R. 683 and [1964] Crim. L. R. 686.
4. *Sockett* (1908), 1 Cr. App. Rep. 101.
5. *Bickley* (1909), 73 J.P. 239; *Mullins* (1848), 3 Cox C.C. 526. Contrast *Brannan* v. *Peek*, [1948] 1 K.B. 68.
6. *Mullins.*
7. *Smith*, [1960] 2 Q.B. 423; [1960] 1 All E.R. 256.
8. *Sorrells* v. *U.S.* (1932), 77 L. Ed. 413; *Sherman* v. *U.S.* (1958), 2 L. Ed. 848.

there is no such defence of entrapment in our law, although the fact of police instigation may mitigate sentence.[1]

Withdrawal from participation

19.21 A voluntary withdrawal from participation by an accomplice excuses him from liability if, before the commission of the principal offence, he expressly countermands his previous encouragement or assistance.[2] Where this is not possible it would presumably be sufficient to notify the police of the proposed offence. In any event a withdrawal does not negative any possible liability for conspiracy.[3]

Uncertainty

19.22 The mere fact that it is not clear which of two or more people was the perpetrator does not prevent the conviction of all of them if each must have been either the perpetrator or an accomplice. Thus, it has been held that where either of two drivers who indulged in unlawful racing, in which each was encouraged by the other, might have run down the deceased, both could be convicted of manslaughter.[4]

Reform of the law of complicity

19.23 The brief outline of the law given above discloses the technicalities involved in the law of complicity and the difficulties which it can produce. One area of difficulty relates to the *mens rea* of an accomplice. It is not easy for instance to say how far the decision in *Bainbridge* goes as regards the number of offences in respect of which the supplier might be convicted as an accomplice.

This and other difficulties have led to the interesting suggestion that the law governing complicity should cease to treat the accomplice as a party to the offence he assists and that there should be a general and separate offence of aiding or encouraging crime. In addition to direct acts of encouragement, it should include the doing of acts known to be likely to assist the commission of an offence by another. The fact that the other would

---

1. *McEvilly* (1973), 60 Cr. App. Rep. 150; *Mealey and Sheridan* (1974), 60 Cr. App. Rep. 59. The possible introduction of a defence of entrapment into English law is discussed in Law Commission Working Paper No. 55, *Defences of General Application*, paras. 65–79. See also the article by Smith, [1975] Crim. L. R. 12.
2. *Croft*, [1944] 1 K.B. 295, [1944] 2 All E.R. 483.
3. See para. 17.7.
4. *Swindall and Osborne* (1846), 2. Car. & Kir. 230; *C. & J. Cases*.

or did fail to commit an offence because of insanity, duress etc. should be immaterial.[1] Anyone who has had to contend with the technicalities of the law of complicity must surely hope that the most serious consideration be given to the suggestion when the proposed criminal code is drafted. It is unfortunate that the Law Commission Working Paper on the subject of complicity does not discuss this suggestion but proposes in essence that the law should be codified very much as it is now, subject to the clarification or reform of certain matters.[2]

Liability for the unauthorised criminal acts of another

4 As we have seen, a person can be guilty under the law of complicity for the offences of another which he has authorised or, if he has a right of control over the perpetrator, which he has deliberately failed to prevent.[3] However, it is a general rule of the criminal law that one person is not responsible for the acts of another which he has not authorised and of which he was ignorant, even if that other person is his employee acting in the course of his employment, so that civil vicarious liability might arise. Thus, in the old case of *Huggins*[4] the warden of the Fleet prison was acquitted on a charge of murdering one of the inmates, as it appeared that death had been caused by confinement in an unhealthy cell by a servant of the accused without any direction from him and without his knowledge.

Exceptions to the general rule

5 In certain limited cases a person can be criminally vicariously liable for the acts of others which he has not authorised and of which he was ignorant. There are only two exceptions to the general rule in common law offences, both of which are essentially civil in character:

a. An employer is criminally liable for a public nuisance committed on his property or on the highway by his employee, even if the latter was disobeying orders.[5]
b. An employer is criminally liable for libels published by his employee unless he proves that he did not authorise the publi-

1. Buxton (1969), 85 L.Q.R. 252.
2. Law Commission Published Working Paper No. 43: *Codification of the Criminal Law: Parties, Complicity and Liability for the Acts of Another*. For comment, see Andrews, [1973] Crim. L. R. 764, and Buxton, [1974] Crim. L. R. 223.
3. Para. 19.8.
4. (1730), 2 Ld. Raym. 1574.
5. *Stephens* (1866), L.R. 1 Q.B. 702, at p. 710.

cation and that the publication was not due to want of due care on his part.[1]

It is of course possible for a statute expressly to impose vicarious liability and this is done in the case of certain statutory offences by putting the words "no person, himself or by his servant or agent" before the definition of the prohibited conduct.[2] However, most of the instances of vicarious liability for statutory offences have resulted not from the express wording of the statute but from judicial interpretation of it. The courts have used two principles of interpretation to impose vicarious liability for a large number of statutory offences—extensive construction and delegation.

Extensive construction

19.26 It has become common for the courts to give an extended construction to certain verbs used in statutory offences, such as "sell" or "use", so that the act of an employee is regarded as the act of his employer and thereby the employer is held to have committed the offence physically performed by his employee. Thus an employer as well as his driver has been held guilty of "using" a motor vehicle with a defective brake.[3] Similarly, an employer has been convicted of "exposing for sale" bags of coal containing short weight, although the short weight was due to the wrongdoing of the employee who exposed them for sale.[4] In *Coppen* v. *Moore* (No. 2),[5] the accused owned a number of shops in one of which an assistant, contrary to instructions, sold an American ham as a "Scotch ham". The accused was convicted of selling goods to which a false trade description had been applied.

The extensive construction principle is not limited to the relationship of employer and employee but has also been used to impose vicarious liability on a principal for the act of his agent[6] and on a partner for the act of a fellow partner.[7] Moreover, the licensee of licensed premises is liable for illegal sales by bar staff, even though they are not his servants but like him employed

1. Libel Act 1843, s. 7.
2. See, for example, s. 59 of the Licensing Act 1964.
3. *Green* v. *Burnett*, [1955] 1 Q.B. 78; [1954] 3 All E.R. 273.
4. *Winter* v. *Hinckley and District Co-operative Society, Ltd.*, [1959] 1 All E.R. 403.
5. [1898] 2 Q.B. 306.
6. *Quality Dairies (York), Ltd.* v. *Pedley*, [1952] 1 K.B. 275; [1952] 1 All E.R. 380.
7. *Clode* v. *Barnes*, [1974] 1 All E.R. 1166.

by the owner of the premises, since the act of selling can only be performed by virtue of the licence.[1]

Although the matter is not free from doubt, it seems that under the extensive construction principle only the act of the employee etc., and not his *mens rea*, can be imputed to the employer etc.[2] Unless the employer himself has *mens rea*,[3] the practical effect of this is to limit this method of imposing vicarious liability to offences where *mens rea* is not required.

Delegation

7 This principle is limited to cases where the holder of a public licence has delegated his responsibilities to another. A public licence is one which is given to control the number, as well as the quality, of persons pursuing a particular activity, such as licences to sell intoxicating liquor and slaughterhouse licences. If a delegate is in breach of any of the statutory responsibilities which have been delegated, his acts and state of mind are imputed to the delegator. Where the offence is one of strict liability, the extensive construction principle normally suffices to impose vicarious liability and the delegation principle generally comes into play only if the statute uses words which import a requirement of *mens rea*.[4] In *Allen* v. *Whitehead*,[5] the licensee of a refreshment house delegated control of it to an employee who, in the licensee's absence and contrary to his express instructions, allowed prostitutes to enter. The licensee was convicted of "knowingly suffering prostitutes to meet together in his house and remain therein", contrary to s. 44 of the Metropolitan Police Act 1839, the acts and *mens rea* of the delegate employee being imputed to him. The delegation principle is not limited to cases where the delegate is the employee of the delegator. In *Linnett* v. *Metropolitan Police Commissioner*[6] it was held that one co-licensee was vicariously liable where his co-licensee, to whom he had delegated the management of a refreshment house owned by their employer, had knowingly permitted disorderly conduct there.

---

1. *Goodfellow* v. *Johnson*, [1966] 1 Q.B. 83; [1965] 1 All E.R. 941.
2. *Vane* v. *Yiannopoullos*, [1965] A.C. 486; [1964] 3 All E.R. 820; *C. & J. Cases*; *Coupe* v. *Guyett*, [1973] 2 All E.R. 1058; contrast *Mousell Brothers* v. *London North Western Rail. Co.*, [1917] 2 K.B. 836; *G. Newton, Ltd.* v. *Smith*, [1968] 2 Q.B. at p. 284.
3. *Ross* v. *Moss* [1969] 2 Q.B. 396; [1965] 3 All E.R. 145.
4. *Winson*, [1969] 1 Q.B. 371; [1968] 1 All E.R. 197.
5. [1930] 1 K.B. 211.
6. [1946] K.B. 290; [1947] 1 All E.R. 380.

19.28 It is necessary that there should have been a complete delegation of the licensee's managerial functions and responsibilities. Thus the House of Lords held in *Vane* v. *Yiannopoullos*[1] that a restaurateur who was permitted to sell intoxicants only to customers consuming a meal and who had told a waitress to serve such customers only, and then withdrawn to the basement, was not guilty of any infringement by the waitress of what is now s. 161 (1) of the Licensing Act 1964 which penalises licensees who knowingly sell intoxicants to unpermitted persons. The restaurateur had retained control of the restaurant and had not delegated this to the waitress, but if there has been a complete delegation of managerial functions and responsibilities it is irrelevant that this only relates to part of the licensed premises or that the delegator licensee is still on the premises.[2] In *Vane* v. *Yiannopoullos*, Lords Morris and Donovan doubted the validity of the delegation principle, but in the light of its continued application it must still be regarded as part of the law[3] which is confused and produces anomalies.

Comments on vicarious liability

19.29 a. Vicarious liability can arise only if the employee or delegate etc. was acting within the scope of his employment or authority. Doing an authorised act in an unauthorised way falls within such scope, but a wholly unauthorised act does not. In *Coppen* v. *Moore*,[4] an employer was held vicariously liable for a sale effected by a sales assistant in an unauthorised manner, but in *Adams* v. *Camfoni*,[5] the accused licensee was acquitted of selling intoxicants outside permitted hours because the sale had been effected by a messenger boy who had no authority to sell anything at all.

b. The liability of the employee or delegate etc. depends on the wording of the particular statute. If it specifies that only a person with a particular characteristic, such as a licensee, can commit the offence, an employee or delegate who actually commits the act can be convicted only as aider and abettor

---

1. [1965] A.C. 486; [1964] 3 All E.R. 820; *C' & J. Cases.*
2. *Howker* v. *Robinson*, [1973] 1 Q.B. 178; [1972] 2 All E.R. 786. Contrast Lords Reid and Hodson in *Vane* v. *Yiannopoullos*, [1965] A.C. 486, at pp. 497–498 and 510.
3. See, for example, *Winson* [1969] 1 Q.B. 371; [1968] 1 All E.R. 197; *Howker* v. *Robinson*, [1973] 1 Q.B. 178; [1972] 2 All E.R. 197.
4. [1898] 2 Q.B. 306. Also see *Allen* v. *Whitehead*, [1930] 1 K.B. 211.
5. [1929] 1 K.B. 95. Also see *Barker* v. *Levinson*, [1951] 1 K.B. 342; [1950] 2 All E.R. 825; *C. & J. Cases.*

of that person, who is vicariously liable as perpetrator.[1] Where the statute does not specify a particular type of perpetrator, the employee etc. can be convicted either as perpetrator jointly with the person held vicariously liable[2] or as an aider and abettor.[3] This distinction is important because, if the offence in question is one of strict liability, the employee can be convicted in the first type of case only if he has *mens rea*, since a person can be convicted as an accomplice to an offence of strict liability only if he has *mens rea*.[4] A person cannot be vicariously liable for aiding and abetting[5] or for attempting to commit[6] an offence.

c. There are several statutory defences which are open to employers and others who may be vicariously liable. The courts have refused to read into statutes, construed by them as imposing vicarious liability for offences, an exception protecting employers who show due diligence in the management of their business, where nothing which they could reasonably be expected to do would have prevented the commission of the offence by the employee. Accordingly some statutes contain an express provision for defences of this nature of which an example is s. 24 of the Trade Descriptions Act 1968.[7] There is much to be said for having a general defence of due diligence in all cases of vicarious criminal liability.[8]

d. Criminal responsibility is generally regarded as essentially personal in nature. The exceptional principles whereby a man can be convicted of an offence of which he was ignorant and which was actually committed by another can be justified only on the basis of the need to enforce modern regulatory legislation, such as that governing the sale of food and drugs or intoxicating liquor.[9] The courts consider that the most effective way of enforcing such legislation is to impose on the employer liability for contravention by employees in order to encourage him to prevent them infringing the legislation.[10] This justification call for two comments. The

---

1. *Ross* v. *Moss*, [1965] 2 Q.B. 396, [1965] 3 All E.R. 145.
2. *Green* v. *Burnett*, [1955] 1 Q.B. 78; [1954] 3 All E.R. 273.
3. *Griffiths* v. *Studebaker*, [1924] 1 K.B. 102.
4. Para. 19.14.
5. *Ferguson* v. *Weaving*, [1951] 1 K.B. 814, [1951] 1 All E.R. 412; *C. & J. Cases*.
6. *Gardner* v. *Akeroyd*, [1952] 2 Q.B. 743; [1952] 2 All E.R. 306.
7. Para. 16.24.
8. Para. 6.11.
9. See, for example, *Gardner* v. *Akeroyd*, [1952] 2 Q.B. 743, at p. 751.
10. *Reynolds* v. *G. H. Austin & Sons, Ltd.*, [1951] 2 K.B. 135; [1951] 1 All E.R. 606; *Tesco Supermarkets, Ltd.* v. *Nattrass*, [1971] 2 All E.R. 127, at p. 151 and para. 6.7.

> assumption that the imposition of vicarious liability is the most effective method of securing compliance with the statute is unproved. Secondly, vicarious liability would be more acceptable if it were limited generally to employers who had been negligent in failing to prevent the contravention. Another justification put forward occasionally is that some offences can be committed only by a particular person, such as a licensee, and that without vicarious liability such offence would be rendered nugatory where that person acted through others: the obvious answer is to amend the statute, not for the judges to impose vicarious liability.

The Law Commission Working Paper on *Parties, Complicity and Liability for the Acts of Others*[1] accepts the idea of vicarious liability but would restrict it to cases where there is an express provision for it, or where the act is described in terms such as "selling" or "using", which in its context applies both to the person who performs the act and the person on whose behalf he acts. Further, where vicarious liability is imposed for offences involving *mens rea*, the person on whose behalf the act is done should not be liable unless he has *mens rea*.

---

1. Law Commission Published Working Paper No. 43. For comment, see the article by Professor Andrews, [1972] Crim. L. R., 764.

20

COURTS OF CRIMINAL JURISDICTION

There are two methods of trying persons accused of criminal offences. One is by judge and jury in the Crown Court after committal for trial on a written accusation of crime called an indictment; the other is summary by a Magistrates' Court without a jury, either on a charge if the accused has been arrested or on a summons if he has not.[1] Over 97 per cent of all offences, including the most trivial, are tried summarily, which means that formality is reduced. The chart on p. 390 shows the outline of the court structure and the following paragraphs explain this, beginning at the bottom.

Magistrates' courts

Magistrates' courts are constituted by any justice or justices of the peace acting under any enactment or by virtue of his or their commission or under the common law.[2] A magistrates' court must be composed of at least two magistrates when trying a case summarily unless there is a special statutory exception,[3] in which case a court composed of only one magistrate has more limited powers of punishment[4] but one magistrate can conduct committal proceedings in his capacity of examining magistrate. The terms "justice of the peace" and "magistrate" are synonymous and henceforth to avoid confusion we shall use the words "magistrate" and "magistrates' court".

The powers of magistrates' courts are almost entirely dependent upon statute. They have jurisdiction over some civil matters which are not dealt with in this book. Magistrates are appointed by the Lord Chancellor or by the Chancellor of the Duchy of Lancaster in the name of the Queen. Each area has an advisory committee which makes recommendations to the Chancellor. There is a separate Commission of the Peace for each county and for the areas of Greater London and the City of

1. Paras. 22.4 and 22.5.
2. Magistrates' Courts Act 1952, s. 124.
3. *Ibid.*, s. 98.
4. *Ibid.*, s. 98 (3) and (5).

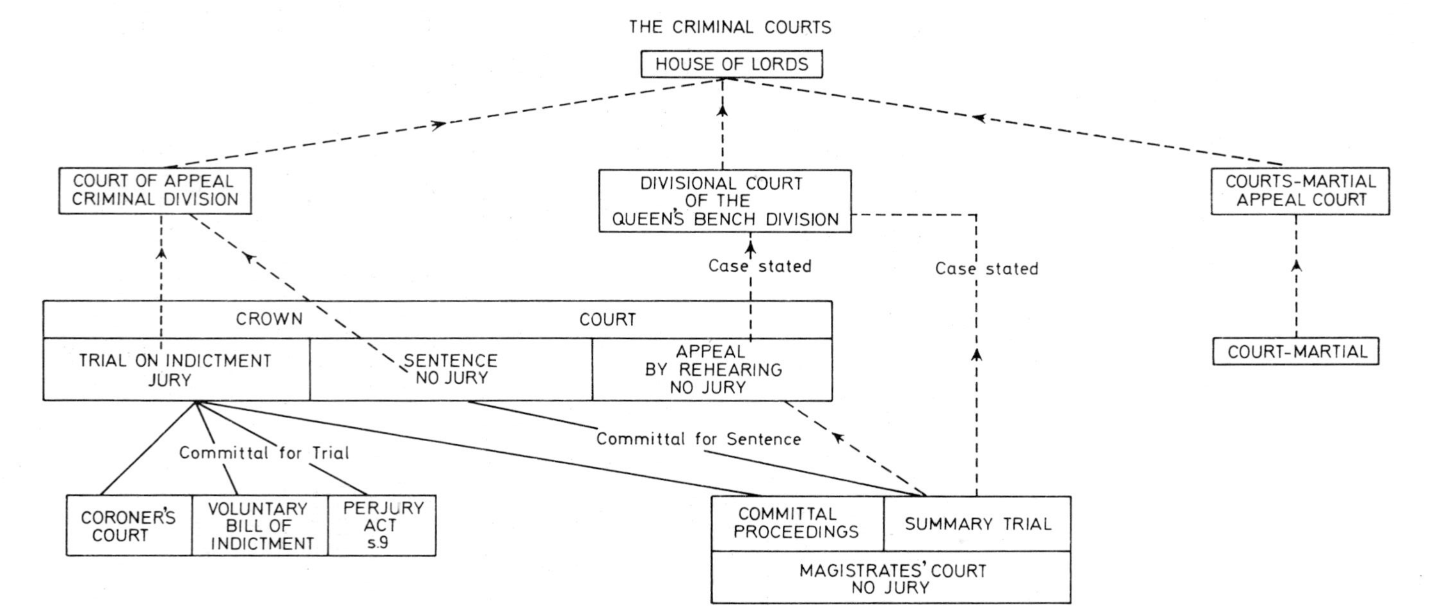
THE CRIMINAL COURTS
HOUSE OF LORDS
COURT OF APPEAL CRIMINAL DIVISION
DIVISIONAL COURT OF THE QUEEN'S BENCH DIVISION
COURTS-MARTIAL APPEAL COURT
Case stated
Case stated
CROWN COURT
TRIAL ON INDICTMENT JURY
SENTENCE NO JURY
APPEAL BY REHEARING NO JURY
COURT-MARTIAL
Committal for Trial
Committal for Sentence
CORONER'S COURT
VOLUNTARY BILL OF INDICTMENT
PERJURY ACT s.9
COMMITTAL PROCEEDINGS
SUMMARY TRIAL
MAGISTRATES' COURT NO JURY
Committals
Appeals

London. Each county is divided into a number of petty sessional divisions.

Lay magistrates are not required to possess any legal qualifications: for legal advice they rely on their clerk, who is usually a solicitor or barrister, but even though the clerk to the magistrates is legally qualified, an individual court may be served by an unadmitted assistant. In the inner London area and in some places outside, jurisdiction is exercised both by stipendiary magistrates, who are barristers or solicitors of seven years' standing or more, and by lay magistrates. Stipendiary magistrates sit alone and have all the powers of two lay magistrates in a magistrates' court. In 1975 there were 39 stipendiary magistrates in London and 10 in the rest of England and Wales.

3 Magistrates' courts have two functions:

a. That of a court of summary jurisdiction or petty sessions, which hears and determines cases without a jury, subject to appeal. Not only do magistrates' courts deal summarily with those offences which are defined in the statute creating them as summary offences but they may also try certain indictable offences with the consent of the accused. Conversely, in most cases, if a sentence exceeding three months' imprisonment may be imposed for a summary offence, the accused, if he has attained the age of 17, has the right to be tried upon indictment and where the accused so elects, the offence is treated in all respects as indictable.[1] The indictable offences which may be tried summarily include:
   i. Destroying or damaging property under section 1 (1) of the Criminal Damage Act 1971 and offences under ss. 2 and 3 of that Act.
   ii. Unlawful wounding under s. 20 and indictable assaults under s. 47 of the Offences against the Person Act 1861.
   iii. All offences under the Theft Act 1968 except robbery, aggravated burglary, blackmail, assault with intent to rob, handling stolen goods from an offence not committed in the United Kingdom and certain cases of burglary in a dwelling house.[2]

   The powers of magistrates' courts as courts of summary jurisdiction are described later.[3]

---

1. Magistrates' Courts Act 1952, s. 25.
2. The full list of these offences is set out in the Magistrates' Courts Act 1952, Sch. I, and the Criminal Justice Administration Act 1962, Sch. III as amended by the Theft Act 1968. For proposals for reform, see Appendix.
3. Paras. 23.18–23.22.

b. That of examining magistrates by whom committal proceedings are held as a necessary preliminary in almost all cases to a trial by jury. The function of examining magistrates is different from that when they sit to hear and determine a case. All they have to decide is whether there is evidence upon which a reasonable jury properly directed could convict. It matters not that the magistrates themselves would not have convicted on the evidence before them. The system has two principal justifications. It should act as a filter so that those against whom there is no evidence on which a reasonable jury could convict are spared the anxiety and expense of a trial.[1] It also enables the defendant to learn and be supplied with a copy of the evidence for the prosecution and thus he has time to consider the weight of the case against him in advance of the trial. The defendant is not asked to plead, although he has the right to give evidence himself and to call witnesses. If the magistrates decide that there is no *prima facie* case against the defendant they decline to commit him for trial and discharge him, but there is nothing to prevent a fresh charge being brought and a new examination held.

The Crown Court

20.4 The Crown Court tries cases by jury on indictment, almost always after committal by examining magistrates, and also hears appeals from the decisions of magistrates' courts unless only a point of law is in issue.

The Crown Court in England and Wales is administratively under the direct control of the Lord Chancellor. It is divided into six circuits and has exclusive jurisdiction over all offences tried by jury on indictment[2] together with jurisdiction:

a. to deal with persons committed for sentence by magistrates' courts;[3]
b. to hear appeals from magistrates' courts including juvenile courts;[4] and
c. to hear original proceedings and appeals in civil matters under certain statutes.[5]

We are not concerned with civil matters which the Crown Court has inherited from the former courts of Quarter Sessions. The Crown Court has power to sit anywhere on any day and at any time in England and Wales according to directions given

1. See Appendix.
2. Courts Act 1971, s. 6 (1).
3. Magistrates' Courts Act 1952, ss. 28 and 29.
4. Courts Act 1971, s. 8 and Sch. 1.
5. *Ibid.*, s. 8 and Sch. 1.

by or on behalf of the Lord Chancellor, and the places at which it sits regularly are listed on p. 394, but the Lord Chancellor reviews the position from time to time so as to ensure that adequate court facilities are provided wherever a need for them is shown so that this list may well become out of date.[1]

The towns on the list are divided into first-tier, second-tier and third-tier centres. The first-tier centres are served by High Court and Circuit judges and Recorders, whom we shall describe later, and they deal with both civil and criminal cases. Second tier centres also are served by High Court and Circuit judges and Recorders but they do not deal with civil cases so that from the point of view of the administration of the criminal law there is no difference between first and second-tier centres. Third-tier centres are limited to criminal cases and are served by Circuit judges and Recorders.[2]

5 Each circuit has two Presiding judges and a circuit administrator together with other staff. Subject to the directions of the Presiding judges of the circuit the chief functions of the circuit administrator are:

a. to assess the need for judges on his circuit having regard to the volume of business;
b. to allocate and reallocate cases within the circuit in order to spread the load evenly;
c. to keep the Lord Chancellor informed about the state of business, congestion, arrears and overwork;
d. to allocate court accommodation in the most economic way;
e. to arrange for the attendance of lay magistrates in the Crown Court.

Under the circuit administrator work courts administrators, each of whom is responsible for organising a group of court centres while at each court centre there is a chief clerk who is responsible for the administrative work of his centre and for summoning jurors. Among his many other duties he signs bills of indictment which become the indictments on which accused persons are tried. Although conditions vary from one circuit to another and none can be described as typical, it may help to see on p. 395 the organisational chart of the Midland and Oxford Circuit as it was on 1 October 1975. There are no geographical limitations on the jurisdiction of the Crown Court to hear cases

1. *Ibid.*, s. 4.
2. Para. 20.6.

Locations of the High Court and Crown Court Centres for the disposal of civil and criminal work as from 1 October 1975

Places described in the following list as first-tier centres deal with both civil and criminal cases and are served by High Court and Circuit judges and Recorders, second-tier centres deal with criminal cases only but are served by High Court and Circuit judges and Recorders; while third-tier centres deal with criminal cases only and are served only by Circuit judges and Recorders.

MIDLAND AND OXFORD CIRCUIT:

First-tier—Birmingham, Lincoln, Nottingham, Stafford, Warwick.
Second-tier—Leicester, Northampton, Oxford, Shrewsbury, Worcester.
Third-tier—Coventry, Derby, Dudley, Grimsby, Hereford, Huntingdon, Stoke-on-Trent, Walsall, Warley, West Bromwich, Wolverhampton.

Peterborough will replace Huntingdon as a third-tier centre as soon as suitable court accommodation can be provided there.

NORTH-EASTERN CIRCUIT:

First-tier—Leeds, Newcastle upon Tyne, Sheffield, York.
Second-tier—Durham, Teesside.
Third-tier—Beverley, Bradford, Doncaster, Huddersfield, Kingston upon Hull, Wakefield.

Beverley will cease to be a third-tier Centre as soon as additional court accommodation can be made available at Kingston upon Hull.

NORTHERN CIRCUIT:

First-tier—Carlisle, Liverpool, Manchester, Preston.
Third-tier—Barrow-in-Furness, Birkenhead, Burnley, Kendal, Lancaster.

SOUTH-EASTERN CIRCUIT:

First-tier—Greater London, Norwich.
Second-tier—Chelmsford, Ipswich, Lewes, Maidstone, Reading, St. Albans.
Third-tier—Aylesbury, Bedford, Brighton, Bury St. Edmunds, Cambridge, Canterbury, Chichester, Guildford, King's Lynn, Southend.

WALES AND CHESTER CIRCUIT:

First-tier—Caernarvon, Cardiff, Chester, Mold, Swansea.
Second-tier—Carmarthen, Newport, Welshpool.
Third-tier—Dolgellau, Haverfordwest, Knutsford, Merthyr Tydfil.

WESTERN CIRCUIT:

First-tier—Bodmin, Bristol, Exeter, Winchester.
Second-tier—Dorchester, Gloucester, Plymouth.
Third-tier—Barnstaple, Bournemouth, Poole, Devizes, Newport (I.O.W.), Portsmouth, Salisbury, Southampton, Swindon, Taunton.

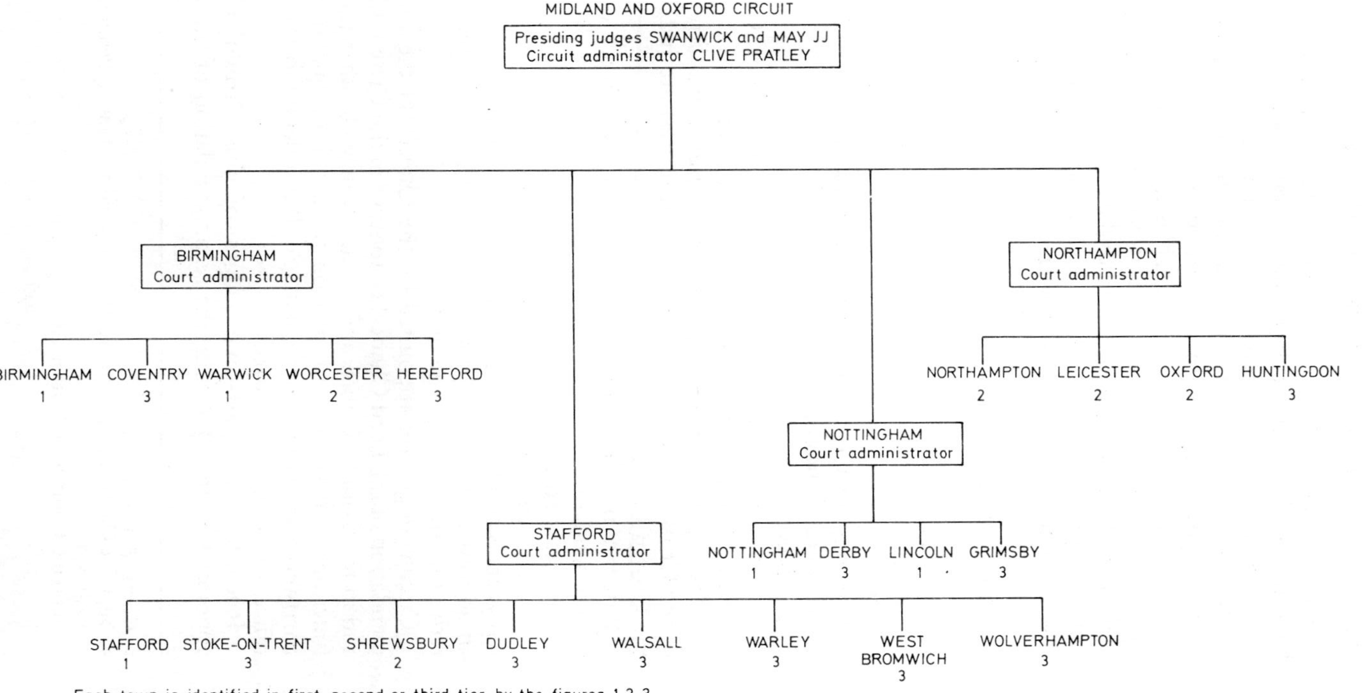

Each town is identified in first second or third tier by the figures 1, 2, 3.

in England and Wales. Local authority boundaries no longer have any significance in determining where a case is heard; the circuit boundaries are there only to define the territorial responsibility of the circuit administrator and cases can be committed for trial by magistrates' courts across circuit boundaries. Section 4 (5) of the Courts Act enables directions to be given by or on behalf of the Lord Chief Justice with the concurrence of the Lord Chancellor with regard to the cases or classes of cases suitable for allocation respectively to a judge of the High Court and to a Circuit judge or Recorder.

20.6 The jurisdiction and powers of the Crown Court are exercised by:

a. any judge of the High Court;
b. any judge of the Court of Appeal who sits and acts at the request of the Lord Chancellor. When so sitting and acting he is regarded as a judge of the High Court;
c. any Circuit judge;
d. any Recorder;
e. in some circumstances any judge of the High Court, Circuit judge or Recorder sitting with lay magistrates.

All such persons when exercising the jurisdiction and powers of the Crown Court (including lay magistrates) are judges of the Crown Court.[1]

Judges of the High Court are appointed by the Queen on the recommendation of the Lord Chancellor and exercise the civil jurisdiction of the High Court as well as the criminal jurisdiction of the Crown Court. Those qualified are barristers of at least ten years' standing. A High Court judge is removable only on an address presented by both Houses of Parliament but must retire on attaining the age of 75.[2]

Circuit judges are appointed by the Queen on the recommendation of the Lord Chancellor to serve in the Crown Court and in the County Courts and to carry out such other judicial functions as may be conferred on them. Those qualified are barristers of at least ten years' standing or Recorders who have held office for at least five years.[3]

Recorders are part-time judges of the Crown Court appointed by the Queen on the recommendation of the Lord

1. Courts Act 1971, s. 4 (2).
2. Supreme Court of Judicature Act 1925, ss. 9 and 11; Judicial Pensions Act 1959, s. 2.
3. Supreme Court of Judicature Act 1925, s. 16.

Chancellor. They must be either barristers or solicitors of at least ten years' standing.[1]

In order to reduce so far as possible any delay in administration of justice in the High Court or Crown Court which is due to the shortage of judges, the Lord Chancellor has wide powers to appoint as a temporary measure deputy judges of the High Court and deputy Circuit judges.[2]

Section 5 of the Courts Act 1971 lays down the circumstances in which lay magistrates act as judges of the Crown Court. They can sit only with a High Court or Circuit judge or a Recorder and not by themselves. They must form part of the Crown Court when it hears appeals from magistrates' courts[3] and also when it is sentencing persons who have been committed for sentence by magistrates' courts but the Lord Chancellor has power to dispense with this requirement. The number of magistrates so sitting must be not less than two nor more than four. Rulings on questions of law are matters for the judge but decisions on other questions, e.g. sentence, are the product of all the members of the court.[4]

Appellate courts

.7 A Divisional Court of the Queen's Bench Division of the High Court, which consists of three judges of the Division, usually but not always presided over by the Lord Chief Justice, has these two functions in the administration of the criminal law:

a. To be a court of appeal only on points of law or jurisdiction from magistrates' courts and from the Crown Court when that court has heard an appeal from a magistrates' court.[5]
b. In relation to the jurisdiction of the Crown Court other than its jurisdiction in matters relating to trials on indictment, and in relation to all inferior courts, to make orders of mandamus, prohibition, or certiorari.[6]

.8 The Criminal Division of the Court of Appeal hears appeals against conviction and sentence from the Crown Court. The Court of Appeal consists of two divisions, civil and criminal. The Criminal Division usually consists of the Lord Chief Justice, one Lord Justice of Appeal and a judge of the Queen's Bench Division. Procedure on appeal to the Court of Appeal is now

1. Courts Act 1971, s. 21.
2. *Ibid.*, s. 24 (1) and (2).
3. Courts Act 1971, s. 5 (1).
4. *Orpin*, [1975] Q.B. 283; [1974] 2 All E.R. 1121.
5. Paras. 24.3 and 24.4.
6. Para. 24.10.

consolidated in the Criminal Appeal Act 1968 and the Criminal Appeal Rules 1968.[1]

Before 1908, a person convicted on indictment had no right of appeal although the trial judge could, in his discretion, reserve a point of law for the consideration of the Court for Crown Cases Reserved and there was also a means of appealing by a writ of error, to which resort was seldom had because it had to relate to a defect in the written record of the case.

The Court of Criminal Appeal was created by the Criminal Appeal Act 1907 and it exercised basically the same jurisdiction as that which is now exercised by the Criminal Division of the Court of Appeal. It consisted of the Lord Chief Justice and the Queen's Bench judges. The major distinction between it and the Court of Appeal (Criminal Division) is therefore the presence in the latter of Lords Justices of Appeal.

20.9 The Courts-Martial Appeal Court, which was originally constituted in 1951, hears appeals from courts-martial of the armed services against conviction anywhere in the world. An appeal lies with the leave of the Court, but only after the convicted person has exercised and exhausted his right to petition the Defence Council, although the Court can dispense with this requirement. The Court is regulated by the Courts-Martial (Appeals) Act 1968 and has powers corresponding in general with those of the Court of Appeal (Criminal Division). Its judges consist of the Lords Justices of Appeal and those judges of the Queen's Bench Division nominated by the Lord Chief Justice, together with judges from Scotland and Northern Ireland and other persons specially appointed.

20.10 The symmetry of the pyramid which has emerged from the Courts Act is distorted by the continued existence of the Divisional Court of the Queen's Bench Division. Logically one would expect that appeals on points of law from magistrates' courts would go to the Criminal Division of the Court of Appeal just as appeals from County Courts go to the Civil Division of the Court of Appeal but the old system has been preserved and appeals on points of law by way of case stated are heard by the Divisional Court from which there is an appeal to the House of Lords. The anomaly is emphasised when it is realised that there is an alternative appeal by way of rehearing from magistrates' courts to the Crown Court and that on a point of law

1. Paras. 24.5–24.7.

there is thence a further appeal by way of case stated to the Divisional Court.

11 The House of Lords in its judicial capacity is the supreme court of appeal in criminal cases.[1]

The right of audience

12 An accused person has complete discretion about whether to conduct his own case or to be represented. While the court may advise him as to the desirability of being represented, it must not force representation upon him against his will.[2] Only a barrister or a solicitor may represent the accused.

Barristers have the right of audience in all criminal courts. Solicitors are limited to appearing before magistrates' courts, except that the Lord Chancellor may at any time direct that solicitors may appear in, conduct, defend and address the court in any proceedings in the Crown Court of such a description as is specified in the direction. Such a direction may be general in extent or be confined to a specified area, region or circuit or to a specified place. The factors to which the Lord Chancellor has to have regard are the shortage of barristers, rights of audience formerly exercised by solicitors and other circumstances affecting the public interest. When the Courts Act 1971 came into operation the Lord Chancellor had given one such direction covering certain kinds of cases, including the trial of certain offences, at Caernarvon, Barnstaple, Bodmin, Doncaster and Lincoln,[3] and shortly afterwards he gave a further direction covering the whole country enabling a solicitor to appear in the Crown Court on an appeal from a magistrates' court or on committal of a person for sentence or to be dealt with, provided that he or a partner in or an employee of his firm appeared on behalf of the defendant in the magistrates' court.[4]

In all cases heard by magistrates' courts, the informant[5] may appear to conduct the prosecution as well as giving evidence himself.[6] As in most summary cases a police officer is the informant, a practice has grown up whereby a superintendent or inspector lays the information, appears and conducts police prosecutions.

---

1. Para. 24.8.
2. *Woodward*, [1944] K.B. 118; [1944] 1 All E.R. 159.
3. Practice Direction, [1972] 1 All E.R. 144.
4. Practice Direction, *ibid.*, 608.
5. Para. 22.3.
6. *Duncan* v. *Toms* (1887), 51 J.P. 631.

The informant himself is not permitted to address the court in trials on indictment, and such cases must in practice be conducted by counsel.

By statute certain persons who are not the informant, nor a barrister nor a solicitor are authorised to conduct prosecutions before magistrates, e.g. an inspector appointed under the Social Security Act 1973, an inspector appointed under the Health and Safety at Work etc Act 1974, and a member or officer of a local authority.[1]

Where a child or young person is not legally represented the court must allow his parent or guardian to assist him (including the cross-examination of witnesses) and in the absence of a parent or guardian the court must allow any relative or other responsible person to assist.[2]

---

1. Local Government Act 1972, s. 233.
2. Magistrates' Courts (Children and Young Persons) Rules 1970, r. 5.

21

PROSECUTIONS

.1 We have seen[1] that usually there is nothing to prevent a private individual from instituting criminal proceedings, but the overwhelming majority of prosecutions are by one of the 47 police forces in England and Wales: there is no official corresponding to the procurator-fiscal in Scotland. A minority of prosecutions are instituted by the Director of Public Prosecutions and by government departments, local authorities or other public bodies or by persons holding official positions.

The Director of Public Prosecutions

.2 The Director of Public Prosecutions has the following principal functions:

a. To institute, undertake and carry on criminal proceedings:
   i. in cases of murder;
   ii. in all cases which are referred to him by a government department in which he considers criminal proceedings should be instituted;
   iii. in any case which appears to him to be of importance or difficulty, or which for any other reason requires his intervention.[2]

b. To consent to and/or to undertake the prosecution of certain offences so designated by statute.

c. To give advice, either orally or in writing and whether on application or on his own initiative, to government departments, clerks to magistrates, chief officers of police and such other persons as he may think right in any criminal matter which appears to him to be of importance or difficulty.[3]

d. To consider reports on complaints against the police sent to him by chief officers of police.[4]

e. To consider reports on proceedings in indictable cases which

---

1. Para. 1.7.
2. Prosecution of Offences Regulations, 1946, reg. 1., S.R. & O. 1946, No. 1467.
3. *Ibid.*, reg. 2.
4. Police Act 1964, s. 49 (3).

have been instituted but no further step has been taken or the prosecution has been withdrawn.[1]

21.3 In spite of his title the Director is responsible for only a small minority of all prosecutions instituted. In 1974 over 56,000 persons in England and Wales were tried on indictment but the Director acted in only 3,390 cases involving 4,180 persons.[2] The Director appeared in 120 appeals and applications to the House of Lords, Court of Appeal (Criminal Division), Divisional Court and Crown Court.[3] The Director may assist prosecutors by authorising the payment of special expenses and may employ a solicitor to act as his agent in the conduct of a prosecution.[4] The chief officer of police of every police district must report to the Director certain offences which are alleged to have been committed within his district including murder, incest, offences under the Official Secrets Act, manslaughter, rape and abortion.[5]

The Directorate is comparatively small. The only significant, consistent and substantial case in which the Director always undertakes the prosecution is murder. Others depend on the circumstances.

Whereas the number of cases in which the Director prosecutes is limited, he receives thousands of applications (16,477 in 1975) for advice, and it is upon the quality of that advice and upon the respect which is given to it that the impact and the contribution which the Director is able to make to the administration of the criminal law is primarily to be attributed.

21.4 At present there are over 50 Acts of Parliament which create criminal offences but which also provide that the consent of the Director is necessary before proceedings can be begun. In this category, as in those described in paras. 21.2 d and e, the Director is required to exercise his discretion about whether it is in the public interest to prosecute. It has never been the rule in this country, as we have already said, that suspected criminal offences must automatically be the subject of prosecution. The discretion works both ways; in cases under para. 21.2 c and d the Director may decide against prosecution although there may be a "paper" case, whereas in cases under para. 21.2 e he may insist on the prosecution going forward. The consent of the Director is re-

---

1. Prosecution of Offences Regulations 1946, reg. 6 (1) (c).
2. Criminal Statistics 1974, Cmnd. 6168, Tables II and VIII.
3. *Ibid.*
4. Prosecution of Offences Regulations 1946, regs. 3 and 4.
5. *Ibid.*, reg. 6.

quired in some cases in order to ensure, among other things, that there will be no frivolous prosecutions. A good example is s. 30 of the Theft Act 1968, which for the first time in the history of the English criminal law makes it an offence for one spouse to steal from the other whom he or she is living with and not on the point of leaving. The consent of the Director is required in order to prevent the criminal courts being congested with connubial squabbles.

The duty of the Director under s. 49 of the Police Act 1964 is to ensure that all complaints against police officers are prosecuted without fear or favour and equally that the complaint against the police is properly the subject of a prosecution and that it is not being instituted merely for the purpose of placating a popular demand.

Unless it is expressly stated to the contrary, none of the foregoing provisions interferes with the right of a private individual to institute criminal proceedings[1] although the Director may intervene at any time.[2]

The Director is the Official Petitioner under s. 41 of the Powers of Criminal Courts Act 1973[3] and cases which are submitted to the Attorney General under s. 36 of the Criminal Justice Act 1972 are channelled through him.[4]

The discretion to prosecute

.5 Not only the Director of Public Prosecutions has a discretion about whether to prosecute: every other body or person in whose hands the decision lies whether to institute criminal proceedings or not has a similar discretion, the existence of which has been not only acknowledged but encouraged by the courts. For example, in *Smedleys, Ltd.* v. *Breed*[5] Viscount Dilhorne said:

> "... although this Act imposes on the food and drugs authorities the duty of prosecuting under s. 2, it does not say—and I would find it surprising if it had—that they must prosecute in every case without regard to whether the public interest will be served by a prosecution. What this litigation has cost I dread to think ..."

1.6 This subject has been examined exhaustively by a former Chief Constable of Hertfordshire[6] who concludes that there are

1. Prosecution of Offences Act 1879, s. 7.
2. Prosecution of Offences Act 1908, s. 2 (4).
3. Criminal bankruptcy.
4. Para. 24.7.
5. [1974] 2 All E.R. 21; para. 16.14.
6. Wilcox, A. F., *The Decision to Prosecute.*

many circumstances in which, although there may be enough evidence on which not only to institute proceedings but to obtain a conviction, it is proper not to prosecute, whether or not it may be desirable to use warnings, advice, cautions and other alternatives to prosecution. The list of circumstances is impressive and includes among 20 categories offences in riots and demonstrations, and against obsolete, controversial, unpopular and absurd laws; trivial, technical and complex offences; offences committed by the young, the old, the infirm and the obsessed. Two facts emerge clearly. One is that it is nowhere suggested that there should be or is a discretion to prosecute in serious and obvious crime, which brings us back to the theme of para. 2.23—the proper scope and function of the criminal law. The second fact is that much conduct which is nominally criminal passes unnoticed and, even if noticed, unprosecuted. This raises the question of what has happened to the Rule of Law and constitutional and sociological questions and happily it is not incumbent on us to deal with these.

Limits of criminal jurisdiction

21.7 *Time.*—At common law a prosecution for an offence can be begun at any time after its commission, but time limits are imposed by statute in the case of certain offences. Apart from those, there is no equivalent in criminal law to the Limitation Acts, which impose general time limits for bringing civil actions. Therefore, a person may be prosecuted for an offence committed by him many years ago and there are several famous instances of prosecutions for murders which were committed twenty or more years before the accused was brought to trial. For certain offences, however, statute expressly provides that a prosecution must be brought within a limited time after their alleged commission. For example, s. 4 of the Perjury Act 1911[1] provides that a prosecution for the making of a false statement in registering a birth or death must be brought within three years. Most important of all, s. 104 of the Magistrates' Courts Act 1952 lays down the general rule, which is subject to relatively few exceptions, that prosecutions for summary offences must be commenced within six months of their commission. This limitation does not apply to indictable offences tried summarily with the consent of the accused or to charges against children and young persons which would be indictable if committed by an adult. If an

1. Paras. 13.4–13.8.

offence is triable either summarily or on indictment at the option of the prosecution[1] it is possible to start proceedings to lead to an indictment even though the period of six months has elapsed.

8 *Territorial.*—As a general rule the jurisdiction of the English criminal courts is confined to offences committed in England and Wales, or the adjacent territorial waters or on a British ship or British controlled aircraft, but there are important exceptions. The extent of British territorial waters for the purposes of criminal law is the subject of technical rules outside the scope of this book, as is the construction of s. 686 and s. 687 of the Merchant Shipping Act 1894 which, in addition to giving statutory effect to the common law rule that English courts have jurisdiction over offences committed on a British ship, deal with the jurisdiction over offences committed by British subjects on foreign ships and offences against the Merchant Shipping Acts.

Unless a statute expressly confers jurisdiction in respect of offences committed abroad, such offences cannot generally be tried by English courts, which exercise criminal jurisdiction on the territorial principle over all offences committed in England, whatever the nationality of the accused may be, and usually do not claim jurisdiction over offences committed abroad, even if they are alleged to have been committed by a British subject resident in England at the time of the trial.

Questions sometimes arise concerning the country in which an offence has been committed, and an offence may be committed in more than one country. Thus, in *Treacy* v. *Director of Public Prosecutions*,[2] the accused was charged with blackmail, i.e. making an unwarranted demand with menaces contrary to s. 21 of the Theft Act 1968. The letter containing the demand was posted in England addressed to a woman in West Germany where it was received. A majority of the House of Lords held that the demand was made in England with the result that the accused could be tried in this country; but the majority were also inclined in favour of the view that, because its consequences would have been felt in England, a demand might likewise have been held to have been made in England, though contained in a letter posted in Germany and received by someone in this country. This view was partly responsible for the decision of the Court of Appeal in *Baxter*[3] according to which someone charged with

1. Para. 23.19.c.
2. [1971] A.C. 537; [1971] 1 All E.R. 110.
3. [1972] Q.B. 1; [1971] 2 All E.R. 359.

having attempted to obtain property by deception by means of faked football pools coupons posted in Northern Ireland and received in Liverpool was held to have been properly tried in that city.

Harden[1] may have to be reconsidered in the light of *Treacy*. The accused was charged with obtaining a cheque by false pretences. The cheque had been posted in Jersey. It was proved that the accused had agreed with a company registered in Jersey that the sending of the cheque in Jersey should complete the transaction and the court held that, as the parties contemplated that the cheque be sent by post, the act of posting the cheque in Jersey, addressed to a place in England, passed the property in the cheque to the accused in Jersey. According to the Court of Criminal Appeal it followed that the cheque was obtained in Jersey which is outside the jurisdiction of the English courts. It is at least arguable that the English courts should have had concurrent jurisdiction because the despatch of the cheque was induced by fraudulent letters posted in England.

In *Millar* (*Contractors*),[2] it was held that the English courts had jurisdiction to entertain an indictment charging the second defendant, a director of the company which was the third defendant, with aiding, abetting, counselling and procuring the first defendant (a lorry driver) to cause death by dangerous driving in England. The allegations against the second and third defendants were that their conduct in Scotland (i.e. causing the first defendant to go on a journey into England with a vehicle which they knew to be defective) made them aiders and abettors of the driver's offence.

The net is large and the mesh is small. In *Markus*[3] the accused was a director of a Panamanian company which printed a prospectus and people in West Germany were induced to subscribe to an investment called Agri-Fund. They were invited to send applications and money to agents of the Panamanian company in London which banked the money in Switzerland. All the acts of the people induced took place in West Germany but their offers to invest were accepted in England. *Ellis*[3] is authority for the proposition that in the case of what is called a result crime in English law, the offence is committed in England and justiciable by an English court if any part of the proscribed result takes

1. [1963] 1 Q.B. 8; [1962] 1 All E.R. 286.
2. [1970] 2 Q.B. 54; [1970] 1 All E.R. 577.
3. [1975] 1 All E.R. 958.
4. [1899] Q.B. 230.

place in England. It was held by the House of Lords that the processing of an investor's application in London on his behalf amounted to a taking part in the arrangements there by him and in this way the investor was induced to take part in such arrangements within the jurisdiction of the English courts.

Exceptions

9 Piracy is an offence by international law and may be tried by the courts of any country, though not committed within its territorial waters. Piracy is roughly armed violence on the high seas, but it now has a detailed definition by virtue of the international convention ratified by the Tokyo Convention Act 1967. By virtue of this statute, piracy may also be committed against aircraft.

The Tokyo Convention Act is now the authority for the proposition that the English courts have jurisdiction over offences committed aboard British controlled aircraft in flight outside the United Kingdom.

Various other statutes give effect to international conventions and provide that the English courts shall have jurisdiction over breaches of the conventions by whomsoever and wheresoever they may be committed. A recent example is the Hijacking Act 1971 punishing with a maximum of life imprisonment the unlawful seizure by force of control of an aircraft while it is in flight, whether or not the aircraft is registered in the United Kingdom. The Protection of Aircraft Act 1973 makes similar provision concerning acts of destroying, damaging or endangering the safety of any aircraft.

A foreigner, as well as a British subject, may be tried for treason committed abroad, provided he owes allegiance to the Crown.[1]

A number of statutes confer jurisdiction on the English courts in respect of specified offences committed abroad by British subjects, including homicide,[2] bigamy,[3] offences against the Official Secrets Acts and, by virtue of s. 31 (a) of the Criminal Justice Act 1948, a British subject employed by the Crown may be tried in England for offences committed in the course of his employment in a foreign country. The above statement with regard to treason and the statutory provisions just mentioned, with the possible exception of s. 31 of the Criminal Justice Act

1. Para. 14.5.
2. Offences against the Person Act 1861, s. 9.
3. *Ibid.*, s. 57.

1948, must be read subject to the provision of s. 3 of the British Nationality Act 1948, which severely limits the criminal jurisdiction of the English courts in respect of offences committed abroad by British subjects who are not also citizens of the United Kingdom and Colonies.

Conspiracy in England to commit a murder abroad is punishable in this country.[1] Under s. 14 of the Theft Act 1968, any person who steals a mailbag or postal packet within the British postal area may be prosecuted in England. The British postal area means the United Kingdom, the Isle of Man and the Channel Islands.

Proposals for reform

21.10 The Law Commission's Working Paper No. 29 raises a number of questions and makes tentative suggestions for reform. Most of these are of a technical nature, concerned for example with territorial waters and offences on British ships. Mention may be made of the proposals that, where any act or omission or any event which constitutes a prescribed element of an offence occurs in England or Wales, that offence shall be deemed to have been committed there, even if other elements of the offence take place outside England and Wales; that, except in cases where the completed offence is not an offence by the local law, an attempt or incitement, wherever it occurs, to commit an offence in England or Wales should constitute an offence against English law; and that, save where the substantive offence is not an offence by the local law, conduct abroad which amounts to counselling and procuring the commission of an offence in England should be an offence against English law. In effect, the second and third proposals confirm the decisions in *Baxter* and *Millar (Contractors), Ltd.* The first proposal would get rid of the decision in *Harden*; it would also give the same answer as did the Criminal Code Commissioners of 1879 to the following questions: "A shot is fired in one place, which wounds a man in another place, who dies in a third place. In which of these places is the crime committed?" The answer was "In each of the three places".

Extradition

21.11 During the last seventy years, this country has entered into extradition treaties with a number of foreign countries under which it is reciprocally provided that offenders who flee from one country to another may, after investigation, be handed back

1. Offences against the Person Act 1861, s. 4. Also see para. 17.9.

to the government of the country in which the offence was committed. Such treaties generally cover the more serious (other than political) offences, and the Fugitive Offenders Act 1967 provides for extradition within the British Commonwealth.

Sovereign and diplomatic immunity

2 The Queen and foreign sovereigns are immune from the criminal as well as the civil jurisdiction of the English courts. Foreign diplomats enjoy a similar privilege but it is that of the government which they represent; therefore it may be waived by or on behalf of the foreign government as it usually is in serious cases[1] but it cannot be waived by an accused person himself unless he does so as an agent and on behalf of the foreign government concerned.[2]

1. *A.B.*, [1941] 1 K.B. 454.
2. *Kanhya Lal Madan*, [1961] 2 Q.B. 1; [1961] 1 All E.R. 588.

22

PROCEEDINGS BEFORE TRIAL

Investigation by police

22.1 It is the function of the police to obtain all possible information regarding offences which have been committed. Although they have no right to detain anyone against his will without making an arrest, they do have the right to question any person regarding the commission of an offence, whether a suspect or not, but, subject to certain statutory exceptions,[1] no one commits an offence merely by refusing to answer. These investigations are mainly governed by the Judges' Rules and administrative directions published with them in 1964.[2] The Judges' Rules were first formulated in 1912; they have not got the force of law, but statements obtained when the Rules have been infringed are liable to be excluded at the trial by the judge in the exercise of his discretion, although there has been no infringement of the strict law governing the admissibility of confessions. According to this law a confession must be rejected unless the prosecution satisfies the judge that it was made voluntarily and the rules of evidence governing voluntariness are very stringent.

22.2 A police investigation is frequently divided into three stages. At the first stage, the police officer has not got evidence affording reasonable grounds for suspecting that the person interrogated has committed an offence. Questioning may continue without any caution being administered, but the person interrogated is generally not obliged to answer and, unless he is arrested, he cannot be obliged to go to a police station or anywhere else.[3] The second stage is reached when the investigating officer has evidence which affords reasonable grounds for suspecting that the person interrogated has committed an offence. A caution worded as follows must be administered: "You are not obliged

---

1. E.g., Official Secrets Act 1920, s. 6; Road Traffic Act 1972, ss. 162 & 165.
2. Home Office Circular, No. 31/1964.
3. *Rice* v. *Connolly*, [1966] 2 Q.B. 414; [1966] 2 All E.R. 649.

to say anything unless you wish to do so but what you say may be put into writing and given in evidence." Questioning may continue (r. II). The third stage is reached when the person interrogated is formally charged,[1] or "informed that he may be prosecuted" (which will occur where and when, in the course of questioning, the police contemplate that a summons may be issued against a suspect who has not been arrested).[2] A further caution must be administered worded as follows: "Do you wish to say anything? You are not obliged to say anything unless you wish to do so but whatever you say may be taken down in writing and may be given in evidence." The Rules are expressly made subject to the principle that, once there is sufficient evidence against a man, he must be charged. Further questioning is only permissible in the most exceptional cases where necessary for the purpose of minimising harm or loss to some other person or to the public, or for clearing up an ambiguity (r. III).

The Rules also contain provisions concerning the recording of statements, and the handing over of a written statement made by one co-accused to another.

There is ground for the belief that the Judges' Rules hamper the police unnecessarily without securing legitimate protection to suspects and it is possible that they will be revised.

Laying the information

3 Criminal proceedings are begun either by an arrest of the person to be charged without a warrant or by laying an information before a magistrate.[3] Any information not on oath may be laid before a magistrates' clerk.[4] Laying an information is the process by which a magistrate is informed of a suspected offence. The informant, who is usually though not always a police officer, may either fill up a form giving a short account of the alleged offence or may give the account orally. The information need not be laid in court and can be laid before a single magistrate at his home or elsewhere. It is not necessary for the information to be on oath or in writing, unless a warrant is required to be issued. Where only a summons is needed, the information may be laid orally and without an oath. The information must contain such particulars as are necessary to give the defendant

1. *Brackenbury*, [1965] 1 All E.R. 960.
2. *Collier and Stenning*, [1965] 3 All E.R. 136.
3. Magistrates' Courts Act 1952, s. 1.
4. Justices' Clerks' Rules 1970.

reasonable information of the nature of the charge.[1] including the statutory provision alleged to have been infringed. Not more than one summary offence may be alleged in each information although several informations may be set out in one document.[2] The time limit of six months imposed by s. 104 of the Magistrates' Courts Act 1952, to which reference has already been made,[3] runs from the date when the matter to which the information refers occurred.

Warrants

22.4 The defendant is brought before the court, unless he is arrested without a warrant, by means of a warrant authorising a police officer to arrest him or by means of a summons addressed to and served upon him. Warrants may also authorise the searching of premises for various purposes.[4] A warrant signed by the magistrate issuing it is directed to all the police officers of the police area. An arrest warrant must state shortly the offence on which it is founded and name or otherwise describe the offender and order the officers to arrest the offender and bring him before the magistrates. The warrant remains in force until it is executed or withdrawn.[5] It is not necessary that the officer who arrests the suspect should have the warrant in his possession at the time of the arrest, but the person arrested may demand to see it and it must be shown to him as soon as practicable after his arrest.[6] The warrant may be endorsed with a direction that the person to be arrested shall on arrest be released on bail, with or without sureties, on such recognisances as may be specified in the endorsement. This is known as "backing for bail".[7] Section 24 of the Criminal Justice Act 1967 provides that a warrant must not be issued in the first instance unless the offence to which it relates is either indictable or punishable with imprisonment or the address of the defendant is not sufficiently established for a summons to be served on him.

---

1. Magistrates' Courts Rules 1968, r. 83 (1) and (2) as amended; S.I. 1968 No. 1920.
2. *Ibid.*, r. 12; *Hargreaves* v. *Alderson*, [1964] 2 Q.B. 159; [1962] 3 All E.R. 1019.
3. Para. 21.7.
4. Para. 22.6.
5. Magistrates' Courts Act 1952, s. 102.
6. *Ibid.* Cf. *Purdy*, [1975] Q.B. 288; [1974] 3 All E.R. 465 (warrant must be in officer's possession in case of arrest for non-payment of fine).
7. *Ibid.*, s. 93.

Summons

5 A summons is issued and signed by a magistrate and is addressed to the offender. It must state shortly the offence or offences alleged together with such reasonable particulars as to enable the accused to know what facts are alleged to constitute the offence, and must require the offender to appear at a certain time and place before the magistrates. More than one offence may now be included in one summons provided that each offence is separately stated.[1]

The summons must be served on the alleged offender:

a. personally; or
b. by leaving it for him with some person at his last known or usual place of abode; or
c. by sending it by post in a registered letter or by recorded delivery service at his last known or usual place of abode.

If the accused is summoned for a summary offence for which there is no right to trial by jury and fails to appear, any of the above methods of service is sufficient and the trial can proceed in his absence. If the offence is one which can be tried on indictment, service must have been personal unless it is proved that the summons came to the knowledge of the accused; such proof may be constituted by a letter or other communication. Service on a corporation is effected by sending it to the registered office.

If the court requires the personal attendance of the accused, and in some cases this is necessary, it may issue a warrant in default of appearance provided that the conditions mentioned in para. 22.4 are satisfied.

Search

6 At common law a search warrant could be issued only in respect of stolen goods but now search warrants may be issued by the magistrates under a great number of statutes which specify the manner in which application shall be made for them and who may apply. Police officers are the normal recipients of the power to search, but certain officials, such as customs officers, are given statutory authorisation in particular circumstances. In some instances a warrant may be granted by specified officers. For example under s. 26 (2) of the Theft Act 1968 a police officer not below the rank of superintendent may grant a warrant where the occupant of the premises has a specified criminal record. The police have powers to search persons and

1. Magistrates' Courts Rules 1968, r. 81 (3).

vehicles without warrant in the case of firearms and dangerous drugs provided they believe on reasonable grounds that the person searched is in possession of these things or that the vehicle contains them.[1] When premises have been entered under a search warrant, the police officer executing the warrant may seize not only the goods which he reasonably believes to be included in the warrant, but also any other goods which he reasonably believes to be likely to constitute material evidence of any offence committed by the occupant of the premises or someone associated with him.[2] There is a common law power to search a person at the time of his arrest, and to retain any goods found in consequence of that search or of a search of the premises on which the arrest was effected, provided that the goods are likely to constitute evidence at the trial of the arrested person or of any other person, or are reasonably considered as weapons of attack or articles which might assist in escape.[3] Where no arrest is effected, and premises are searched without a warrant, goods may be seized only if they are reasonably believed to be the fruit of serious crime, or the instrument with which such crime was committed or to be likely to constitute material evidence of it and it is reasonably believed that the person in possession of them either committed the crime or was implicated in it.[4] Unlawful search and seizure do not result in the inadmissibility of the evidence obtained, subject to the trial judge's discretion to exclude it,[5] but they may result in civil or criminal liability on the part of the searcher.

Arrest without warrant

22.7 Section 2 of the Criminal Law Act 1967 provides powers of arrest in relation to "arrestable offences" which are divided into two groups.

a. Offences for which the sentence is fixed by law or for which a person (not previously convicted) may under or by virtue of any enactment be sentenced to imprisonment for a term of five years, and attempts to commit any such offence.[6] The sentences for treason (death) and murder (life imprisonment) are fixed by law. In other cases maximum terms of imprisonment are generally prescribed by statute although the

1. Firearms Act 1968 s. 47; Misuse of Drugs Act 1971, s. 23.
2. *Elias* v. *Pasmore*, [1934] 2 K.B. 164.
3. Stephens, Search and Seizure of Chattels, [1970] Crim. L. R. 74, 139.
4. *Ghani* v. *Jones*, [1970] 1 Q.B. 693; [1969] 3 All E.R. 1700.
5. *Kuruma* v. *R.*, [1955] A.C. 197; [1955] 1 All E.R. 236. See Haydon, Illegally Obtained Evidence, [1973] Crim. L. R. 603, 697.
6. Criminal Law Act 1967, s. 2 (1).

judge has a discretion whether to impose the maximum and does so only in the worst cases. Most serious offences are punishable with five years' imprisonment or more. For example, manslaughter (life), theft (ten years) and unlawful wounding (five years') are all arrestable offences along with many others. Some common law misdemeanours, e.g. conspiracy and public nuisance, are punishable at the discretion of the court up to imprisonment for life, but they are not arrestable offences because they are not punishable "under or by virtue of any enactment". Although there are some anomalies in the maxima for several offences, the distinction between arrestable offences and other offences does bear some relation to the seriousness of the offence and is therefore to be preferred to the former distinction between felonies and misdemeanours.

Any person may arrest without warrant anyone who is, or whom he, with reasonable cause, suspects to be in the act of committing an arrestable offence. Where an arrestable offence has been committed, any person may arrest without warrant anyone who is, or whom he with reasonable cause suspects to be, guilty of the offence. Where a police officer with reasonable cause suspects that an arrestable offence has been, is being, or is about to be committed, he may arrest without warrant anyone whom he with reasonable cause suspects to be guilty of committing or about to commit that offence.

To effect an arrest under these powers a police officer may enter, if need be by force, and search any place where the person to be arrested is, or is with reasonable cause suspected by the officer to be.[1] An important distinction, based on the common law,[2] between the powers of a police officer and a private individual to arrest without warrant is that an arrest on reasonable suspicion is permissible in the case of the officer, even though the offence has not been committed, whereas to justify an arrest on reasonable suspicion in the case of a private individual it is essential that the offence should actually have been committed, though not necessarily by the person arrested.

b. Offences deemed by statute to be arrestable offences.

A statute sometimes declares an offence to be an arrestable offence although the maximum punishment is less than five years', such as the offence of taking a conveyance without authority.[3]

1. *Ibid.*, s. 2 (6). 2. *Walters* v. *W. H. Smith & Son, Ltd.*, [1914] 1 K.B. 595.
3. Theft Act 1968, s. 12 (3).

22.8 Some serious offences, as well as a very large number of less serious ones, being punishable with less than five years' imprisonment, are not arrestable offences, such as indecent assault on a female and cruelty to children (two years'), but sometimes statute gives a police officer power to arrest without warrant on specified conditions a person found committing a particular offence. Such a power of arrest is provided for some offences, such as the unlawful possession of an offensive weapon in a public place,[1] by their governing statutes, and in addition such a power is provided for a wide range of petty offences by local Acts and bye-laws. Such provisions do not make the offence an arrestable offence in its technical sense and the powers of arrest are more limited than for an arrestable offence.

For instance, any person who, having been sentenced to imprisonment, or Borstal training, or ordered to be detained in a detention centre, or having been committed to a remand centre, is "unlawfully at large" may be arrested by a police officer without a warrant.[2] In addition, any person may arrest without warrant a person found committing an indictable offence by night and a police officer may arrest a person found loitering whom he reasonably suspects of having committed or being about to commit offences under a variety of statutes. If a statute gives power to police officers to arrest without warrant in certain conditions, these conditions must be strictly fulfilled.[3]

Arrest

22.9 An arrest occurs when the arrester states in terms that he is arresting or when he uses force to restrain the individual concerned.[4] Unless authorised by the Criminal Law Act or other statute, an arrest without warrant is unlawful and may be the basis for proceedings for false imprisonment at the suit of the person arrested. However, even if the circumstances are such that an arrest may lawfully be made without a warrant, it is nevertheless generally unlawful if the person arrested is not informed of its grounds unless the circumstances are such that the person arrested knows.[5] Even if the original arrest is unlawful because the arrested person is not so informed, it becomes lawful

---

1. Prevention of Crime Act 1953, s. 1 (3).
2. Prison Act 1952, s. 49; para. 21.7.
3. *Dumbell* v. *Roberts*, [1944] 1 All E.R. 326.
4. *Hussein* v. *Chong Fook Kam*, [1970] A.C. 942, at p. 947, *per* Lord Devlin.
5. *Christie* v. *Leachinsky*, [1947] A.C. 573, at pp. 586–587; [1947] 1 All E.R. 567, at pp. 572–573.

as soon as he is.[1] It is enough that the arresting officer has done everything that a reasonable person would do if, for example, the person arrested is deaf or cannot speak English.[2] An arrest by the use of force is unlawful if the force is unreasonable in the circumstances.[3]

Committal proceedings

A person who is summoned or arrested for an offence and who is to be tried on indictment by a jury must, subject to rare exceptions,[4] appear before a magistrate or magistrates whose duty is not to try the case but to decide whether there is enough evidence on which a reasonable jury if properly directed could find him guilty and, if so, to commit him for trial to the Crown Court. These are committal proceedings and the magistrates who conduct them are called examining or committing magistrates or justices.[5] When a person accused of an offence which can be tried on indictment comes before a magistrates' court, the procedure differs according to whether the offence is indictable but can be tried summarily with his consent, or whether it must be tried on indictment, or whether the offence is summary but the accused has the right to claim trial by jury.[6] Whichever category the offence is in, if the magistrates' court is not going to deal with it summarily, the accused is told what he is charged with but is not asked to plead. The court has two courses open to it depending on the circumstances:

a. If the prosecution informs the court that:
   i. all the evidence consists of written statements which have been served on the accused;
   ii. the accused is (or all are) legally represented;
   iii. none of the defending advocates objects to the use of the written statements or requests the court to consider a submission that the written statements disclose insufficient evidence to commit the accused for trial; and
   iv. the accused does not wish to give evidence

   the court may, though it is not obliged to, commit the accused for trial without looking at the statements. The safeguard for the accused is that this procedure cannot be used unless he is legally represented and he can object without giv-

1. *Kulynycz*, [1971] 1 Q.B. 367; [1970] 3 All E.R. 881.
2. *Wheatley* v. *Lodge*, [1971] 1 All E.R. 173.
3. Criminal Law Act 1967, s. 3.
4. Paras. 22.13 and 23.4.
5. Magistrates' Courts Act 1952, ss. 4–8.
6. See Appendix.

ing reasons to any of the evidence being given by means of a written statement and it is assumed that his advocate will advise him on his proper course. This procedure is called committal without consideration of the evidence and cannot take place without written statements.[1]

b. If the foregoing procedure is not used, the prosecuting advocate opens his case by giving a summary of the facts and then calls the witnesses for the prosecution one by one; they are examined in chief and may be cross examined by the accused or his advocate and then re-examined. The whole of the evidence of each witness must be taken down as nearly as possible in his own words and read over to and signed by him; this becomes his deposition and the statements are collectively known as the depositions. This procedure is time consuming but, even if it is not possible to use the procedure of committal without consideration of the evidence, it is still possible to shorten the proceedings by using s. 2 of the Criminal Justice Act 1967 which enables written statements to be used instead of oral evidence on certain conditions. In practice they are read aloud or summarised. The statements take the place of depositions and the makers may be ordered by the committing magistrates to attend the trial conditionally or unconditionally just like a witness who has given oral evidence in the proceedings.

When all the evidence for the prosecution has been given the court must consider whether a *prima facie* case has been made out. The defendant's counsel or solicitor may submit that there is no case for his client to answer. If the court decides that there is a case to answer the charge must be written down if this has not already been done and read to the accused and its nature explained in ordinary language; he must be asked whether he has anything to say, and if he is not represented, he must be told that he need not say anything and that he has the right to give evidence and call witnesses.[2]

Whatever the accused may say in answer to the charge must be taken down, unless it amounts to an oration,[3] read over to him and (if the accused wishes) signed by him and transmitted to the court of trial with the depositions or written statements or both. The court must also give the accused a warning about any possible alibi; this must also be

1. Criminal Justice Act 1967, s. 1 and Magistrates' Courts Rules 1968, r. 3.
2. See Appendix.
3. *Morry*, [1946] K.B. 153; [1945] 2 All E.R. 632.

done in the procedure outlined in a.[1] Usually the accused says nothing and reserves his defence until the trial.

1 Whichever method of committal is used in committing the accused for trial at the Crown Court, the magistrates must specify the place at which he is to be tried and in selecting that place must have regard to the convenience of the defence, the prosecution and the witnesses, expediting the trial and to directions given under the Courts Act 1971 relating to the cases or classes of cases suitable for allocation to a judge of the High Court and to a Circuit judge or Recorder.

All the depositions and written statements, together with the statement of the accused and other papers, must be sent to the Crown Court. Copies of the written information, of the depositions and of the list of witnesses[2] must be supplied to the accused on his application and are usually sent to him or his solicitor as a matter of course. The procedure where a corporation is charged with an indictable offence is slightly different.

Reporting

2 The Criminal Justice Act 1967 contains stringent restrictions on the publication of reports of committal proceedings. Under s. 3, the general rule is that only purely nominal matters such as the identity of the court and magistrates, the names of the parties and the nature of the charges may be published in a written report or broadcast. There are two exceptions: reporting must be authorised by an order of the magistrates on the application of the accused or any of the accused if more than one, and reporting is permitted after the magistrates have decided not to commit, or after the trial where there has been a committal, or after the magistrates have decided to deal with the case summarily.

Coroners

3 The coroner is an officer whose duty it is to hold inquests into death where there is reasonable cause to believe that the deceased died either a violent or unnatural death, or has died a sudden death the cause of which is unknown, or has died in prison. The coroner's court is not a criminal court. The procedure is inquisitorial and no one has the right to be heard. In some cases the coroner must sit with a jury.

The findings take the form of an inquisition, and when a

1. Para. 23.12.
2. Magistrates' Courts Rules 1968, r. 10.

coroner's jury makes an inquisition which charges murder, manslaughter or infanticide against a named person, the coroner must issue a warrant for the arrest or detention of such person and may commit him for trial before the Crown Court.[1] In this way a person may be committed for trial without the necessity of appearing before the examining magistrates, although this is rare, but if it does occur the person concerned is tried before the Crown Court upon the inquisition (which is equivalent to an indictment) without an indictment being preferred. The law relating to coroners' inquisitions has given rise to public disquiet and the government proposes to introduce a Bill to prevent an inquisition charging an offence of homicide against a named person and to abolish the coroner's duty to commit that person for trial.[2]

Bail[3]

22.14 Examining magistrates have the power to grant bail to all persons aged 17 or over who are committed for trial for any offence except treason.[4] It is very unusual to grant bail in murder cases. Those who are not granted bail by examining magistrates may re-apply[5] or apply either to the Crown Court[6] or to a judge of the High Court in chambers.[7]

The only case in which examining magistrates are required to grant bail is specified in s. 18 (3) of the Criminal Justice Act 1967 which provides that where a person is charged with a summary offence which is to be tried by a jury the court must grant bail if the committal proceedings are adjourned or he is committed for trial unless he is unable to provide proper recognisances or sureties or unless certain other conditions are fulfilled, such as the fact that he is charged with other offences, punishable with six months' imprisonment and he has previously been sentenced to imprisonment or borstal training. A defendant who is granted bail is required to submit to the condition that, if he fails to appear to stand his trial or at an adjourned hearing as the case may be, he will be liable to forfeit a stated sum of money.

1. Coroners Act 1887, ss. 3 and 5, as amended by the Coroners (Amendment) Act 1926 and Courts Act 1971, Sch. 8 para. 15 and Sch. 11.
2. *The Times*, 24 July 1975 and 7 August 1975.
3. Zander, Bail: a Re-appraisal, [1967] Crim. L. R. 25, 100, 128.
4. Magistrates' Courts Act 1952, s. 8; para. 21.7.
5. *Ibid.*, s. 7 (3).
6. Courts Act 1971 s. 13 and Crown Court Rules, rr. 17 and 18.
7. Criminal Justice Act 1967, s. 22.

This is called entering into a recognisance. A further condition may be that other persons, known as sureties, are required to enter into recognisances which may be forfeited if the defendant does not appear. No actual deposit of money or security is, or may be,[1] required. The technical name for the forfeiture of a recognisance is "estreating".

The principal test to be applied by the magistrates when considering whether to admit an accused person to bail is whether he will appear to stand his trial but they should also refuse bail if the accused is charged with a serious offence such as burglary and does not dispute his guilt, and it appears probable that the offence will be repeated if he is released,[2] or if it seems probable that there will be interference with witnesses. Section 21 of the Criminal Justice Act 1967 provides that the conditions on which bail is granted may include conditions appearing to the court to be likely to result in the appearance of the accused at the time and place required, such as reporting to the police at stated intervals, or to be necessary in the interests of justice or for the prevention of crime.

If the examining magistrates refuse bail they must inform the accused of his right to apply to a judge of the High Court unless the accused is legally represented. The court must also tell him the reason for the refusal in any event if he is not represented and, if he is represented, upon request. The Crown Court may admit to bail any person who has been committed in custody for appearance before it.[3] At least twenty-four hours' notice in writing must normally be given to the prosecution and to the Crown Court office. The application is made to a judge of the Crown Court in chambers.[4]

A person who is released on bail and fails to appear in court may be arrested on a warrant.[5] A police officer may arrest without a warrant a person who has been admitted to bail if the police officer has reasonable grounds for believing that that person has broken, is breaking or will break any condition of his bail.[6]

---

1. *Harrow Justices, Ex parte Morris*, [1973] 1 Q.B. 672; [1972] 3 All E.R. 494.
2. *Phillips* (1947), 32 Cr. App. Rep. 47.
3. Courts Act 1971, s. 13.
4. Crown Court Rules, rr. 17, 18 and 22.
5. Magistrates' Courts Act 1952, s. 97 and Courts Act 1971, s. 13.
6. Criminal Justice Act 1967, s. 23; para. 21.7.

Legal aid[1]

22.16 At each stage of criminal proceedings an accused person whose means are such that he cannot afford immediate legal representation may be granted legal aid out of public funds if it appears to the appropriate court to be desirable in the interests of justice to grant it.

The only cases in which legal aid must be granted are either where a person is committed for trial on a charge of murder or where the prosecutor appeals or applies for leave to appeal from the Court of Appeal or the Courts-Martial Appeal Court to the House of Lords. In all other cases the decision lies within the discretion of the court to which application is made, provided that if there is any doubt about whether legal aid should be granted or not the doubt must be resolved in favour of the accused.

Legal aid normally consists of representation by solicitor and counsel and includes advice on the preparation of the case, but this is subject to limitations and extensions in particular circumstances. For example, a person who is granted legal aid in a magistrates' court, whether for a summary trial or for committal proceedings, normally has a solicitor only; a person who is granted legal aid for a trial in the Crown Court may, if he is convicted, receive advice on whether there are grounds for an appeal and, if so, assistance in the preparation of an application for leave to appeal or in giving notice of appeal.

A person to whom legal aid is granted is liable to make such contribution as the court may order in respect of the costs incurred on his behalf as appears to the court to be reasonable having regard to his resources and commitments and sometimes he may be liable for the whole cost. Payment may be ordered to be made in one sum or by instalments. Most applications must be made to the court before which the proceedings are pending or in progress, although in some cases there is a choice; the regulations made under the Act prescribe the forms which are to be used both for the purpose of applying for legal aid and also for making statements of means; it is always possible for an application to be made orally to the court although the grant is subject to receipt of a written statement of means.[2]

Dock briefs

22.17 In a very small and dwindling number of cases it is still possible as a last resort for a person charged with a criminal offence

1. Legal Aid Act 1974, ss. 28–40.

2. Legal Aid Rules, r. 1 (3).

on indictment to ask for a dock brief; if his request is granted the accused may choose any barrister who is present and robed in court who is bound to act for him at the request of the judge on payment of a small fee which may be waived. This ancient practice is based on custom and has been rendered mostly obsolete by statutory legal aid.

23

TRIAL

Trial on indictment

23.1 An indictment is a written accusation of crime to be tried by a jury. A bill of indictment charging any person with an indictable offence may be preferred before the Crown Court, and where a bill of indictment has been preferred, the proper officer of the court must sign the bill whereupon it becomes an indictment.

As soon as the clerk at the Crown Court receives from the clerk to the magistrates the depositions, recognisances, list of exhibits and such exhibits as can be conveniently sent and other documents, he proceeds to draft the indictment, or to refer it to counsel for the prosecution.

The indictment must be in the form in Schedule 1 to the Indictment Rules 1971,[1] or in a form substantially to the like effect. Specimens of the forms which are used in practice are shown on pp. 426–427. The prosecution and the accused may inspect the indictment, or the draft indictment if the indictment has not been signed.

23.2 In accordance with the Indictments Act 1915 and the Indictment Rules 1971 referred to above, an indictment is divided into three parts—the commencement, the statement of the offence and the particulars of the offence. The commencement consists of the name of the case, the court of trial and a statement that the defendant is charged with the offence or offences which follow.

The statement of offence must describe the specific offence shortly, together with such particulars as may be necessary for giving reasonable information as to the nature of the charge.[2] If the offence is one created by or under an enactment, the statement of offence must contain a reference to the section of, or the paragraph of the schedule to, the Act creating the offence,

1. S.I. 1971 No. 1253 (L. 31), r. 4 (1).
2. *Ibid.*, r. 5 (1).

and if the offence is one created by subordinate legislation the statement must specify the relevant provision of the statutory instrument or other subordinate legislation.

The particulars of offence must disclose the essential elements of the offence such as the date on which it is alleged to have been committed and a description of the goods alleged to have been stolen or of the injuries caused as the case may be, but the omission of an essential element does not matter if the accused is not prejudiced or embarrassed in his defence by the failure to disclose it.

3 If the alleged offence is one to which the relevant statute provides a defence, by way of exception, exemption, proviso, excuse or qualification, it is not necessary for any of these to be specified or negatived either in the statement or particulars.[1]

If it is necessary to describe a person whose name is not known, such as the owner of goods or a fellow conspirator, it is enough to describe him as a person unknown.[2]

Where more than one offence is charged in an indictment, the statement and particulars of each offence must be set out in a separate paragraph called a count.

Where more than one person are charged with being engaged in the commission of an offence it is permissible for them to be jointly indicted and the usual course is for this to be done.[3] An application may be made by any one or more of them for a separate trial, and it lies within the discretion of the judge to order a separate trial where the interests of justice demand it.

4 Although the normal practice is for an accused person to be committed for trial by examining magistrates, it is possible to dispense with this requirement and to apply to a judge of the High Court in chambers for a voluntary bill of indictment. This may be necessary where magistrates have refused to commit for trial or where it is desired to add further charges and join other persons to an indictment already in existence so that all may be tried together.[4] An indictment may also be preferred by the Court of Appeal, where it orders a fresh trial,[5] or by the order

1. *Ibid.*, r. 6.
2. *Ibid.*, r. 8.
3. *Assim*, [1966] 2 Q.B. 249; [1966] 2 All E.R. 881.
4. Administration of Justice (Miscellaneous Provisions) Act 1933, s. 2; Indictments (Procedures) Rules 1971, rr. 4–9, S.I. 1971 No. 2084.
5. Criminal Appeal Act 1968, s. 8.

SPECIMEN INDICTMENTS

These specimens are based on indictments which have been preferred in the Crown Court but the facts referred to in them are fictitious.

INDICTMENT

No. 1

THE CROWN COURT at BARCHESTER

THE QUEEN v. T.P.

T.P. is
charged as follows:—
Statement of Offence: Murder
Particulars of Offence: T.P. on the 24th day of January 1975 murdered O.S.

GEORGE WALKER
Officer of the Crown Court
21 March 1975

INDICTMENT

No. 2

THE CROWN COURT at BARCHESTER

THE QUEEN v. F.A.

F.A. is
charged as follows:—

Count 1 *Statement of Offence:* Wounding with intent, contrary to Section 18 of the Offences against the Person Act, 1861.

Particulars of Offence: F.A. on the 18th day of December 1974 wounded C.D. with intent to do him grievous bodily harm.

Count 2 *Statement of Offence:* Wounding, contrary to Section 20 of the Offences against the Person Act, 1861.

Particulars of Offence: F.A. on the 18th day of December 1974 unlawfully and maliciously wounded C.D.

GEORGE WALKER
Officer of the Crown Court
21 March 1975

INDICTMENT

No. 3

THE CROWN COURT at BARCHESTER

THE QUEEN v. D.B., F.M. and G.D.

D.B., F.M. and G.D. are charged as follows:—

Count 1 *Statement of Offence:* Burglary, contrary to Section 9(1)(*b*) of the Theft Act 1968.

Particulars of Offence: D.B., F.M. and G.D. on the 19th day of January 1975 having entered as trespassers a building known as 49 Trollope Close, Barchester, stole therein one record player, fourteen records and approximately seven feet of electric flex.

Count 2 *Statement of Offence:* Damaging property, contrary to Section 1(1) of the Criminal Damage Act, 1971.

Particulars of Offence: D.B., F.M. and G.D. on the 19th day of January 1975 without lawful excuse damaged a dwelling-house, the property of the District Council of Barchester, intending to damage such property or being reckless as to whether such property would be damaged.

GEORGE WALKER
Officer of the Crown Court
21 March 1975

of the judge trying a case where it appears that a witness has committed perjury.[1]

Arraignment

23.5 After the indictment has been signed, and provided that there has been no successful motion to quash it, the next step in the trial is the arraignment of the accused which means that he is called to the bar (i.e. the front of the dock) by name, and after each count of the indictment has been read out, asked by the clerk of the court whether he pleads guilty or not guilty.

23.6 At this stage the question of whether the accused is unfit to plead, discussed earlier[2], should be considered. Where the accused has been committed in custody for trial, the Home Secretary may order his detention in a mental hospital without trial. The Home Secretary can only make such an order if he is satisfied by medical reports that the accused is suffering from mental illness or severe sub-normality which warrants his detention in a mental hospital for treatment.[3] This seemingly wide power to detain without trial is used on average less than once a year, since the Home Secretary exercises it only when it would be a scandal or an inhumanity to bring the accused to court.[4]

When the accused is arraigned he may be found unfit to stand trial, or as it is often put, "unfit to plead", in which case he will be detained during the Queen's pleasure pending his recovery.[5] It is possible in theory for him to be tried after recovery, but this is never done in practice. The issue of fitness to stand trial may be raised by the defence, the prosecution or the judge.[6] A jury is then empanelled to decide on the evidence, which of course is largely medical, whether the accused is capable of understanding the course of the proceedings so as to make a proper defence, of challenging a juror to whom he might wish to object, and of understanding the details of the evidence.[7] However, an attack of hysterical amnesia rendering it impossible for the accused to remember what happened at the time of the

1. Perjury Act 1911, s. 9.
2. Para. 5.16.
3. Mental Health Act 1959, s. 73.
4. Royal Commission on Capital Punishment, Cmd. 8932, para. 219.
5. Prevezer, Fitness to Plead and the Criminal Lunatics Act 1800, [1958] Crim. L. R. 144.
6. *MacCarthy*, [1967] 1 Q.B. 68; [1966] 1 All E.R. 447.
7. *Pritchard* (1836), 7 C. & F. 303.

events in respect of which he is charged has been held not to make him unfit to stand trial.[1]

Where the accused has raised the issue of unfitness to be tried he has the burden of proving this, although he only has to satisfy the jury of his unfitness on the balance of probability.[2] However, if the issue is raised by the prosecution or, presumably, by the judge it must be established by the prosecution beyond reasonable doubt.[3]

.7 Where the issue of fitness to stand trial is raised the procedure is governed by s. 4 of the Criminal Procedure (Insanity) Act 1964. Normally the question must be determined as it is raised, i.e. before the trial itself. However, to prevent the accused being found unfit and deprived of his right to trial where he may be entitled to acquittal of the offence charged, s. 4 (2) provides that the judge has a discretion to postpone the question of fitness to be tried until the opening of the case for the defence, where he considers it expedient to do so and in the interests of the accused. In applying this provision the judge should consider the strength or weakness of the prosecution case as disclosed in the depositions or statements as the case may be and the nature and degree of the suggested disability; he should then ask himself whether postponement is expedient and in the accused's interest.[4] The prosecution case may be so strong and the accused's condition so disabling that postponement of the trial would be wholly inexpedient. Conversely, the prosecution case may be so thin that whatever the degree of disability it clearly would be expedient to postpone.[5] If there is a reasonable chance that the prosecution case will be successfully challenged, postponement will usually be in the accused's interests.[6] If the issue of fitness to be tried is postponed and the prosecution evidence is insufficient to convict, the jury will be directed to acquit the accused and the issue of fitness is not determined. If there is sufficient evidence to convict, the postponed issue of fitness will be determined before the defence case is opened. Generally the issue of fitness to be tried and the criminal charge (if the trial proceeds) are determined by separate juries. There is a right of appeal against a finding of unfitness to stand trial. For the accused the possibility of being

1. *Podola*, [1960] 1 Q.B. 325; [1959] 3 All E.R. 418.
2. *Ibid.*
3. *Robertson*, [1968] 3 All E.R. 557.
4. *Burles*, [1970] 2 Q.B. 191; [1970] 1 All E.R. 642.
5. *Ibid.*
6. *Webb*, [1969] 2 Q.B. 278; [1969] 2 All E.R. 626.

found unfit to stand trial is a mixed blessing since he is sent indeterminately to a mental hospital without being tried for or convicted of an offence. On the other hand, it would be wasteful and inhumane to try a person who is incapable of standing trial. On balance the argument is in favour of the present procedure, even though, if the issue is raised by the prosecution or the judge, the accused may be detained indeterminately against his will, without having been convicted of an offence. In 1974, 32 persons were found unfit to stand trial.[1]

23.8 In answer to the clerk's question the accused may plead "guilty" or "not guilty" or enter a special plea. If he admits the truth of the charge, he pleads guilty. In this event, the court hears a statement of the circumstances of the offence and evidence of his character and circumstances.

The following reports on the offender may be provided for the court.

a. A police officer gives an account of the previous convictions and general character of the offender which are called "the antecedents". In doing so, the officer should confine himself to such facts as are admitted by the defence or which can be strictly proved.[2] A proof of evidence is prepared containing a factual statement of the previous convictions, particulars of age, education and employment, the date of arrest, whether the offender has been on bail and, if previously convicted, the date of his last discharge from prison if known. It may also contain a short and concise statement of the offender's domestic and family circumstances, his general reputation and associates and, if it is to be said that he associates with bad characters, the officer giving evidence must be able to speak of this from his own knowledge.
b. There may be a report from the governor of the prison where the offender has been awaiting trial.
c. Medical or psychiatric reports may have been prepared between conviction and sentence on the direction of the judge, the offender having been detained in custody or on bail according to the judge's order.
d. There may be a social inquiry report, often prepared before trial with the consent of the offender, by a probation officer.

---

1. *Criminal Statistics*, 1974, Cmnd. 6168. For proposals for reform see the Report of the Butler Committee on Mentally Abnormal Offenders, Cmnd. 6244.
2. *Van Pelz*, [1943] K.B. 157; [1943] 1 All E.R. 36.

> Such a report may be required by the judge in any case, and it is normally essential for juvenile offenders.[1] The Home Secretary may make rules requiring the court to consider a social inquiry report before passing sentence in specified cases,[2] but the Home Secretary has so far preferred to deal with the matter by means of recommendations contained in Home Office circulars. At present (October 1975) the relevant circulars are No. 28, 1971, applying to Magistrates' Courts and No. 29 applying to the Crown Court. They recommend that a social inquiry report should be considered in all cases in which the offender is aged seventeen or more before he is sent to a detention centre or Borstal, and before he is sentenced to imprisonment for two years or less (including a suspended sentence) when he has not previously been sentenced to imprisonment or Borstal training. The circulars also provide that social inquiry reports should be considered before a woman is sentenced to imprisonment, whatever the circumstances may be.

These reports are followed possibly by witnesses as to character on behalf of the offender, the court then hears the offender or his counsel in mitigation and proceeds to sentence him.

3.9 If the accused denies the charge, he pleads not guilty, and the case proceeds.

The accused is not limited to pleading guilty or not guilty. If he has already been tried for the same offence and convicted or acquitted, he may plead "*autrefois convict*" or "*autrefois acquit*", as the case may be. These pleas are available only if the accused has previously been in peril on a charge for the same or practically the same offence, and he must show that on a former occasion there had been a verdict delivered by the jury.[3]

An accused person is not in peril merely because he appears before examining magistrates. If they find that there is no *prima facie* case, this is no bar to his being brought up on a subsequent occasion.

He may plead not guilty of the offence specifically charged in the indictment but guilty of another offence of which he might be found guilty on that indictment. If he refuses to plead

---

1. Children and Young Persons Act 1969, s. 9, as modified by Children and Young Persons Act 1969 (Transitional Modifications of Part I) Order 1970, S.I. 1970 No. 1882.
2. Powers of Criminal Courts Act 1973, s. 45.
3. *Robinson*, [1975] Q.B. 508; [1975] 1 All E.R. 360.

or will not answer directly to the indictment, the court may order a plea of not guilty to be entered on his behalf.

The jury

23.10 If the accused pleads not guilty, jurors are called from the panel, which is the name given to the list of persons summoned to serve as jurors.

A person is eligible for jury service if he or she is between the ages of 18 and 65, is included on the electoral register for parliamentary and local government elections, and has been resident in the United Kingdom, the Channel Islands or the Isle of Man for any period of at least five years since the age of 13.[1] There are certain exceptions. Some persons are ineligible for jury service, including judges, barristers and solicitors, police officers, clergymen and the mentally ill. Certain ex-prisoners are disqualified and persons such as peers, soldiers and doctors are excusable as of right.[2] The ineligibility of those associated with the administration of justice continues after they have ceased to be occupied as such but, except in the case of judges and certain others, only for ten years.[3]

The Lord Chancellor is responsible for summoning jurors in the Crown Court, and the officer who actually summons jurors is the chief clerk at each location of the Crown Court.[4] Although there is no legal restriction on the places in England and Wales at which a person may be required to attend or serve as a juror, the Lord Chancellor and his officials must have regard to the convenience of the persons summoned, to where they live and in particular to the desirability of selecting jurors living within daily travelling distance of the place of trial.[5]

23.11 As the name of each juror is called, the accused has the opportunity to challenge. Not more than seven jurors may be challenged without cause.[6] This is called peremptory challenge. There is also a right of challenge for cause, and this may be in respect of the whole jury ("to the array") which is virtually unknown, or be confined to an individual or individuals ("to the polls"). The prosecution has the right to challenge without cause to an unlimited extent by saying "Stand by for the Crown".

---

1. Juries Act 1974, ss. 1 and 3.
2. *Ibid.*, Sch. 1.
3. *Ibid.*, s. 2 (1).
4. Para. 20.4.
5. Juries Act 1974, s. 2 (2) and (3).
6. *Ibid.*, s. 12 (1).

These jurors stand by and can be called upon again if the panel is exhausted, whereupon the prosecution must show cause. A challenge for cause of an individual juror may be on the ground that he is an alien or under 18 though by mistake his name has been put on the jurors' books. A more frequent cause is that the juror is related to the accused or may be suspected of being prejudiced for some reason either in his favour or against him. Any challenge for cause is tried by the judge.[1]

Provided that there is no successful challenge, each member of the jury is sworn or affirms individually, and the accused is then given in charge to the jury. If after this he wishes to change his plea to one of guilty, the verdict of the jury must be taken. If a juror dies or becomes ill the trial may continue as long as the number of the jury is not reduced below nine but this does not apply to trials for murder unless the prosecution and the accused assent in writing; in any event the court may discharge the entire jury if one or more of them dies or becomes ill.[2]

The conduct of the case

12 As soon as the accused has been given in charge to the jury, counsel for the prosecution makes his opening speech. The witnesses for the prosecution are then each called, examined in chief, cross-examined and re-examined. In trials on indictment, it is almost an invariable rule for counsel to be briefed for the prosecution, although in certain locations of the Crown Court or for certain purposes solicitors have a right of audience.[3] A prosecutor who appears personally has no right to make a speech, but is confined to giving evidence if he is a material witness. It is a tradition of the bar that counsel for the prosecution should conduct his case moderately, stating the facts as objectively as possible, and he must confine himself to matters which he intends to prove. If the defence has informed him that it is intended to dispute the admissibility of certain evidence, it is his duty not to refer to that evidence in his opening speech, in order that there shall be no disclosure to the jury of matters which it may not be possible to prove.[4] After this opening speech is concluded, each witness is called.

At the end of the case for the prosecution, the accused, or his counsel if he is represented, may submit that there is no case for

1. Juries Act 1974, s. 12 (1) (b).
2. *Ibid.*, s. 16.
3. Para. 20.12.
4. *Hammond*, [1941] 3 All E.R. 318.

him to answer. He may address the court upon this submission and counsel for the prosecution may be heard in reply. If the submission is accepted, the judge directs the jury to return a verdict of not guilty and the case is at an end. If no submission is made or if the submission is rejected, the case for the defence is opened.

Where the accused himself is the only witness who is to be called on the facts, he must give his evidence immediately after the close of the case for the prosecution and before his counsel makes his speech. If there are witnesses other than the accused on the facts—i.e., not witnesses as to character—counsel for the defence, or the accused if he is unrepresented, opens his case with a speech. When this is finished, the accused is called, if he wishes to give evidence, and then any other witnesses are called. If the accused does not wish to give evidence, he may nevertheless make an unsworn statement from the dock upon which he cannot be cross-examined. Obviously, it is unlikely that much weight will be given to such a statement. Counsel for the prosecution may not comment to the jury on the failure of the accused to give evidence, although the judge may do so. When the accused and his witnesses, if any, have given their evidence the closing speeches follow.

Where in the course of the case for the defence evidence has been given of some matter which the prosecution was unable to foresee, it lies within the discretion of the judge to allow the prosecution to call further evidence. This power to admit additional evidence after the close of the case for the prosecution is very sparingly exercised. A common instance in which evidence in rebuttal used to be readily admitted was the case of the surprise alibi raised by the accused for the first time at the trial, but under s. 11 of the Criminal Justice Act 1967 the accused is not allowed without the leave of the court to adduce evidence in support of an alibi unless he has given notice of particulars of the alibi within seven days from the end of the committal proceedings. A warning to this effect must be given to the accused on committal.[1]

The defence always has the right to the last word to the jury.[2] It is a breach of natural justice not to allow an accused appearing in person to make a speech after giving evidence in his defence.[3]

In some cases the point at issue is not wholly, or at all, one

1. Para. 22.11.
2. Criminal Procedure (Right of Reply) Act 1964.
3. *Middlesex Crown Court, Ex parte Riddle* (1975) *Times*, 8 October.

of fact but whether the facts proved constitute the offence charged or whether evidence is admissible. Legal argument may be heard at any stage of the trial which may be convenient; if the interests of justice so require (e.g., to avoid the jury hearing evidence in dispute), it takes place in the absence of the jury. If the defence wishes to submit that the facts proved by the prosecution do not in law amount to the offence charged, the argument usually takes place on a submission by the defence at the close of the case for the prosecution and the prosecution has the right of reply. Alternatively, the question of law may not arise until after the evidence of the witnesses for the defence has been heard, so that the submission is made at the close of the case for the defence but before the closing speeches.

The summing up

3 After the closing speeches for the prosecution and the defence, the judge sums up. No evidence must be received after the judge begins to sum up.[1] There are no precise rules about summing up and different judges have different methods. Usually the judge begins by explaining to the jury that they are the judges of the facts and that whatever he may say about the witnesses or the accused or the way in which either the prosecution or the defence has been presented they remain the judges of the facts and that it is for them to decide whether they believe or do not believe the witnesses. He usually stresses more than once in the course of his summing up that the burden lies on the prosecution to prove the guilt of the accused beyond reasonable doubt and that if at the end of the case, after hearing the evidence both for the prosecution and for the defence, they do not feel sure of the guilt of the accused they must acquit him. The judge summarises the evidence which has been given on each side and analyses it as he goes along; he may suggest the amount of weight which the jury may give to vital parts of it and draw the attention of the jury to inconsistencies and omissions. He may comment on the demeanour of a witness and in particular he may comment on the fact that the accused has not elected to give evidence if he has not done so, although he must stress the fact that the accused is under no legal obligation to give evidence.

It is the judge's duty to direct the jury on the law and its application to each of the charges before the court. If the jury are

---

1. *Owen*, [1952] 2 Q.B. 362; [1952] 1 All E.R. 1040; *Sanderson*, [1953] 1 All E.R. 485; *Lawrence*, [1968] 1 All E.R. 579.

not so directed, any conviction on a count in the indictment upon which there has been no direction will be quashed.[1]

A particularly important part of the judge's duty in summing up on the law is to direct the jury about any legal rules relating to the evidence. For example, he must warn them about the danger of convicting the accused on the uncorroborated evidence of an accomplice and tell them what in law amounts to corroboration.

Verdict

23.14 After the judge has summed up, the jury retire to consider their verdict. They choose a foreman to speak for them and retire under the supervision of a jury bailiff. The verdict is announced by the foreman in open court.

There are four types of verdict open to the jury:

a. The general verdict, which is one of guilty or not guilty on the whole indictment.
b. If there is more than one count a verdict is taken on each count separately and the jury may find the accused guilty on one or more counts of the indictment and not guilty on others.
c. The jury may find the accused not guilty of the offence charged but guilty of some other offence on which it is open to them to bring in a verdict of guilty. Section 6 of the Criminal Law Act 1967 lays down the general rule but some statutes provide specific alternatives. The effect of s. 6 (2) is that on a charge of murder the accused may alternatively be convicted of manslaughter, causing grievous bodily harm with intent, infanticide,[2] child destruction,[3] an attempt to commit these offences, or assisting an offender. For all other offences, apart from treason, s. 6 (3) provides that the jury may find the accused not guilty of the offence charged in the indictment but guilty of another offence, where the allegations in the indictment amount to or include (expressly or by implication) an allegation of that other offence. The allegations in the indictment expressly include an allegation of another offence when, if all the averments which have not been proved are struck out of the indictment, there remain particulars of another offence. If an accused is charged with burglary, in that he entered a building as a trespasser and stole, and the theft is established but the trespass is not, he can be convicted

1. *Lester* (1938), 27 Cr. App. Rep. 8.
2. Infanticide Act 1938, s. 1.
3. Infant Life (Preservation) Act 1929, s. 1.

of theft.[1] The allegations in the indictment impliedly include an allegation of another offence when the latter is an essential ingredient of the former,[2] but a man charged with wounding with intent cannot be convicted alternatively of assault since the former offence does not necessarily involve an assault.[3]

d. The jury may bring in a special verdict, which either consists of a finding upon certain facts and leaves it to the judge to apply the law to these facts, or else is a verdict of not guilty by reason of insanity. Special verdicts of the former type are most exceptional.[4]

5 Where the verdict of a jury is clear and unambiguous, the judge ought not to question the foreman of the jury about the grounds upon which it was reached. Thus it has been held that if a jury return a verdict of manslaughter, the judge should not put questions in order to discover whether it was on the grounds of the accused's criminal negligence or because his unlawful act caused the death of the deceased,[5] but it has since been held that the question can be asked when either diminished responsibility or provocation might justify a verdict of manslaughter.[6] On the other hand, when the verdict is ambiguous on the face of it, the judge may question the jury in order to discover the true nature of the verdict. Where a verdict appears clear but is followed by words which are contradictory, the contradictory words are regarded and a verdict of guilty may thus easily become one of not guilty. For example, when a jury returned a verdict of "guilty of dangerous driving on the ground of an error of judgement", this was held to be tantamount to a verdict of not guilty because something more than an error of judgment at that time was required to support a conviction for dangerous driving;[7] it has since been held that if driving is in fact dangerous, and that the dangerous driving is caused by some carelessness on the part of the accused, then however slight the carelessness it is dangerous driving.[8] Under s. 17 of the Juries Act 1974 the verdict of the jury need not be unanimous. If, after two hours in a case where there are not less than 11 jurors, 10 of them agree,

---

1. *Lillis*, [1972] 2 Q.B. 236; [1972] 2 All E.R. 1209.
2. *Springfield* (1969), 53 Cr. App. Rep. 608.
3. *Austin* (1973), 58 Cr. App. Rep. 163.
4. *Bourne* (1952), 36 Cr. App. Rep. 125.
5. *Larkin*, [1943] K.B. 172; [1943] 1 All E.R. 217; *C. & J. Cases*.
6. *Matheson*, [1958] 2 All E.R. 87.
7. *Howell* (1938), 27 Cr. App. Rep. 5.
8. *Evans*, [1963] 1 Q.B. 412; [1962] 3 All E.R. 1086.

or in a case where there are 10 jurors, 9 of them agree, a majority verdict may be accepted.[1] If, even after allowing for this provision, the jury are unable to agree they will be discharged and a new jury called to try the case. If at the second trial the jury still disagree, it is theoretically possible for the accused to be tried for a third time, but the usual practice is for the prosecution to offer no evidence at the third trial so that the accused is acquitted.

23.16 After a verdict of guilty has been given, accepted and recorded, evidence is given of previous convictions and of the general character of the accused in the same way as in a plea of guilty, in order to enable the court to determine the appropriate sentence. A plea in mitigation of sentence may be made by the accused or his counsel. The accused's mental condition at the time of his conviction may have to be considered in order to determine whether the procedure contemplated by s. 60 of the Mental Health Act 1959 which empowers the court to make a hospital or guardianship order, or s. 3 of the Powers of Criminal Courts Act 1973 (probation on condition of treatment) should be followed.

Before the court proceeds to sentence, the accused may ask that certain other offences for which he has not yet been tried shall be taken into consideration and a comprehensive sentence passed to cover both the substantive offence or offences of which he has been found guilty, and also the others which he wishes to be taken into consideration. This practice is very convenient, in that it enables outstanding offences to be cleared and allows the accused, after he has served his sentence, to start with a clean sheet instead of being charged and tried again.

The court is not bound to take such offences into consideration, and usually declines to do so when they are of an entirely different nature from the specific offence for which the accused is before the court.[2] In no circumstances may a sentence be passed which is in excess of that which could be passed in respect of the offence or offences of which the accused has been found guilty although compensation for injury or loss sustained as a result of these offences may be ordered.[2]

The usual practice is for the police to take the initiative and to present a list of such other offences to the accused who should

1. Practice Direction, [1967] 3 All E.R. 137; Practice Note, [1970] 2 All E.R. 215.
2. *Collins*, [1947] K.B. 560; [1947] 1 All E.R. 147.
3. Powers of Criminal Courts Act 1973, s. 35.

personally and in open court be asked if he admits them and agrees that they shall be taken into consideration.

The court may decide to remand the convicted person in custody for a medical or social enquiry report before deciding on the sentence.

Summary trial (other than juvenile offenders)

7 In a summary trial the accused usually appears in answer to a summons, although he may have been arrested. The first step is for the clerk to the magistrates to read out the offence with which the accused is charged.[1] Although the accused frequently appears, s. 1 of the Magistrates' Courts Act 1957 made a fundamental change in the law by enabling the accused to plead guilty without attending and without the need to call evidence. Provided that the offence is not one which can be tried on indictment or which carries a sentence of more than three months' imprisonment there may be served with the summons a notice stating the effect of s. 1 of the Magistrates' Courts Act 1957, together with a concise statement of such facts relating to the alleged offence as will be placed before the court by or on behalf of the prosecution if the accused pleads guilty without appearing in court. The section does not apply to juvenile courts. If the court is satisfied that these documents have been served and the clerk of the court has received notification in writing purporting to be given by the accused or by a solicitor acting on his behalf that the accused desires to plead guilty without appearing, the court may hear and dispose of the case in the absence of the accused. If the case is dealt with in this way the prosecution is limited to the concise statement served on the accused who may send to the court a statement in mitigation.

If the prosecutor does not appear, the magistrates may dismiss the case, unless for some reason they think it proper to adjourn the hearing.[2]

8 If the offence is one which is triable either summarily or on indictment, it is necessary to ascertain which is to be the form of trial. As magistrates' courts are the creation of statute, they have practically no powers at common law and therefore no offence may be tried summarily unless there is express statutory

1. Magistrates' Courts Act 1952, s. 13.
2. Magistrates' Courts Act 1952, s. 16.

authority. When they do try cases summarily they are described as courts of summary jurisdiction. The other important function of the magistrates' courts so far as the criminal law is concerned is to act as examining magistrates in order to ascertain whether a *prima facie* case has been made out where the actual trial will take place on indictment.

Because of the historical development of the magistrates' summary jurisdiction, the simple division of offences into indictable and summary is no longer possible, since there are a large number of offences which by statute fall between these two extremes. Leaving aside the special provisions relating to the trial of children and young persons,[1] the following categories of offences can be distinguished:

a. Some indictable offences are triable only on indictment; examples are murder, rape and robbery.
b. Many indictable offences, which are listed in the First Schedule to the Magistrates' Courts Act 1952 as amended, must be tried on indictment unless the accused consents to summary trial and the magistrates decide, having regard to the nature of the charge and the circumstances of the case, to deal with it summarily.[2] Examples are theft, criminal damage and unlawful wounding.
c. Some statutes provide that an offence shall be punishable either on summary conviction or on indictment and are called hybrid offences. For the purposes of the Magistrates' Courts Act 1952 these offences are both indictable and summary, although for other purposes, such as the question of whether a person should forfeit his directorship of a company because he has committed an indictable offence, they should be regarded as indictable.[3] Hybrid offences are sub-divided as follows:
   i. Those in respect of which the accused has a right to elect trial on indictment. These are offences which carry a maximum sentence of more than three months' imprisonment on summary conviction. They must be tried in the Crown Court unless the magistrates decide to deal with the case summarily, either on the application of the prosecutor before evidence is called, or during the committal proceedings (in the light of any representations

1. Paras. 23.22–23.24.
2. Magistrates' Courts Act 1952, s. 19.
3. *Hastings and Folkestone Glass Works, Ltd.* v. *Kalson*, [1949] 1 K.B. 214; [1948] 2 All E.R. 1013.

made by the prosecution and the defence and of the nature of the case) and the accused, having been informed of his right to trial on indictment, consents to summary trial.[1] Examples are unauthorised possession of a controlled drug and dangerous driving.

ii. Hybrid offences in respect of which the accused has no right to elect trial on indictment. These are offences which do not carry more than three months' imprisonment on summary conviction. The procedure here is the same as in the previous type of hybrid offence except that, if the magistrates decide on summary trial, the accused's consent is not required.[2] An example is possession of an offensive weapon in a public place without lawful authority or reasonable excuse.

d. There are some purely summary offences (with certain exceptions such as common assault) which carry a maximum of more than three months' imprisonment and which are triable summarily unless the accused appears, and having been informed of his right to elect trial on indictment, claims that right.[3] An example is selling intoxicants without a licence.

e. Finally, there are offences which are triable only summarily. Generally these are summary offences which are not punishable with more than three months' imprisonment. They can only be tried in the magistrates' court. Examples are careless driving and selling adulterated food contrary to the Food and Drugs Act 1955.[4]

9 Where a case is to be dealt with summarily, the clerk asks the accused if he is guilty or not guilty. The same rules apply as in a trial on indictment. There may be circumstances on a plea of guilty which make it desirable to hear evidence on oath and this is a matter for the magistrates to decide,[5] but normally if the accused pleads guilty the court convicts him without hearing evidence.[6] With the leave of the court the accused may change his plea at any time before the final disposal of the case, and in exceptional circumstances even between conviction and sentence.[7] If the accused pleads not guilty, the next step is for the

---

1. Magistrates' Courts Act 1952, ss. 18 and 25.
2. *Ibid.*, s. 18.
3. *Ibid.*, s. 25.
4. See Appendix.
5. *Recorder of Grimsby, Ex parte Purser*, [1951] 2 All E.R. 889.
6. Magistrates' Courts Act 1952, s. 13 (3).
7. *S. (an infant)* v. *Manchester Recorder*, [1971] A.C. 481; [1969] 3 All E.R. 1230.

prosecution to prove its case, and basically the same rules apply as in a trial on indictment.

23.20 At the end of the evidence and speeches the magistrates may retire in order to consider their decision. Any communication by any party with the magistrates after they retire should be open and revealed to the other party. The clerk should not retire with the magistrates as a matter of course, but only if they request him to do so or send for him after they have retired in order that he may advise them on the law,[1] mixed law and fact, matters of procedure and powers of sentence. The decision is reached by a majority, and the chairman has no casting vote. Where there is an equality of voting, the case may be adjourned to be re-heard before another court. Where the magistrates cannot reach any conclusion, they should dismiss the information. There is no power on summary trial to return an alternative verdict.[2] If the court decides to dismiss the information, this is announced and the accused is free to go. If the court decides to convict, it enquires into the accused's previous record and hears the defence in mitigation in the same way as in a trial on indictment. The court need not decide upon the sentence at once, but may adjourn the case, never for a single period exceeding three weeks if the accused is in custody, four if on bail, to enable inquiries to be made or to determine the most suitable method of dealing with the case. In such circumstances the court which passes sentence need not consist of the same magistrates as found the accused guilty, but if it is not it must enquire into the circumstances of the case before passing sentence.[3]

23.21 The maximum sentences for summary and hybrid offences tried summarily are laid down by the relevant statutes. Consecutive sentences of imprisonment must not exceed six months in aggregate in the case of summary offences[4] or the maximum for the hybrid offence in the case of conviction for such offences.[5] Where an indictable offence is tried summarily the

---

1. *East Kerrier Justices, Ex parte Mundy*, [1952] 2 Q.B. 719; [1952] 2 All E.R. 144; *Welshpool Justices, Ex parte Holley*, [1953] 2 Q.B. 403; [1953] 2 All E.R. 807; *Barry (Glamorgan) Justices, Ex parte Kashim*, [1953] 2 All E.R. 1005; Practice Direction, [1953] 2 All E.R. 1306.
2. *Lawrence* v. *Same*, [1968] 2 Q.B. 93; [1968] 1 All E.R. 1191.
3. Magistrates' Courts Act 1952, ss. 14 (3) and 98 (7).
4. Magistrates' Courts Act 1952, s. 108 (1).
5. *Ibid.*, s. 108 (3).

magistrates may not impose more than six months' imprisonment[1] or an aggregate of 12 months where there is a conviction for at least two indictable offences.[2] There are limits on the fines which magistrates may impose.[3]

If a person of not less than 17 years of age has been tried summarily and convicted of an indictable offence and if the court, on obtaining information as to his character and antecedents, is of the opinion that some greater punishment should be inflicted than it has power to inflict, it may commit him in custody or on bail to the Crown Court for sentence. There is no appeal against such an order of committal, although of course the accused may appeal against the conviction. The words "character and antecedents" mean that the court is not confined to considering previous convictions alone.[4] The accused then appears before the higher court and is dealt with as if he had been convicted on indictment.[5] If the gravity of an offence is apparent to magistrates from the nature of the charge and nothing emerges from the facts as stated by the prosecution which increases this gravity or which reflects in the character of the accused more than is reflected in the charge itself, the magistrates have no power to commit for sentence.[6]

Magistrates' courts are given powers by the Mental Health Act 1959 to make orders for the admission to and detention in hospital of persons convicted by them. They can also make such orders without proceeding to conviction so long as they have embarked on the trial and are satisfied that the accused did the act or made the omission charged and they would have power to make the order if they had convicted him. If the accused appears unfit to plead and is charged with an indictable offence, he must be committed to the Crown Court. In 1974, 525 hospital orders were made by magistrates' courts.[7] If the magistrates consider that the discharge of the accused from hospital ought to be restricted they must commit him in custody to the Crown Court for the necessary order to be made.[8] A magistrates' court

1. *Ibid.*, s. 19 (6).
2. *Ibid.*, s. 108 (2).
3. See Appendix.
4. *London Sessions, Ex parte Beaumont*, [1951] 1 K.B. 557; [1951] 1 All E.R. 232; *Vallett* [1951] 1 All E.R. 231.
5. Magistrates' Courts Act 1952, s. 29 as amended by Criminal Justice Act 1967, s. 20 and Sch. 6, and Powers of Criminal Courts Act 1973, s. 56 and Sch. 5.
6. *Tower Bridge Magistrate, Ex parte Osman*, [1971] 2 All E.R. 1018.
7. *Criminal Statistics*, 1974, Cmnd. 6168.
8. Mental Health Act 1959, ss. 65 and 67.

can vary or rescind a sentence or other order within 14 days from the day on which it was imposed or made.[1]

The trial of juveniles

23.22 A child is any person under the age of 14; a young person is any person who has attained 14 and is under 17.[2] A magistrates' court before which a person under 17 is charged with an indictable offence must deal with it summarily unless:

a. the charge is one of homicide; or
b. he is a young person and the offence is so grave that under specific statutory powers he, if found guilty, may be sentenced to be detained for a long period;[3] or
c. he is charged jointly with a person who has attained 17 and the court considers it necessary in the interests of justice to commit them both for trial.[4]

Subject to a few exceptions, all charges against a person under 17 which are dealt with summarily must be heard by a juvenile court.[5]

Juvenile courts have power to make orders for the care or supervision of persons under 17 on several grounds including the fact that they are guilty of an offence or offences. Although these offences under this procedure are not the subject of charges, the juvenile court in dealing with them must give the person under 17 the same protection as if it were dealing with the offences as such.[6]

Substantial alterations to the procedure for dealing with juvenile offenders were made by the Children and Young Persons Act 1969 and the Magistrates' Courts (Children and Young Persons) Rules 1970. Most of the 1969 Act and all the rules came into operation on 1 January 1971 but one vital change has been held in suspense. Section 4 of the Act provides that a person must not be charged with an offence, except homicide, committed while he was a child. This would mean that children alleged to have committed offences would be dealt with as being in need of care or control so that no one under 14 would be subject to

1. Criminal Justice Act 1972, s. 41.
2. Children and Young Persons Act 1933, s. 107 (1).
3. *Ibid.*, s. 53 (2), and Children and Young Persons Act 1969, s. 6.
4. Children and Young Persons Act 1969, s. 6.
5. Children and Young Persons Act 1933, s. 46, as amended by Education Act 1944, Sch. 9, Part I, and Children and Young Persons Act 1963, s. 18.
6. Children and Young Persons Act 1969, s. 3.

the criminal law except in cases of homicide. Section 4 is not yet in operation but the provisions relating to care proceedings are, and so the situation remains as described earlier[1] except that not only may a person who has attained the age of 10 be charged with an offence but in the alternative care proceedings may be taken. The procedure for dealing with both children and young persons is thus the same. It is understood that the government's present intention is in due course to exempt from criminal liability (apart from homicide) children up to the age of 12 only.

23 A juvenile court is composed of magistrates specially appointed for the purpose who must retire at 65. Whenever possible the court must consist of at least one man and one woman and not more than three persons in all. It must not sit in a room in which sittings of a court other than a juvenile court are held if a sitting of that other court has been or will be held there within an hour before or after the sitting of the juvenile court. The only persons who are permitted to be present in court are members and officers of the court, parties in the case and solicitors, counsel and witnesses, newspaper reporters and other persons specifically authorised to be present.[2]

No newspaper report of any proceedings in a juvenile court may reveal the name, address, or school or include any particulars calculated to lead to the identification of any child or young person who is accused or is a witness, and no picture of any such child or young person may be published in a newspaper, except by direction of the court or of the Home Secretary.[3] The words "conviction" and "sentence" must not be used in relation to children and young persons: instead the terms "finding of guilt" and "order made upon a finding of guilt" must be used.[4]

The parent or guardian of a child or young person who is charged or is for any other reason brought before a court may be required by summons or warrant to attend at the court at all stages of the proceedings and must attend at any stage where the court thinks it desirable, unless the court is satisfied that it would be unreasonable to require his attendance.[5] The court

1. Para. 5.3.
2. Children and Young Persons Act 1933, s. 47 as amended by Children and Young Persons Act 1963, s. 17.
3. *Ibid.*, s. 49.
4. *Ibid.*, s. 50.
5. Children and Young Persons Act 1933, s. 34 substituted by s. 25 of Children and Young Persons Act 1963; Magistrates' Courts (Children and Young Persons) Rules 1970, r. 26.

may order the parent or guardian to pay any fine, compensation, damages and costs, and must do so if the offender is a child unless the court is satisfied that the parent or guardian cannot be found or that he has not conduced to the commission of the offence by neglecting to exercise due care of the child or young person.[1] Apart from the restrictions on publicity the summary trial of a juvenile corresponds in most respects to the trial of an adult except that the court must allow the parent or guardian of the accused to assist him. If there is a finding of guilt the court is required to receive the fullest possible information from a variety of sources.[2]

23.24 Where the proceedings before the juvenile court take the form of an application for a care order alleging an offence, the court must inform the minor who is the subject of the application of the general nature of the proceedings and of the grounds on which they are brought, of the substance of the alleged offence or offences in simple language, and ask him whether he admits to being guilty. If he does not the proceedings must continue as if they were a summary trial and as in a summary trial the parent, guardian, relative or friend is allowed to assist. Although it is possible for the court to hear some evidence in care proceedings in the absence of the minor, all evidence relating to his character and conduct and to the commission or otherwise of the alleged offence must be heard in his presence.[3] At the end of the care proceedings the juvenile court, if satisfied that the application has been substantiated, may require the parent or guardian to enter into a recognisance or may make a supervision, care, hospital or guardianship order but must not impose any penalty in respect of any alleged offence,[4] although if the offence is indictable, e.g. theft, it may order compensation for loss or damage.[5]

---

1. Children and Young Persons Act 1933, s. 55 and Criminal Justice Act 1961, s. 8 (4).
2. Children and Young Persons Act 1969, s. 9.
3. Magistrates' Courts (Children and Young Persons) Rules 1970, rr. 14–20.
4. Children and Young Persons Act 1969, s. 1 (3).
5. Children and Young Persons Act 1969, s. 3 (6) and Powers of Criminal Courts Act 1973, s. 35.

24

APPEALS

1 There is no right of appeal from any conviction or order of a court of criminal jurisdiction unless it is specially conferred by statute, with the exceptions that at common law an accused person before conviction who is refused bail by the magistrates may apply direct to a judge of the High Court and the orders described later,[1] although now governed by statute, were preceded by writs which were not statutory.

From a Court of Summary Jurisdiction to the Crown Court

2 a. A person convicted by a court of summary jurisdiction, if he did not plead guilty or admit the truth of the information, may appeal to the Crown Court against conviction, or against sentence, or against both;[2]

b. a person convicted by a court of summary jurisdiction who pleaded guilty or admitted the truth of the information may appeal to the Crown Court against sentence only.[3]

The appeal to the Crown Court takes the form of a re-hearing of the case, i.e., the case is tried all over again, witnesses being called etc., without any reference to the proceedings in the magistrates' court except that the Crown Court may have regard to inconsistencies in the evidence given in the magistrates' court compared with that given in the Crown Court. Where the appeal is founded upon a question of law alone, it is usually thought preferable to ask the magistrates to state a case for the opinion of the High Court, as described later.[4]

There is no limitation on the grounds upon which an appeal may be made to the Crown Court with the exception that a person who has pleaded guilty deliberately and intentionally and who understood what he was doing may appeal only against

1. Para. 24.10.
2. Magistrates' Courts Act 1952, s. 83 (1) as amended by Courts Act 1971, Sch. 9.
3. *Ibid.*
4. Para. 24.3.

sentence. The term "sentence" does not include a probation order, an order for conditional discharge, an order for payment of costs, an order for the destruction of an animal or an order which the court is bound to make but includes other orders such as a disqualification. The Magistrates' Courts (Appeals from Binding Over Orders) Act 1956 confers a right to appeal against orders to enter into recognisances to keep the peace or to be of good behaviour.

Normally only a convicted person may use this method of appeal but an exception is the power of a customs and excise[1] officer to appeal against a dismissal of an information laid by him.

From magistrates' courts to the Queen's Bench Division

24.3 Either the prosecution or the defence, or any other party to a proceeding before a magistrates' court, if aggrieved by a conviction, order, determination or other proceeding of that court on the ground that it is wrong in law or is in excess of jurisdiction, may apply to that court to state a case for the opinion of a Divisional Court of the Queen's Bench Division.[2] The court may refuse to state a case if it is of the opinion that the application is frivolous, but in any event a court which refuses to state a case may be compelled to do so by an order of *mandamus* issued by the Divisional Court.[3] If this method of appeal is chosen, an appeal to the Crown Court is excluded. The application must be in writing and signed by or on behalf of the applicant and must identify the question or questions of law or jurisdiction on which the opinion of the Divisional Court is sought. Within 21 days after receipt of an application, the clerk of the magistrates' court whose decision is questioned must, unless the magistrates refuse under the power mentioned above to state a case, send a draft case in which are stated the matters required to the applicant or his solicitor and a copy to the respondent or his solicitor.[4] Within 21 days each party may make representations, and within a further 21 days after the latest date for making representations the magistrates must make any necessary adjustments to the draft and then state and sign the case which the clerk sends to the applicant or his solicitor. The case must

1. Customs and Excise Act 1952, s. 283 (4).
2. Magistrates' Courts Act 1952, s. 87.
3. Para. 24.10.
4. Magistrates' Courts (Amendment) (No. 2) Rules 1975, S.I. 1975 No. 518 (L.8), replacing rr. 65–68 of the Magistrates' Courts Rules 1968, S.I. 1968 No. 1920.

state the facts found by the magistrates and the question or questions of law or jurisdiction on which the opinion of the Divisional Court is sought. There are provisions for extending the time limits.[1]

From the Crown Court to the Queen's Bench Division

4 When the Crown Court has decided an appeal against conviction or sentence from a magistrates' court, either the prosecution or the defence may, if dissatisfied with the determination of the Crown Court as being wrong in law or in excess of jurisdiction apply to the court to state a case for the opinion of the Divisional Court of the Queen's Bench Division.[2] The procedure is similar to that described in para. 24.3.[3]

From the Crown Court to the Court of Appeal

5 A person convicted on indictment before the Crown Court may appeal to the Court of Appeal (Criminal Division):

a. Without any leave, against conviction on a question of law alone.
b. With leave of the Court of Appeal (Criminal Division) or of the trial judge, against conviction:
   i. on a question of fact alone, or
   ii. on a question of mixed law and fact.
c. With leave of the Court of Appeal (Criminal Division), against conviction on any other ground which appears to the court to be sufficient.
d. With leave of the Court of Appeal (Criminal Division) against sentence, unless the sentence is one fixed by law.[4]

As we have seen, the Court of Criminal Appeal was set up by statute in 1907; it was replaced in 1966 by the Criminal Division of the Court of Appeal, and the governing statute is now the Criminal Appeal Act 1968. Only a convicted person may appeal: the prosecution has no right to appeal against an acquittal upon indictment.[5]

6 The more important powers of the Court of Appeal (Criminal Division) are:

a. To allow the appeal on the following grounds:
   i. that the verdict of the jury should be set aside on the

---

1. *Ibid.*
2. Courts Act 1971, s. 10 (3).
3. Crown Court Rules, r. 21 and Rules of the Supreme Court, Order 56, rr. 1–4.
4. Criminal Appeal Act 1968, s. 1 and ss. 9–11.
5. But see s. 36 of the Criminal Justice Act 1972; para. 24.7.

ground that under all the circumstances of the case it is unsafe or unsatisfactory;

ii. that there was a wrong decision on any question of law; or

iii. that there was a material irregularity in the course of the trial.[1]

The most common allegations upon which an appeal is founded are misdirection on a point of law by the judge, and the wrongful admission of evidence. A person who pleaded guilty, but wishes to appeal against conviction, very rarely satisfies one of these three grounds.[2]

b. To dismiss the appeal. Even though the court is of opinion that the ground of appeal is good, it may dismiss the appeal if no miscarriage of justice has occurred.[3] The test is whether the court is satisfied that, on the whole of the facts, and with the correct direction, the only proper verdict would have been one of guilty.[4] This is sometimes called "applying the proviso".

c. To order a new trial where an appeal against conviction is allowed by reason only of evidence received or available to be received by the court under s. 23 of the Criminal Appeal Act 1968, and it appears to the court that the interests of justice so require.

d. To make an order in the nature of *venire de novo*, i.e., if the trial was in fact no trial at all and was a complete nullity, the court may order a proper trial to take place. In *Cronin*[5] a purported trial had taken place before a deputy recorder who was not qualified to be appointed as such, and therefore the whole proceedings were a nullity. The Court of Criminal Appeal made an order in the nature of *venire de novo* for a proper trial to be held.

e. On appeal against sentence to reduce it, but not to increase it except that when a conviction for one or more offences covered by the indictment is quashed, the sentence on the part of the indictment on which the appellant remains convicted may be increased up to the total sentence passed on the appellant at the trial.[6]

---

1. Criminal Appeal Act 1968, s. 2.
2. *Director of Public Prosecutions* v. *Shannon*, [1974] 2 All E.R. 1009.
3. Criminal Appeal Act 1968, s. 2 (1) proviso.
4. *Stirland* v. *Director of Public Prosecutions*, [1944] A.C. 315; [1944] 2 All E.R. 13.
5. [1940] 1 All E.R. 618.
6. Criminal Appeal Act 1968, s. 11 (3).

f. To substitute for a conviction for one offence a conviction for another offence if it was open to the jury at the trial to find the accused guilty of the latter offence, and if the court considers that the jury must have been satisfied of the facts which were necessary to prove the accused guilty of that latter offence.[1] In an appeal against acquittal by reason of insanity there is a corresponding power[2] to substitute a verdict of guilty of the offence charged or of some other offence of which the jury must have been satisfied that, apart from the question of insanity, the accused was guilty.

g. To order the appellant to be admitted to a specified hospital on the ground that the verdict should have been one of not guilty by reason of insanity,[3] or to make a hospital or guardianship order under the provisions of s. 60 of the Mental Health Act 1959.[4]

h. To vary or annul an order for the re-vesting or restitution of property.[5]

If a convicted person appeals without leave on a question of law alone he is not allowed in the course of appeal to argue questions of fact or mixed law and fact without leave.[6]

7 The court has power to admit fresh evidence, but this power is usually exercised only when such evidence was not available at the trial or otherwise there is a reasonable explanation for the failure to adduce it.[7] In *Dashwood*[8] the appellant at his trial refused to call evidence as to his insanity although it was available. It was held that he could not do so before the Court of Criminal Appeal. By s. 17 of the Criminal Appeal Act 1968 the Home Secretary may, at any time after a conviction on indictment or acquittal through insanity, refer either the whole case or a particular point to the Criminal Division of the Court of Appeal which in these circumstances more readily allows evidence of his insanity although it was available at the trial. It may admit fresh evidence[9] but the court confines itself to the grounds

1. *Ibid.*, s. 3.
2. *Ibid.*, s. 13.
3. *Ibid.*, s. 6.
4. Para. 23.16.
5. Criminal Appeal Act 1968, s. 30.
6. *Robinson*, [1953] 2 All E.R. 334.
7. See *Parks*, [1961] 3 All E.R. 633 for a full description of the principles on which the Court of Appeal will admit fresh evidence; Criminal Appeal Act 1968, s. 23 (2).
8. [1943] K.B. 1; [1942] 2 All E.R. 586.
9. *McGrath*, [1949] 2 All E.R. 495 and *Sparkes*, [1956] 2 All E.R. 245.

on which the Home Secretary has referred the case and does not go beyond them.[1]

By s. 36 of the Criminal Justice Act 1972, the Attorney-General may refer to the Court of Appeal a point of law arising at a trial on indictment where the person tried has been acquitted. The opinion of the court does not affect the acquittal but provides authoritative guidance for the future.

From the Court of Appeal or the Divisional Court to the House of Lords

24.8 After the determination of an appeal by the Court of Appeal or by the Divisional Court of the Queen's Bench Division or of the Courts Martial Appeal Court either the prosecution or the defence may appeal to the House of Lords provided that the necessary conditions are fulfilled and leave is granted either by the court below (i.e. the Court of Appeal or the Divisional Court or the Courts Martial Appeal Court) or by the House of Lords. An important and unusual feature is that either the prosecution or the defence may appeal. The conditions which must be fulfilled are:

a. The court below must certify that a point of law of general public importance is involved.
b. Either the court below or the House of Lords must be satisfied that the point of law is one which ought to be considered by the House of Lords.[2]

If the court below refuses to certify that a point of law of general public importance is involved that is an end of the matter, whatever the House of Lords might have thought.[3] Once an appeal is before the House of Lords it seems that the House is not restricted to considering the particular point certified by the court below.[4] If the court below certifies that a point of law of general public importance is involved but refuses leave to appeal to the House of Lords, an application to the House of Lords for leave must be made within a period of 14 days after refusal by the court below.

Points of law referred to the Court of Appeal by the Attorney-General may be further referred to the House of Lords.

---

1. *Caborn-Waterfield*, [1956] 2 Q.B. 379; [1956] 2 All E.R. 636.
2. Administration of Justice Act 1960, s. 1; Criminal Appeal Act 1968, s. 33.
3. *Gelberg* v. *Miller*, [1961] 1 All E.R. 618n.
4. *A.G. for Northern Ireland* v. *Gallagher*, [1963] A.C. 349; [1961] 3 All E.R. 299.

Time limits

In all the above appellate procedures, written notice of appeal must be given within a certain time of the decision appealed from; 14 days in the case of appeals to the Divisional Court or House of Lords; 21 days for appeals to the Crown Court, and 28 days for appeals to the Court of Appeal. Generally, these time limits may be extended by the appellate court in question. It is possible for an appellant to be released on bail pending the determination of his appeal.

Other proceedings in the nature of appeals

Independently of any right of appeal proper, all inferior courts of criminal jurisdiction are subject to control by the Queen's Bench Division by means of orders of *mandamus*, prohibition, or *certiorari*.[1] An order of *mandamus* is used to compel any body, whether acting in a judicial capacity or not, to carry out a definite duty imposed on it by law. The order cannot be used to compel the body to exercise its discretion in a particular way, but it may be used to compel it to hear and determine a case,[2] or to state a case for the opinion of the High Court.[3] Orders of prohibition and *certiorari* will issue only to bodies which are acting in a judicial or quasi-judicial capacity. This does not mean that they will issue only to courts, for many other bodies, such as local authorities, may sometimes act in such a capacity. Conversely, there are rare occasions on which courts act in an administrative and not a judicial capacity.

The order of prohibition is used to prevent such a body from doing something improper, and covers much the same ground as an order of *certiorari*, but before, and not after, the damage is done. The order of *certiorari* is used where such a body has already done something and it is desired to review it and, if necessary, quash it on the ground that there is an apparent defect, or want of jurisdiction, or clear evidence of fraud, or a denial of natural justice. As the orders issue only to inferior courts, the Crown Court is not subject to them in respect of trials on indictment. In respect of other matters, such as appeals from magistrates' courts which were inherited by the Crown Court from Quarter Sessions, the powers of the High Court survive.[4] A per-

---

1. Administration of Justice (Miscellaneous Provisions) Act 1938, s. 7.
2. *Adamson* (1875), 1 Q.B.D. 201.
3. Magistrates' Courts Act 1952, s. 87 (6).
4. Courts Act 1971, s. 10; *Leeds Crown Court, Ex parte Bradford Chief Constable*, [1975] Q.B. 314; [1975] 1 All E.R. 133.

son who has been convicted or sentenced by a magistrates' court and has applied for an order of *certiorari* may be released on bail by the High Court,[1] but not by the magistrates' court. The application for an order is made to a Divisional Court of the Queen's Bench Division. During vacation, the application is to a judge in chambers from whom there is an appeal to the Divisional Court.

---

1. Criminal Justice Act 1948, s. 37 (1) (d).

APPENDIX

The Distribution of Criminal Business between the Crown Court and Magistrates' Courts. Summary of the more important recommendations in the Report of the Interdepartmental Committee under the chairmanship of Lord Justice James. Cmnd. 6323. November 1975. The references to paragraphs are to those in the Report.

1. The primary criterion determining whether a case should be triable on indictment is the seriousness of the offence and the test should be the seriousness in the eyes of society and not the importance to the defendant (para. 41).
2. At present there are cases tried in the Crown Court which, on this criterion, are not serious cases while in other cases the defendant elects trial on indictment for secondary reasons, such as a wish to defer the date of conviction and disqualification in driving offences or to ascertain the evidence on which the prosecution intends to rely without disclosing, except in the case of an alibi, the nature of the defence (paras. 51–52 and 76).
3. There should be three categories of offences:
   - 3.1 Indictable: triable only on indictment;
   - 3.2 Intermediate: triable either on indictment or summarily;
   - 3.3 Summary: triable only summarily (paras. 43–45).
4. A person charged with an intermediate offence should have the right to elect to be tried on indictment (para. 61) except for:
   - 4.1 Certain offences of theft and related offences of dishonesty, including attempts and incitement to commit those offences, where the value of the money or property involved does not exceed £20 (paras. 78–100);
   - 4.2 Offences of criminal damage, including attempts and incitement to commit those offences, other than arson, where the value of the damage does not exceed £100 (paras. 101–104).

In these two exceptional categories the trial should be summary with no right to trial on indictment (paras. 77 and 248).

5. The following offences at present triable only on indictment should be transferred to the intermediate category:
   - 5.1 Burglary in a dwelling if entry was effected by force or deception (para. 115);
   - 5.2 Unlawful sexual intercourse with a girl aged between 13 and 16 years (para. 117);
   - 5.3 Bigamy (para. 118);
   - 5.4 Offences under ss. 16, 26, 34, 36 and 38 of the Offences against the Person Act 1861 (para. 119);
   - 5.5 Causing death by reckless or dangerous driving (if the offence is retained) (para. 124); see para. 10 below;
   - 5.6 Those offences of forgery and using false documents which are at present triable only on indictment. Existing offences should be replaced by a single offence of forgery and a single offence of using false documents, as recommended by the Law Commission (paras. 125–127);
   - 5.7 Perjury, other than perjury in judicial proceedings (paras. 128–129);
   - 5.8 Certain other offences (para. 132).
6. The following hybrid offences should be transferred to the summary category:
   - 6.1 Any hybrid offence for which the maximum penalty on indictment is within the normal powers of a magistrates' court to impose (para. 136);
   - 6.2 All drinking and driving offences (paras. 146–148);
   - 6.3 Using threatening, abusive or insulting words and behaviour etc. under s. 5 of the Public Order Act 1936 and related offences (paras. 151–154);
   - 6.4 Homosexual soliciting (para. 169).

   All other hybrid offences including reckless and dangerous driving (if the offence is retained in its present form), possessing an offensive weapon and assault on the police should be in the intermediate category and carry a right to elect trial on indictment (paras. 135, 144–145, and 155–156).
7. The normal maximum fine which magistrates can impose should be increased to £1000 which should be the standard maximum fine on summary conviction for intermediate offences (para. 201).
8. There should be a greater measure of disclosure of the prosecution case to the defence in advance of summary trials (para. 212). A person charged with an offence in the inter-

mediate category should have a statutory right to receive, on request, copies of the statements of the witnesses on whose evidence the prosecution proposes to rely, if written statements have been taken (paras. 213–228). If the prosecution considers that it would be against the interests of justice to provide copies of the statements, it should be able to apply to a magistrate for a direction that they should not be served (para. 227). If witness statements have not been prepared or if a court directs that a statement should not be served, a summary of the facts upon which the prosecution intends to rely should, on request, be supplied to the defence instead (paras. 224 and 227).

To ensure that the evidence is examined more thoroughly before a person is committed for trial under s. 1 of the Criminal Justice Act 1967, both the defence advocate and the person conducting the prosecution should be required to sign a certificate to the effect that they have examined the witness statements and are satisfied that the case is suitable for committal for trial under s. 1 without consideration of the evidence by the court (paras. 235–238).

The offence of causing death by reckless or dangerous driving should be abolished (Appendix K, para. 2). There should be a new offence of reckless driving which should be in the intermediate category (Appendix K, paras. 3–4). There should be a single composite summary offence not punishable with imprisonment to replace the existing offences of dangerous driving, driving without due care and attention and driving inconsiderately (Appendix K, para. 7).

INDEX

All references are to paragraph numbers

All references are to paragraph numbers

All references are to paragraph numbers

All references are to paragraph numbers

All references are to paragraph numbers

All references are to paragraph numbers

Printed by Butler & Tanner Ltd, Frome and London